R/1817/4x/9-15 July Vol 38

D1326958

POLITICAL PHYSICIST

POLITICAL PHYSICIST

Terence Price

The Book Guild Ltd
Sussex, England

First published in Great Britain in 2004 by
The Book Guild Ltd
25 High Street
Lewes, East Sussex
BN7 2LU

Typesetting in Times by
Keyboard Services, Luton, Bedfordshire

Printed in Great Britain by
Antony Rowe Ltd, Chippenham, Wiltshire

A catalogue record for this book is available from the
British Library

ISBN 1 85776 828 0

For Ned, Rozzie, Anna and Kasia

Contents

Foreword

by Rt. Hon. Lord Healey
Secretary of State for Defence 1964–1970

Besides ranging widely over energy, transport and industrial policy, this book provides an invaluable insight into the work of scientists at the Ministry of Defence at a time when the development of nuclear weapons was transforming strategy throughout the world. The work of Solly Zuckerman, John Kendrew, Patrick Blackett and William Penney was particularly important. Terence Price worked with them all as Zuckerman's assistant. Later Price worked as his representative on a new tri-service Operational Analysis Committee, and became Director of the Defence Operational Analysis Establishment when it was set up at Byfleet.

Price also worked closely with American experts in the field such as Jerry Wiesner, Isidor Rabi, Harold Brown and Leo Szilard. His work with a hundred defence scientists from the NATO countries in support of a NATO Long Term Planning Group was of crucial importance. He was also a member of Britain's Joint Intelligence Committee, which led him to a role in Mountbatten's JIGSAW – the Joint Interservice Group for the Study of All Out Warfare. Thus his book gives a clearer insight into the development of Britain's nuclear strategy than anyone else still living could achieve.

Preface

Why write a memoir? Immodesty, perhaps. To inform the grand-children, certainly. Not least to remind today's younger professionals that attempts to plan life tidily may be thwarted by the unpredictable on-rush of events.

I wish, too, to illustrate what the Russian academician Lev Artsimovitch had in mind when he observed that 'science is the best way of satisfying one's own curiosity at other people's expense'. Science is the greatest promoter of change that the world has seen. Some of those changes can be so significant as to create issues of major political importance. When that happens there are few more intriguing places to work than at the interface of science and politics.

That interface is the setting for my central chapters, which deal with the processes of government and the way they are influenced by powerful personalities. The issues facing the United Kingdom in my time included the cold war, nuclear deterrence, disarmament, withdrawal from Empire and economic decline; together with the beginnings of nuclear energy, transport policy and the burgeoning problems of the environment. I make no pretence of offering a comprehensive analysis of the many conflicting issues. I shall be content if these chapters are accepted for what I have tried to make them: a balanced account of what I observed from my privileged position as a scientific adviser in central government. Students of British politics may also find some interest in the references to the beginnings of the Thatcher revolution. The closing chapters chronicle the difficulties encountered in the eventually successful creation of the Uranium Institute, since reconstituted as the World Nuclear Association.

I am grateful for the unstinted help I have received from many friends. I particularly wish to thank Fergus Allen, Peter Bayley, Katherine Bell, Reuben Clark, Joan Cull, Norma Dixon, David Farrell, John Garlick, Monica McAllen, Peter Mountfield, Neil Peck, John Peyton, Maria Sachs, Peter Smart and Alan Wickens for doing their best to guide me. If, despite their efforts, there are errors the responsibility is entirely mine.

Jordans, Buckinghamshire, UK

May 2004   T.P.

Chapter 1

Growing up in Gloucester

Nous entrons dans l'avenir à reculons...
demain est une puissance cachée

La politique de l'esprit
Paul Valéry (1871–1945)

Valéry neatly summarises life's central problem: we walk backwards into the future, knowing where we have come from, uncertain where we are going, surrounded by perpetual change. As a boy in the early 1930s I could in no way have foreseen my involvement, only twenty or thirty years later, with atomic energy and its political fall-out; with cosmic-ray research on French mountain-tops; with policy debates in Whitehall on defence and disarmament and transport; or, briefly, with international spies. How could I have anticipated my prolonged – albeit innocent – entanglement with American anti-trust litigation, or involvement with Japanese industry? What could be further from the gentle Cotswolds than the wildernesses of mining sites in Kakadu or Saskatchewan? No-one has a rear-view mirror to see into such unknown futures. All that one can do is seize opportunities as they occur, and prepare oneself accordingly.

My upbringing reflected the values and disciplines of a working-class town in the years following the 1914 war. Socially Gloucester was poles apart from its geographical twin, Cheltenham, with

1

its Regency terraces and educational establishments, where life for many was easy and pensioned. Gloucester lived on its industry and sheer hard graft. People counted their pennies. Children's clothes were often hand-me-downs, shoes soled-and-heeled several times. Shop prices were keen enough to warrant a nine-mile bus or train journey for Cheltenham's poorer folk. Gloucester people helped each other as a matter of course. The streets were absolutely safe after dark, dishonesty almost unknown.

It was the county town, the trade centre for a rural hinterland. On market days cattle from Severn water meadows were driven through the streets to the market near the twin railway stations. Sheep came in from the Cotswolds. People helped them on their way with shouts tinged with traces of the West Country. Gloucester had its own local words. A 'pitch' was a long slope where cyclists would dismount, a 'tump' a small rounded hill, a 'nobby' the crusty end slice of a loaf. There were verbs I have not heard since I left the city. 'You are' could become 'thee bist', the negative 'thee bisn't'. Granny would still use the archaic 'I'd as lief do that'.

The city was undeniably inward-looking, though there were romantic whispers of the outside world. The Gloucester and Berkeley Ship Canal brought sizeable timber ships from the Baltic. The Wagon Works sent railway carriages to the colonies and dominions. Red coaches for the London Underground were shunted backwards and forwards from the works sidings across the Bristol Road, sometimes for ten minutes at a time – exciting train spotters and frustrating motorists, whose holiday-time mile-long queues (even in the 1930s) stretched back along Southgate from the Cross. Looking down on them a huge poster confusingly and memorably proclaimed for many weeks the beneficial properties of a well-known tonic drink: REFRESHING, INVIGORATING, ENERVATING.

Sport was an active ingredient of city life: rugby in winter (soccer was thought cissy), cricket in summer. Gloucester's cricketers – Hammond, Barnett, Goddard – carried its name as far as Australia. In return visiting Test sides were welcomed at

2

the Wagon Works sports ground in Tuffley. For three days work all over the city was disrupted, as everyone tried to be there. The roar of the crowd could be heard a mile away. State nannyism and the Health and Safety Executive were still things of the future. So on nearby Coopers' Hill round wooden 'cheeses' were rolled down its steep slopes on Whit Monday by a Master of Ceremonies in a beribboned white hat, and young men and women came to grief in pursuit. Under its steep escarpment the Brockworth aircraft factory made Gloster Gauntlets and Gladiators for the RAF.

With no television and little radio the townspeople made their own entertainment. Culture depended on two operatic societies, a couple of good drama groups, school plays, and an Orpheus male voice choir. Several concert and variety parties provided a trickle of entertainment for the city and surrounding villages. Once every three years the cathedral, with its Norman nave, fan-traceries, and matchless tower, played host to the Three Choirs Festival.

Civic pride and a sense of community were almost tangible. Lucky children learned of it early through the Mayor's Party, held in the now-abandoned Guildhall to mark the New Year. The ballroom offered glorious opportunities for sliding on the chalk-powdered parquet floor, before the party photograph was taken from the gallery with the help of a smoking magnesium flare. Opposite the Guildhall in Eastgate Street was the covered fruit, fish and flower market, lost in a fire in 1994. Next to it was Blinkhorn's, where crowds of children and parents blocked the December traffic to see Father Christmas finish a journey that had begun on the ship canal aboard the pleasure steamer *Wave*. His final act was to climb a ladder thirty feet to the roof of the store, and shower gifts on the tumult below. Processions were part of civic life – for a new Mayor, for Remembrance Day (the Kaiser's war was still only yesterday to the men of the Fifth Gloucesters), and for any other occasion that could be discovered or invented.

Religion still mattered. Every Sunday the Salvation Army

could be seen – and heard – marching to the Citadel: 'Onward Christian Soldiers'. There were the imitators in the Church Army and the Boys' Brigade with their drums and fifes. Methodism was strong, despite its competing sects: Primitive, Wesleyan, and (ignoring evidence to the contrary) United. There were Presbyterians, Congregationalists, Unitarians, Christian Scientists, Plymouth Brethren, Seventh Day Adventists and Jehovah's Witnesses. The Anglicans' fifteen churches provided à-la-carte Christianity, bridging the entire spectrum of ritual from frill-free low church to near-Catholicism, complete with incense. Gloucester had fostered the first Sunday School, founded by Robert Raikes in 1783 in a Tudor half-timbered building in St Catherine's Street. Alas, the devout citizens' interests did not extend to protecting the city's cultural inheritance, and in my life-time the already decaying building was finally swept away.

London broadcasts had not yet cast their shadow over provincial music-making. Few chapels and churches did not boast a choir whose celebrations of the great festivals made up in fervour what they lacked in musicianship. Little was heard of Bach or even Byrd, except at the Three Choirs Festival. Monteverdi was still unknown. But there was *The Messiah* at Christmas, Stainer's *Crucifixion* at Easter, Maunder's *Olivet to Calvary* on Good Friday for choirs of lesser accomplishment, and Elgar's *For the Fallen* on Remembrance Day in November – preceded by wreath-laying by a uniformed veteran of the Great War and a lone bugler sounding Last Post and Reveille. A cohort of soloists went from church to church. They included my father, Ben, whose light tenor could be heard on Sundays singing Merbecke's choral eucharist in high-church St Mark's. He also sang every autumn in the Three Choirs chorus, and the oratorio repertoire was as familiar in the home as Welsh rarebit or cribbage. My earliest musical memory was asking father to sing 'the clock gets straight' – a childish corruption of 'the crooked straight' in the 'Every Valley' aria from *The Messiah*. Later, at the Three Choirs Festival, I saw Elgar and Vaughan-Williams – who once trod on my foot – and had a glimpse of the long-haired Kodály.

In my teens I would follow the festival through its three-year cycle to Hereford and Worcester. The railways were cooperative: evening returns to Worcester, thirty miles away, cost a mere one shilling and nine pence – one-eleventh of a pound.

Except for the Festival the cathedral, in its glorious protective close, stood apart from the life of the working town, unless great ceremonial was needed. Then the temporary lifting of this very separation added significance to services of remembrance or celebration. But for the greater part of the year the see of Gloucester catered more for the surrounding country gentry than for the townsfolk – or so it seemed to us Methodists.

Social layering was in any case part and parcel of the city's life; and the engine of its principal recreation, gossip. At the top there was that mysterious group, the 'county'. There were a few doctors and other professionals, distinguished by their possession not just of cars – itself something still remarkable – but cars that anyone might envy: Armstrong-Siddeleys, Wolseleys, Lanchesters, even Bugattis. These were so far removed from the Austin Sevens, Morris Eights, and £99 Fords that were just beginning to cater for the mass market, that the sight of one parked outside a neighbour's house would provoke anxious inquiries whether someone might be ill.

The city's magistracy carried great prestige. It was the Justices of the Peace who operated the system of deterrence that kept the streets so safe that an unlocked bicycle could be left leaning against a tree by a forgetful teenager – myself – and still be there when he returned from holidays a fortnight later. It was father's greatest reward that in later life, after years of unstinting and unpaid public service, he could place the coveted letters, JP, after his name.

Cutting across the layers, and adding to the city's cohesion, were the interlocking interest groups: Masons and Rotary; the British Legion and Toc H, where men could drink beer and tell tales of Flanders and Gallipoli. For some the Workers' Educational Association offered a kind of pre-radio Open University. Further social glue was provided by *The Citizen*, the oldest daily newspaper in the land, which dropped through letterboxes in the late afternoon bringing news of the latest hatches, matches and despatches.

My parents married in 1919, and I was born on 7 January 1921. We lived in a terraced house in Clegram Road, one of the unpretentious streets leading off Bristol Road opposite Price Walker's timber yard. In that part of Gloucester life was regulated by factory hooters. Price Walker's siren was thin and reedy, and the Wagon Works' not much better. But along the Bristol Road was Moreland's Match Manufactory which made non-safety England's Glory matches and packed them in boxes of fifty, with a highly stylised warship on the front and a joke of the kind still found in Christmas crackers on the back. Moreland's had a deep, ship's siren that blew at 12.25p.m., again at 12.30p.m., and twice again an hour later, after dinner – Gloucester working-folk did not eat 'lunch'.

Clegram Road felt itself a cut above the next street, Alma Place, but definitely further down the social scale than Bloomfield Road, where we were to move a few years later; and still more so than middle-class Tuffley, on the edge of glorious Robinswood Hill. The Clegram Road house had no indoor toilet and no bathroom. Money did not always run to toilet paper, and I learned early in life that squares of newspaper, if carefully crumpled, could provide an adequate and absorbent alternative. If a bath was needed an oval galvanised contraption would be brought into the kitchen, and kettles boiled on the gas stove. Cleanliness being hard to come by, it was naturally placed next to Godliness by mother.

She had been brought up by Granny to be a true believer. Granny had been in the Salvation Army, and had worn her poke-bonnet with pride. Mother – we called her Mamie – preferred a less ostentatious religion. She was a pillar of nearby Wesley Hall, whose packed timetable regulated our lives on Sundays. Her strong contralto voice won her a place in the choir, at a time when the chapel was a thriving society with congregations of a hundred, morning and evening, on Sundays. But, apart from choral music, culture was a closed book to her. She read hardly at all, except for the most popular of magazines, and the house was poorly provided with books. She did not enjoy good looks, having had her nose broken during a dangerous challenge at hockey while still a girl. Nor did she have the conventional social graces. Her virtues lay elsewhere: honesty, hard work, self-discipline, tidiness, frugality, dedication to the family and, not least, a willingness to help any friend, without thought of self. She had been apprenticed as a milliner, after a primary school education which taught house-craft with the same thoroughness as I was later taught physics: I still have her needle-work examination pieces as evidence.

She had enormous vitality, which remained undimmed until well into her seventies. She took the gruelling round of cooking, cleaning, mending and making beds in her stride, with no help and almost no modern aids to ease the load. As a young mother she would cycle for miles around country lanes on a sit-up-and-beg machine fitted with a pillion seat. On it she took me or my younger brother Michael for many picnics when we were small. She found inspiration in villages like Cranham and Painswick, and in consequence we boys knew what glories the Cotswolds had to offer years before the world read Laurie Lee.

In her middle years her contribution to the community lay in supporting father in everything he did or asked for, her efforts making possible and sustaining his active participation in local public life. But when war came, and Michael and I had left home, she became a vigorous member of the community in her own right. She worked with the Womens' Voluntary Services, and Meals on Wheels, as lynchpin rather than leader. When in 1947 I brought home a bride from a different social background Jean was overwhelmed with admiration for mother's extraordinary mixture of energy, competence, self-reliance, and generosity – qualities she had never previously found in one person in like measure.

Mother was a passionate gardener, and had the greenest of fingers. She made the tiny garden in Clegram Road blossom like Kew, despite the occasional bottles thrown over the fence by our neighbour, Ginney (whether that was a name or a comment I never found out). On the other side, at number 10, the Triggs were almost 'family'. Edith was a kind and handsome woman, with a glorious contralto voice. But she was a victim of the sex imbalance created by the Great War and never married, remaining a strait-laced spinster. Every Christmas she sang in the choir at Wesley Hall, with evident conviction, 'Behold a virgin shall conceive...' Her brother, Percy, had a prodigious appetite. Once I saw him devour thirteen slices of bread and jam for his tea – and, being four years old, said as much, numeracy triumphing over diplomacy.

In the summer of 1926 Mamie achieved her dream when we moved to Bloomfield Road. Moreover, the house was ours; mortgaged it is true, but not rented. It was not far from Clegram Road, where Granny remained for a time, and still within earshot of the factory hooters. Nor was it any further from Wesley Hall, so there was no loss of chapel friends. Our new abode, which rejoiced in the grand name of Kingsley House, had a bathroom and inside toilet, but no central heating or running hot water. There was however a geyser, which avoided the exercise with kettles in the kitchen, though it took nearly twenty minutes to fill a small bath and made the walls run with condensation. We now had three bedrooms, a sizeable garden where Mamie could exercise her skills, and good neighbours. My enormous rocking-horse found a new home in the garden shed. A cherry tree produced magnificent black fruit and exuded gum that made a serviceable glue. From the back bedroom we could spy on walkers on Robinswood Hill through a telescope, and from just down the road we could see the masts of tall ships coming up the canal into the town docks.

It was time to start school. There must have been some element of parental choice, as Calton Road was not the nearest primary school. But since its foundation twenty years earlier it was unquestionably the place where ambitious but impecunious parents placed their young. So there I went. It had the cachet of its own cap-badge with a Latin motto: *Age Quid Agas* – 'Do what you can.' There was no transport in family cars, which hardly existed; though some children travelled two miles by ordinary bus four times a day. Those, like me, who lived nearer walked – in my case three-quarters of a mile each way. After the first week, at the tender age of five, I did the four journeys daily unaccompanied. There was no risk: traffic was light and child molesters almost unknown.

Getting to school on time was a serious business. Coming back offered the chance of more social activities, not least calling in to see mother's friend Ruth, and announcing that Mamie said I could have a piece of cake. Once, in mid-winter, because of the factory chimneys and coal-burning domestic grates, there was a pea-soup fog so thick that we could play hide-and-seek across the street. And for a happy couple of weeks, after the workmen had gone home, we commandeered a light railway carrying concrete for an extension to Calton Road, and sent the trucks off down a slight hill until they derailed. Then we set them back on their rails again, and restored them to their rightful place. Bliss!

More often there were games of marbles, played by two or three boys in the gutters as we made our way home, after calling in at Denley's to buy and share the best dripping cakes in the world. Such sharing, alas, too often taught us more of the laws of the jungle than of equity, particularly when cream buns were involved. From marbles we learned basic economics. Small clay marbles, which ran badly and stopped soon, could be bartered for the better-performing glass 'alleys', or larger and even more wonderful 'pritts', with multi-coloured stripes. But the exchange rate of twenty or more ordinary marbles for a single good pritt was a deterrent. Gutter-marbles had its own vocabulary and involved much shouting. If a player who was not doing well managed to shout 'lags' before his opponent could block him with 'no lags', he could have an extra turn. Vocal agility counted as much as a good eye. Peter Bayley, a future Professor of English and Chairman of the Oxford Playhouse, made a formidable opponent.

The prestige of the two older universities was such that by the age of nine every Gloucester boy had chosen one or the other as his favourite. The Boat Race had much to do with it, especially after the arrival of crystal sets, whose cat's whiskers brought us John Snagge's live running commentary. Little boys peeing against the school urinal wall would simultaneously launch Oxford and Cambridge matchsticks down the descending streams and watch as they floated away to see which came off best. In this, at least, boys had the advantage over their less well-arranged sisters. Two of the contestants in my year later achieved the university of their choice – the hard way, with scholarships.

Our progression up the school, from Infants to Juniors, was helped by kind, dedicated Miss Hunt. She dressed primly in Victorian fashion, always with a high lace neck to her blouse. She was stern, but attentive to the needs of her flock. One girl struck her as being a little sickly, so the saintly pedagogue paid for regular supplies of Iron Jelloids. A similar offer of Parish's Food offended one mother, who took it as a slight on her maternal care. In the light of the modern clamour from educational-ists for classes of thirty or less, it is worth recording that Miss Hunt, like the rest of the staff, kept perfect order in classes as large as forty-two.

The school did its best with scant resources during the Great Depression of 1929. For a time writing-paper was in such short supply that we were driven to turning pages through ninety degrees after filling them, and starting again – latter-day palimp-sests. The result was well-nigh indecipherable for teachers trying to allot marks, and the experiment did not last long.

Eventually those who stayed the course reached the Scholarship Class of twenty-five eager nine- and ten-year olds – ten of them girls – who studied under the watchful eye of 'Groggy' Gardner. He was short, scarcely taller than his pupils, fifty-ish and wore spats. He had a cane, but used it less for discipline than as a symbol of authority, like an officer's swagger-stick. As a pedagogue he was extraordinarily successful. His pupils spoke and wrote

English grammatically and knew something of geography. Most were adept at mental arithmetic – nowadays a lost art. He implanted some knowledge of world affairs by requiring a duty reporter to choose the most significant event of the previous day and show the class on a world map where it had happened. All except one of his pupils in my year won scholarships to local secondary schools; and of the fifteen boys, all from ordinary working or lower-middle class households, three eventually made it into *Who's Who*. Groggy would have been delighted.

Meanwhile there was religious schism in the family. Both Granny, who had joined us in Bloomfield Road, and Mother were loyal Methodists. Father was Anglican. Mother's writ ran regarding Sundays, which brought a gruelling regime of betterment, starting with Sunday School for us boys at 10.00a.m. and again in the afternoon. A huge wall-scroll asserted 'Thou God Seest Me' – intimidating if believed, but an early cause of scepticism. Then followed the ritual of collecting missionary money from my parents' friends until dinnertime: a ha'penny here, sometimes tuppence from the very generous, all to send missionaries to convert the heathen in India and China. If we were in luck some particularly virtuous Christian might offer a slice of cake. For Mother there was morning service at 11.00a.m., after preparing dinner and making the beds, and an evening service at 6.30p.m.

Even during the working week Wesley Hall still strongly influenced our lives. There were Sunday School outings in blue charabancs, choir festivals, choir rehearsals on Wednesdays, and the Womens' Social Circle on Thursday afternoons. On Mondays Granny helped with the Band of Hope. It was strictly teetotal, but this did not prevent her from making the most delicious blackberry wine. She argued, in all innocence, that as all she had done was to add sugar to the fruit there could be no harm in it: God had done the rest.

It was as a boy treble in the Wesley Hall choir that I had my first experience of choral music. My voice had an extraordinary range: from a contralto F to D or even E *in alt*. Tears came to people's eyes when, as an eleven year old, I sang 'Oh for the wings of a dove' and 'Hear my prayer'. At the Cheltenham Eisteddfod I won the boy soloists' section with ease. But I came to value this gift properly only when my voice was on the point of breaking into an indifferent baritone; until then singing had seemed rather cissy.

Neither father's work nor his inclinations could mesh with the time-consuming Wesley Hall regime. He was manager of the main local dairy – a place full of the clatter of churns and the noise of pumps, pasteurisers, coolers, cream separators and bottling machinery. A fearsome boiler provided process steam. Fifteen feet high, it radiated heat, filling me with dread lest it should explode. Cows take no weekends, so work went on seven days a week. Drab work it was too, with long hours, directed from the twelve-feet-square Dickensian office father shared with George Kingscote, 'The Boss'. Short, stocky and moustached, he sat at a desk smoking a cigar while father worked standing up at a high desk, doing the accounts. A coal fire blazed summer and winter, while three original Old Master paintings looked improbably down from the walls. One was reputedly by El Greco (the Boss called him 'El Greeko'). There was also an 'Ecce Homo'. Memory is uncertain, and searches in the Witts Library of the Courtauld Institute have failed to provide further details of the Kingscote collection. The Boss had started it in the Great Depression, when luxuries were cheap and works of art a potential store of future value.

In summer, when there was a glut of milk, cheese-making added to the work-load: father once won first prize at the London Dairy Show for his Double Gloucester. Often he had no lunch break, and in my teens I used to cycle the mile into town carrying his hot meal in a basket on the handlebars. After a sixty-hour week he came home on Sunday afternoons, drained of energy, to collapse in front of the fire for a snooze, before going to St Mark's at the other end of the town, where his parents lived, to sing in the evening service. Afternoon Sunday School for my younger brother and myself was mandatory – as much to get us out of father's way as for spiritual improvement:

'The Lord help you if you come home and disturb Daddy.' His passionate love of the theatre – he was for years chairman of the Gloucester Operatic and Dramatic Society – and his devotion to the Three Choirs Festival were his personal antidotes to the semi-slavery on which we depended. His one vice was smoking. We children eagerly collected the cigarette cards that came with the packets, knowing nothing of the risks. He died from lung cancer when still only sixty.

As a child I did not feel comfortable with his side of the family. Granny Price was a formidable woman who occasionally came to see us in her Bath chair, pushed by her devoted spinster daughter and slave, Ethel. The opportunity of steering this three-wheeled juggernaut down the street as she left was the only highlight of her visit. Poor woman: she was the second wife of my grandfather, whose main distinction was his virility. She had herself borne him eleven children. He had also fathered an earlier brood of at least half a dozen by his first wife. Consequently I had a huge number of paternal uncles, aunts and cousins, to none of whom I felt particularly close – except for father's younger brother, David, who lived with us for a time. Granny Price, as I later learned, had brought up her family to the strictest moral standards. She was poor, and the children's pocket-money was only a ha'penny a week, doled out by 'Grampy' on Saturdays round the dinner table. But she was never in debt. It was half a century after her death before I learned of her virtues.

Grampy Price had been a strong man in his prime. When living at Maisemore, outside the city, he regularly walked nearly three miles to and from the Wagon Works. His day there as a carpenter began at 6.00a.m. and lasted for eleven hours. During his occasional visits to Bloomfield Road he would announce, with the air of someone distributing largesse, that he had a present for me. As often as not this turned out to be half a dozen broad beans: 'Plant these and you'll have a fine crop!' I was underwhelmed.

Granny Barnes, mother's mother, was a widow, her husband

having died young. He had been a crane driver at the Wagon Works, and had once taken the King of Siam for a ride in his crane. The family spoke of this as one of the great occasions. When I was very small I vaguely remember him taking me fishing, after equipping me with a stick and pepper-pot. I was told to sprinkle the pepper on the water and hit the fishes on the nose as they came up to sneeze. Granny lived with us, and to help pay for her keep she worked as a night nurse. With the money she scraped together she bought me a magnificent Meccano set.

Granny's half-brother, Thomas Perkins Curtis ('Tom'), kept a bicycle shop near Wesley Hall. He spoke with an extraordinary accent, more cockney than Gloucester. He had long ago married his childhood sweetheart, Lucy. When she died in 1975, aged 88, he followed only two days later.

On her eighty-seventh birthday I recorded Tom's reminiscences. He told me something of my maternal great-grandfather, Jim Thomas Curtis – a bad lot who married twice. Granny was a product of the first marriage, along with two brothers, one of whom bummed his way around the Far East and came home with a Chinese wife. When Granny's mother died young she was looked after first by her grandparents, and later by an uncle in Dublin. Meanwhile JTC – my great-grandfather – married Nell, a Sunday School teacher, whom he rapidly corrupted into a drunkard. Eighteen more children were the inevitable result, one of them being my informant, Tom. Eight died young, possibly not all from natural causes:

'At about that time – '84 or '86 – the nurse ... well it wasn't the nurse, it was the old lady with the black bag ... and of course they didn't have proper schooling on the job, and that's why they lost so many. On the other hand, if there was a lot of family she would say "Do you want to keep this one or not?" And if the mother said "I can't have any more family now" she'd take it away with her, and it'd be "still born" – see?'

Here at last was an explanation of why mother had threatened me when I misbehaved as a small boy with the ultimate sanction of sending for 'the lady with the black bag'! These were the unpromising beginnings that had produced the teetotal and impeccably honest Tom, and had led him to treasure his life-long happiness with Lucy.

Chapter 2

Grammar School

The summer of 1931 was one of fevered excitement. Never mind the depression that was afflicting the city, with dole queues and university graduates glad of a chance to drive buses or do a bit of gardening. I was on my way to the Crypt Grammar School, whose maroon and gold cap I had long coveted.

Like other ancient grammar schools, its foundation was partly a consequence of the dissolution of the monasteries by Henry VIII. It began in 1539 as an educational charity established by John and Johanne (Joan) Cooke in the parish of St Mary de Crypt. John had died earlier and his will, dated 1528, included the provision that:

> the said Johanne should establishh and ordeyn a contynuall free scole of Grammer for the contynuall erudicon and teaching of childern and Scolers ther forever.

In making this provision he may have intended to contest the educational dominance that had been enjoyed since the twelfth century by the priory and convent of Llanthony, whose ruins can still be seen at the western edge of the city. The priory was finally expropriated in 1539, and his widow Joan seized the opportunity of purchasing its lands from the Crown.

The new school began in 1540 in a small, specially-built house next to the church of St Mary de Crypt, from which it took its name, and whose rector was John Cooke's attorney. The church was known as originally Blessed Mary of Cryste – to distinguish it from St Mary de Lode and St Mary de Grace – but the similarity of the medieval 'f' and 's' probably led to the corruption of the name into 'Crift' and eventually Crypt. Within a few years the school had established a reputation for scholarship. We know that from Richard Willis, who was at school there in 1571, and who later became secretary to the Chancellor of the Exchequer: 'And this I note, that though I were no graduate of the University, yet (by God's blessing) I had so much learning as fitted me for the places whereunto the Lord advanced mee.'*

The school's great period was associated with the site at Friars' Orchard, into which it moved in 1889. Although in the very centre of the city, only a quarter of a mile from The Cross, its two acres of lawn were screened from the noise of traffic by splendidly mature shrubberies. This academic calm, worthy of an Oxford college, attracted a succession of truly great headmasters. Alas, the city fathers seized Friars' Orchard and razed its century-old trees to build a new technical college, and in 1943 the Crypt moved to Podsmead on the southern outskirts of the town. A decline set in. It need not have happened: there was after all a connection between the manor of Podsmead and the original Cooke bequest that could have been used imaginatively to maintain tradition. A second Friars' Orchard could have been laid out – there was ample space on the new site – but almost nothing was done. It was as though World War II had left a legacy of institutional fatigue even greater than that which followed the Kaiser's war. In addition, like many other once-great foundations, the Crypt had become a victim of the politically-inspired attack on the grammar schools in the 1960s. Although the name was unchanged, I could no longer feel that it was the school that had nurtured me, and to which I owed so much.

All this lay far in the future. For me the immediate and most

---

*The Crypt School 1539–1939 by Roland Austin (John Bellows, 1939).

important fact was that the school was ruled by a benevolent despot. Williams was a classicist who governed mainly by example, and only occasionally through the terrifying discipline of semi-public caning, known as 'the dabs'. The ceremony was timed to take place at morning break, when the full awfulness of the lecture to the miscreant that preceded the punishment could be seen through the glass door of his study. The lesson was not lost on the school, which for the rest of the break became silent and withdrawn.

Bill could write elegant Latin verse. The school still sings his 'Carmen Cryptiensis', set to an adaptation of the melodious carillon tune that the cathedral clock strikes out. And he could be master of the light touch. He once marked an essay:

> Dear Scott,
> Don't talk rot.
> Sorry to trouble you.
> Yours,
> DGW.

He also had the skill, essential in any manager of men, of being able to attract and hold a staff that was outstanding, even in subjects of which he knew little. His dry humour did not always endear him to the City Fathers. Nor did the fact that he wore suede shoes – in the eyes of those who had gone through World War I the very hall-mark of a bounder who wished to skimp on shoe-cleaning. His mistaken belief in Hitler's integrity (he had a German wife) and his pacifism did not help either. Nor perhaps the way in which he would cycle through Gloucester, trailing his tattered gown as a signal that he was not a tradesman but an academic, and as a symbol of the need to prepare the minds of the young for something greater than mere commercial technicalities. Under his guidance this small school of 370 pupils, almost all from unprivileged homes, regularly won three or four scholarships and exhibitions at Oxbridge and London, at a time when universities were far smaller than today and admission correspondingly more difficult. I knew from my first day that if there was to be any way to Cambridge it would be through Friars' Orchard.

Bill Williams had assembled a remarkable collection of personalities to teach us. For French we had 'Burglar' Whiteley, whose soubriquet was popularly attributed to an occasion when he had locked himself out of his classroom and had had to climb in. His broad Yorkshire accent when speaking English did not sully his immaculate French vowels. We began with hours of learning how to produce genuinely French sounds, using small mirrors to check that we were forcing our mouths into quite un-English positions.

Herbert Siggee taught physics by a combination of clear exposition and a variety of tricks designed to keep the class awake – including hurling chalk at offenders, or calling them to the dais and pinching their thighs when they got the answers wrong. It was all an act; but one wonders just how far he modified his techniques when he moved to St Felix's, Southwold – a girls' school. He was also the driving force in the school Scouts, and could enthusiastically 'hold down Swazee warriors' in camp-fire sing-songs.

'Laz' Whitehouse, a natural gentleman whose ability to keep discipline was not his strongest point, taught physics to the lower school and to the sixth form, which was considered mature enough not to cause him trouble. In my last couple of years he gave me individual supervision, Cambridge-style, writing while he taught, and passing me his notes afterwards. He fired my interest in astronomy, into which he had done some research after graduating from Queens'. And it was partly because of his benign influence that I later chose that college as my own.

Laz owed his nickname to his gaunt skeletal figure, of which it was said that there was insufficient liaison between the extremities, and that their articulation left much to be desired. Despite a frail constitution he lived to the age of 102. He was a great walker, and loved the Lake District. One afternoon he had the misfortune to break his glasses while on the fells, but just had time to scramble down to the nearest post-office before it closed and dispatch a telegram to his oculist in London. A letter from his son to *The Times* records that a new pair was delivered by the overnight sleeper train to Windermere and arrived at 8.00a.m. the following morning! The oculist had received the telegram by motorcycle delivery just as he was closing. Knowing the prescription, he made the new pair immediately, sent his boy round to Euston, and had them delivered into the safe hands of the guard. No story better supports the widespread conviction of the elderly that 'newer' means 'worse'.

Mathematics was under the wing of 'Dan' Fletcher, who was also Second Master. He planned the school timetable with immaculate efficiency. I found him a brilliant teacher, though to the weaker brethren he could be acerbic. 'What's the answer? No, don't tell me. Change it. Change it again... That's *right!*' Dan produced a steady stream of scholarships to Cambridge. He had a sweet daughter, Betty, whom I met at the highly respectable dancing class run by Margery Deavin. One night I was seeing her home, the two of us riding abreast on our bikes and engrossed in conversation, when we failed to notice that a bus had stopped. A crash ensued, and I had the embarrassment of explaining to Dan that his daughter had broken both wrists.

My English essays merited at best beta markings, but some culture was absorbed from Wilfred Hook's remarkably eclectic lessons. He did not confine himself to the written word. Occasionally there were recordings of Shakespeare by Henry Ainley or the young John Gielgud. Sometimes he would read Chaucer, using the original Middle English pronunciation. Through his forays into the world of art we were introduced to impressionism, cubism and pointillism. But most memorable was the magnificence of his invective. It was never vulgar: if he wished to castigate a miscreant he drew on the whole panoply of the English language, reducing the offender to pulp and the rest of us to helpless laughter.

'Wilf' produced a steady stream of remarkably accomplished English scholars. They included Derek Brewer, who had chosen the Crypt against his parents' wishes for the most whimsical of reasons: he rejected the blue and yellow cap of Sir Thomas Rich's school in favour of the Crypt's maroon and gold. Thus casually was the education determined of a future Professor of English at Cambridge and Master of Emmanuel College.

Hook, like Siggee, was a scoutmaster. The school scouts existed partly because of Bill's pacifism: he would not countenance a school Cadet Corps. Scouting took its place as a part of the curriculum. And marvellous fun it was – erecting engineering structures to take us over ditches in the shrubberies, using only poles, sisal, rope and a few pulleys. 'Wide Games' on Painswick Beacon against other schools taught us how to penetrate territory held by the opposition, leading inevitably to good-natured scrums at the end. The annual camp provided opportunities to see Devon and Cornwall, and later, as we became more adventurous, France, Switzerland and Germany. Being a hard-working and reasonably intelligent bunch, badge-hunting presented few difficulties, and our uniforms were soon festooned with symbols denoting proficiency in forestry, map-reading, and the couple of dozen other skills that help men fend for themselves. My own 'patrol' of seven boys – I was not the leader – included four who were King's Scouts, and therefore invited to the annual march-past before George V and Queen Mary at Windsor.

One of the skills learnt in the Scouts was estimating distances. So I was gratified but not particularly surprised when, about 1935, I won a height-judging competition at Sir Alan Cobham's air circus, and was rewarded with a flight in an Avro 504K. This was a biplane that had been built during, or immediately after, the 1914–18 Great War. We took off from a field at Highnam, to the west of Gloucester, and made a stately tour of the city in perfect weather. I resolved one day to learn to fly. A year or two later I heard an unusual roar of engines approaching our house from the north-east. I rushed into the garden, and was rewarded by the astonishing sight of the Graf Zeppelin, flying almost directly over the house at a height that could not have been much greater than 1000 feet. At that height the hull subtended an angle of nearly 40 degrees. Nothing we see flying today remotely approaches such an airship in magnificence.

Out-of-school Gloucester was a marvellous place for a boy in his teens. Towns are sometimes classified by population – whether they are large enough to maintain a professional theatre, a good art gallery, or a symphony orchestra. Gloucester in the 1930s had only fifty thousand inhabitants – in such terms scarcely worth a second thought. No matter: fifty thousand is a good number for the young. There are one thousand in every age-year; perhaps one hundred potentially congenial companions. And with no traffic problems for cyclists who knew the side streets, their homes would all be only a few minutes' cycle ride apart. Gloucester's youth suffered none of the loneliness of a great city. Moreover, the Cotswolds were at our door. The beauties of Cranham, Slad, Sheepscombe and Painswick – since discovered by London society – were all within easy cycling distance.

To the west the city is bounded by the Severn, that thrilling river which several times a month erupts in fury as the Bore sweeps in from the sea, carrying assorted flotsam and sometimes dead cattle that have failed to reach safety before its onslaught. At Stonebench, a few miles south of Gloucester, the five-feet-high wave breaks on a shallow ledge of rock – the 'Bench' – before reforming and sweeping on to Lower Parting, just outside the city. There the river splits into two channels. One can stand at the southern tip of Alney Island and have the wave rush by on both sides. The huge tidal range made salmon fishing easy. I was introduced to putcheons at the age of three. These were tapered wicker-work baskets mounted in the wider part of the estuary just above low water mark, through which the rising tide swirled, trapping salmon swimming upstream to their spawning grounds. When the tide fell the harvest was waiting there for collection. As a method of fishing it was totally unsporting, but effective. Perhaps too effective: putcheons were outlawed in 2001. The tide also brought in vast shoals of elvers: baby eels two inches long, caught with an oversize butterfly net. Eaten fried, like whitebait, they were a local delicacy. Life near the Severn was never dull.

In summer cricket was a family obsession. We watched county cricket whenever possible, hoping to see Wally Hammond opening his shoulders and driving fours and sixes. On other days there was home cricket down the side entrance – nine yards of concrete instead of twenty-two of grass, but as sacred as Lord's to those with sufficient imagination. In my early teens my younger brother Michael and I played our own 'Test Matches' – eleven a side, scores properly kept, the various fictional players each carefully endowed with his own identity and individual skill. At the end of the season averages would be worked out, to decide which of our 'players' had been most effective.

Another staple pastime was trainspotting, in the great days of that sport. Two railway lines ran through the town, to stations that Bradshaw's timetable classified as 'almost contiguous' – thereby adding another word to my vocabulary. The Great Western Railway's locomotives wore a splendid green and gold livery, and were named after romantic people and places: King George V, Iron Duke, Waverley, Windsor Castle, Tre Pol and Pen. Many happy days were spent ticking off their names in our locomotive books. In contrast the Midland's engines were smaller and, having no names until the late 1930s, at least on our line, were hardly worth consideration as collectors' items. But it was still exciting to get as close as possible to these minor monsters at level crossings and smell the clouds of steamy smoke. At Tuffley the two lines ran alongside each other, which doubled the chance of making a capture before returning home to tea. And there was excitement to be had in placing small stones on the line at the White City foot crossing, and marvelling at how easily the great wheels crushed them. We were experimentally inclined, and the size of stones grew until prudence called a halt. I sat instead with Peter Bayley on a line-side stile, wondering what might be meant by 'going off the gold standard'.

A few years later the quiet waters of the canal became equally familiar, as we learned to handle the Rowing Club's skiffs and coxed fours. Even walking down the towpath was fun: with luck one would see several motor barges on their way to the Midlands, some of a hundred tons or more. Trows – flat-bottomed dumb barges, well adapted to taking the ground between Severn tides if need be – were hauled by *Stanegarth* or *Mayflower*. (The latter can still be seen in the Bristol Industrial Museum. She is probably the oldest steam-driven tug in the world, having been built in Bristol in 1861.) Occasionally a vessel of several hundred tons looked huge as it squeezed through the elegant wooden swing bridges on its way to the city docks. There it would berth not far from the fire-float *Salamander*, bought after a series of disastrous fires were started on the timber-wharves by an arsonist. The name was a graceful allusion to the legendary ability of these lizards to withstand fire. The docks were a constant joy, with their smells of freshly sawn timber, malted grain and tarred hemp. Powered barges in dry dock, and an occasional tall ship like *Garlandstone*, were reminders that we were only sixteen miles from a navigable estuary. A network of railway lines served the dockside warehouses, cluttering the roads with wagons. They were left untouched sometimes for days, with no signs of management attempting to make its capital work hard. They provided an enjoyable Sunday-afternoon challenge to our ability to move twenty tons a foot or two by muscle-power. The canal's sixteen feet depth provided swimming that was good, if hardly safe by modern standards. Apart from the dangers of deep water, and detritus from the shipping, no-one warned us of rat-borne Weil's Disease. But we survived.

At the age of sixteen a desire to have my own boat took hold, and with the minimal tools left behind by Grampy Barnes I managed to construct a two-seat scout kayak, steered by pedals, aircraft style. Long hours were spent on the loo, reading Pears' *Dictionary of Mythology* in search of a suitable name. Eventually one was chosen for its mellifluous sound: *Lesbian*. I was stencilling this on the hull when father arrived. His explosion gave no clue as to why he was so angry, but the message was clear: the name had to be changed. Eventually *Galatea* seemed a safe choice –

a statue of a woman so beautiful that the sculptor King Pygmalion asked the gods to bring her to life. She found a riverside home at Stonebench, where more than once, after particularly high tides, she was floated in through the front door of the former Stonebench Inn and out again at the back. She still survives, hung on beams in my garage.

At eleven I started to learn the piano, under the Crypt's head of music, Harry Dawes. It was a relief to discover at last what those mysterious numbers placed above the notes meant. A year or two earlier, when mother had given me some rudimentary lessons, I had been confused by so much mathematics. I had read that the figure 3 over a group of three notes meant that they should be played in the time of two, and similarly for the figure 4. But the pieces I was given to learn were festooned with numbers, and I could not imagine how performers could be clever enough to do all this rhythmic adjustment and still make a piece sound convincing. The discovery that they were, after all, no more than fingering instructions was an early reminder that a little knowledge can be dangerous.

Under Harry Dawes progress was rapid, and by the time I was fourteen he introduced me to the organ. Soon afterwards I found myself for a time the village organist at Highnam, close to where I had my first flight. It meant a longish cycle ride in winter over the bleak, exposed causeway to the west of the city. The church was dark, the walls blackened by decades of candle smoke. When I returned there sixty years later I found to my astonishment that all was clean and sparkling, the walls a riot of Victorian frescoes as brilliant as the day they were painted. The artist was Gambier Parry, local landowner and father of the composer. My return had been intended as a pilgrimage to see the little tracker-action organ on which I had done my young best, and on which doubtless Sir Hubert Parry, some time Director of the Royal College of Music, had played before me. That too had changed, replaced by a modern electronic wonder.

Soon afterwards Wesley Hall needed an organist, and I gladly accepted the offer of its more modern electric-action instrument.

25

But for me the organ remained tiring, difficult, and non-intuitive, lacking the piano's immediate correlation between touch and effect. It was also embarrassing to practise with people listening to one's errors, particularly if they were trying to pray. It was not until retirement, fifty years later, that the arrival of a good practice instrument in my own sitting room gave me both the opportunity and the time to get seriously to grips with the instrument.

Being a reasonably competent pianist I was pressed into service accompanying father and his concert-party friends. They sang Victorian ballads with strong moral overtones, like 'Watchman, what of the night?' and 'Excelsior'; humorous duets such as 'Tenor and Baritone'; and love-songs of commendable purity and classicism like Handel's 'Where'e'er you walk' or Coleridge-Taylor's 'Onaway, awake beloved'. It was all done 'straight', with no lampooning, and the audience loved it. It is a genre that has completely vanished.

There were other, more earthy, accompaniment tasks. I occasionally provided background music for conjurors like 'Corky' Manning – the only man I have ever known personally who could spin plates on two billiard cues simultaneously. His family had run a cork-importing business, with a base in the Docks where Spanish cork was unloaded. During the Civil War their imports had sometimes seen previous service as improvised defences: bullets would often be found embedded in the sheets of cork bark. But technology was changing, and the demand for cork falling. When I knew him he was living in an often-flooded house in lower Westgate Street, and supplementing his income by refurbishing car clutches, which at that time still used cork as the friction material. He had been a motor-cyclist since his youth and I was fascinated by his tales of the early machines: how on cold days he warmed up the cylinder with a blow-torch before starting, and how he always wore a bowler hat as a rudimentary form of crash helmet. He had a sweet and beautiful daughter; she married the RAF squadron-leader who became my best man. Fifty years later Joyce and David helped us to celebrate our Golden Wedding.

Once I cycled the ten miles to Newent, to help with a strong-man act at the small theatre. My job was to play – as best I could, and for as long as necessary – 'Gee, but you're wonderful', while the strong man lifted my piano and carried it round the stage. He ended his act by inviting the audience to watch him pulling a double-decker bus along the street with his teeth on the following day.

At sixteen I started piano lessons with Herbert Sumsion, the cathedral organist. He was a natural teacher, who knew how to pass on his considerable technical competence and musical insight. I began to tackle more difficult piano works. Once, when we had finished a lesson on Franck's *Prelude, Chorale and Fugue* he remarked sadly: 'They don't write pieces like that any more.' He was a superb accompanist, who taught me, for instance, to breathe with a singer when accompanying, so as to know when a breath was necessary. He insisted that when sight-reading one should read a bar ahead of what was being played. And he pointed out that one can always find a few bars that define the speed at which a given piece should be played: it is simply a matter of searching for clues.

He was one of those rare people with a sense of absolute pitch. When as a boy soprano he went for an audition he told the then cathedral organist, Herbert Brewer, of this gift. Brewer was intrigued, though sceptical. But just then – it was half past twelve – Gloucester's factory hooters started to blow. Brewer took the young Sumsion out into College Green, and asked him to say what note each siren was sounding. He did so without difficulty. But later, in World War I, this sense of absolute pitch proved an unexpected stumbling block. As a subaltern he had been asked to give a recital to the troops. A piano had been found, and even someone in the regiment to tune it. But it was an old instrument, and the tuner did not dare take it up to the normal pitch. Sumsion started confidently enough, but his mind expected notes quite different from those he actually heard. He broke down, and had to explain to the disbelieving troops that he could not continue.

27

We lost touch after I went to Cambridge. Half a century later I was buying music in a London second-hand shop, just off St Martin's Lane – appropriately in the house where Mozart had stayed during a visit to London in 1764 – when I heard the proprietress, Valerie Emery, put down the phone saying, 'No, I'm afraid we have no works of Herbert Sumsion in stock.'

'He was my teacher,' I said, 'long ago. He must by now be dead.'

'Not so,' she replied, 'he's ninety-three, and I've just been staying with him.'

A heart-warming small-world story. But even Sumsion was mortal. At his memorial service in Gloucester Cathedral we heard how, after the Second World War, he had been offered the post of organist at Westminster Abbey. He had refused, preferring to stay close to his roots, his cathedral, and his beloved organ. When at last I had the chance of playing it for myself, in 1997, it had been refurbished, losing in the process the majestic tubas that had been Sumsion's pride and joy.

I became accompanist to the grandly named Gloucester Amateur Operatic Society which, under father's chairmanship, put on a major musical show every year. By then Gilbert and Sullivan's light operas were regarded as a little passé, and the society concentrated on shows like *The Desert Song* and *The Student Prince*. Its musical director was the genial Arthur Cole, a splendid musician and a close friend of the conductor John Barbirolli. He directed a small orchestra at Cheltenham, and from him I learned some of the practicalities of light orchestral work – tricks like thickening the sound of a small orchestra with the judicious use of a harmonium, without making it obtrusive. Finding a harmonium tuned to the standard pitch of $A = 440$ proved unexpectedly difficult. Most had been built in the late nineteenth century – not then far in the past – at a time when the English Philharmonic pitch was a semitone higher, at $A = 453$ to 455. 'Uncle' Arthur also taught me the importance of producing a strong, easily-read beat. He introduced me to Hermann Scherchen's monumental *Handbook of Conducting*. Discouragingly, it states on page four that '... it is indispensable

28

that the student should play a stringed instrument well enough to be able to sit in an orchestra.' That is a privilege denied me: on my eleventh birthday the gift of a new penknife led, before the morning was out, to a severed tendon in the middle finger of the left hand. Micro-surgery being then unavailable, I could no longer bend the end joint of that finger. This is of little importance for playing a keyboard instrument; but strings are impossible. Nevertheless, Scherchen dispenses wisdom so copiously that acquiring a modicum of conducting technique is not difficult. One then needs practice. The chance came later, at the musically-talented Harwell nuclear research station.

Meanwhile I had reached the Sixth Form, had done reasonably well in the Cambridge Higher School Certificate, and was preparing to have a second try with a state scholarship in mind. Only a very few hundred were awarded each year, equally divided between boys and girls, and competition was intense. Those who succeeded were assured of funds sufficient to take them to Oxbridge with no further drain on their parents' income. In August 1938 we were on holiday in Paignton on the day the results came out. The previous night I could not sleep. I rose at 5.30, went to the station to await the arrival of the newspaper train, bought a paper, and saw that I had achieved three distinctions and a state scholarship. I ran all the way back to the hotel, woke my parents, and told them I was going to Cambridge.

With hindsight I should have gone up that autumn. A war was clearly coming and I should have been better placed to make a full contribution. As it was I decided to stay at the Crypt for another year, to try for a college scholarship at Queens'. That too was successful, and for the remaining two school terms I lived a privileged life, reading more physics and chemistry, learning some astronomy from Laz, running the school Wolf Cubs, and generally preparing for university.

By the time term began the war was a month old. Life went on unaltered except for the blackout. I was not to know, in the autumn of 1939, that I should lose two of my closest friends in naval disasters that had nothing to do with enemy action, or that one-third of my class-mates' names would be engraved on the school war memorial. The future seemed bright, and all was still to play for.

Chapter 3

Undergraduate

I first saw Cambridge one freezing December morning in 1938, when I went to sit the scholarship examination. The college made its decision within ten days. Despite rumblings of war, Christmas that year was unusually jovial.

I had chosen Queens' on the advice of two of my teachers who had both been there. My family was far from rich, so they counselled against places like Trinity, home of the affluent. Queens' then was more modest – academically as well as financially. It is only more recently, following a successful television series, that it has taken its place amongst the academic leaders. There may also have been another reason for this renaissance. When Queens' was founded in 1448 by Margaret of Anjou it had as one of its purposes 'to laud and honour the sex feminine'. Eventually – five and a half centuries later, in 1980 – women were admitted.

The college has lovely, mellow brick buildings and the fabulous Cloister Court. When my physics teacher, 'Laz', had been there before World War I the Long Gallery had been completely plastered on the outside; by the time I first saw it the plaster over the timber members had been removed, adding greatly to its beauty. (Total plastering, I learned later from the city conservationist of Rouen, had been a medieval precaution to protect the timbers against fire; it had ceased to be so important after the coming of powered fire-engines.) A further attraction of Queens' was the river. In spring and early summer the riverside Grove was ablaze with tens of thousands of flowering bulbs. I saw no reason then to regret my choice – nor have I done so since.

When term started in October 1939 Cambridge was still almost untouched by the 'phoney war'. True, chapels and halls had lost their stained glass windows as a precaution against bomb damage, and there was blackout at sunset. But freshmen were still deluged with invitations to join university clubs. We still fed tolerably well. Saturday morning coffee at the Dorothy remained a great occasion. Fitzbillies' marvellous chocolate cakes, at a mere three shillings and sixpence, still provided a cheap and reliable source of satisfying guests. Socialites still strolled along King's Parade with their retinues, wearing monocles and cloaks, and carrying gold-topped swagger sticks. Friends' faces had not yet begun to disappear from Hall table. This easy life continued for three terms, until it was rudely shattered by Dunkirk. We were ordered to leave Cambridge at one day's notice to make room for the troops being evacuated from the beaches. When we reassembled in the autumn of 1940 it was in a harsher world.

During that first year Queens' freshmen had to share rooms, since the college was host to 160 pre-clinical students from St Bartholomew's Hospital (Bart's) who had been evacuated from London in case of bombing. It was one of a myriad adjustments that had been made unobtrusively in the few weeks since war was declared. Having Bart's with us meant that dinner – 'Hall' in college terminology – was an unavoidably compressed experience. To gain space, benches at two of the long refectory tables were set hard against the walls, and could only be reached by walking across the tables. Gowns were a hazard, tending to sweep cutlery from the table; but the manoeuvre quickly became second nature. When the commotion subsided a gong would sound, we would stand, the dons would enter, and the duty scholar would read Latin grace:

Benedic, Domine, nos et dona Tua, quae de largitate Tua
sumus sumpturi...

The grace ran to twenty-seven words – not as long as some, but long enough for shuffling to begin by the time it was half finished. The more socially conscious scholars did the whole thing in one breath, in about twelve seconds. There was one exception, who was so entranced by the sound of his perfect diction – he was not English – that his carefully articulated periods lasted considerably longer. Hunger pangs and impatience combined to make his last words inaudible, as a hundred beefy bodies began to sit down.

Throughout the war the Steward, the aptly named Mr Chamberlain, kept his gentlemen reasonably well fed. The meat ration was supplemented by off-ration venison, presumably from some herd owned by the college. Queens' pudding provided an appropriate and welcome change from soggier wartime desserts. Sugar was not easy to come by, and porridge in the morning was filling rather than enjoyable, until I discovered that marmalade (which for a time was unrationed) provided an excellent substitute. Waistline problems have since weaned me from breakfast oatmeal, but I could return to this wartime habit with relish.

The Cambridge staircase system has much to commend it. Those living on a staircase get to know each other well. They mould each other into something like a family, in a way that is impossible in the corridors or high-rise blocks of more modern colleges. If there is a don on the staircase he provides a link between generations. For a time my rooms were immediately below those of Professor Bailey, a specialist in oriental languages of such immense distinction that when he died at the age of 97, knighted and full of honour, he was proclaimed as Queens' greatest scholar since Erasmus. Once, when travelling in the Caucasus to attend the celebrations marking the 800th anniversary of the Georgian poet Rustaveli, he astonished his audience by delivering a short speech in both the local Ossetic languages. His obituary recalled that it was as if a Japanese had addressed a Welsh assembly in Welsh. He kept his diary in verse form in a private language concocted from classical Sarmatian inscriptions. When a colleague remonstrated that his lifetime experiences might be lost forever should he die before they were transcribed, he remarked that they were not particularly obscure: 'There is hardly a line that could not have been understood by any Persian of the fourth century.' For all their immensely greater importance in nature's scheme of things, how can knowledge of the Second Law of Thermodynamics or nuclear physics compete with that kind of erudition?

Coming from a family of modest means, and from a grammar school, I at first felt some difficulty in squaring up to better-heeled public-school men. How could one contribute to a conversation extolling the sybaritic delights of running hot water, central heating and telephones when home had none of these things? It was not a problem that should have worried me. But I was a freshman in a new society, and still uncertain. I quickly learned the chameleon skills of protective colouring.

What I did not experience was the slightest scintilla of awkwardness with the dons. For them a good school was just that, irrespective of the depth of its coffers. Coming from the Crypt I was *persona grata* with my tutor, a don who had just marked the English essays in the Cambridge Higher School Certificate. The best had come from two of my school friends. I immediately wrote to Peter Bayley, suggesting that a scholarship at Cambridge would be a virtual certainty. He preferred to hold fast to the Oxford option: the opposing ambitions we had cherished since those matchstick races at primary school were not to be lightly cast aside. In due course he became a don at University College. Tom Stock, the other star, became Senior Demi at Oxford's Magdalen College. He went to the war in Burma as one of Wingate's Chindits, was captured, and had a gruelling time in prison. Philip Stibbe, chronicler of that ill-fated expedition, says of him: 'When people question whether there is such a thing as pure unselfishness, I quote this action of Tom Stock's as an example.' He had surrendered part of his water ration to a colleague in greater need.

Perhaps the most heartening feeling on arrival at Queens' was that I was now officially adult, or as near as made no difference.

Notices posted on the screens were addressed to 'Gentlemen'. True, we were still *in statu pupillari*, which meant that our tutors were *in loco parentis*. But the rules were administered with a light touch, except as regards women in college: they had to be out by seven, unless there was written authority to the contrary. The penalty for doing on College precincts what is no doubt taken as an inalienable right by the present mixed undergraduate population was, at best, rustication for the rest of the term, at worst, being sent down permanently.

A factor that I had not fully weighed was the number of hours that had to be devoted to lectures and laboratory demonstrations. Chemistry, physics, mathematics and crystallography were my intellectual diet for three years. The work was concentrated and dry, and although I loved science I did sometimes regret that it did not feel like culture in the same way as an arts course. It was hardly material for arresting conversation. Our lecturers were mostly sound enough, but few had star quality. As teachers some were downright failures. The Cavendish Professor of Physics lost his audience almost completely after only four lectures.

A few moments have survived as memories. Searle, an aged demonstrator, found one of his women pupils having difficulty with her experiment in magnetism. 'Well, you're wearing stays. Take 'em off!' And there was the moment when the genial, but elderly, Alex Wood demonstrated that one's ability to hear high-frequency sounds diminishes with age. He started a particularly piercing Galton's whistle deliberately pitched just above his limit of audibility. He was undisturbed, while our younger ears were in pain. This was the same Francis Galton who published his 'Statistical Inquiries into the Efficacy of Prayer' in the *Fortnightly Review* in 1872. He concluded, on the basis of the thoroughly ordinary expectation of life of royal families, that prayers on their behalf were ineffectual. However, as a letter to *The Times* observed in 1997, one factor he might have overlooked was interference in the experiment by God.

While lectures were time-consuming, they were not at first

35

arduous, since, like others who came from grammar schools, I had done virtually all the first year's work while still at the Crypt. We literally had to wait for those from public schools to catch us up. So I welcomed the cultural pursuits that Cambridge showers on its members. The Music Club was an obvious choice. It met in the Music School, which boasted a perfect concert room in miniature. It also had a number of splendid pianos, amongst which was a Bösendorfer whose tone and touch still remain in the memory half a century later. In my three years at Cambridge I took part in half a dozen concerts, giving performances that Miss Jean Brodie might have described as 'serviceable'. At Gloucester they would have been commendable; but a chastening feature of Cambridge is that however good one may be there is always someone better. This became clear at the Freshmen's Concert a few weeks after term started. David Willcocks, the new organ scholar at King's, gave an immaculate performance of Ravel's *Jeux d'Eau*. Although he was not yet twenty years old, it was immediately evident that he would become a force in British music.

The first time I performed at the Club was with Cecil Pearce, a Bart's student. We played a Grieg violin sonata. Soon afterwards we ran over it again in the panelled rooms of Stephen Wilkinson, the Queens' organ scholar. While we were doing so he sat on the floor, his back to the wall, writing on music manuscript paper. When we had finished he asked if he might try out what he had written. It was a small one-movement Sonata, in a highly personal idiom that had absolutely nothing to do with what we had just been playing. It was the most vivid demonstration I ever had of what is meant by the 'inner ear' – that ability to 'hear' music simply by reading a written page. Later I gave his piece its first performance at the Music Club.

Stephen went down at the end of my first year, reappearing from time to time in naval bell-bottoms. We lost track of each other after the war ended, until one summer evening in 1972, when I was giving a talk on current affairs for the BBC Third Programme, in the interval of a Promenade concert. As the red light started winking I heard the closing announcement at the end of the first half: Stephen had been conducting the BBC Northern Singers.

Despite wartime upsets, Cambridge fought hard to keep its musical traditions intact. One was the annual madrigal concert given by a choir of nearly forty in punts moored to exploit the echoing vault of King's Bridge. Wartime austerity had not touched the programme, which was a beautifully printed twelve-page affair. It contained the warning that:

> ...during the last madrigal, 'Draw on sweet night', the singers in their punts move down the river ... the procession is of the width of six punts ... boats are asked to move out of the way.

But the war could not be entirely discounted:

> In the event of an Air Raid, all college gates ... will be thrown open.

The concert in 1941 was undisturbed, and the singers floated off into the distance without mishap. Not so on an earlier occasion, when the Madrigal Society fell prey to some wags from Queens', which is just upstream from King's Bridge. The culmination of the concert was upstaged by a procession of chamber pots carrying lighted candles, floating serenely down the Cam.

My closest friend in the first year was Kenneth Buttemer. He had been at Bryanston, and some of the musical education acquired in that culture factory rubbed off onto me. Talking to him made me realise how restricted was my knowledge of the repertoire. At Gloucester I had known only piano pieces and large-scale choral works. Suddenly orchestral and chamber music acquired new significance. Until Queens' I had not even known what was meant by 'the Brandenburgs'; now I did. Kenneth left after the first year, and became the first of several close friends in the Armed Forces to die by accident rather than enemy action – in his case from unattended appendicitis in the Middle East.

Another source of musical knowledge was Christopher Terry. His uncle had been the first organist to be appointed to Westminster Cathedral when it was built in 1901, and consequently received many records for review. These he passed on to Christopher, who had shelves full of albums. Listening to gramophone music was not as easy then as now. The records each lasted only four or five minutes, and before playing there was an elaborate ceremony of sharpening fibre needles to avoid damaging the surface. It was in his rooms that I first learned to listen with proper attention to string quartets: Haydn, Mozart, the intellectually charged late Beethovens, the ever-fresh Ravel.

Douglas Victor Abraham Suriarachi Amarasekara (he enjoyed intoning his full name) was a brilliant fellow-student from Ceylon. He was a man to whom all things came easily. He gained a triple starred first in the Mathematics Tripos, was an actor and debater of distinction, and an artist good enough to be hung on the line at the Academy. His pastel portrait of the bearded L.J. Potts, my tutor, captured the man's personality with total assurance. Douglas too decided to grow a beard and to record the fact for posterity:

> So polished, so pretty,
> This excellent ditty,
> Celebrates in terse and elegant verse
> The charm of the beard
> Which at length has appeared
> (Having taken its time)
> In its fullness and prime,
> Adorning my chin and inspiring this rhyme.

And so on for several verses.

Sharing rooms with Stephen Wilkinson in that first year was a namesake and poet, Stephen Coates. I owe to him my introduction to the pleasures of hearing poetry read aloud, as verbal music.

Two dozen of us sat cross-legged on the floor while he read *Old Possum's Book of Practical Cats*, which had not long been published. T.S. Eliot dedicated it to his god-children, one of whom became a neighbour of mine many years later. He also referred to a mysterious 'man in white spats' who, her mother told me, had been a proofreader at Eliot's publishers, Fabers.

With such an abundance of riches it was easy to spread one's time too thinly. Saying 'No' was a discipline not yet learnt. So I went, purely speculatively, to a first meeting of a proposed Ballet Society, and came away with the job of college representative. As men went off to the war I later found myself, for a time, impressed into acting as its secretary. This was an enjoyable distraction, though sometimes a chore: asking speakers to travel to darkened, war-time Cambridge for no recompense strained my powers of persuasion.

The duty of entertaining these visitors was a further encroachment on the 168 hours that are all that nature allows per week, even to Cambridge undergraduates still in the first flush of youthful energy. Once an entire corps de ballet came to tea; relations with my bed-maker remained strained for several days, owing to the amount of washing-up. A punting expedition with other Ballet Society members in honour of the fine dancer, Lisa Serova, revealed that she was as English as myself. For the Ballet Rambert I did a little rehearsal playing and became friendly with David Martin, who danced an immaculate *L'Après-midi d'un faune*. He was killed in a tank battle in North Africa. Marie Rambert herself was often in Cambridge and – on the principle that I ought to know something about ballet – I took a couple of lessons from her. I am no dancer, but this did lead to a memorable afternoon at her house in Holland Park, when she brought out her archives and showed me how the *Illustrated London News* had fêted her during the First World War. The Ballet Society also put me in touch with Kurt Jooss whose ballet, *The Green Table*, was a biting commentary on the futility of disarmament conferences in a world of fully-armed and determined nation-states, as Europe was in the 1930s.

I went as often as possible to the recently completed Arts Theatre, with its pentagonal auditorium symbolising the five arts of drama, opera, ballet, music and cinema. It frequently played host to London actors driven out by the Blitz. Donald Wolfit's company introduced me to much of Shakespeare, and to Elizabethan plays like *Volpone* and *'Tis Pity She's a Whore*. Their performance of this latter was the first since Pepys saw it on 9 September 1661. Generations of students owe Keynes a debt for having made the Arts Theatre financially possible.

Then there was sport. I played tennis frequently with an Indian whose name was so unpronounceable that he was universally known as 'S'. I was as frequently beaten comprehensively. And there was that refuge for those who have no eye – rowing. In my final year I coxed the first eight in the May races. Perhaps because I was a full stone too heavy our performance was only middling, and there were faster boats behind us. As we came up to Grassy Corner it was clear that we could not long avoid being bumped. I used the rudder to wash off the bow of the Christ's boat for as long as possible, but the bump was made just at the corner. We drew quickly into the bank to allow room for the dozen other boats that were chasing behind. The boat that had bumped us spent a moment too long in mid-stream savouring victory before doing the same. Its pursuer just scraped round in the remaining clear water. The following boat was not so lucky: it drove up the bank, breaking its back. The same thing happened to the next, which had been about to make its own bump. The boats were following each other at about ten-second intervals, so all this was happening faster than it takes time to tell. I sat there helpless, watching disaster unfold.

It was some years after I went down before Queens' rowing improved to the point at which the College went Head of the River. At the annual reunion that summer Archie Brown, the elderly don who encouraged and protected the Boat Club, rose and declaimed in his asthmatic voice: 'For fifty years I have waited for this day. Now all that I have to hope for is that we shall never make another bump.' Alas for Queens', fortune has no favourites.

40

The wartime blackout encouraged the gentle sport of night-climbing. A book, *The Night Climbers of Cambridge*, had appeared in 1937. Its illustrations, taken at dawn on the roof of King's Chapel, were a standing challenge to all undergraduates. That went for graduates as well: a Swiss metallurgy supervisor was rumoured to be the Stephan mentioned in its Preface, who had climbed St John's Chapel tower. Whether this was true or not his standing in the university greatly benefited. My own exploits were minor in comparison. They did not even include climbing in over the college gates after they had been locked at 11.00p.m. because the river provided an easier entry. There were spiked iron railings projecting over the water as a deterrent; but they could not extend far without being a navigational obstruction, so it was easy to swing round in a matter of seconds. The porters knew, the dons knew; but this essential social safety valve remained unaltered and fully operational throughout my time at Cambridge.

From 1940 fire-watching and military service were added to our weekly timetable. Inspired by my schoolboy ride in the Avro 504K I chose the University Air Squadron. We paraded up and down Chaucer Road at a brisk 120 paces to the minute, learned the rudiments of airmanship, and were rewarded by a few hours' dual instruction in Tiger Moths. They were delightful aircraft, with a gentle rise-and-fall motion in the summer air, like good-tempered sailing dinghies. On my last flight the instructor, in the front cockpit, put out his hand to caress an inter-plane strut. It was loose to the point of danger. We were back on the ground in record time.

By my third year the University Air Squadron had instituted guest nights, to which we invited officers from neighbouring RAF stations. They were rowdy occasions, which finished with rugger scrums using cushions in place of balls. Our invitation was returned by the Waterbeach station, which put on a display by Army Cooperation Typhoons. Three of them made a series of very low high-speed passes, never more than ten feet above the ground, simulating the way in which they would 'beat up' enemy tanks. During the final pass one of the pilots made the mistake of getting into the wake turbulence behind his leader. He momentarily lost control, his propellor hit the ground, and divots flew. We were grateful that he was thirty yards to one side of our party. The plane flew on, climbing, and aiming to complete a circuit before landing. But it turned onto finals too hastily, stalled, dropped a wing, and spun into the ground. It was the first time I had seen a fatal accident. A sober group made its way back to Cambridge that night.

Fire-watching, in case of incendiary bombs, was another duty. All the colleges had taken appropriate precautions. On King's Parade, outside the Chapel, a large 'static water tank' had been constructed on the sacred lawn. One morning Cambridge woke to find two punts floating there.

There was no shortage of air-raid alerts: I kept a log that showed twenty-four in the month of October 1940. But most were precautionary, and I remember only one night when bombs actually fell on Cambridge. I was on fire-watching duty on the roof of the Porter's Lodge with Harding, the head porter. He kept up a running commentary as though it were a football match: 'They've got the station.' Only then did he remember that he lived in that direction. A second bomb fell near the Catholic church. My friend, Alice Heim, lived close by. She was a Medical Research Council psychologist, who specialised in aptitude tests. Warm, chubby, with an infectious laugh, she cycled round Cambridge on a bicycle that was as near thief-proof as could be devised in that city of kleptomaniacs: with admirable application of applied psychology she had painted it, uniquely, with all the colours of the rainbow. When I called the morning after the bomb she was unhurt, though some glass had gone.

Alice had come into my life as a dancing partner of Betty Hughes. Betty was slim, beautiful, and altogether impressive: not for nothing had she been Head Girl at Roedean. The two were due to dance 'Bomber and Fighter' in a revue, and wanted me to play Rimsky-Korsakov's *Flight of the Bumble-Bee* as accompaniment. Alice entered stage left, and slowly crossed while flapping her arms – a veritable harbinger of death from the skies – while Betty made darting attacks. Alice doubled back behind the backdrop, and re-entered as the next bomber. This never failed to raise a laugh. On her third pass, just before the music ran out, Betty succeeded in shooting her down, and performed a triumphant victory roll. Alice collapsed melodramatically and rolled out of sight off-stage.

One of Alice's special achievements was to train dogs to understand human speech. Her best performer was Robin, mongrel of mongrels, who responded to about 70 commands. He did not rely on eye movements, nor on her voice alone: he performed equally well for me. Robin was killed crossing the road; Alice immortalised him by writing *Barking up the Right Tree.*

Much of my first summer vacation was spent in a Birmingham refrigerator. This unlikely way of passing the time arose because, in the bitter winter of 1939, the British Army had found difficulty in keeping its transport operational. It was before the days of thin engine oil, and the viscosity of the lubricants was such that the starter motors could not turn the engines once they had cooled for more than a few hours. As an ad hoc measure engines were run every three hours throughout the night, but clearly starters needed to be improved. Joseph Lucas not only made the starters, but also had a huge cold-room where whole lorries could be frozen.

This vacation job coincided with the first Blitz on Birmingham. By the standards of what Dresden was to suffer later it was peanuts, but it became wearing because of lost sleep. In one fortnight there were eighteen alerts, ending typically at 4.00a.m. I was unfortunate in living close to an anti-aircraft battery in a park just across the road. Once it opened fire further sleep was impossible.

If there was a plus side to this period of wartime tribulation, it was a sense of comradeship that was almost tangible. Helping or sheltering complete strangers became a matter of course; indeed, a matter of pride. Crime was rare, and the streets were safe, despite the absence of any lighting. We felt a sense of homogeneity that transcended class or social position. A feeling of Englishness stiffened our sinews. It was patriotism in its least jingoistic sense.

During subsequent vacations I did several spells of driving taxis that had been modified to burn coal gas. They carried huge rubber bags on their roofs which, given the low pressure of Gloucester's gas-mains, took twenty minutes or more to fill. They could travel about twenty-five miles on one gas filling, after which one switched back to petrol. Their performance on town gas was poor, but at least they were using an indigenous fuel that put no-one's life at risk from being torpedoed.

At the end of my last term I was interviewed by a Board chaired by C.P. Snow, of 'two cultures' fame. It was the Board's job to decide where scientists should do their war work after graduation. Inevitably, their decision was something of a lottery. How could it be otherwise, since none of us was old enough to have an established track record? I expressed a preference for nuclear work, as I had done earlier in the term to Kowarski during a conversation on Cambridge station. He was the man who, along with von Halban, had brought the precious French supplies of heavy water to England when France fell, and was still engaged on nuclear research. But the Board's decision was that I should join the Admiralty for electronics work, about which I knew nothing. It was not until 1969, during another chance conversation with Kowarski, this time during a visit to the Dragon high-temperature nuclear reactor at Winfrith in Dorset, that I learned that he had asked for me to join him. Had his request been granted I should have been part of the allied wartime nuclear effort, I should never have met the girl whom I married, and the grandchildren for whom these memoirs were written would never have been born.

Contemplating university life from a distance of more than half a century I have only one major regret: I never joined the Union. Politics remained a closed book throughout my time at Cambridge. But not forever. Hiroshima catapulted physics into the political arena. Although I was never a politician in the parliamentary sense, at least I was to have the privilege of a ringside seat on more than one occasion.

Chapter 4

Naval Electronics

Most scientists had an easy war. Those who had gone up to Cambridge in 1939 to read Natural Sciences had been allowed to stay for the full normal span of three years (later entrants were not so lucky). On graduating we were not only allowed to pursue our chosen professions, provided the work contributed to the war effort: we were directed to do so. Some of my colleagues went on operations involving personal risk, particularly in the North Atlantic. But only a few faced dangers like those of the celebrated Commando raid to capture key technical items from the German radar station at Bruneval: on that occasion the military escort's secret orders were to kill the expert should his capture appear imminent! London in the Blitz, and a chance bomb that fell 100 yards away in soft ground in the country, were my own nearest brushes with death at Hitler's hands. It was difficult not to feel that in some way I was cheating. Those of my scientific friends who did try to join the Forces got a dusty answer, and were told to get on with their war work. We had an exceptionally privileged position and, in the hope that whatever we did might help to save our friends' and brothers' lives, we worked long hours as a matter of course.

I was appointed to Admiralty Signal Establishment (ASE), which had moved from Portsmouth to Haslemere to minimise the risk of bomb attack, at a princely initial salary of £270 per year. Work on high-frequency direction-finding (H/F D/F) occupied my next few years. It was part of the background to the submarine war. Against the U-boat any extra piece of intelligence was worth its weight in gold. We needed especially to know the locations of the attacking submarines engaged in convoy battles. If we could take bearings on their reports to base, and do so from a number of direction-finding stations, then by plotting cross bearings we might hope to direct our escorts onto the U-boat wolf-packs.

There were considerable difficulties. Bearings on often rapidly-fading stations were not easy to measure accurately. Convoy battles could take place a thousand miles or more from the British Isles, and an error as small as one degree could result in a fixing error of twenty miles. A more normal uncertainty of two or three degrees might require convoy escorts to search an area one hundred miles across. Should an escort turn north or south to find the enemy? And what might the enemy do meantime?

As the war progressed so did our techniques. High-frequency direction-finding stations were placed at the extreme ends of the British Isles, in Cornwall and in Caithness, to give the longest possible base-line. Groups of stations were used rather than single stations, in the hope that errors might be reduced by averaging. The method depended on assuming that radio waves travelled in straight lines from the transmitter to the receiver. But they reached us only after bouncing off the ionosphere many miles above the earth's surface. If its base had been smooth and level like a mirror we should have had fewer problems. But in practice it seemed to be canted and variable, with the result that radio waves could arrive from directions that could change rapidly by several degrees within a few seconds. Even with these constraints the direction-finding network was far from useless; but for the distant Atlantic battleship-borne systems on the escort vessels were needed if the enemy was to be pinpointed sufficiently well for an attack to be successful.

My task was the modest one of helping to build up the land-based direction-finding chain during its expansion phase. I was a very small part of a truly impressive network. Listening-rooms

47

at Winchester and Scarborough maintained a 24-hour watch on German transmissions. When something of interest was identified H/F D/F operators hundreds of miles away were alerted. The approximate position of a U-boat target could be known within a few minutes.

Meanwhile the U-boat fleet was being re-equipped with an automatic transmission system that sent extremely compressed reporting signals, complete in one-third of a second. Fortunately we had by then a new generation of cathode-ray equipment that could take a bearing no matter how short the transmission, provided we had warning of the frequency. It was a surprise to some of us how frequently such a warning was available. It now seems that the information came from 'Ultra' decrypts, but during the war great care was taken to protect the source.

This work occupied a large section of ASE, located in Nissen huts on the cricket pitch of Lythe Hill House. My new colleagues, mostly civilian, included some of the most engaging characters one could wish to meet. Prominent amongst them were a number of Polish army officers, all electronic engineers. They included my own boss, Matuszewski. When Poland fell he travelled first to the Balkans, where he was interned. There he became friendly with his captors, with whom he whiled away the time playing cards and gambling. Eventually, he was owed so much that he was allowed to escape, as a practical way of settling a debt of honour. From there he travelled to Paris; but when France fell he commandeered a taxi and drove to La Rochelle, sometimes standing on the running-board, waving a pistol and trying to look terrifying (he was the most gentle of men). He managed to board one of the last ships to leave for England. Like his fellow-countrymen he was homesick for Poland and terrified about what might be happening to his family. When, in January 1945, I made the mistake of congratulating him on the 'freeing' of Warsaw by the Russians, his sad reply was that Stalin was as bad as Hitler: 'For us it's the same.' The confirmation of the massacre at Katyn bore out his worst fears.

The most impressive of the Poles was Struszynski, the former head of direction-finding in the Polish State Telecommunications Establishment. 'Stroos' was responsible for ship-borne D/F, a technology that had problems so serious that the Germans assumed they were insoluble. Although the signals were from relatively short ranges – up to 100 miles – where no ionospheric reflection was involved, the ship's own structure 're-radiated' and interfered with the incoming waves, thus introducing substantial new errors. However, any submarines likely to be of interest to the escorts would not be far away, and even with large errors a fair indication of direction could still be obtained. Struszynski succeeded in devising a practical system. His cage-like structures at the top of the escorts' main-masts were essential pieces in the tactical battle. The Germans knew of their existence, but failed to identify their function.

Another cricket pitch denizen was Eric Mendoza, a small, chubby, immensely happy man who later emigrated to Israel. In the build-up to the Normandy invasion he was in charge of navigational aids for the mine-sweeping leaders. The radio-navigation methods he was using enabled distances and positions on the globe to be fixed with greater accuracy than had previously been possible. He was intrigued to discover that the Normandy coast was up to a couple of hundred metres from its previously charted position. The summer of 1944 was exceptionally hot, and one day he came to work without a tie. Although D-day was imminent, and he still had much to do, he was sent home – twenty miles by public transport – to get himself properly dressed! During the turmoil of the invasion one of the precious technical instruction books was mislaid, and EM received a letter informing him that he had incurred Their Lordships' (of the Admiralty) extreme displeasure, and would be fined. Some time later the book was found – someone else had mis-filed it. EM wrote to Their Lordships saying *they* had incurred *his* extreme displeasure, and asking for his money back.

Some of the work on the cricket pitch was concerned with communications. One system which died a rapid death involved making use of the principle that two complementary colours reaching the eye simultaneously give the appearance of white light. This is true whether the colours are red and green, or blue and yellow. The system was intended as a simple security device for Morse code messages transmitted between surface ships. Instead of the usual flashing, what the viewer would see would be a continuous white light. But this would actually be two sets of complementary colours, interchanged according to the sequence of Morse dots and dashes. The message could be read normally if the light was observed through an appropriately coloured filter. All went well until a visitor asked why a light was flashing. A colourblind man had found the system's Achilles heel!

Working closely with the electronics scientists was a group of mathematicians. At the neighbouring Witley establishment, helping with the development of radar, were people who would later be leaders in their profession, like Hermann Bondi, future Master of Churchill College, or Maurice Pryce, who (if legend is to be trusted) later became the first Wykeham Professor of Physics to be challenged by the proctors in the vicinity of an Oxford women's college.

Our own mathematicians at Haslemere explored the physics of re-radiating ships' structures, the propagation of radio waves, theoretically optimal aerial arrangements, and ways of improving the signal strength against the ever-present background of radio noise. Easily the most idiosyncratic was Ray Whipple. He came from a scientific family, his father having been Director of the Kew Observatory. His skill as a mathematician and his amiable otherworldliness excused his errors of noncomformity. During ship trials he had been known to hand an oily rag to the first pair of hands he could find – 'hold this' – even if they happened to be the captain's. Once he was arrested for pushing a bicycle across a field, carrying binoculars, a camera and a one-inch map, in a prohibited area near Chichester. His protestations that he had not been dropped by parachute but was an Admiralty scientist only added to the apparent implausibility of his story.

Life with Whipple could be exciting, though for the wrong

reasons. The civilians at ASE were enrolled in the Home Guard. One day during firing practice I was lying on the ground, about to shoot. Whipple was standing, holding his loaded rifle, safety-catch off, when he accidentally pulled the trigger. A bullet thudded into the ground inches from my head. On another occasion, in a bombing pit, he mishandled a hand-grenade, and was only saved by the alertness of his sergeant, who got rid of it just in time. Despite being so clumsy he was an enthusiastic climber. Alas, his technique was not equal to his ambition and, to the sadness of his friends, this uncharacteristic pursuit led, after the War, to his early death.

Whipple had given much thought to the physics of re-radiation as it affected ship-borne direction-finding. It seemed possible that a different aerial system, more like a miniature version of that used on land, might reduce bearing errors. An experiment at Haslemere seemed to confirm this hope, and a sea trial was arranged. I and my new aerial were hoisted in a huge bucket by the giant hammerhead crane at Vickers' Barrow ship-yard, and it was bolted onto the top of the mast of *Saltburn*, a small mine-sweeper which was our trials ship. We sailed for the Isle of Man in a mounting gale and beam sea. The bridge roll indicator several times recorded more than 45 degrees, before we reached the welcome shelter of Douglas Bay. These further trials confirmed the improved accuracy of our bearings, but the signal-to-noise ratio was much poorer than we had hoped. This had been a worry from the start. What we had not foreseen was that seagulls alighting on the aerial would play havoc with the bearings. That approach was abandoned. *Saltburn* did not long survive the war. Forever hyperactive, she broke away from a tow in the Bristol Channel and finished high and dry on Hartland Point.

Back at Haslemere the war-time routine of fire-watching and Home Guard duties helped to fill our time. Despite flying bombs nights were normally uneventful – except when a German bomber in difficulties jettisoned a bomb which landed just behind my laboratory hut. I heard it coming, and threw myself on the ground. A shower of white-hot fragments flew over my head. In the morning there was a large piece of shrapnel a few feet from where I had been lying. I still have it – a personal reminder that, despite fine words and patriotic sentiments, the essence of war is to rip human beings apart. The Dornier crashed in Fernhurst woods. I went looking for it the next night, but a nightingale began singing a few yards away with such intensity that I gave up the search and enjoyed the concert instead.

By 1944 priorities for the Navy were changing. Germany was nearing defeat, but Japan remained. My Gloucester friend Denis Condick, commanding a Landing Ship (Tank), set off for the Far East across the Bay of Biscay, and was lost in a gale. He was my third close friend to die from causes associated with the war rather than enemy action itself.

The Fleet Air Arm needed a major expansion if it was to make a significant contribution to the war in the Pacific. New training airfields were being constructed, and some that the RAF no longer needed were being taken over. I became involved with the siting and commissioning of radio navigation aids for a couple of dozen naval air stations. Almost all were out in the wilds, and could be reached most easily via the calibration flight, which was stationed at Hinstock in Shropshire. The pilot who flew me most often was the meticulously careful Ian MacDonald. When I took up flying a quarter of a century later a kindly providence decreed that it should be 'Mac' who became my instructor.

All over the country new aerials sprouted at my behest, usually on hills with miles of cable-runs back to the airfield. Whether securing the best possible 'view' was strictly necessary I now doubt. Certainly we did no cost-benefit analysis. It was wartime, and resource availability was taken for granted. Speed of decision and certainty of good performance were the over-riding requirements.

The navigational-aids siting parties visited extraordinary places. In the Orkneys the Navy had three air stations, the most northerly having the ludicrous name of Twatt. This inevitably encouraged suggestions for crests and mottoes that were unlikely to commend themselves to Their Lordships. Twatt's winters were so harsh that cattle on neighbouring farms were kept indoors from autumn until spring. At Macrihanish I tried for a time to find a suitable site on a mountain near the southern end of the Mull of Kintyre. But the equipment lorry was twice caught in a peat bog, and escaped only thanks to a farmer and his team of huge horses. There was Dale on the Pembrokeshire coast, where the runway terminated at the cliff edge; Ronaldsway in the Isle of Man, where to the surprise of the airmen we settled on the middle of the airfield as the preferred site for a homing beacon; Anthorn on the Solway Firth, where one could marvel at the speed of the incoming tide; and Culdrose on the Lizard. There we designed the airfield from scratch. It was sad to envisage those Cornish fields, with their stone hedges and the patina of centuries of farming, giving way to a bleak airfield. It is still operational; only the heart-warming name reminds us of what was bull-dozed in the national interest.

Maydown was the aerodrome nearest to Londonderry. Just beyond was neutral Eire. The area must have been a happy hunting-ground for spies and counter-espionage. But everything looked peaceful, and when I set about calibrating the Maydown navigational direction-finder in a field overlooking the naval base my only preoccupation was with a bull grazing peacefully some way off. A car stopped and a man in US Army uniform vaulted over a gate and started walking towards me. I welcomed this new arrival – he might divert the bull's attention. He pulled out a handgun. I was surprised that the bull was so dangerous. Then he pointed it at me, took off the safety-catch, invited me to put my hands up, marched me towards the radio hut, and accused me of 'transmitting with an antenna'. This was indeed true, there being no other way of doing the calibration. I suffered the indignity of being vouched for, on British soil and to a foreigner, by my laboratory assistant. The thought that he might have been my accomplice fortunately did not enter the gun-toting military policeman's mind. Whipple apart, that was probably my single most dangerous moment of the war. It has coloured for ever my views on the American gun-lobby and on that country's light-hearted approach to other nations' sovereignty.

The abstract mathematical nature of some of the research on direction-finding was something for which I never had much aptitude. I was more at home with practical matters – which may have been why I was sent off to the Far East in the hot summer of 1945, to refurbish the Far Eastern chain of stations. This involved being commissioned as a Lieutenant RNVR. I had previously worn Army uniform in the Home Guard, and RAF uniform in the University Air Squadron. Now I was to wear navy blue – and all this while remaining, legally, a civilian.

A week before leaving England I voted in my first General Election. Victory had been won, and Churchill deemed it politically necessary to regularise the constitution of Parliament. However, those of us who supported the man who had seen us through the European war were appalled to hear him describe Labour as having its own Gestapo – he pronounced it 'Jestapo'. Something seemed amiss with his judgement: these were people who had supported him in a National Government for the past five years. It was only later that we learned from the Churchill archives of the tensions that had existed between him and Attlee.

There could have been no better preparation for the heat of the tropics than wearing my heavy new uniform for several days in London in mid-July, while completing the appointment formalities and waiting for an air passage to Colombo. Some relief came with departure from the capital on 12th July, via an air-line office at Victoria station. Passengers checked in, walked through the building, and there waiting was a short Pullman train of a luxury otherwise unknown during the war years. We spent that night at Poole. The following day a Dakota flew us to Istres, near Marseilles – where an Arab waitress with purple lipstick served lunch – then to Malta for supper and overnight to Cairo.

The meticulous checking of baggage and papers by immigration officials reminded me that although Egypt was still marked red on school maps, no allegiance to the Crown was felt in its citizens' hearts. This was confirmed the following morning, when I had the utmost difficulty in shaking off the attentions of a teen-age shoe-black, who was eying my brand-new white tropical uniform shoes with gleefully malicious intent.

The onward journey was in the Imperial Airways flying boat *Carpentaria*. It carried about thirty passengers in the greatest of luxury. So great, indeed, that there were moveable wicker armchairs, and a promenade deck with massive windows. These were structurally possible because the plane was unpressurised. I was told years later by an elderly BOAC air steward that the galley windows could be opened 'so we could peel spuds out the window'.

We took off from the Nile, somehow finding a clear course through the countless small boats. The aircraft was confined to routes where such water 'runways' were available at intervals of a few hundred miles, so our first stop was on the Dead Sea near Jericho. People were floating nearby in the brackish water, sitting as if in armchairs, umbrellas hoisted against the fierce sun, reading. Taxying to the mooring buoy the Captain opened a small hatch and hoisted a Royal Mail pennant. By such symbolism the British proclaimed Empire and political solidarity to the watching natives.

From Palestine (as it then was) a further 500 miles brought us down from the cool upper air to Lake Habbaniya for lunch in a tent where the temperature was 115 degrees Fahrenheit. Again there was the mail pennant ceremony. Then 300 miles down the Euphrates and its marshes for a night-stop at the Shatt-al-Arab Hotel at Basra. Unfamiliar and exotic fruits graced the dinner table. A hardened expatriate lectured me as he downed his gin and bitters on the importance of keeping up my salt intake.

With our modest cruising speed India was still a long day's journey away. After a dawn take-off we hopped our way down the Gulf, stopping briefly at small settlements called Bahrein and Dubai, and then at Jiwani, almost at the western frontier of India. For the last few hundred miles we hugged the rugged southern coastline of what was then Persia and, further east, what is now Pakistan, arriving eventually at Karachi. The town was only nominally under British influence. Our laws were certainly insufficient to deter petty theft, and my room-mate warned me that the locals were skilled at using fishing-lines through open hotel windows to extract one's valuables. He also taught me the morning ritual of making sure that my shoes did not contain curled-up scorpions before putting them on. An expedition into town to see the sights resulted in a race between our garry and another, whose horse slipped and fell in a mangled heap. Our driver did not stop. We had reached the Far East!

From Karachi an RAF Sunderland flying boat took us low along the palm-fringed coastline, past the straits separating India from Ceylon, and so to the flying boat base at Koggala, in the south of the island. By the time I reached Colombo the following morning the journey from London had taken eight days all told, three of them in the air.

My appointment was to HMS *Anderson*, a 'stone frigate' where the signals intelligence effort was concentrated. It was a place of contrasts. Outside the unexciting huts women gardeners squatted on the grass, cutting it by hand with nail scissors. Indoors a highly competent organisation functioned on a round-the-clock basis, as it had done for the past two years. In a listening room a dozen operators transcribed Japanese signals. Linguists and cryptanalysts from Bletchley Park were making progress in their difficult art. Most were of my own age. One, John Sharman, I already knew.

Because of the distances involved my tasks were more easily listed than accomplished. The H/F D/F station in Cocos needed recalibration. That in Mauritius was due for a total overhaul. A site for a station in Ceylon needed to be identified. There might be intelligence to be picked up when we recaptured Singapore, and it too would need a suitable H/F D/F site. So would post-liberation Hong Kong. The distances involved were vast, and the day of long-distance aircraft had not yet dawned.

Four days after my arrival in Colombo the news broke that

Churchill had been defeated, the electorate having taken fright at his 'Jestapo' speech. Barely a fortnight later, on 6 August, the first atom bomb was dropped on Hiroshima, followed three days later by one on Nagasaki. Being a physicist I was told to report to the Commodore of the base to explain how these devices worked. Fortunately, what I already knew about the fission process made some intelligent guesses possible about both the bomb and future peaceful uses for atomic energy. I left the meeting with a feeling that a degree in physics had suddenly increased in value.

My first visit was to Cocos, an atoll in the middle of the Indian Ocean, 1,500 miles from Ceylon. The RAF took me there in a Liberator. For most of the crew it was their first time over the Equator, as it was mine, so a message to Neptune, dropped as we 'crossed the line', seemed appropriate. The landing strip, made of metal tracking, was laid out along the curving, narrow West Island, one of several forming a perfect coral atoll. The rudimentary nature of the facilities remained in my memory. Twenty years later, when the Ministry of Defence was debating the feasibility of projecting massive British air power world-wide at virtually no notice, via an island-hopping strategy that included Cocos, one simple question regarding the area available for hard-standings brought a crucial meeting to a rapid close.

Surf thundered on the seaward side of the landing strip. On the east side the lagoon was calm. The D/F station lay six miles away on Direction Island. Further round the atoll was Home Island, where the natives lived. It had very sensibly been put out of bounds to British troops. The islands had first been inhabited in 1823, when the adventurer, Alexander Hare, set up a harem and a retinue of slaves brought from Malaya. Four years later Clunies Ross, a Scot, settled on Direction Island with his family. Until World War II his descendants continued to direct the island's affairs under the distant control of the Straits Settlements. There was virtually no disease or crime. Football was the local passion, played in bare feet by the whole community, including the women. This I learned at a victory party. One of my lasting regrets is that I did not make time to accept an invitation to visit Home Island as a specially privileged guest.

A steady stream of warships came and went, and it was not difficult to borrow a Loch class frigate to carry a calibrating transmitter round the station. That took about a day, and there was not a great deal else to do – except swim, read with considerable nostalgia Robert Gibbings' gentle travelogue *Sweet Thames run softly*, and attend to the painful fungal skin infections which in those days seemed inseparable from life in the tropics. I hope and expect that medication has since improved. For us the best cure appeared to be gentian violet, even though it played havoc with our white uniforms.

I joined the queue to get back to Ceylon, but before I could do so VJ day (Victory over Japan) was proclaimed. The destroyers *Caesar* and *Cleopatra*, travelling very naturally in company, set off at high speed in the hope of reaching Perth before the celebrations were over. It was twenty years before I met the captain of *Caesar*, by then long since retired. Robin Maurice entered my life as a much-loved relative of my future sister-in-law, Wendy.

There were in fact two VJ days. On the first, 15 August, a short-wave radio brought us the sounds of cheering crowds in Piccadilly, during a break from watching a Veronica Lake film under the stars on the beach. On the second I flew back to Koggala, where a riotous party was in full swing. A posse of war correspondents had arrived en route to Rangoon and Singapore, which they hoped to reach in time to cover the Japanese surrender. By the end of dinner few were in a fit state to travel, but somehow they were shoe-horned into a Sunderland. It was nearly midnight when it started its take-off run. The night was calm, with no wavelets on the lake – not the best conditions for inducing a heavily loaded flying-boat to become airborne. We heard the engines suddenly cut out, and after a pause the sound of the aircraft taxying back for a second attempt. Someone said: 'That'll sober the bastards!' They need not have hurried. It was nearly two weeks before the surrender was signed in Rangoon, and another fortnight before Mountbatten received the Japanese commander's sword in Singapore.

Meanwhile, Mountbatten was in Kandy, the old capital in the hilly centre of the island, where by a happy coincidence the season had arrived for the Esala Perahera. The war was over, there were no more blackouts, people wished to celebrate, and Mountbatten loved ceremony. By common consent this annual procession, which had been temporarily abandoned because of the war, once again took its place in the Buddhist calendar. It is a parade of the casket reputedly containing a tooth of Lord Buddha himself, though there is, unsurprisingly, some dispute about its authenticity. The casket is taken on an enormous sacred elephant from the Temple of the Tooth around the streets of Kandy as the central element of a huge procession at the time of the Buddhist New Year. It culminates in a ceremony in which a boat carries the priests up the Mahaweli Ganga until, at the first blush of dawn, the river is cut with a golden sword. The water below the cut is last year's; that above belongs to the new year.

The elephant was not allowed to walk on the ground: a carpet was unrolled before him – and rolled up again to be re-used immediately he had passed. The organisers were not averse to the use of modern technology. His form was outlined by fairy lights. Behind him in the procession I counted sixty-eight other elephants, together with scores of dancers, jugglers, torchbearers, fire-eaters, princes, priests, judges and other notables riding in howdahs. Apart from the modern electric trappings it was instantly recognisable as the same ceremony that was recorded in 1821 by a Dr Davy.

Our party was fortunate in having seats immediately below Mountbatten's dais. As the participants came level with us they took pains to show off their special skills to the Supreme Commander. It was almost midnight before we set off back to Colombo. Half-way there our native driver fell asleep, and I watched with mounting disbelief as we bumped our way, seemingly in slow motion, over a small ditch, up the steps of a road-side bungalow, and into the front door. But we were travelling only slowly, and no great damage was done. Two days later Colombo had its VJ parade on Galle Face Green, with Mountbatten for the Navy, Slim for the Army, Keith Park for the Air Force and the Governor of the island all on the saluting base.

Some weeks elapsed while the consequences of the Japanese defeat for the signals intelligence network in general, and my itinerary in particular, were being considered. The days passed pleasantly, indeed at times idyllically, thanks to my meeting Jean Vidal on 29 August. It was on that day that John Sharman introduced me to his fiancée, Margaret, a 'Wren'. The Wrens took part in radio-eavesdropping operations, operated the Hollerith machines that provided a rudimentary computing service for the cryptographers, and generally helped to keep the show on the road. Margaret in turn introduced me to her closest friend, Jean – they had been at school together. I was captivated.

Before the war St Thomas's mess had been a large private house. It was on the waterfront, separated from the beach only by a railway line, whose ancient steam-hauled carriages carried as many passengers outside, or on the roof, as ever squeezed inside. We lived in 'bandas' – huts with half-walls, and roofs thatched with palm-leaves. Large overhangs shielded the interior from the frequent rains, but salt spray from the pounding surf rapidly turned our gold braid green with verdigris. Mosquito nets were essential; as a further precaution against malaria we took mepacrine pills, which rapidly turned us as yellow as any Chinaman. Arrivals fresh from the UK were almost comically pink in contrast.

Three days after I first met Jean the mess put on a ball. She came as my partner, wearing a glorious dress. After supper we strolled across the railway line onto the beach. By the time we rejoined the party thoughts of engagement were in our minds.

Jean had been on the island long enough to know her way about, in both senses. It was not long before she arranged for us to go up-country together to spend a few days away from the humidity of Colombo on the Norwood tea-plantation. This was at Hatton, in the middle of the island, at a height of 3000 feet. Here the temperature was Mediterranean rather than tropical. Strawberries grew in the garden. The air was right for tennis. Our hostess, Mrs Jeffery, pampered us. By the time we returned Jean was ready to write to her parents telling them what was happening.

The war had stopped, work was light, and time off generous. Jeanie introduced me to some of her Dutch friends aboard their depot ship *Plantius*. It was lunch-time, and a 'rijsttafel' was served. I had never seen such food and set about doing it justice under the mistaken impression that the many starters were the meal itself. Then the main course arrived: twenty-four separate dishes, and still two more courses to follow! Evening was well on its way before the meal ended. I have since learned that as rijsttafels go ours was a modest affair – in the best hotels in post-war Batavia they sometimes ran to two hundred dishes.

There was swimming at Mount Lavinia and hitch-hiking down the coast road as far as Bentota, which then had just one small rest-house. The beach was empty and inviting. At least, it looked empty – though if one turned round sharply one might glimpse a dozen small heads disappearing behind coconut trees. Our relationship prospered. Jeanie's love of music, and her wide knowledge of the repertoire, provided a strong bond. We went to a music club meeting in the Da Costas' elegant house and to a concert given by the local virtuoso pianist, Clifford Huntsman. He made a practice of interspersing his playing with spoken programme notes. Before a piece from Granados' *Goyescas* – 'the Maja and the Nightingale' – he mentioned that the word 'Maja' might possibly need some explanation: 'She was more than a woman, but not quite a lady.' The audience smiled knowingly.

There was another recital – two pianos this time – by Cyril Smith and Phyllis Sellick, which sticks in the memory for the worst of reasons. It was a particularly hot night, and although the verve with which they performed the Arensky suite (Opus 15) should have kept me awake the climate was a more potent influence. I fell gently into a semi-hypnotic coma, which ended the moment the applause began. I woke to the sight of a crown and three stars on a khaki background, very close to my eyes – I had fallen asleep on the shoulder of an amused Brigadier!

A week after returning from Hatton Jeanie celebrated her 21st birthday. I had known her for barely four weeks – twenty-six days that helped to shape the rest of my life. The following night I boarded the train for Trincomalee, on the eastern side of the island, bound at last for Singapore. Just before it was due to start the Railway Transport Officer came along the platform, looked into my carriage, and announced that I 'would do'.

'For what?'

'You will be OC train.'

I asked what my duties might be.

'If the train is derailed in the jungle, make sure the troops don't stray too far.'

As dawn broke I saw that the train had lost half its carriages. Anxiously seeking out the guard, I asked what had happened to the rest. 'Massa, this section too steep. Train go next junction, then back for other half.'

I took passage to Singapore in the destroyer *Caprice*. We sailed in company with her sister ship *Volage*, which a year later was to be the victim of a tragic encounter with an Albanian mine in the Corfu channel. We were carrying the Dutch administrator for the northern half of Sumatra, who was to disembark at Sabang. His first administrative act was to bar the ship's company from stretching their legs ashore. The next day we reached Penang. The officers went ashore and were taken on trishaws to the New World Dance Hall. Taxi-girls were available as dancing-partners for a trifling fee; but I had only recently left Jeanie, and the delights of oriental flesh were not for me. I drank beer instead and watched. A well-spoken young Chinaman joined me and, after twenty minutes of pleasant conversation, I remarked on his excellent English.

'I read law at Cambridge – at John's.'

'I was at Queens'. What are you doing here?'

'Oh, I run this place. Would you like a bed-woman?'

I thanked him for his Cantabrigian solidarity, but said I was quite happy just talking to him. He had been at the Singapore bar, but after the Japanese invasion there was little work and considerable danger. So he came up-country, and found brothel-keeping as good a way as any of staying out of trouble. With his initiative and energy he doubtless did well in the post-war capitalist world.

A day and a night running down the Malacca Straits brought us to Singapore, where it was so humid that we slept on deck. Ashore, Japanese prisoners were being used as labourers. When they passed a British officer whole lorry-loads would bow low. Was this truly the much-feared enemy?

My task was to investigate Japanese direction-finding technology. I reported, accurately but complacently: 'The receiver is hopelessly out of date ... workmanship shoddy throughout.' Interrogation of a Japanese officer led me to believe that such stations were all that the Japanese had. As with the Germans there were no ship-borne systems. It was all very low-key and professionally unexciting. A week's work saw the job done. I joined the queue for a flight back to Koggala in a Sunderland flying boat.

While waiting I seized the opportunity to play the organ in the Cathedral, and bought Jeanie's engagement ring. I also went to hear Clifford Huntsman, who had followed me from Ceylon. For one of his encores he chose the same Granados piece that he had played in Colombo, and was half-way through his well-rehearsed introduction about the Maja when a cockney voice shouted: 'Speak up, can't yer. We can't 'ear a bleeding thing back 'ere.' Rarely has a sophisticate been so disconcerted.

During my stay a sizeable portion of the American fleet paid a courtesy visit. Fortunately, they arrived just after, a number of people had died as a result of drinking locally produced firewater, which contained a potentially lethal quantity of methyl alcohol. Two tots gave a 50% chance of death within two days; any who survived were likely to go blind. I went on board a US destroyer and warned the captain, who took the point – US ships are 'dry', so that drinking ashore tends to be excessive. He asked if it were true that the British allowed alcohol on board. I confirmed this was so. He pondered for a moment, then asked, in an incredulous voice: 'Gee, how d'you run the ship?'

Back at Anderson I learned that my next visit would be to Mauritius. By the time I returned Jeanie would be on her way to England. I was given only three days' notice, but our farewells were less painful through being cut short. We had time for one last, delicious day in Bentota, sailing in a borrowed native catamaran, swimming in the lagoon, and eating our usual Bentota lunch of poached eggs, with guava jelly on toast for dessert. On the last afternoon I squeezed in a sailing race at the yacht club, but the wind died and we drifted ignominiously. Late that evening, after a farewell supper, I joined *Natal*, a South African frigate. South of the Equator we passed through the tail of a tropical storm and for a couple of days the quarter-deck was awash, but by the time Mauritius rose above the horizon the weather was set fair.

The harbour at Port Louis was little more than an open bay with a single jetty. Behind it, providing a dramatic backcloth, was a jagged ring of mountains. Moored offshore with a string of attendant barges were two sugar boats. We berthed, and were greeted by Commander Pennefather, who drove me to Naval HQ at Vacoas. This was 1,300 feet above sea level and delightfully cool – like an English May. Pennefather had already retired once from the regular Navy, and had farmed in Kenya before being recalled. I came to value his robust common-sense.

The H/F D/F station at Vacoas had a bad record for inaccuracy. It certainly had technical problems, but the voyage out had alerted me to another possible cause. Also on board *Natal* had been a draft of naval ratings who would be relieving some of the operators. Two-thirds of them had no previous experience of direction-finding, and only limited training. This led me to analyse the accuracy of individual operators. It soon became clear that eliminating the worst performers would greatly improve the value of the station, even with no technical improvement.

Thereafter reported bearings were accompanied by the names of the operators responsible, so that the people at *Anderson* could, if they wished, discount a bearing that made no obvious sense. Operator accuracy correlated well with general intelligence.

The station overhaul took little more than a fortnight and, once again, I was stranded without transport back to Colombo, this time for several weeks. It was a fate easily borne. The island was green and beautiful, with mountains to climb and magnificent waterfalls to explore. There was little urban development, and the semi-tropical jungle that covered most of the island held few dangers. The importation of the mongoose a century earlier had effectively exterminated snakes. When walking in rough country the biggest hazard was from the huge thorny leaves of the sisal plants. Along the coast were beautiful beaches and lonely rocks from which to dive into a clear blue sea – like the waters off Cornwall, but mercifully warmer. One could walk or swim at will, and be on one's own. Hunger and thirst were dealt with by carrying a supply of succulent litchis, costing a penny a pound. Mauritius in 1945 was a paradise.

The inhabitants fell into five racial groups: Creoles, Tamils, Chinese, French and British. The Creoles were descendants of the African slaves who had been liberated by the British in 1835. The Chinese were the entrepreneurs. Instead of speaking of a general store, people would ask the way to a 'Chinaman's shop'. The Tamils, who were brought in to replace them on the sugar plantations, included my servant, Mardi. He was a faithful retainer who, despite his poverty, ironed rupee notes from my wallet without ever stealing a cent. When I left he begged me to take him with me to England. He had no concept of the austerity facing us back home, nor could he have been expected to, given our well-heeled colonial life-style.

In 1945 this mix of coloured races had not yet swollen in numbers sufficient to swamp the French, who mostly lived at Curepipe, in the centre of the island, a few miles from Vacoas. They kept themselves apart from the English, being separated not only by language, but also by their Catholicism and the still lingering memories of the British capture of the island during the Napoleonic Wars. Their quasi-independent existence had been guaranteed by the Treaty of Paris of 1814. I did, however, succeed in making contact with members of a French climbing club, and came to realise how insular many of their compatriots were. One young woman expressed incredulity at the scenes shown in Hollywood films. Could buildings possibly be so high? Was it conceivable that trains could travel at a mile a minute?

As for the English, their linking theme was sport, for which the Vacoas Club catered. It also served as the main-spring of the English social round. Through a contact made there I was invited to the house of the Director of Prisons, Mr Hamilton. His wife, Ruth, had a quite outstanding voice and had performed Brahms' demanding *Alto Rhapsody* at a Promenade concert under Sir Henry Wood, as an autographed photo bore witness. I had the pleasure of accompanying her more than once. My own voice was a light baritone. She suggested that it might be worth having some training when back in London, and gave me the name of her teacher.

The naval mess was another useful source of contacts, one of which resulted in an invitation to join a minesweeper that was engaged in lifting a minefield controlling the approaches to Grand Port, in the south of the island. All went well at first. A dozen mines were recovered and stowed on deck, ready for dumping in deep water twenty miles offshore. But the last defied our efforts for more than an hour, and when the trawl finally snagged on an object it brought up not a mine but a massive anchor with a twelve-foot stock. Once that was out of the way the remaining mine was raised without further difficulty. We speculated that our anchor must have dated from the Battle of Grand Port between the British and French navies a century and a quarter earlier. The captain presented it to the local Army mess.

One day Mardi begged me to photograph him fire-walking. The ceremony was clearly religious, with a ritual period of purification for ten days beforehand. The fire-pit was about twenty feet long. By the time the fire-walkers arrived it had been raked out, and though still hot was no longer red. As the sun began to set Mardi appeared, his face and body daubed with yellow paint, seemingly in a kind of trance. Some of his friends had more extreme decorations, including skewers through their cheeks, and wires holding out their tongues. As the fire-walkers braved the embers an ecstatic crowd kept up a rhythmic drumming. As I left a man was starting to dance on large knives held by Mardi and his friends.

1946 was still only five days old when I sailed for Colombo in a sugar freighter. The *Fort Wellington* was slow but stable; there was no risk of seasickness. She became slower still when the engine-room staff went on strike a couple of days out, and for thirty-six hours we averaged only three knots. Flying fish had no difficulty in overtaking us. I fretted at the delay. While we wasted time drifting the United Nations were holding their first meeting in Westminster. The world was changing fast and I wanted to be part of it. When we were still twenty miles south of the Equator the BBC World Service broadcast the voice of one of my father's best friends, from the Kingsholm rugby football ground in Gloucester. He was Tom Voyce, who, with Father, had organised the city's 'Holidays at Home' during the war years. Tom had been England's rugby full-back in the twenties. He had the largest hands I ever saw, and could pick up the oval ball single-handed as easily as I could an orange. His broadcast was one of the few incidents that broke the monotony of being a passenger without duties on a ten-day voyage. On reporting to *Anderson* I was not sorry to be greeted by the news that I was to go to Hong Kong in a couple of days. Jeanie and her splendid companions were already on their way home. My circle was breaking up.

As we climbed out after a night take-off from Negombo in a particularly spartan Dakota, Adam's Peak and the highlands were silhouetted against the first flecks of dawn. Breakfast at Bangalore was in a tent on the airfield. No-one imagined for a moment that before the end of the century this town would be one of the world centres of computer programming. Who would have known anyway what computer programming might be? The journey continued to Vizagapatam, then across the Ganges delta to Calcutta.

Apart from the swimming club, which was magnificent, though the water was surprisingly cold, my most vivid memory of Calcutta is of a holy man, smeared with ashes and completely naked, executing a solemn dance in the middle of Chowringee, the main thoroughfare. The traffic politely gave him space. No-one apart from me was giving him a second glance, and I was suddenly aware that by staring I was committing an unpardonable solecism.

Another plane took me to Rangoon, where the arrangements fell apart. The stopover had been planned to last only two nights, but the RAF were on strike. Aircrews were fed up with ferrying men back to the UK while their own release was held back. Day after day I hitch-hiked to Mingaladon airfield to see whether the strike had been called off, but it held. I filled in the time with visits to the glorious Shwe Dagon Pagoda, its golden spire rising nearly four hundred feet, and with sailing on nearby Victoria Lake in carvel-built cutters that comfortably held three.

On one occasion I took a Brigadier in the military government as companion and sailing pupil. I believe he was Vernon Donnison, who became Secretary of the Government of Burma prior to independence. Vernon certainly remembered being taught to sail by a young naval officer. A few years later, when we were all back in England, he became our friend, sailing companion and musical collaborator.

Forty years later he told me that he regarded as his most significant act of statesmanship his recommendation that Aung San should head the Burmese government after independence. It was not a popular recommendation in Whitehall, since Aung San had collaborated for a time with the Japanese as commander of the Burmese Independence Army. That, said Donnison, was because he was above all a Burmese patriot. More important, he was an honest man. Donnison's view prevailed, and Aung

San negotiated Burma's independence with Attlee. But on 19 July 1947, six months before the British finally handed over, he was assassinated in the Council Chamber, along with six colleagues, by a gang wearing British uniforms. For those who never knew him the qualities that he stood for can be seen again in the struggle against oppression carried on half a century later by his daughter Suu Kyi.

Over a week went by before we were finally flown out, escorting a lone Spitfire over wickedly mountainous jungle as far as Saigon. And so, finally, to Hong Kong. Kai Tak was then a small airfield, with a mountain at one end hampering any overshoot. The runway extending into the harbour had not yet been built. We got down safely, and there were no landing formalities. Knowing nothing of the local geography, I looked· for transport which might take me to naval headquarters. By good fortune I managed to stop an amphibious lorry which, to my surprise and delight, took me to the harbour, down a ramp, across the water past the battleship *Duke of York* and an armada of junks, to Hong Kong Island and so to Naval HQ. I received a frosty reception from Commander Courage for having travelled in khaki, as was normal in the rest of South-East Asia. I was brusquely told to 'get those things off and come properly dressed in whites'.

It was February, the best time of the year in Hong Kong. The days were dry and the climate Mediterranean. We wore white shorts by day, and 'Red Sea Rig' in the evening: short-sleeved shirt, blue trousers and cummerbund. I stayed in the Junior Staff Officers' Mess in a large house in Conduit Road. It was the highest contour-following road on the peak, about half-way up. Immediately behind the house the ground rose alarmingly. Looking up, I wondered whether there was any danger of a land-slip. My question was answered twenty years later, when commuting into London with Kevin Nash, the Professor of Civil Engineering at King's College, London. Soil mechanics was his speciality. Not knowing that I might have a personal interest, he showed me a photograph in that day's *Times,* of Hong Kong houses swept away after heavy rains. It looked like Conduit Road.

Living in the mess brought me a life-long friendship when I found an Engineer Lieutenant playing records of Walton's *Belshazzar's Feast* on a wind-up gramophone. This, by any standard, was a remarkable encounter. Few people were familiar with the work, fewer still in the Navy. So we got to know each other, and *inter alia* became bridge partners. The partnership was dissolved once we had won a Grand Slam, there being little hope of ever repeating the performance. He was David Garstin, with whom I subsequently motor-rallied, sailed, and enjoyed opera at Glyndebourne.

The town – the district which was later christened Central – was within easy walking distance of the mess, as long as one was on the way down. Coming back involved a climb of several hundred feet. There were bargains to be struck, jade and ivory to be bought at very reasonable prices, narrow lanes to explore, the occasional wedding or funeral to watch, ferries to take to Kowloon or the outlying islands. The skyscraper revolution had not yet taken root. The highest building was still the old Hong Kong and Shanghai Bank, which today stands dwarfed and insignificant. Even so, it overshadowed the cathedral where, a couple of times, I was allowed to play the organ.

One evening the mess invited Admiral Sir Bruce Fraser, Commander of the British Pacific Fleet, to dinner along with senior members of his staff. I gave him news of Charlie Wainwright, the mechanic who had taught me the rudiments of workshop practice at Haslemere and had always spoken with affection of the admiral. Fraser remembered him well; they had been shipmates together in *Resolution* in the First World War. As was naval custom, dinner was followed by a sing-song in a large room on the first floor. All went well until we came to the musician's song: 'Ich bin ein Musikant, aus dem Vaterland...' The musician sings that he can play various orchestral instruments, and the song imitates them in turn, with the verses growing steadily longer. All went well until we came to the orchestral bass. Fifty strong male voices sang 'Zumpa-zumpa-zumpa-ZA...' while plucking imaginary strings and tapping the floor with their feet in time with the music. The rhythm coincided exactly with the resonance frequency of the floor. The repeated foot-taps, though small in themselves, combined to produce a large up-and-down movement – several inches in the centre of the room. I retreated to the doorway in case the floor collapsed. It held – but on the ground floor several beautiful chandeliers and almost the whole of the plaster ceiling lay in ruins.

I was in Hong Kong to find a site for a new H/F D/F. This had the agreeable consequence of allowing me to visit the whole colony at a time when much of it was undeveloped, the population then being only half a million. By the end of British rule it had grown twelve-fold, but in 1946 Hong Kong resembled the western Scottish islands, brought south into tropical seas. It did not take long to rule out the main island as a suitable site, and the lesser ones as well. That left the New Territories: a peninsula twenty miles long leading to China that was technically more promising. I took the opportunity of visiting the frontier, with its regimental badges carved in the rock and, on my return, wrote a favourable recommendation.

In a colony with so much water, and with the weather set fair, there was no difficulty in amusing oneself. The Yacht Club on Kellet Island was reached in a sampan propelled by an elegant Chinese woman skilfully wielding a single oar over the stern. The island has long since been caught up by land reclamation, which has taken the shoreline further and further out into the harbour. There were regular one-design dinghy races. The fleet also included a couple of Teak Ladies – seventeen-foot cutters with small cabins, ideal for pottering round the islands so long as there were no gales. The many sailing junks, with eyes painted on their bows and chickens in cages hung over the stern, were always ready for a challenge to a race. They were ungainly but fast, and it was hard to outsail them in a small boat. The principal hazard was fog. Having no compass, I once had to find my way back without entering Chinese waters, using as my only guide the sun shining through a sea-fog that was thick horizontally but thin vertically.

The war was now over. Like most people I wanted to go home and get on with life. I wrote to Colombo complaining of under-employment, and also to the Civil Service about a job in nuclear energy. I eventually obtained a passage to Colombo by flying boat. While refuelling at Penang high-octane fuel overflowed from the wing tanks and started dripping into the overheated cabin just as a passenger took out his matches to light a forbidden cigarette. I snatched them away in time to avoid incineration. Another casualty would have been the Bishop of St Asaph, who had confirmed my future wife. Back at *Anderson* I learned that I was booked on the first ship home. I was not sorry to be leaving. Once March arrives humidity, temperature and rain make life in Colombo less than ideal.

There was time for one last brief visit up-country to the Norwood tea plantation; and for one last sail in a Water-Wag, the local racing dinghy class, originally an Isle of Wight design. I was drifting in light airs off the harbour when the upper-works of a large passenger ship became visible. It was *Orion*, my transport home.

As we left harbour I reflected on the crowded eight months that had enlarged my horizons and found me a fiancée. Never again would I have the bizarre experience of accompanying half an hour of Welsh songs on Colombo radio. There would be no more rides in a rickshaw. Should I ever again hear the 'chi-chi' dialect of the inhabitants, see Tamils squatting fully clothed in the sea doing their ablutions, watch bullock-cart drivers kicking the genitals of their animals as encouragement to go faster, give the dhobi-women my clothes to pound on river-side boulders, step carefully on pavements red with beetel-juice, pass the ancient banyan-tree on the way to the office, eat mangosteens, or smell the salt spray drifting over Galle Face Green from the ceaselessly pounding waves?

When *Orion* left Colombo she was already carrying three thousand troops, and we embarked a further two thousand at

Bombay. I ate in the first-class restaurant, but conditions on the crowded troop-deck were spartan. It was only a couple of days before the other ranks started complaining about the food and demonstrating outside the first-class quarters. The *Daily Express* led with the story on our return: 'Hunger Strike Staged in a Troopship.' When it was my turn to be duty commanding officer I did 'rounds' with considerable apprehension; fortunately all passed off quietly.

We were alongside in Bombay for four nights, the stop giving me the opportunity of having a meal at the Royal Bombay Yacht Club and of reclining after a memorable curry lunch while being cooled by the resident punkah wallah. It was a moment redolent of the great days of the Raj. So, later in the day, was the ceremony of Beating Retreat. The Royal Marines were impressive and, though I am not a colonialist at heart, I could not help feeling proud that it was carried out with such style. In less than two years British sovereignty over India was to become a matter of history.

Lying off the port of Bombay was a three-funnelled liner, which I was told was the *Strathnaver*. Later, back in London, when walking past a shipping office on the south side of Trafalgar Square, I noticed a model of this ship, but it had only one funnel. Intrigued, I went in and asked whether my recollection was faulty. The receptionist explained that two of the war-time funnels were dummies. *Strathnaver* had been masquerading as the three-funnelled *Queen Mary*, to confuse the enemy.

Concert-parties kept me busy most of the way home. For one I learned Adinsell's *Warsaw Concerto*. For Noel Brophy's revue, *Thanks a Million*, I wrote a chorus song – musical clichés loosely strung together – and did some accompaniment. The review was playing as we passed through the Suez Canal, so I missed some of the excitement. Before then, while still in the Red Sea, there was a memorable half-hour in which a whale came close, with porpoises playing around it, while two huge sharks overtook the ship from stern to bow as though we were standing still. The steady stream of British naval vessels still travelling east as reliefs for the Pacific Fleet flashed challenges in Morse: 'What ship?' Passing Cape Bon, where the Italian army had surrendered, and later Gibraltar, it was easy to believe that we still controlled a substantial part of the globe.

It was a cold April morning when *Orion* berthed at Liverpool, after a night standing off the Mersey estuary while a smallpox case was disembarked. Mother was on the quay, waving a letter. It was from Jeanie. She had changed her mind and would not marry me after all.

Chapter 5

Musical Interlude

It was difficult to settle after returning to Admiralty Signal Establishment at Haslemere. I was not the only one in that position. No-one could say what would become of us in peace-time. The only certainty was that research funds would be sharply cut. I was far from sure that I wanted to spend more time as a servant of the Navy. Other more exciting things were coming up over the horizon, in particular atomic energy. I asked my colleague, Heinz Paneth, to put in a good word for me; his father, a distinguished chemist, seemed to have the right connections. And I began to look at the vacancy notices that were starting to appear. They were the first-fruits of peace, so far as I was concerned.

There was a good deal of report-writing to do, the gathering together of wartime experience. Some captured German equipment added a frisson of interest: there was, for instance, a magnetic tape machine that enabled us to listen to our own speaking voices, in my case for the first time. The Fleet Air Arm produced a smidgeon of work which, in the high summer of 1946, took me to Malta, where the Navy was planning to maintain no fewer than three airfields. That was extravagantly unreal, but no-one had any idea of how the post-war world would be shaped.

It was time for serious reflection on how to survive in this new state called 'Peace'. I had two strings to my bow: physics and music. A physics degree had become a potentially valuable asset, with a new atomic energy industry about to be born. Musically, although a competent pianist, I was not good enough to be a professional performer, so science looked the safer bet. The Ministry of Supply, which held the keys to a nuclear appointment, left me without a reply for so long that I doubted whether they were interested. Then I heard that the BBC was looking for people who straddled music and science. I wrote, and had a reply by return of post.

One day in late August 1946 I found myself in a large room near Broadcasting House along with twenty other hopefuls, all facing aptitude tests. These included listening to recordings and identifying which instruments were playing orchestral solo passages, how many different voices made up a chord, and so on. We were lectured about microphone arrangements, including the appalling problems presented by the Albert Hall echo. With my radio direction-finding experience in mind I suggested that an array of microphones could be made directional, so as to minimise the effects of the echo – '...like a cardioid antenna array,' I said. There were blank looks, embarrassed coughing, and we passed on. Half a century later I understand that something like this is now in common use.

I got the job, and became a Music Programme Engineer at the 'London station' – which meant anywhere from Maida Vale in the west to the People's Palace in the Mile End Road. The MPEs were the intermediaries through whom the musical great and good communicated with their audiences. At that time the word 'engineer' carried weight in the BBC, as in the country. It is symptomatic of our national change of culture that my successors are known as Studio Managers.

While the structure of each day was different, there was the ever-present discipline of the clock. Until joining the BBC I had not been the world's best timekeeper. Now there was no choice: programmes were expected to start to the second. I managed never to fail, and learned that if one really has to be punctual all that is needed is forethought and self-discipline.

There was little that was routine about the job. Every day

was different. Keeping us on our toes were occasional operational challenges, usually with happy endings made possible by the BBC's superb backup system. One day just before Christmas I was in the People's Palace in the Mile End Road – one of the main music studios at that time – for the first broadcast performance of Benjamin Britten's *Ceremony of Carols*. A secretarial error had sent the announcer to Maida Vale, six miles away across London. No matter – the 'continuity' announcer in Broadcasting House was there to deputise. On another occasion, after a morning's rehearsal in Maida Vale, I was asked to go urgently to another studio. I arrived at 1.24p.m., to find the band of the Plymouth Division of the Royal Marines – the same band that I had seen beating the retreat a year earlier in Bombay. No announcer had arrived, nor a programme engineer. The microphone cables lay neatly coiled. A broadcast was due to start in six minutes. To make matters worse, this 'Bandstand' concert was to start with an exchange between announcer and brass: 'Ladies and gentlemen' (brass flourish) 'we present' (another flourish) 'Bandstand!' – and away would go the band with the opening number. That presented no difficulty when the announcer was in the studio, but this time we would have to rely on the continuity people in Broadcasting House. There was just time to tell the band where to set up the microphones, guess a 'level' setting, bundle the bandmaster into the control room – its sound-proof window giving onto the studio – and warn the continuity announcer. The bandmaster conducted the opening announcement through the window, taking his cue from the announcer's voice over the linking loudspeaker; the band stayed cool under fire – they were Marines – and the breathless opening minute passed off successfully.

While I admired the BBC's organisation, its integrity and its sense of public service, I was worried about my pay, which was a pittance. On my first day Ivor Wadsworth, a senior programme engineer, asked how I was going to survive, adding: 'I compose.' I had no such talents, and life proved financially restricted. But there were congenial companions all in the same boat, and I was blessed in my choice of landlady. Lisetta Lagatolla was a slim, kind, rather sad, middle-aged Italian widow, who looked after me like a son. My bed-sit had a boudoir grand piano, and she did not object to the noise of practising. Although there was still rationing we did not go short – possibly because her son was a restaurateur with a growing reputation. As companions she had a family of cats, among whom incest was entirely normal.

It was all very congenial, but it did not take me long to realise that being in this part of the BBC was essentially life at second hand. The audience was not interested in me, only in my mistakes. It was the performers who mattered. I resolved to stay no longer than necessary, but meanwhile to enjoy this window on the musical world. And there was much to enjoy.

There were the conductors. Boult would occasionally come into the control room during a rehearsal and listen for obscure parts like the third violas (we always worked with full scores to keep us aware of the inner parts). Klemperer I encountered only once. One morning we were rehearsing Beethoven's seventh symphony on the Covent Garden stage, and he was not satisfied either with the orchestra's attack or with its rhythm at the beginning of the last movement. 'It's easy. All you have to do is to say my name twice: KLEMperer... KLEMperer.'

And of course there was Beecham. The day he performed Berlioz's *Damnation of Faust* in the Maida Vale main studio remains fresh in the memory. In one place Berlioz moves the action to the plains of Hungary as an excuse for including the Rákóczi March. This begins with a prolonged fanfare on a solo trumpet. Beecham was in a bad temper and was not satisfied with the trumpeter's first attempt, nor the second ... nor the tenth. Finally, the poor man's lip gave out. Beecham threw the stick at him.

The soloist that evening was to be Lilian Stiles-Allen, but she had the remains of a cold; so the Australian soprano, Marjorie Lawrence, was drafted in at short notice. A victim of infantile paralysis, she was in a wheelchair. As she was brought through the door of the studio Beecham stopped the orchestra and, with a sweeping gesture, announced: 'Behold the Queen of Sheba'. Marjorie Lawrence was outraged, and vowed she would not sing for 'that man.' In the event Lilian Stiles-Allen recovered sufficiently for the performance to proceed as planned.

The day's dramas were not yet over. In the final scene Margaret is in Heaven, Faust on his way to the other place. A bell tolls periodically. At rehearsal Beecham was dissatisfied with the tubular bell and asked Jimmy Blades, the percussionist, to find a louder one. For the performance Blades found a truly massive bell, nearly a foot in diameter, and equipped himself with what can only be described as a maul with which to strike it. When the time came he gave a mighty blow. The bell tottered and started to fall. Immediately below the percussion were the tenors. One of them, out of the corner of his eye, saw it falling, and with a save that would have done credit at Twickenham managed to catch it, silently. In the control room I heard nothing untoward. With superb aplomb Blades moved to the smaller bell, which was still on the platform, and came in exactly on the beat for the next stroke. The tenor remained holding the monster until the red light went out five minutes later.

Encouraged by life in this musical environment I started taking music lessons again. I was still interested in singing, though after my voice broke I was only a passable baritone. To try to improve matters I went to Marcus Thompson, as Ruth Parry had suggested in Mauritius. Apart from voice production he had a particular interest in diction. He liked to point out that the English language, unlike Italian, contains many diphthongs which, when sung, need to be stretched out in time. This is not a process that comes naturally so, as an exercise, he would make his pupils whisper the words, dragging out the s-t-r-e-t-c-h-e-d vowels to fill the whole of the musical space.

My sense of pitch was unfortunately not wholly reliable. So I was interested to note when Elsie Suddaby was broadcasting that in the dry acoustics of the studio even this famous soprano had some difficulty with intonation. Her solution was to place the score on a music stand, leaving her free to cup her hands around her ears. Like this she was able to hear more of the direct pure sound, rather than the distorted sound transmitted through the head. The voice sounds different, and control is easier.

Occasionally there were counter-tenors. Once, when two were singing a duet, a soprano waiting to be rehearsed came into the control room to listen – and to ask a delicate question. 'Are they ... real' – she paused, summoning up her courage – '...men?' I set her mind at rest.

Broadcasting was a service that ran twenty-four hours a day, and we could find ourselves working at any hour. We might have to transmit an orchestral programme to South America at 2.00a.m. But the out-of-normal-hours task that I most enjoyed came on Saturday evenings: the singing of Compline by the Temple choir. Their discipline, the unworldly quality of the plainchant, the intensity of the religious experience, all stay with me these many years later.

More routine were the 'lift up your hearts' programmes that I did regularly with George Thalben-Ball, organist at the Temple, and the tenor, René Soames. Plump and jovial, Thalben-Ball was perfection itself as an organist. Soames was a consummate radio artist with splendid diction, though his unamplified voice was slight. We did the programmes in Maida Vale like competent journeymen, without much religious uplift. That was more easily found in the little chapel studio in Broadcasting House, where the immaculate BBC Singers sang for the Morning Service. Alas, they fell victim to the 'bean-counters' in 1994; but for nearly half a century they were living examples of how English church music should be sung.

It fell to me to transmit the first musical item in the new Third Programme – a recital by Wanda Landowska, the harpsichordist. The Third Programme had no worries about appearing overtly elitist. It was to be free of all pressures and devoted to the care and nurture of the arts. If programmes under-ran there would be no tedious filling-in, but 'artistic silences'.

Of course, the idea did not last. Listeners were confused. If they switched on during a silence, how could they know whether their set was working? But for a time a Third Programme transmission was a happy and relaxing assignment.

From time to time I found myself in the Concert Hall of Broadcasting House, a room smaller than its grand name implies. The control room had two buttons, 'Up' and 'Down', which appeared to be without useful purpose. I learned the reason from an old hand. When the Hall was built in the 1930s the architects thoughtfully included a small lift for raising grand pianos from the floor of the hall onto the stage. One day a visitor was in the control room during a broadcast and, asking what the buttons were for, pressed 'Down', without waiting for an answer. The piano suffered a disastrous list. Thereafter the buttons were disconnected, and pianos moved by the more predictable 'heavy gang'.

Our duties included putting on gramophone concerts. It was in the days of the old 78s, which played for an average of just over four minutes per side. A string quartet might easily need six sides, a long symphony even more. The joins had to be as nearly indistinguishable as possible. The manufacturers did their best to assist by making the changes at long held notes, but there was an inherent uncertainty of just under a second, even if one put the needle into exactly the right groove. To help us we always had the full score, and rehearsed, sometimes for half an hour, beforehand. The results were, at best, adequate; even if the joins were perfectly timed, a careful listener could always tell when a fresh side had been started, because the surface noise was different at the two ends of the record. Thank God for LPs, cassettes, and CDs.

Occasionally there were outside broadcasts, like the recording I engineered for the pianist, Michelangeli, on a Broadwood piano that had once belonged to Chopin. It was in poor condition and had to be retuned after every movement, making a live broadcast out of the question. That visit to the Broadwood showrooms was made doubly memorable by being shown a letter from

Beethoven in which he thanked Broadwoods for their gift of a piano incorporating a sustaining pedal: 'This is the altar on which I shall dedicate my music.' In celebration he wrote the 'Hammerklavier' sonata, Op 106.

While all this was going on my relations with Jeanie had taken a turn for the better, and she occasionally joined me in the studios. She successfully survived a severe test of sang-froid when she agreed to turn over for Millicent Silver who, with the Sylvan Trio, was giving the first performance of a work that was still in manuscript. Jean had not been at the rehearsal, when there had been turning difficulties. Halfway through the actual performance, to her horror, she lost her place, and only just in time found that the action had shifted, without warning, to a modified passage in faint pencil lower down the page.

Early in 1947 the Ministry of Supply suddenly wrote, asking if I could go for an interview the following day. It was an implausible display of urgency after six months' failure to answer my letter. Fortunately, I had no clashing transmissions and attended, with the result that at the end of February 1947 I engineered my last broadcast. A few days later I motor-cycled to Harwell from my parents' home, across Cotswold roads six inches deep in rutted ice – it was a desperately hard winter. By the end of the day I had been given responsibility for radiation shielding calculations for the new nuclear 'piles' (as reactors were then called) that were beginning construction. I had found my way back from the delightful cul-de-sac of the BBC onto my career highroad.

Chapter 6

Harwell

The former airfield at Harwell, fifty miles west of London, was being transformed into the greatest of British applied research stations as fast as the government could manage. When I arrived the establishment was little more than a year old, but the staff already numbered close on a thousand. Twelve months later this figure had almost doubled – a pace of development reflecting the need to build an experimental reactor. It was the first step towards a British nuclear weapons programme. However, that aspect of the work received little emphasis. For the vast majority of the staff, and certainly for myself, what attracted us to this bleak and windswept site on the Berkshire Downs was the chance of being in at the very beginning of a new form of useful energy.

I found myself in a unique international assembly of some of the brightest scientists of the day. At the top was John Cockcroft, soon to be knighted and awarded a Nobel prize for his pre-war work on the artificial transmutation of atomic nuclei. From November 1943 he had been head of the Montreal Laboratory of the war-time Anglo-Canadian Atomic Energy Project and, since the war ended, had been planning Harwell's development for almost two years. He displayed effortless competence in absorbing the stream of information flowing from the efforts of hundreds of American and British researchers. My own division – nuclear physics – was headed by Egon Bretscher, a Swiss physical chemist who had come within an ace of discovering fission when he noticed what seemed to be evidence of barium in uranium that had been irradiated with neutrons. He had to live with the frustration of knowing that what he had assumed was an impurity was in fact proof that the uranium had been split into lighter elements – the 'fission fragments'.

For a time his deputy was Otto Frisch who, with colleagues Meitner (his aunt), Hahn and Strassmann, had in 1938–39 helped to make the necessary leap of imagination that established the existence of the fission process that Harwell had been created to exploit. Like Bretscher, Hahn had also found indications of barium. Meitner regarded him as far too good a chemist to be mistaken. Frisch's key experiment took place in Copenhagen on 15 January 1939. As he later noted, this was the clinching observation that established that uranium atoms could indeed be fragmented – 'fissioned' – by neutrons. Because additional neutrons are produced during fission there was a possibility that a chain reaction could be made to act as a new source of energy. Frisch and Rudolf Peierls, both expatriates living in England, drew attention to the potential implications for future weaponry. Only seven years later their speculation became reality.

Frisch did not stay with us long and, after he moved to Cambridge to take the Jacksonian professorship, his place was taken by John Dunworth, himself a product of the Cavendish Laboratory. Besides being a first-class physicist, he was unusually astute in matters political. He later became Director of the National Physical Laboratory.

The other divisions were equally star-studded. Resources were pouring into the site, exciting envy in Oxford, forty minutes away along the twisting old A34. 'All the money and none of the brains' was the university's verdict. To those of us from Cambridge this seemed like sour grapes. In fact, the research divisions – engineering, chemistry, chemical engineering, metallurgy, theoretical physics, nuclear physics – were overflowing with talent. We were young and energetic. Even Cockcroft was only just fifty. Work went on far into the night. Taking work home was the norm. One's social standing was determined by one's contribution to nuclear progress.

Construction continued apace. Harwell was becoming a showplace for VIPs, so gardeners from Kew were drafted in to clear up as each area was finished. There was an air of excitement and expectation about what lay ahead. We knew we were standard-bearers for the country – and needed no further proof than the 'mystery tours' run by London Transport. At weekends these brought red double-decker buses to the Harwell runways, for passengers to gape at scientists digging their gardens, as though we were denizens of a zoo. Newspapers ran headlines like 'Atom Man Was There' when one of us attended any meeting that was remotely in the public eye. It was all very heady and enjoyable.

Married members of the staff lived in the houses left over from RAF days, or in factory-made aluminium bungalows – 'prefabs' – erected on the site. These were intended to last for only a few years, but they were not finally removed until the 1990s, more than forty years later. The luckier unmarried people lived in the old officers' mess, known as Ridgeway House after the ancient track that runs along the escarpment of the Berkshire Downs a mile to the south. The whole site was like a university campus, but with more singleness of purpose than is commonly found in academia.

The weather during the first few weeks was arctic. Henry Arnold, the Security Officer, was seen with his feet in the lighted gas-oven of his prefab, to ward off frostbite. The snow that had started shortly before my arrival lay on the ground until late April, and traffic over the Berkshire Downs along the A34 to Newbury was cut off. This for me was fortunate, because I had been billeted on a Newbury hairdresser, whose only bath was a portable tin contraption on the floor of the kitchen. Pleading the difficulties of travel during the blizzard I was able to worm my way into Ridgeway House as a resident. There I found perhaps forty people who were to be my new colleagues. Outstanding amongst them was Brian Flowers, who later became Rector of Imperial College, Vice-Chancellor of London University, and a life peer.

His future cousin by marriage, Derek Behrens, was a mathematician with an impish sense of humour. On April Fools Day 1948 he produced a spoof 'report' in exactly the style of official Harwell publications. It was the densest gobbledegook which, on close reading, turned out to be an analysis – deliberately and amusingly meaningless – of the statistical behaviour of the canteen mice. Like any genuine scientific report it ended with a mass of references – including one to 'Galli-Curci's Expansion' (Behrens was a musical buff), and another, which gave the game away, to a paper by 'O. Hooke, B. Lyne and Ahevi Synka'. The report duly appeared in the accessions list of the Science Museum. When this came to light he was reproved for wasting public money. He had done nothing of the sort, the 'report' having been published at his own expense. Derek was splendidly and incorrigibly idiosyncratic. Once he submitted his income tax return in verse, and was overjoyed to receive a reply from the Inspector in like vein. One particularly cold day he was stopped by the guard at the gate, who pointed out that he was still wearing his dressing gown. 'It's warmer than my overcoat,' said Derek, and swept on.

For someone about to get married the timing of my arrival could not have been happier. More prefabs were nearing completion, and a word with the housing officer produced an abode at the very reasonable rent of 17/6 a week. It was minuscule – about 600 square feet all told and with only two bedrooms – but it was a home that would be available from Day One of married life, though not earlier (the key was withheld until the week of the marriage). The knot was tied in London that summer at St Mark's, Hamilton Terrace and, after a honeymoon sailing and motoring in Cornwall, I returned to a frenetic schedule.

A major inheritance from the RAF was four huge hangars and their adjoining office blocks, some of which were quickly converted into laboratories. Each hangar covered about two acres. Hangar 7 was earmarked for a cyclotron and other miscellaneous physics equipment, Hangar 9 for the main workshop, and Hangar 10 for a large experimental reactor. Hangar 8, where I first had my office, was home to the nuclear physicists. In it there was a high energy Van de Graaf accelerator and a small experimental reactor that became operational in August 1947. It was called GLEEP – Graphite Low Energy Experimental Pile – and was used for checking and refining the reactor physics calculations for the larger BEPO. Harwell thrived on acronyms, and this one stood for British Experimental Pile, with a final letter added either in the interests of euphony or possibly as a salute to one of the Marx Brothers. In those days nuclear reactors were known as 'piles', because their cores were assemblies of carbon blocks literally piled one on top of another. With the coming of alternative designs, using water rather than graphite, the name was dropped.

I was to be responsible for radiation shielding, including some aspects of the shielding of BEPO, whose construction had already started, and its associated 'coffins'. These were lead containers where highly radioactive materials could be temporarily stored after irradiation in the reactor. I knew nothing about protection from nuclear radiation, and the available information was scanty, so an early task was to assemble a 'shielding handbook'. There was not much to go on – just a few notes brought back from North America, and scattered references in physics journals. Fortunately, it was always possible to devise ways of over-designing that were certainly safe. The fact that thicknesses and weights might not be optimal hardly mattered in the rush to get the nuclear energy programme started. A few years later, along with co-authors Cliff Horton and Ken Spinney, I expanded the small shielding handbook into a full-length textbook.

The colleagues who built and commissioned BEPO were a remarkably congenial group. The chief designer was Dick Moore. When in the Navy he had been awarded a George Cross for work on magnetic mines. 'I just happened to be the only chap around that day,' he explained with his unfailing modesty. It was only when he died in 2003 that I learned from a *Times* obituary that, in fact, he had dealt with no fewer than five. Once the reactor was built the man in charge of operations was Jimmy Grout, who had been Peter Scott's engineer officer in gunboats during the war. He must have been specially chosen for his balance and coolness under fire. Even so he commented that Scott's determination to live up to the standards of his father, the explorer, had led to an unusually fraught war, which he was glad, and somewhat surprised, to have survived.

His deputy, Bob Jackson, was equally agreeable in his very different way. Many holiday-makers have used the special vehicle, which he designed as a spare-time exercise, that assures communication with the hotel on Burgh Island in South Devon at all states of the tide. It uses a hydraulic drive that can survive in a difficult salt-water environment.

The naval flavour extended to the watch-keeping operators, who were all ex-Navy. The nuclear requirements of reliability, technical skill and unflappability were exactly those that had been needed in wartime engine-rooms.

The reactor in its concrete shield was completed and painted in a colour that I had not previously encountered – heliotrope. Although years of work around the reactor have imprinted the colour on my memory I have never had any opportunity to make use of this one and only piece of decorative expertise. On 3 July 1948 BEPO was officially started up in the presence of a number of VIPs. The commissioning trials that followed were not without incident.

The reactor's purpose was to provide an intense flux of neutrons for nuclear physics experiments, and to learn something of the effect of radiation on materials. Unfortunately, this could not be done without also producing an embarrassingly large quantity of heat – 6,000 kilowatts of it – that had to be removed if the structure was not to melt. This was done by pumping a blast of air through channels in the reactor and up a 200-foot chimney. It had to be that high because the argon in the air would become slightly radioactive during its passage through the reactor and needed to be dispersed. Such direct discharge to the atmosphere would not be countenanced today. Between the reactor and the chimney was an expansion joint. When the blowers were switched on for the first time this vibrated, exciting the chimney as though it were an organ pipe. But what a pipe! It must have been the largest in the world and, moreover, one driven by 2,500 horsepower. Several hundred yards away, on the steps of the staff mess, the noise was so loud that shouted conversation could be carried on only with the utmost difficulty. Inside the blower house it was as though a giant were shaking one's chest. An acoustics expert from the National Physical Laboratory quickly found that the expansion joint at the base of the chimney was acting like an oboe reed. A small re-design silenced the Harwell organ.

The reactor performed as intended, except that too much radiation was escaping from one of the shielding faces. A hurried re-examination of the drawings showed that the shielding was too thin over a limited area; the conventional sections used in the drawings had concealed the defect and led to the oversight. To avoid obstructing a large fuel-charging machine, any patching of the shielding had to be limited in thickness, so it was necessary to use special high-density concrete. An urgent request went to the Ministry of Supply for 20 tons of steel scrap, to be used in place of conventional ballast. What arrived was box upon box of surplus aircraft spares: bolts, nuts, washers, etc. Not all were needed, so the surplus was 'liberated' by the handy-men of the team for use in their own workshops. Fifty years later my own supply seems almost undiminished.

BEPO provided the first abundant source of neutrons in the UK, and enabled a commercial radioactive-isotope industry to be started. That was the foundation of what became the highly successful operation of Amersham International. The Navy began to take an interest. They needed to understand more about the implications of nuclear warfare; in particular, how far a ship's structure might provide shielding during a nuclear attack for the crew of a command centre deep in the hull. Early in 1949 we were asked whether we could provide a large gamma-ray source, which would then 'shine' at a decommissioned cruiser, the *Arethusa*, afloat in Portland Harbour. I was told to make the necessary arrangements. I roughed out the shielding requirements for transport between Harwell and Portland, and the dockyard built a suitable 'coffin'. Highly radioactive pellets would be arranged in rows of tubes, which could be wound up and out of the coffin to shine at the ship. The operator would expose the source while he himself was protected by a thick shield. Care was needed, because once the source was exposed he could collect a lethal dose of gamma rays in no more than twenty minutes if he stood in front of the coffin.

As part of the preparation for the trials I made use of some radiation measurements, taken at the July 1946 American Bikini weapons trials, which had just come into my possession. The head of the theoretical physics division expressed an interest – they were new to him – and as he was my senior I naturally passed him a copy. He was Klaus Fuchs, of whom it was written in *Harlequin*, the Harwell Magazine:

> Fuchs
> Looks
> An ascetic
> Theoretic.

He became the most famous of British nuclear spies. No doubt the information went straight to Moscow.

In one of the experiments radioactive sodium was used as the source. This has a short half-life: the intensity falls to half in just under 15 hours, to a quarter in 30 hours, to an eighth in 44 hours, and so on. Speed was therefore essential. The source was unloaded from BEPO at about 2.30a.m. on the morning of 16 June 1949, placed in its coffin – which weighed about 15 tons – loaded onto a naval lorry, and surrounded with several more tons of concrete to bring the radiation level within acceptable limits. We set off, but a hill between Newbury and Andover defeated the heavily laden lorry, which stalled. The driver, being a resourceful man, invented ways of levering most of the concrete off the lorry onto the side of the road – it may still be there for all I know – and we managed to get to Portland by about

6.00a.m. The coffin was loaded onto a large barge, which was towed into the middle of the harbour, and a couple of motor launches were stationed to keep pleasure boats away from the danger area. The experiments started on board *Arethusa*, which was moored about a hundred yards away, where the radiation was easily measurable but no longer dangerous.

Work being finished for the day, I returned to the barge to close down the source. But when I turned the handle, which should have lowered the array of tubes by means of a worm-gear drive, the mechanism seemed unusually stiff. Suddenly something broke, and the handle became useless. It was clear from my radiation monitor that the source was still exposed. I could not safely look from the front, but the gamma-rays scattered backwards from the air molecules were enough to make quite clear that we had a problem on our hands. The Navy looked expectantly at me. I retired to the depot ship to take thought, after arranging for safety patrols to continue. Having cobbled together a periscope arrangement that would allow me to take a peep at the source, and armed ourselves with an assorted collection of things with which to poke it in the hope of making it move, my party returned to the barge. More by luck than skill I managed to loosen the source, which had jammed in its slide, and, no longer driven by the handle, it crashed down into the coffin, where it was at least safe. Whether it could ever be withdrawn again was at that point uncertain. Fortunately, we were then able to get at the mechanism and found that a taper pin had sheared. We trooped back to the depot ship and work started on another. Meanwhile, I was entertained – too well – in the wardroom. By the time the taper pin had been finished I was hardly in a state to deal with the wretched broken source. It was already dark and I turned in early. In the morning everything went smoothly. It proved possible to withdraw the source, and the experiment proceeded.

Apart from helping the Navy I also had responsibilities, as a kind of in-house consultant, for the shielding aspects of two much larger reactors which were to be built at Windscale, on the Cumbrian coast. They were intended to produce military plutonium, but this purpose was still secret. Those of us who were engaged in their construction hoped they would also prove a useful step towards a world powered by nuclear energy. We were sustained in that hope by the speculations of people like Oscar Bunemann, of the theoretical physics division, who explored the possibilities of a power programme that would lean heavily on 'breeder' reactors – for which plutonium would be an essential fuel. However, his exploration took no account of economics or practicalities, of which we knew very little at the time. Fifty years later his hopes were still uncrowned by convincing commercial designs.

A month after joining Harwell I became a member of the Production Pile Design Committee, which had already held five monthly meetings under the chairmanship of Leonard Owen. He was a Yorkshire engineer whose feet were firmly planted on the ground. Two and a half years and thirty-one meetings later the committee's job was done; I had not missed a meeting.

Before I joined, the committee had already begun to consider what type of reactor could best meet the required production rate of around 100 kilograms of plutonium a year. The choice was broadly between reactors that used water as the coolant and those which used a gas – either compressed carbon dioxide or air. In both cases the main structure would be of graphite, which would serve as a 'moderator' to slow down the neutrons created in the fission process, thus making it easier for them to be captured by more uranium. A preliminary assessment by an advisory panel had recommended water-cooling. While those deliberations were proceeding, and because of the political pressures, it was decided to construct earth-mats of concrete large enough and thick enough to provide the foundation for two units of any possible reactor design.

The arguments about reactor design continued. Even at this early stage in the British military programme some thought was given to the possibility of eventually using nuclear energy for electricity production. One of the apparently telling arguments in favour of gas-cooling – the final choice – was that it was believed to have more development potential. The Minister of Supply, John Wilmot, wrote in May 1947, in a minute to the Prime Minister:

'(with gas-cooling) we should be taking a short step in the right direction to the development of industrial power (the water-cooled pile is not, so far as can be foreseen, in the line of future development).'

With half a century of hindsight it is clear that it was at this early stage we became committed, almost accidentally, to gas-cooled power-reactor policies, which were destined to be overtaken by the more competitive water-cooled system developed in America. In 1947 we do not seem to have considered the possibility of a reactor system in which water acted as both coolant and moderator. This is what happens in the Pressurised Water Reactor (PWR) which, three decades later, so strikingly outsold our own designs. We can, however, be forgiven for overlooking the possibility in 1947. Easy loading and unloading is needed for military plutonium production, and this the PWR does not offer. Moreover, optimisation for a PWR is more difficult than for air-cooled reactors, where nuclear physics considerations can be dealt with almost independently of heat-transfer problems. It required the persistence of Admiral Rickover, and resources on an American scale, to solve its technical problems. What is almost certainly true is that the British choice of gas-cooling – later simplified to straight-through air cooling – was the easiest way for us at that time to produce the plutonium the military needed.

It also seemed the safer route. The Americans had used a water-cooled graphite-moderated design for producing their military plutonium. This choice was rejected on the prescient grounds that if for any reason – mechanical failure, corrosion or blockage – one channel were to lose its coolant water, the power output of the reactor might rise uncontrollably. There would be a steam explosion, which could hardly fail to spread radioactivity around our small country, so creating a national disaster. Nearly forty years later that is just what happened with the somewhat similar reactor at Chernobyl. Instead, in July 1947 it was decided to build three scaled-up versions of the Harwell reactor, whose nuclear safety was justifiably regarded as more certain. In the event only two were built.

Since the purpose of the reactors was to provide military plutonium rather than useful energy, the heat generated – over 100 megawatts per reactor – was a nuisance rather than an asset. It was decided to throw it away to the atmosphere, with the help of six megawatts of blowing power. In its passage through the pile the cooling air would become slightly radioactive from neutron bombardment, just as at Harwell, so to minimise any health hazard the air was to be discharged up stacks each 400 feet high.

The design engineers worked under the direction of Jim Kendall who, until his sad early death, was a close friend who shared my love of sailing. As with any engineering design there was always more than one way to do the job, and choices had to be made. Moreover, every solution raised fresh issues. Jim's philosophy was always to choose the more certain route. He did not expect elegance from his design team, but he did expect their designs to work.

The reactors were to have some new features, including a new design of charge machine for inserting the uranium into the reactor. However, design problems arose owing to the size of the finned uranium cartridges: if one hole in the shield were provided for every fuel channel in the reactor, the shielding wall would be dangerously weak. So it was decided to design a charging machine that could service four reactor channels via one access hole in the shielding. But then difficulties arose over the length of machine, which was partly determined by the thickness of the reactor's concrete shield. I suggested that a way out might be to house the machine in a special charge room, separated from the reactor core by a shield that was much thinner than usual but still sufficient to shield the operators from the less intense radiation coming from the pile once it had been shut down. The charge room would, of course, be out of bounds during reactor operation. Its outer wall would form the remainder of the 'biological shield'. This idea simplified the design and was accepted. It was this charge room, with its direct access to the reactor core, that was used by Tom Tuohy when he took the heroic decision to play a hose on one of the reactors when it caught fire in October 1957, during a routine operation intended to remove any damage to the graphite structure from the intense radiation. Before doing so he had to consider the possibility that inflammable 'water gas' might be produced in a reaction with the red-hot graphite. Any explosion would have spread radioactivity far and wide. He judged correctly, however, and disaster was averted.

Settling the final details of the Windscale reactor took many months; meanwhile the reactor structure, including the chimney, was rising from the earth-mat. As each day progressed the design became more and more set in concrete – literally. I began to worry about the problem of access to the reactor core for diagnostic purposes, should there ever be a malfunction. Before the top of the reactor shield was cast I managed to have inserted a large number of inspection tubes, one above each reactor cooling channel. They later provided one of the few ways of observing what was going on in the runaway reactor when it started to burn out of control.

The fact that the reactor was destroyed by fire was not due to any neglect of the fire hazard at the design stage. There had been frequent discussions, though the exact sequence of events that led to the disaster was not foreseen. Uranium catches fire if exposed to air at too high a temperature. Normally the fuel elements would be protected by aluminium sheaths. Aluminium was used because, unlike steel, it does not absorb the neutrons needed in the nuclear chain reaction to any great extent. But it is a poor engineering material, with an uncomfortably low melting point. If a channel became blocked for any reason, so that the cooling air supply was reduced, the temperature might rise outside safety limits. Then, if the aluminium were to melt, the unprotected uranium would burn, and its radioactivity would be blown out of the chimney and dispersed around the countryside. The first chimney was already rising above ground level when I made a speculative calculation about the possible extent of the radiation hazard – assuming, as we had done until then, that the outlet air would remain unfiltered.

Just how the dispersion would take place once the contaminated air left the chimney was outside my knowledge. But the Porton Chemical Weapons Establishment had a limited amount of information from studies of smoke plumes, and there was some published work by Sutton. It was not much to go on, but it served. I found my calculations disturbing, and announced at the next meeting of the Production Pile Design Committee that the air coming out of the chimney needed to be filtered. Leonard Owen leant back in his chair and looked sternly at me. 'Don't be so silly, lad,' he said in his blunt Yorkshire manner. 'Two tons of air go up chimney every second. Can't filter that.' I returned to Harwell a little chastened and consulted Dunworth, who took the case to Cockcroft. He was persuaded and, after some argument, he managed to change Owen's mind.

Further study showed that filtering the air was, after all, just about feasible. By then the only possible place for filters was at the top of the chimneys, where they would be serviced by dedicated vehicles running around little balconies. That is why the bulges in the Windscale chimneys were nearly four hundred feet above ground level, instead of being in the logical place, near the bottom. The filters were known in the Risley design offices as 'Cockcroft's folly'. But when the reactor did catch fire they trapped at least the larger flakes of contaminated uranium oxide, which would otherwise have been blown out of the chimney. By chance I first heard of the Windscale fire from the radio as I came ashore at Plymouth from the USS *Nautilus*, the first nuclear-propelled submarine, having spent the day cruising along the bottom of the English Channel. It was a day not to be forgotten.

Kendall's skill as a mechanical designer failed him only once to my knowledge. It was over the design of the Windscale control-rod drives. Because of the size of the reactors it was necessary to start up slowly, to avoid loss of control over the neutron reaction. But in case of malfunction the reactors needed to be shut down very quickly. The control was carried out quite normally, using neutron-absorbing control rods that could be withdrawn from the reactor for start-up and reinserted for shutdown. However, it was decided to use *two* control-rod drives: the first a slow drive for motoring-out the rods, and a second fast-acting drive for shutdown. There would then be two freewheel arrangements, so that the drives did not interfere with each other. The gearboxes were manufactured and assembled, but seemed to be jammed solid. They were stripped and rebuilt, with the same result. Kendall was called to Windscale from Risley to see what was wrong. After burning up the road in his high-powered Allard he found things just as reported. As he later told me, with a wry smile, it took him another couple of days to realise that two freewheel systems cannot operate back-to-back – they necessarily jam solid. He and his highly skilled design team had been misled by mere words.

While all this was happening Jeanie and I were putting down roots. She joined the library staff, where her knowledge of the Hollerith sorting machines used in wartime code-breaking was put to good use. We planted our garden and, while the windbreaks were growing, evolved a method of escaping from the never-ending gale that hurled itself across the bleak airfield. This was simply to dig down a couple of feet below ground level and make a 'dell', sheltered by ramparts built from the spoil. A new micro-climate was thus created, where sunbathing was possible for at least six months of the year. The dell had room for two or three, who were out of sight of the neighbours. Once, having lent the prefab to a couple of our friends, we returned to find interesting rumours circulating about what might have happened there.

Harwell continued to grow, until it was the size of a small

town. A decade after its inception there were six thousand people working on the site, and a graduate population that matched any university. We revelled in its cultural breadth. Jean took cello lessons from Brian Flowers. He was a good performer, and I welcomed the opportunities for making chamber music with him and half a dozen others. One who added greatly to our enjoyment of life was Sebastian ('Bas') Pease. I had first noticed him at the 1940 Freshmen's Concert in Cambridge, when he performed the Mozart two-piano sonata with a friend. He was also a concert-class clarinettist. Once, with the help of a soprano from the BBC Singers, we performed a varied programme in nearby Wantage: two-piano works by Mozart and Milhaud, a Brahms clarinet and piano sonata, some lieder and, finally, Schubert's *Shepherd on the Rock* with all three of us. I have continued to make music with Bas ever since. In later years he headed the UK fusion research programme, was made a Fellow of the Royal Society, and became the British chairman of the Pugwash movement for international reconciliation.

With so much musical talent it was inevitable that ambitions should extend to a Harwell orchestra. I played no orchestral instrument, so was invited to wield the baton, which I had done previously only for small choirs. In preparation I re-read Scherchen's magisterial book on conducting. With its help, and the aid of a large mirror that provided a depressingly accurate commentary, I managed not to disgrace myself. The orchestra began life a couple of years after my arrival at Harwell.

Meanwhile, Brian Flowers ran the choir, which took Fauré's *Requiem* in its stride, but found more difficulty with 'Jesu, priceless treasure' – Bach has no mercy on his tenors. When Brian left to go to Birmingham to study theoretical physics I took over. After joining forces with the orchestra, augmented by professionals from Newbury, we produced a creditable *Acis and Galatea*. A local priest, Father Nash, implausibly attired in a cassock, sang the part of the hero. Norman Platt, who later directed Kent Opera with great distinction, was the monster Polypheme. But the high point of Harwell music in my time was Haydn's *Creation*, performed on

7 May 1953 with an orchestra of thirty and a choir of sixty. Nothing I have since done compares with the excitement of swinging through the final chorus, with the soloists, choir and orchestra all going flat out, and realising that we were about to succeed – on only two full rehearsals!

Nor were our surroundings in Berkshire an intellectual wilderness. A friend put us in touch with Herbert and Paulise Lugg who, at their house in nearby Aston, had restarted their annual open-air Shakespeare plays after a six-year wartime gap. Herbert had been involved in the highly successful original production of *Journey's End* and knew almost everyone in the theatre, including some of the young up-and-comers. So we had the joy of seeing people of the calibre of Robin Baillie acting like angels, before they made their name in front of a wider public. A 'boy' prince in Macbeth was played by a very young Prunella Scales, years before her many stage and screen successes. It was at a Lugg play, on a clear starlit night, that I saw one early Russian satellite flashing regularly overhead as it rotated, still in the sunlight, while iambic pentameters four centuries old were being declaimed on the brightly lit stage below.

The next village to Aston was Hagbourne and there, through Jeanie's formidable Aunt Dorothy, we were put in touch with Vernon Donnison. By a happy chance he turned out to be the Brigadier with whom I had briefly sailed at Rangoon. He and his wife Ruth took Jeanie to their hearts, and much of my subsequent career can be traced directly to contacts that arose from their friendship. So too, for the next decade, could my spare-time music-making, for it was Vernon who enlisted my help with another small choir, formed ad hoc to sing at a village wedding. From that developed the Sabrinas – an *a capella* group of friends – of which more later.

Just as Vernon helped to shape our lives, so did our next-door neighbours on the Chilton prefab estate. Martin Fishenden was a scientific administrator who became a wise counsellor of first recourse when I unexpectedly found myself advising the Foreign Office on political aspects of nuclear energy.

Martin owned a vintage Aston-Martin tourer. My resources ran only to the cheapest Ford 8 saloon, and I frequently found myself breaking the tenth commandment. The annual Harwell driving tests did something to restore my self-esteem, as I regularly beat him, despite his powerful mount. The secret lay in the narrowness of the Ford. When necessary I could sit in the left-hand front seat and still reach the controls, even when looking rearwards out of the near-side window. It was verging on cheating, but gave a decisive advantage when reversing at speed round left-hand corners through narrow gaps. For four consecutive years my cheap Ford carried the day.

Naturally, Martin and I tried our hands at motor-rallying. I introduced him to David Garstin, who also loved beautiful cars and knew how to look after them. Since we first met in Hong Kong in 1946 David had acquired a $4\frac{1}{2}$-litre Bentley, in which he visited the Naval Liaison Officer at Harwell. We met again quite by chance. The result was an invitation to join him in a Hants and Berks Motor Club rally.

It was no ordinary club. Every imaginable device was used to make rallying more than a series of dashes from one six-figure map reference to the next. In those days one could indeed dash, there being no out-of-town speed limit. H & B rallies were often strenuous, and some participants excelled in their ingenuity. This added spice to rallying, but two basic problems remained. Having a fast car was almost essential, and the order of events was pre-ordained – choice did not come into it. After a few such experiences even H & B rallies could become a little boring. Martin and I decided to make our own contribution to motor sport – a rally in which there would be a strong built-in element of personal choice, giving the man in the little car as good a chance of winning as the owner of a high-powered Lagonda. We enlisted David's help, and he invited the H & B to take part.

The underlying idea was simple. Instead of being stationary, our marshals would move continuously, so that the tactical situation constantly altered. But there were difficulties, the most obvious being to find enough marshals. As there needed to be an ideal solution for the sake of fairness, the marshals would need to follow a timetable. Finally, they had to be instantly recognisable.

We were discussing these points when someone said 'buses'. Instead of using marshals in the ordinary sense why not use the number plates of the Newbury and Oxford bus companies? A pilot attempt quickly showed how to make the rally interesting. The ideal was for encounters between drivers and buses to take place at T-junctions, with cars coming up the vertical stroke of the 'T' at times when buses should be travelling across the top. If, on arrival at the junction, no bus was in sight, the rally crew had to decide immediately whether to go to meet it, or whether it had already gone. If they chose wrongly, they risked being forced further and further from the ideal solution. To add tension the competitors would also have to pay three visits to a fixed marshal (David) in the centre of the competition area, at any time of their choosing, on condition that they came back again twice exactly 50 and 85 minutes later. There would be heavy points losses for failures in timing the visits. The scoring system favoured elegant solutions over rushing around without much thought.

The police and the Royal Automobile Club gave us their blessing. So one fine afternoon in December 1954 eighteen competitors met at the Harwell Social Club to receive instructions. Not since School Certificate days had so many appeared so completely mystified. The rules listed the timetables of fourteen buses, and also asked for the names or numbers of the engines of two trains, one being a West Country express leaving Didcot, five miles away, soon after the start of the rally. With calculated malice this was mentioned last of all.

The rally proved to be all that we had hoped for. There was no doubt about the strong influence of personal choice – the timing of the first arrivals at the central marshal varied by as much as two hours, in a rally lasting less than five. Some regular Monte Carlo rallyists found it altogether too much and gave up.

101

By a happy chance the winning car was the slowest in the competition: a two-cylinder Jowett, with a top speed of 55 m.p.h. – but its crew came from the Harwell theoretical physics division. The only untoward aspect of the afternoon concerned industrial relations. The bus drivers noted many people taking their numbers and concluded that management was engaged in a secret efficiency check. A local bus strike was narrowly avoided.

Chapter 7

Les Cosmiques

The first Windscale reactor was finished in December 1950. But a year before that the design was complete apart from minor details, and the workload was falling off. I wondered what to do next. Because of the war I had missed the normal post-graduate training of an experimental physicist and needed to extend my experimental technique if I was not to lose my place in the scientific rat-race. For that is what it was – there were more scientists alive and working than the total who had lived and died since science began.

An opportunity came in January 1950, when Bruno Pontecorvo, an Italian physicist with an international reputation, joined Harwell from Canada, where he had worked on nuclear energy during the war. He had been one of the celebrated Rome team, led by Fermi which, in the mid-thirties, had explored the artificial radioactivity induced by slow neutrons. This had been one of the stepping-stones towards the discovery of fission. My request to work under him was approved, as part of his 'Independent Research Group', which was intended to provide a nursery for experimental physics: people would join 'Ponte' for a limited period, do work that was intellectually stimulating regardless of immediate utility, and move back to more directed work when they had profited from the contact. It was a generous concept but, apart from myself, few of the team came and went as intended – life in IRG was too congenial to be abandoned lightly.

There was the question of what research to pursue. Science does only what it knows how to do. New techniques pave the way for new discoveries. Pontecorvo had a reputation for making and using 'proportional counters', which seemed potentially useful for analyzing the cosmic rays that stream into the atmosphere from outer space. New particles, mesons, had recently been discovered. Although nowadays they can be made in giant accelerators in the laboratory, in 1949 the easiest way to study them was to go to the top of a mountain and catch them before they had been attenuated by the atmosphere. I set about making proportional counters and the necessary recording apparatus. Pontecorvo consulted possible collaborators who had high-altitude laboratories. There were four in Europe: on the Jungfraujoch in Switzerland, on the Pic du Midi in the Pyrenées, at Cervinia on the Italian side of the Matterhorn, and in France, 12,000 feet high, near Mont Blanc. Pontecorvo made friends with the Ecole Polytechnique in Paris, and I was invited to plan an expedition to their Aiguille du Midi laboratory at Chamonix.

In the intervening months it became increasingly clear that Pontecorvo was not intending to stay long at Harwell. He was fretting that so many chairs of physics were being filled by those who had led the country's scientific effort in wartime. As a recently naturalised citizen he felt at a disadvantage. Back in Italy there were two vacant chairs of physics, in Pisa and in Rome – but they were for Italian citizens, and he was now officially British. He was still making up his mind when an offer came from Liverpool. Excellent facilities were available, but he was not sure that he wanted to work in the cold north-west.

On 3 February 1950 I was listening to the BBC lunch-time news when the jolting announcement came that Klaus Fuchs, head of the theoretical physics division, had been arrested for espionage. I walked back to Hangar 8 and told Pontecorvo. His immediate reaction was to speak to Fuchs's secretary. Reassured, he told me that Fuchs was at a meeting in London. Indeed he was, but no longer as a free man. The Fuchs trial led Pontecorvo to confess to Henry Arnold, the security officer (whom we have already met with his feet in the oven), that his brother, Gilberto, was a communist. That alone might not have undermined his position; but in March came a report from Sweden that both Pontecorvo and his wife had been communists themselves. He was in danger of becoming *persona non grata*. Liverpool suddenly looked attractive. He accepted the offer and arranged to take up a professorial appointment at the beginning of 1951.

I knew little of this at the time and busied myself with preparations for the exciting prospect of working in a mountain environment. Our French collaborators paid us a visit; the experiments to be performed were settled. The Aiguille du Midi laboratory was equipped with a large cloud chamber that produced magnificent pictures of the passage of cosmic-ray particles through the atmosphere. This was done by suddenly expanding the volume of the chamber, which contained a saturated gas, and photographing droplets condensing on the electrons wrenched from the atoms by the cosmic rays. A strong magnetic field bent the tracks of the particles and enabled their momentum to be measured. In conjunction with our own equipment we hoped to be able to measure the mass of each cosmic-ray particle.

The French team was under Paul Chanson, the deputy director. Although nominally number two, in practice he was the genial but absolute boss. The formal holder of the title 'Director', Professor Leprince-Ringuet, having a poor head for heights, had only once made a visit. Chanson and his team went on to play an important part in the French atomic bomb project, but I knew nothing of this while making my preparations. I have since wondered whether the weapons connection influenced Pontecorvo's choice of collaborators.

Harwell provided me with a three-ton lorry and enough electronic and mechanical spares to make us self-sufficient. Pam Rothwell, another member of Pontecorvo's group, persuaded him to send her also, and a third member, David West, with whom I had been at Cambridge, came along for a holiday. He motor-cycled, which opened up the possibility of Jeanie coming too, on the pillion. She endured the first 100 miles, but with 500 still to go I took pity on her and moved her into the lorry, regardless of insurance problems.

Having a three-ton vehicle simplified the problem of negotiating the traffic maelstrom at the Etoile. We made stately progress down the Champs Elysées and garaged the lorry for the night at the Embassy. The following day we called on one of Chanson's colleagues, Professor Nageotte. He was an elderly, somewhat pinched figure, married to a sculptress who specialised in decorating swords for Academicians. As we arrived at the floor of his flat the lift door was opened by a patriarch in a red velvet cloak, with a matching hat of the kind popular amongst artists. We commented on this striking figure. 'Yes,' said Nageotte, 'he's an artist who lives opposite. I don't expect you've heard of him. His name's Matisse.'

Approaching Chamonix we had our first sight of Mont Blanc, dazzling white in the August sun. It was to be my home for an incident-filled three months. I would return twice more, in 1951 and 1953.

The laboratory was served by the old Téléférique de l'Aiguille du Midi, long since decommissioned. It started from Les Pélerins, on the Geneva side of Chamonix, and proceeded in two conventional stages as far as Plan des Aiguilles at about 8000 feet. We then transferred to the 'petite benne', a small steel tray about six feet by three feet, with sides perhaps ten inches high. This carried us up in one dizzy span to a rock spur about 2000 feet higher. There we transferred to another benne for the second part of the journey. The transfer needed to be made with care. It involved climbing perhaps thirty steps that were often ice-covered, with no protection in case of a slip. Once seated in the upper benne one touched a metal wand onto the supporting cables, which gave Péderot at Plan des Aiguilles the signal to start.

The second span provided an unforgettable journey close alongside the western face of the Aiguille du Midi. Its dramatic qualities had been exploited a year earlier in the Claude Rains film, *The White Tower*. At the upper terminus there was another

Heath Robinson station, escape from which involved walking twenty feet along a plank above a sheer precipice; the plank had no handrail and was also frequently covered with ice. Then a few safer steps, and we were in the dazzling whiteness of the Vallée Blanche in high summer, at the Col Simon. From there it was a scramble up a snow slope to the laboratory building, a quarter of a mile away. Jeanie, who had come up for the day, took it all in her stride.

The laboratory was built on a rocky ridge about half a mile long that formed the northern boundary of the Vallée Blanche, then a lonely plateau not yet accessible to skiers. At its eastern end it was just wide enough for a building with rooms for a laboratory, a kitchen/dining-room, two dormitories, a diesel-generator house, and a basement which held the reserve batteries in case the main power supply coming up from Chamonix was cut, as occasionally happened. Facing the Vallée Blanche was a balcony, from which a vertical wooden wall ran some thirty feet down to the snow-field. In this wall, at basement level, were cut a couple of square holes, into which one's rear end could be inserted when necessary. Sanitation by gravitational removal was the only option at this height, where there could be no running water because of the cold. The arrangement forced one to choose between internal discomfort or frostbite. In fine weather watchers leaning over the balcony could speculate on the owner of the buttocks when they came into view. Disputes could be settled by means of a well-directed snowball – protesting voices are not easily disguised.

Apart from this interesting detail, and the absence of tourists and skiers, the view from the balcony was much the same as from the top station of today's Aiguille du Midi téléférique. To the north, on a clear day, the Palais des Nations at Geneva could be seen. So too could the huge fountain in the harbour. To the south stretched the seventy miles of Italian Alps. The sun rose behind the Matterhorn, Monte Rosa and the Grand Combin. When it set Mont Blanc turned pink and a long shadow stretched away to the east. It was, and is, a magical place.

The 'labo' normally housed a team of about a dozen. There were five or six research staff from the Ecole Polytechnique, all active or reserve officers in the army engineering corps. There was one laboratory technician, Reposeur, whose skill as a raconteur enlivened our hermit existence. The intensity of the shared experience in this mountain refuge forged the strongest bonds of friendship. That with Chanson was cut short by his early death; but when I met his colleague, Jean Becker, forty years after leaving Chamonix it was as though time had stood still. I confirmed then what I had just learned from a BBC documentary: that he had been one of the courageous defenders of the Dunkirk perimeter, before being made a prisoner of war. It was characteristic of the man that he had never mentioned this in the laboratory.

Chanson himself was an engineer-colonel. He had considerable Alpine experience, gained from a period at the beginning of World War II when he was responsible for building a number of high-altitude forts on the Italian frontier. They formed a defensive chain, but had one weak point: in a sufficiently determined attack a few skilled commandos could lob grenades through the gun-ports. Chanson himself was once under such an attack and had lost sight of the enemy, who were already close to the walls. Having confidence in his own engineering, he called up the next fort and asked for fire to be concentrated on his own position. The raiders fled. This was the man who now ran the laboratory.

Two Chamonix guides, Jacques Burnet (Jacquot) and Alfred Ravanel, did the hard labouring and portering – made harder by the reduced atmospheric pressure. Jacquot was the elder of the two. He was short, stocky, and immensely strong. As a guide he was as good as the best, and had the confidence that comes from surviving for a lifetime in Chamonix's hostile mountains. He had been in the upper benne with the Italian director of the Aiguille du Midi téléférique, then under contruction, when the traction cable broke. There was no safety brake. The benne started to accelerate towards the intermediate station. Jacquot knew that there was but one slim chance of survival: to jump onto a small snow-field half-way down, which involved a fall of at least one hundred feet. The Italian was paralysed with fear and refused to jump. Jacquot took the risk and survived. The Italian died.

Alfred Ravanel was not from the same heroic mould. He too acted as guide in summer and ski-instructor in winter, and supplemented his income with a bit of forestry and occasional contraband – taken over the Col de Balme, higher up the Chamonix valley, into an Italy which had not yet coordinated its tariffs with the rest of Europe. In retirement he kept a small hotel, and was surprised and gratified when I called on him forty years later.

Our cook was Alice, a good-looking young Swiss from Zermatt. She kept her distance from the men. Tittle-tattle to the contrary in the Chamonix valley annoyed her. She would start her preparations for lunch before breakfast ended, wielding a cleaver to slice large carcasses while the British were still struggling to wake up. Her cooking was basic, but we were well fed. Her reputation as a chef perhaps benefited from the fact that our meals were always accompanied with wine. A week's supply was reckoned to be five full jerry-cans – three of red, two of white. That was 125 litres for an average of ten people, or two bottles per head per day. Despite this, and perhaps because of the low pressure, the team remained adequately sober.

It did not take long to discover the considerable delights of drinking French liqueurs, in particular Chartreuse; but there was the problem of stopping Jacquot and Alfred from raiding one's stocks. One Sunday I bought a bottle of the milder yellow variety and decided to teach them a lesson. Yellow Chartreuse was the same colour as a washing-up liquid I had brought from England. Decanting the Chartreuse, I half filled the bottle with Stergene, then labelled it 'POISON' and placed it prominently on a shelf in the living room. On Monday morning, just after breakfast, Jacquot came up and was immediately attracted by the bottle. He read the notice, decided – correctly in one sense

– that it was a deliberate deception, and placed the bottle to his lips. The resulting shower of bubbles would have done a child's heart good. Chanson whispered, 'Terry, go as far away as you can – quickly.' When I returned half an hour later Jacquot – who could have killed me with his bare hands – came up, clapped me on the shoulder and said, 'Monsieur Price, it was my fault.' We all loved him for that.

Life in the laboratory resumed its normal course. It would be wrong to suggest this was always placid, for the low oxygen pressure had the effect of inducing both fatigue and short temper. Pam had astonishing energy, but even at sea level she could be difficult. Now, at the altitude of the lab., she could be positively obtuse. I too was suffering from hypoxia, and found this difficult to bear. One day, quite calmly, I set about trying to strangle her – it seemed the most appropriate solution. Fortunately for us both, Chanson was there. He suggested we should spend the rest of the day visiting Geneva, where there was a good scientific library in which we could explore the point of contention.

The guides had a different response to Pam's occasionally acerbic tongue and waited for a chance to even the score. One morning, soon after dawn, they rose, carried her outside, still in her sleeping bag, and dumped her in the snow a hundred yards away. I was woken by her furious screams. 'I think Miss Rothwell is calling for you,' said Alfred. I had to dress at that ungodly hour and carry her back.

It was difficult to think properly much above 8000 feet. Experimental problems at the lab. sometimes seemed insoluble, though if one simply went down a few thousand feet all would suddenly become clear. In this respect there seemed to be no acclimatisation. Our routine was therefore to spend the working week in the lab. and to take Saturday afternoon and Sunday off down in the valley.

Once we had acquired a head for heights these up-and-down trips were enjoyable – at least when the weather was good. Even standing up in a large cement bucket, which sometimes replaced the little benne, became a normal way of travelling.

But one always had to be prepared for electrical failures, as the French grid at that time was overloaded and unreliable. Moreover, hoar frost could form around the overhead power lines which came up from the valley, sometimes swelling them to as much as four inches in diameter. In a gale the pounding of the wind, coupled with the weight of the hoar frost, could snap the cables and cut off the power supply. A failure at dusk might mean being stranded overnight in mid-air, with a freezing wind blowing. We therefore always took our mountain gear, even in the hottest weather, and for extra protection a bundle of old newspapers. Tucked under our outer clothing they might stave off hypothermia. I never had to use the bundle myself, but others were not so fortunate.

Our base at Les Pélerins was a chalet run by the energetic and worldly-wise Mère Couttet. The Couttets were one of the leading Chamonix families. Indeed, James Couttet was the current world downhill ski champion. With Madame C. as our link, little happened in the village that we did not soon know about.

We were studying cosmic rays and so were dubbed 'les cosmiques' by the locals. The subject was special, as was the fact that we were the highest working team in Europe, beating by a few hundred feet the Swiss at the Jungfraujoch. The name stuck. Even though the lab. burned down in the 1980s, the new mountain refuge that replaced it was still called Les Cosmiques. Forty years after my time on the mountain I had only to mention that I had been one of the chosen few to receive a quite unusual degree of consideration and, if need be, help from people twenty miles or more down the valley.

Chamonix at that time was little more than a large village and getting to know the inhabitants was not difficult, especially for a 'cosmique'. Chanson was welcome everywhere and sometimes took me with him. Once we visited an old man, well on into his eighties, who, if I understood correctly, had been a guide on the first ascent of Mont Blanc by women. Another time Chanson took me to Geneva to visit a watch-maker who was assembling Rolex watches in his sitting room. In the 1950s Swiss watch-making was still largely a cottage industry, dependent on the skills of individual craftsmen.

The laboratory was a special place, not only for science but also for the view. Just as the Aiguille du Midi téléférique does today, it attracted many visitors for that reason alone. The year before I arrived Field-Marshal Montgomery had turned up in his much-decorated battle-dress. A young princess from the royal house of Denmark had also been there.

Journalists came to research articles about us, one of which unexpectedly helped me on my return journey through the Geneva customs zone. The lorry was carrying a large amount of goods that would normally attract duty, and I had lost my special permit. The douanier listened to my tale without showing much willingness to assist. But when I mentioned 'les cosmiques' he asked me to wait, rushed indoors, and emerged a moment later clutching a copy of the *Dauphiné Libéré*. Pointing to a picture of the lab. he asked if the person in the background was me – as indeed it was. No further documentation was needed!

Scientifically the most interesting visitor was Willard Libby, the pioneer of radio-carbon dating. His technique works because a small fraction of the carbon circulating in the biosphere is weakly radioactive; as all living creatures contain carbon all of us are also radioactive. When we die we no longer breathe or otherwise absorb this slight radioactivity, and that which is already in our bodies slowly decays, falling by one half every 5,730 years. Given that one basic assumption is valid, the age of a mummified corpse, tree or fossil – anything that has lived – can be found by measuring the residual radioactivity.

The assumption is that all living creatures, whether animals, fishes or plants, contain the same proportion of radioactive carbon during their lifetime, irrespective of where they live. Verifying this assumption was a necessary step towards proving the method. Libby collected as many samples as possible, including some Antarctic seals that spent the summer in a large refrigerator. The assumption having been proved valid, Libby then compared the results of his method against museum specimens whose date was already well established from historical evidence. Once again the validity of the method was strikingly upheld – though he did have some difficulty persuading the curator of a Cairo museum that an allegedly 'pre-Christian' boat was unquestionably a nineteenth-century fake.

The warm dry summer of 1950 invited exploration of the surrounding countryside. I had brought from England, in the three-ton lorry, my BSA motor-cycle. The first time I rode it in Chamonix on an otherwise empty road I noticed that everyone was shouting and waving their arms. Enquiring what was the matter, I was told that I was driving on the wrong side of the road. This problem had not arisen when driving the lorry because the orientation of the steering wheel and the presence of other traffic had been constant reminders, but the mental connections had to be learned afresh for the motor-cycle.

Jeanie was bored with her solitary life in the valley during the working week, and happy to join me on a 200-mile circuit of Mont Blanc, sitting on the far from comfortable pillion seat. Our tour included climbing the then fearsome Forclaz pass between Argentière and Martigny (it has since been tamed). Very reasonably she did not relish staying in Chamonix on her own while I worked nearly two miles above her head, and decided to return to England.

It was time to prepare for an inspection visit from Pontecorvo, who was due to return from a holiday in Italy. His parents had not been to Chamonix for years, and it was arranged that we should all meet in the valley for dinner. Pam and I met the parents, but Pontecorvo and his family failed to turn up; so the dinner went ahead without them. The following morning came news that he had been delayed by a minor car crash, but that there was nothing to worry about. The elder Pontecorvos went back to Milan, and we returned to the mountain.

A couple of weeks later I received a letter from Pontecorvo's father, asking if I had any news of his son; he had heard nothing further. I rang Henry Arnold, the security officer at Harwell. He sounded worried but tight-lipped. He knew something of

Pontecorvo's movements from the travellers' cheques that had been cashed, but there had been no clues during the last few days. We now know that it was on the day we should all have had dinner together that Ponte flew from Rome to Stockholm on his way to Moscow. At the time, nothing was further from my thoughts.

A couple of weeks later I was about to make my usual Monday trip up the mountain when Antoine Pocachard, the téléférique manager, said that a policeman wished to interview me on behalf of Interpol. I was questioned informally about Ponte's disappearance, but could give no useful information. The conversation then turned to Klaus Fuchs, whose arrest had been well publicised in France. Before the interview ended I agreed that the two men knew each other – as indeed, all of us at Harwell did.

One lunchtime soon afterwards I received a delayed radiotelegram asking me to meet Egon Bretscher at Geneva airport. He was my Harwell division head and Pontecorvo's boss. As the rendezvous was for an hour earlier than the arrival of the telegram there was little to do but wait for him to ring, while wondering why he should want to see me. Eventually, he found his way to Chamonix and telephoned from the bottom station of the téléférique asking me to come down and talk to him. 'It's a splendid day. Why don't you come up and spend the night here instead?' At first he demurred, but finally agreed; by tea-time he had arrived. As chance would have it Alice's friend, Hugo, from Zermatt was also staying. He was the guide who had doubled for the hero in the film *The White Tower*, jumping over spectacular crevasses and climbing vertical pitches. Far from being able to perform such feats, the leading man in the film had suffered vertigo so badly that he had had to be strapped into the little benne before going down the mountain.

The following morning Bretscher and Hugo set out to climb the west face of the Aiguille du Midi, which involved several hundred feet of fairly exposed rock. I still did not know why he had come, though on his return I had the impression he was concealing something. Eventually, he asked if I would go for a short walk to a nearby hut, used by the Italian workers who were building the Aiguille du Midi téléférique.

We sat in the porch, and Bretscher took off his shirt in the sun. He then asked: 'What's this about Fuchs?' I had no idea what he was referring to, so he explained. 'When you spoke to the French police you said you thought that Pontecorvo was an accomplice of Fuchs. The French police are too close to their newspapers for our liking. We are trying to negotiate a new agreement with the Americans. If that kind of thing gets into the papers we could kiss all that goodbye.' A chasm was opening beneath my feet. Could I possibly be regarded as a security risk?

I told him I had no recollection of saying anything as definite as that. The policeman had asked if Pontecorvo knew Fuchs. I had said yes, and in response to a further question had probably said that they were friends. I had not long arrived in France, and my French at the time was still far from fluent – 'friend' came more easily than 'acquaintance.' While the policeman had clearly embroidered my reply, it seemed to be no more than a matter of emphasis or misunderstanding that had brought Bretscher all the way from England, where his wife was about to give birth. He listened sympathetically and told me to write down for the Harwell security people what I had told him. He stayed another night, and a number of us accompanied him down the mountain and had lunch in Mère Couttet's garden.

Bretscher was speaking German with one of the French team, and Switzer Dütsch with Hugo. Our electrician, Locatelli, occasionally dropped into Italian. There was the French contingent and Pam and myself. Our lively multilingual conversation was noted by a Hungarian lady sitting at the next table. Mère Couttet whispered that she scraped a living teaching bridge to visitors. As we broke up she singled me out. 'Que vous parlez bien l'Anglais!' I thanked her and admitted that I had spent some years in England.

After Bretscher left I spent three weeks wondering whether my Harwell career had been irretrievably blighted. Then the téléférique office rang to say that there was a letter for me. It was late October and winter had already closed in at the lab. After an interminable wait at the 12,000 feet upper station the benne emerged from cloud, carrying a letter from Henry Arnold, weighted down by a snow-ball: 'Dear Terry. I quite understand.'

Life at Les Cosmiques was never dull for long. During my 1951 visit we were about to sit down to lunch when Radio-Genève announced that an attempt would be made to land a small aircraft on Mont Blanc, in pursuit of a large prize offered by an Italian newspaper. Sure enough, there was a Piper Cub climbing up over Les Houches. I remembered that in the attic there was a pair of magnificent Zeiss artillery binoculars, mounted on a tripod and magnifying thirty times. The plane made its approach to the Dôme du Gouter, about three miles from the laboratory. A team of guides had climbed up to prepare a rudimentary landing strip in hard-packed snow, but the plane was above its normal ceiling and unable to climb at the critical moment. Instead of landing on the prepared strip – whose value to a wheeled aircraft was in any case doubtful – it landed to one side. The wheels dug in, the propeller hit the ground in a flurry of snow, and the plane turned over onto its back. The guides rushed to extricate the pilot and passenger, and soon had the plane back on its undercarriage, in the normal attitude.

All this could be easily seen with the binoculars. I rushed back into the dining room with the news. Just then Radio-Genève announced that a four-engined Constellation aircraft had arrived on the scene, and was circling Mont Blanc. 'The first part of the adventure has been successfully completed,' said a commentator in the aircraft. 'The plane has landed, and soon will be taking off again.'

At this point Chanson, alert to the possibility of a bargain, asked the Chamonix exchange, over the radio link, to put him through to Radio-Genève. Chanson explained that the observer in the Constellation had given information that was incorrect, that the Cub had crashed, and that if Radio-Genève agreed to let us have a case of good Swiss wine, we should be glad to keep them in touch. At that moment the airborne observer said that the word 'hélice' (propeller) had been written in the snow. Our version was clearly correct, and the deal was agreed.

Nothing happened for an hour. Then we learned from the radio that the famous Swiss pilot, Geiger, would try to parachute a new propeller, so that a quick repair could be made. His plane soon arrived overhead, but the parachute drop was a failure; the propeller finished thousands of feet down the mountain.

The Cub was clearly unflyable, and the skyline just below the gale-ridden summit of the highest mountain in the Alps was no place for an aircraft with a take-off speed of less than 50 m.p.h. The guides tried to coax it downhill to a safer place but, as the slope steepened, the plane broke away, dug in its wheels, turned over once again onto its back and slid upside down on its wing for perhaps half a mile. The group skied after it, righted it again and started to push once more, but the same thing happened again. In this bizarre fashion the plane was eventually manoeuvred into a relatively sheltered combe at a height of about 11,000 feet.

Two weeks later we learned that Geiger was to make an attempt to recover the plane. The tail was lashed to a stake driven into the ice and the engine tested. Then an elastic launch-rope was passed behind the undercarriage and drawn into a V, kept taut by a dozen helpers immediately downhill. The engine was run at full power; the launch party tugged. Geiger cut the anchor rope – and the plane flew. A lump came into my throat as I saw it fly away to the east as though nothing unusual had occurred.

Three miles away across the Vallée Blanche, in Italy, lay the Torino hut, at about the same height as our lab. It exercised an irresistible attraction for Jacquot and Alfred. They claimed that the Cinzano was better in Italy. The rest of us suspected that contraband – or perhaps the ladies – might also have something to do with it. At all events, they often spent their weekends there instead of going home to Chamonix.

Chanson decided that we should join them one weekend, to

sample the experience. The day-time instability of the Glacier du Géant immediately below the Torino hut meant that we needed to start while it was still cold and dark. In bright star-light we set off down the slope to the Vallée Blanche, then roped up for the mile walk across ice as hard and smooth as Piccadilly, before tackling the 1,000 feet climb to Torino through séracs larger than houses. Dawn was breaking as we reached the hut, and the enormous vista over the Italian Alps to the south was already visible in its full glory. Down below was the sleepy Courmayeur valley, soon to be brought into the modern world by the opening of the Mont Blanc tunnel. We had a leisurely breakfast before returning to the lab. It was high summer, and the danger of weakening bridges over the huge crevasses meant that it would be wise to complete the journey well before midday.

Not long afterwards Alfred and Jacquot spent another weekend at Torino. They were due to return on the Sunday evening, but when nightfall came without any sign of them we concluded that the drinking had warranted their staying for another night. However, around 10.00p.m. we heard footsteps on the balcony and Jacquot appeared, alone. He was without gloves, goggles, crampons, rucksack, iceaxe, or Alfred, and had been drinking heavily. He managed to mutter that Alfred was in a crevasse somewhere near Torino; then collapsed insensible.

Chanson decided that a rescue must be organised. The Italians who were building the new Aiguille du Midi téléférique, and who lodged close by, agreed to send out a search party. Wanting to make some contribution, however small, I got out a large searchlight from the attic, and rigged it up so that the Vallée Blanche was illuminated. In its light we saw the Italians setting off in search of Alfred. We waited for another couple of hours before turning in.

About 11.00 the following morning the Italians returned, carrying one of their number on an improvised stretcher. He had fallen into a crevasse and broken his leg. An hour later Alfred turned up, safe and sound, to face an inquisition. His story was that they had set out at nightfall from Torino after a heavy drinking session. Jacquot was much the worse for wear. He had fallen into a crevasse and it was only with difficulty that Alfred had been able to extricate him. Fearing that it was too dangerous to proceed with Jacquot in this condition, Alfred tried unsuccessfully to persuade him to return to Torino. In the dark they lost each other and Alfred began to despair of finding him. Then our searchlight came on, and Alfred correctly deduced that Jacquot must have reached the lab. after all and raised the alarm. It would have been possible for Alfred to return by its light, but that would have involved a breach of a primary safety rule: never go into the mountains alone. So he went back to Torino and spent the night in jollity. Reflecting on these events, Chanson commented that by his single-handed escape from more than one crevasse Jacquot had probably demonstrated as never before his excellence as a mountain guide.

These extraordinary events enlivened our off-duty hours. Meanwhile, the results of our work were a little disappointing, though not wholly without value. We had hoped to identify the various kinds of cosmic-ray mesons by combining the French cloud chamber measurements with our own measurements of ionisation (the electrical charges liberated in the rays' passage through our counters). In the event, an unforeseen lack of precision in our apparatus made that impossible, and we were forced to look for other targets. We found one in an obscure consequence of the theory of relativity.

The sense of adventure continued until the last. We had all left the mountain early in November, after shutting up the lab. for winter. The following day I was packing the lorry at the lower téléférique station, which I understood had closed at the same time. Cable cars travel silently and it was only by good luck, in a moment of silence between moving heavy packages, that I heard a slight whistling sound. Looking up I saw an empty car swinging low over the ground no more than a hundred yards from the lorry, which was directly in its path. Never have I started a vehicle so quickly. If there had not been that moment of silence there would have been the first recorded collision between a cable car and a Ministry of Supply lorry.

The Chamonix work led to a couple of published papers that amounted to a further verification of the theory of relativity, which predicted how the ionisation of particles travelling at near the speed of light should behave. This we were able to verify. I had not quite finished with the subject. A different apparatus for measuring the momentum of cosmic-ray particles existed at Manchester, and thither we took our equipment. Another couple of papers resulted; but for me the most valuable consequence was forming a life-long friendship with John Maddox, who carried out the statistical analysis. He was later knighted for his distinguished work as editor of the scientific magazine *Nature*.

It was a great sadness that my friendship with Chanson was cut short when he developed a paralysing disease, which led to his hospitalisation a decade later at Montpellier. From there he continued to direct his scientific work, which had become involved with nuclear weaponry. For this he had been promoted to General. I felt duty bound to visit him, but there were constraints of time and cost. Finding myself in Paris for a NATO meeting in September 1966 I asked a French Air Force officer if by any chance military planes flew regularly to Montpellier, hoping to hitch a lift. He thought not, but promised to make enquiries. The following day he sought me out. 'Any friend of Chanson is a friend of France. A plane will be at your disposal tomorrow morning at Villacoublay. It will be yours for the day.' Would my own country, I wondered, show such generosity in similar circumstances? And would the RAF do as much for the Army?

In the couple of hours I was able to spend with Paul I witnessed an extraordinary demonstration of the will to live. He was in an iron lung, totally immobile except for his eyelids. Unable to speak, his only channel of communication with the outside world was through his wife, to whom he signalled in Morse code: dot for one eyelid, dash for the other. She was astonishingly quick to understand and, with her help, we had an easy, and even light-hearted, conversation. After we had exchanged our personal news he asked me about Pam. I told him that she had left Harwell, had worked in the Italian laboratory at Cervinia, and had taken part in a geophysical expedition that involved sailing round Africa. More recently she had tried to join the Royal Society's expedition to the South Pole – only to be rebuffed with the comment: 'Miss Rothwell, you don't seem to realise that our team down there won't have seen a woman for a whole year.' Paul's eyes danced with amusement and the eyelids got to work. 'Tell Pam that I think she will be the first woman in the Moon.'

The nurses came to attend him and I had a word with his wife. She was loyal but strained. She was his only communication channel and Paul was understandably inclined to panic when she was out of the room. For both their sakes I could not wish even such a heroic existence as his to continue for long.

During a short visit to Geneva I took the opportunity to visit Chamonix. As I approached Les Pélerins who should be coming down the road with his usual rolling gait but Jacquot. He greeted me warmly. 'Monsieur Price, vous n'avez pas bougé.' I told him about Chanson, and he looked saddened and serious. 'Chanson,' he said, 'était un homme.' He emphasised the last word. Paul could have wished for no finer epitaph.

Chapter 8

Nuclear Safeguards

After returning from Chamonix for the second time in November 1951 I began an extended programme of measuring the fissile properties of uranium and plutonium nuclei, as part of a general drive towards refining the data underlying nuclear reactor design. When uranium and plutonium absorb neutrons useful amounts of energy can be produced from fission (the splitting of atomic nuclei). However, the process follows rules that have no analogue in everyday life. Everything depends on a neutron's exact speed, so measurements have to be made with equipment that can separate neutrons of different speeds. For some of the work I used the Harwell reactor as the neutron source; also a linear accelerator, which produces neutrons by bombarding a target with high-energy electrons and, incidentally, creates high intensities of gamma rays. Inside its massive concrete shield a human being would receive a lethal dose within a few seconds. The precautions we adopted would horrify today's Health and Safety Executive. They consisted merely of a cardboard notice hung on the master switch: DO NOT SWITCH ON – MEN INSIDE.

To work out some of the properties of four kinds of nuclei took more than three years, after which the results were published and compared with similar measurements in other countries. There was reasonable agreement, though for a time there were no other published data on plutonium-241 (a fissile isotope of plutonium produced during irradiation in a reactor). However, at the first Atoms for Peace conference in Geneva in 1955 the Russians promised to declassify their own Pu-241 measurements. Would they agree with mine? I awaited their paper with interest; agree they did.

Meanwhile, although the Mont Blanc experience was a matter of history, it was starting to influence my life in an unforeseen way. At the Aiguille du Midi I had, perforce, learned to speak French. The words I used were not always those normally heard in Paris salons, as my tutors had included two hard-swearing Chamonix guides. But I was fluent and idiomatic and could interpret for my colleagues during the many exchanges we were having with nuclear scientists from across the Channel who, unlike their countrymen today, rarely spoke English. I fell into the rôle of someone who, though still primarily an experimental physicist, also kept an eye on the wider world.

Harold Macmillan once said – and Paul Valéry would certainly have agreed – that unforeseen events are the most difficult things to deal with when backing into the future. But sometimes, with luck, they provide a springboard, as they did for me on 8 December 1953, when President Eisenhower addressed the General Assembly of the United Nations. He proposed that an International Atomic Energy Agency be created, and 'to the extent permitted by elementary prudence', offered to contribute to an international pool of nuclear material for the peaceful development of atomic energy. Fifty kilograms of uranium-235 would provide an initial endowment. His speech gave my life a new theme, which was to remain a significant influence for the next decade.

Eisenhower was speaking immediately after meeting Churchill in Bermuda, where he had discussed the intended speech in detail. However, it appears that, during the flight to New York, very little of the original text survived intact; indeed, there was a flurry of secretarial activity on board Air Force One to get the speech retyped in time for the landing. The result was that the British Permanent Representative to the United Nations, Sir Gladwyn Jebb, had no warning of the proposal. The Foreign Office was soon in touch with Harwell, asking for advice and, a day or two later, my boss John Dunworth took me with him to call on the Under-Secretary concerned. I cannot be certain, but he was probably Paul Mason. He ran over what the President had said and asked for help in understanding the implications. We talked the matter over for nearly an hour, but just as we were about to leave a thought struck me. 'What about security?' He appeared not to follow my drift. 'U-235 can be bomb material.'

I was possibly overstating the problem, because the figure of 50 kilograms might have been intended to refer to the U-235 content of dilute rather than concentrated fissile material, such as would be needed for bombs. Be that as it may, few remarks of mine have had a more gratifying effect. The Under-Secretary sat up; there was work to be done. At the very least the Americans would have to spell out the details so that the implications could be fully measured. It seems curious in retrospect but, although there had been intermittent discussions both within Whitehall and with the United States since World War II about what are euphemistically known as 'safeguards' – the prevention of the diversion of fissile material from civil uses – I had the clear impression that the part of the Foreign Office most closely concerned with United Nations issues had yet to consider that aspect of the Eisenhower proposal. We spent a few minutes in further explanation, were thanked, and left.

The Foreign Office is an extraordinarily effective administrative machine and it did not dawdle. A high-level meeting was held on 18 December to take stock of the situation. As a result it was agreed that the British Ambassador, Sir Roger Makins, should press the Americans for more details of what they had in mind and that the Foreign Office should prepare a policy paper covering, in particular, what our attitude should be to Russian participation (or non-participation) in the new Agency.

There had been a young secretary in the room at the time, and it must have been he who telephoned me a few months later asking if I would be able to 'advise the Minister of State'. No further explanation was given, except that the Minister's name was Selwyn Lloyd. A few days later, on 10 May 1954, I found myself back in the Foreign Office, dressed in a new suit bought for the occasion but, regrettably, fifteen minutes late, my train having chosen on that of all mornings to run far behind time. As I was ushered in Selwyn Lloyd murmured, 'We've been waiting for you'. Around the Minister of State's table were a number of distinguished foreigners. Jules Moch was there from France, chain-smoking Gauloises. Canada was represented by the High Commissioner in London; the USA by Ambassador Morehead Patterson. I was slightly alarmed at being introduced as the Minister's scientific adviser, and wondered what Cockcroft would make of it.

It soon became clear that this was a briefing to settle the policy line of the Western powers, prior to meeting the Soviets at a four-power sub-committee of the United Nations Disarmament Committee. Selwyn Lloyd brought me up to date on the present state of Western disarmament thinking. The starting point was that all nuclear material should be surrendered as a first step. Then, having removed the nuclear threat, conventional disarmament could begin. He invited me to comment. I was totally unbriefed, something which today would be inconceivable at a ministerial meeting. Moreover, I knew nothing of military matters. But, in those days, Whitehall was engagingly amateur, unbureaucratic and refreshing.

In the circumstances there seemed only one comment worth making: 'Minister of State, the Western proposal appears to stand or fall on our ability to track down the fissile material which has so far been produced. I am not at all sure that we are in a position technically to ensure that this can be done to the accuracy national security would require.' An awkward silence followed. It was broken by Selwyn Lloyd saying, 'Well, that's unfortunate, but we shall have to go ahead for political reasons.' So go ahead we did, in the opening sessions of the Lancaster House conference, and it was left to the Russians to point out in their own good time that tracking fissile material is bound to be a rather inexact affair.

I walked out into Whitehall in something of a daze. I was still a fairly junior research worker, whose main job was as an experimentalist. No-one at Harwell, still less in the London headquarters, yet knew why I had been asked to go to the Foreign Office. We had assumed that it was probably a follow-up to the December meeting. I walked the short distance to the Atomic Energy headquarters in Charles II Street, and asked if I could see the Chairman, Sir Edwin Plowden. He happened to be free, so I was able to put the matter straight there and then. He heard me out, laughed, and said, 'Well, you'd better continue to hold the baby.' A few days later the *News Chronicle* carried a short item on its front page noting the start of the conference, under the caption: 'Atom man will be there'. Father, who had only a few months to live, was delighted.

The meetings in the gilded halls of Lancaster House were amongst the most boring of my life. Mercifully, I was not needed for more than a couple of days a week, and in between donned my white coat and continued measuring fissile properties. Some enjoyment came from conversations with Bertrand Goldschmidt, a French scientist whom I already knew slightly from contacts at Harwell and who occasionally came to advise the French delegation. His wife was English, and his English was faultless. I knew him as a distinguished chemist; but his astuteness only became clear years later when he told me how the French had found out which solvent the British were using to extract plutonium at Windscale (we were prevented from telling them by our agreement with the Americans). Goldschmidt solved the puzzle quickly and cheaply by instructing two young researchers to find out which solvents had recently disappeared from the open literature in the UK.

After the initial stimulus of meeting the Russians had worn off there was little to do except try, as a loyal official, to support a politically attractive but practically unattainable position. There were some background papers from earlier discussions, but they shed little light. Discussions went on inconclusively on what should be covered by a comprehensive disarmament agreement, the nature of the controlling machinery and the timing or phasing of the reductions on which agreement might be reached. There was particular emphasis on nuclear weaponry, about which I knew almost nothing. Semantic difficulties sometimes intruded – in French and Russian the word for 'control' has less of a flavour of overall management than in English, more a sense of monitoring. But the principal problem was that the Soviets were too paranoid about inspection, which we regarded as essential, to allow any progress to be made.

The Disarmament Conference broke up on 22 June 1954 after twenty meetings, having achieved nothing of substance. The West, whose political preoccupation had been to respond to the widely held view that something should be done about nuclear weapons, had little to point to. But the subject was too important to drop. On my return to Harwell, with strong encouragement from Cockcroft, I formed a small discussion group to mull over the problems with complete informality and no holds barred. It included the Deputy Director, Basil Schonland, who had been Montgomery's scientific adviser during the war. Martin Fishenden, my next-door neighbour on the Chilton prefab site, was another member. All that summer Martin and I argued the problems endlessly, while gardening or shaping asbestos panels for a shared garage that we were erecting on the old airfield runway.

Our conviction grew that whatever else might be possible, the doctrine of 'no critical risk' should be over-riding. I discussed our conclusions with the Foreign Office, where I was still welcome. Kit Silverwood-Cope of the United Nations Political Department, in particular, was always willing to listen. He was the embodiment of the perfect English gentleman: courteous, elegant and modest. It was only years later that I learned of his wartime record from his *Times* obituary. He had been captured during the retreat to Dunkirk and maltreated by the Gestapo, escaped from a prison camp, spent a year in Warsaw before being recaptured and, finally, as the ultimate accolade for courage, been imprisoned in Colditz Castle. Assisting him was Michael Jacomb, the brightest mind and most articulate speaker that I encountered in twenty years in and around Whitehall. Alas! He was posted to the Middle East, fell ill one morning, and was dead that same afternoon from a raging form of polio.

This dual existence – experimental physicist and diplomatic adviser – occupied 1954 and early 1955. Shortly after the end of the 1954 conference Kit Cope tried to move the Foreign Office away from public support of a policy based on the total elimination of nuclear stockpiles, with little success. The Disarmament Sub-Committee was re-convened in the spring of 1955, again in Lancaster House. This time it was the Russians who pointed out that some fissile material might not be traceable – my point exactly. But with the world split into East and West camps that were still engaged in a vicious cold war nothing useful could be achieved.

That might well have ended my interest in the political control of atomic energy; but it received an unexpected boost later in 1955, when the first Atoms for Peace Conference was held in Geneva from 8–20 August. I naturally hoped that my paper on plutonium-241 might qualify me for a place in the British delegation. But numbers were limited, and my contribution was subsumed into a more general statement by a colleague. However, shortly after the conference started I was unexpectedly summoned to join Cockcroft for a 'Little Geneva' meeting, at which the national nuclear leaders of East and West would attempt to make a contribution to world stability. They were to '...consider the problems of safeguarding or guaranteeing the peaceful uses of atomic energy against diversion of materials. The discussions will be concerned with the technical aspects of these problems.' The press reacted critically, reporting 'growing uneasiness' among the diplomatic representatives of countries that had not been included. There was even talk of 'an atomic Yalta'.

Preparations had been in train behind the scenes for some weeks. On 29 July the USA had sent a note to the government of the USSR suggesting that the opportunity should be taken of using the assembly of so many nuclear experts in Geneva to call a small private 'technical' meeting. The same note enclosed a draft statute for the planned International Atomic Energy Agency, which – following Eisenhower's 1953 proposal – was to be set up in Vienna. It already had some support from the USSR but, after twenty months, its functions and powers were still undefined. For its part the British Foreign Office had made an attempt, through an inter-departmental working party, to crystallise its thoughts on the possibilities of control.

I arrived at Geneva and settled in at the Beau Rivage Hotel, the traditional home for British delegates and one that I was to get to know well in later years. It was summer, and I particularly enjoyed breakfasting in the open air. It was there one morning that I beheld a unique assembly: Dick Moore, Bob Hurst and Peter Danckwerts, all members of the British delegation, all holders of the George Cross or George Medal, breakfasting together.

Nuclear experts from six nations met privately at the Palais des Nations from 22–27 August. Isidor Rabi – Nobel laureate in physics – led for the USA, Francis Perrin for France, and Skobeltsyn for the Soviets, who were backed up by Czechoslovakia. The West had, in support the genial W.B. ('Tubby') Lewis – an expatriate Englishman, now representing Canada. Cockcroft led for the UK. The cast was star-studded, but the meeting had been convened with preparations that were merely political and diplomatic. There had been no technical study of what was unquestionably an intractable issue, one on which there was no established consensus. It was hardly surprising that there was no effective agenda.

The opening sessions presented no problems. All the delegations were ready with expressions of goodwill and hopes that their 'work' would prove fruitful. Procedural matters were also useful face-savers and consumers of time. But problems arose once the preliminaries had been dealt with and matters of substance could no longer be avoided. No-one wished to speak. Several times we sat for minutes on end, eyes cast down, doodling. The stenographer's fingers remained poised over the keys. The interpreters sat alert but silent in their booths. The tension grew.

Occasionally a delegate would make a short comment, but nothing ran, and Trappist silence would descend once more on the conference chamber.

The ice was suddenly broken by Isidor Rabi, who argued that since the problem was to know where stocks of uranium – potential bomb material – were being kept, one way might be to 'tag' them with small quantities of an isotope (uranium 232) that is easily detectable through the penetrating gamma rays emitted by its daughter-product, thorium C". It was not an idea with much practical substance, and raised more questions than it answered. Who would do the tagging? Who the monitoring? What about past production? How would chemical separation be dealt with in a reprocessing plant? The scientists present – Rabi most of all – knew the hollowness of the proposal, but gave no sign. Their professional reputation within the world of diplomacy was at stake. The diplomats, interpreters and UN officials knew nothing of thorium isotopes or of tagging, and assumed this must be a breakthrough of the kind that could shape careers.

Immediately Rabi spoke the UN machine leapt into action. His fellow scientists did what they could to help spin the web, heaping hypothesis on hypothesis, taking care whenever possible to use incomprehensible jargon while conceding only a minimum of clarity. Most of the subsequent discussion came from the US team, who took as their theme the kind of 'safeguards' that might be incorporated in the, as yet, ill-defined International Agency. They assumed that it would have a high degree of authority over the design and operation of nuclear chemical plants, so as to make clandestine diversion as difficult as possible. There would be stringent security, and so on. Their scheme was technically sound but politically non-negotiable.

This splendid game could not last. After barely a week the conference adjourned for further study by officials. In the car on the way back to the Beau Rivage I let off steam with Jim Stewart, from the Industrial Group of the Atomic Energy Authority, who had also taken part. We vowed that we would never again go into a conference with so little preparation.

If the interaction between nuclear energy and world politics was so significant, then it should be given serious study. Scientists should at least be in a position to offer reliable estimates of how accurately fissile material production could be monitored and what such monitoring would involve. We decided, if possible, to mount an exercise at an operating British nuclear plant, to see whether management could actually 'steal' plutonium in the face of simulated international inspection. By the time we arrived at our hotel the outline of what was to become Operation CIRCUS had been sketched.

What we had in mind was arguably against the spirit of the Atomic Energy Act – and possibly against the letter. Certainly it could not be done without permission from the Atomic Energy Executive; this, however, was duly forthcoming. But there were also practical difficulties. We would be using an actual nuclear reprocessing plant, Sellafields – or Windscale as it was then still called. We would need a team of inspectors willing to live there for whatever time was needed to deliver useful results – possibly up to three months. They would need to be mature, professionally qualified chemical engineers and physicists, preferably with no previous connection with Windscale. These were not easy conditions to meet: many of the country's relevant professionals had already been involved with the plant in one way or another. Moreover, there was a general shortage of professional manpower in the rapidly-growing atomic energy industry. But, eventually, we found four suitable candidates and, by dint of explaining the growing political importance of nuclear issues, we persuaded them to live apart from their families during the week for whatever time it took. In addition, there were three non-resident inspectors, who widened the professional base. Jim Stewart was to referee the management's actions and I would do the same for the inspectors. In parallel, the UKAEA prepared a technical appraisal of the possibilities of control, on which the Foreign Office based a political appreciation of future options.

Planning for CIRCUS was still incomplete when I was asked

to join Cockcroft's party for discussions at the US State Department on the shape and functions of the nascent International Atomic Energy Agency. I flew to New York in February 1956 with Ivor Porter, from the Foreign Office, in a noisy Stratocruiser that took 18 hours for the journey, with one landing at snow-covered Goose Bay in Labrador. It was an aircraft that still retained a semblance of social togetherness – at least for First Class passengers, who could use the crush bar downstairs. This was abreast of the inboard propellers and the noise was deafening, creating an authentic cocktail party ambience even before the first drink was served.

I was in the States for a week – my first visit – and in that time managed by happy chance to run into David Garstin, my motor-rallying companion. I also formed what was to become a lifelong friendship with Max Isenbergh, who was then General Counsel to the United States Atomic Energy Commission. We met at the final working meeting in the Embassy, at which Sir Roger Makins chalked up a point for Britain by announcing, in confidence and with a certain panache, that we were planning a field exercise. The Americans were impressed, and I was asked by Max – whom I had not previously met – to join him and and his wife, Pearl, at a concert in the Library of Congress. He must have been told by our Science Attaché of my interest in music. On the way into the hall I was able to admire the Library's great collection of Stradivarii.

When the concert was over we went back to the Isenberghs' beautiful house on Massachusetts Avenue – the only house I know whose address and telephone employed the same four-figure number. In the elegant double-cube sitting room was a piano on which lay a copy of Brahms' F Minor clarinet sonata, which I had only recently performed in Wantage with Sebastian Pease. Max noticed my interest and asked if I would like to play it with him. Without admitting that I would not be sight-reading, I sat at the piano; he picked up his clarinet and, as we later agreed, for the next two hours we both enjoyed some of the best music-making of our lives. He was a concert-standard instrumentalist, whose summer holidays in France frequently included chamber music broadcasts for French radio. We desisted only when my remaining sleeping-time had been reduced to less than four hours. I returned to my hotel, got up at six, caught a plane to New York and flew home.

Meanwhile, the Windscale management had been trying to devise ways in which the plant records could be falsified so as to deceive an inspection team without jeopardising control of plant safety. Safety in a nuclear chemical separation plant is concerned not only with the ordinary aspects of fire that are always important whenever solvents are present, but also with nuclear safety. There must be no accumulation of nuclear material large enough to start a nuclear chain reaction. The risk is not of a military-size explosion; but careless management could cause explosions large enough to damage equipment, scatter radioactivity around the plant and possibly place a few lives at risk.

For their part the inspectors had to devise an approach that would minimise any need to breach commercial secrecy – to do otherwise would be politically unacceptable, no matter where such inspections might be undertaken – while at the same time giving reasonable confidence that no diversion was occurring. The obvious approach was boundary control: provided the inspectors knew about every pipe-run, their work would become a matter of checking inputs against outputs plus material-in-progress.

It took eight months to set up the exercise, which started on 11 April 1956 and ran for a further three months. It ended when the supervisors had become reasonably confident that there were no more important lessons to be learned. By then the factory managers felt that they understood the extent – the relatively small extent – to which they could deceive the inspectors. They were also aware that continuing to run two parallel material accounting records might, before long, lead to confusion amongst the employees in a situation where safety demanded the utmost clarity. It would become progressively more difficult for the factory management to falsify plutonium records, especially if tight residential inspection was maintained. All in all CIRCUS confirmed our earlier expectations, but put inspection on a much firmer basis.

The exercise had been carried out under a tight cloak of secrecy, with the minimum number of employees in the know. Nothing was published at the time lest it should lead to banner headlines of the kind: BRITAIN RESEARCHES NUCLEAR CHEATING. Some workers had, of course, noticed the inspectors at work and were becoming worried lest an unannounced time-and-motion study were being carried out; but the anxieties of union officials fortunately did not escalate into what is euphemistically, and misleadingly, known as 'industrial action.'

A month after CIRCUS reported I went with Basil Schonland to Paris to discuss our findings with European colleagues. While there we had a memorable dinner in a velvet-lined *cabinet particulier* at Lapérouse, as guests of Francis Perrin, head of the French Atomic Energy Commission. Homi Bhabha, who was in charge of the Indian nuclear project, was also there. Bhabha made it quite clear that India would resist any attempt on the part of the international community to control her own future plutonium production. While he wanted a strong International Atomic Energy Agency, he could not agree to discriminatory controls. He was not asking the Big Three to abolish all their stocks of nuclear weapons, because that would be unrealistic. He would, however, be impressed if they agreed to supervision of their own future production, because it would remove the element of discrimination that India found so objectionable. A Norwegian scientist expressed a somewhat similar fear, that the Agency could be used to hamper the nuclear progress of smaller nations.

The outlook for nuclear control was hardly propitious but, nevertheless, the thinking continued in Whitehall. Other organisations needed tight controls over certain products, notably Customs and Excise in their supervision of bonded whisky stocks, and, above all, the Royal Mint. In April 1957 a Working Party on Inspection and Control, under the chairmanship of Sir

William Penney, invited these organisations to offer their guidance. The Master of the Mint described how his controls worked. With the CIRCUS experience in mind we asked about boundary control and materials accounting. Having listened to his response we suggested one way in which there might be leakage. His face clouded. 'It's very confidential, but we suspect that is what is actually happening.' We were beginning to understand the subject of inspection.

It was several years before this work could be used to produce a useful political dividend. A chance came at the 1962 Disarmament Conference in Geneva (see Chapter 12). A paper outlining the CIRCUS results – without admitting that such an exercise had been mounted – had the effect of helping to transform an arid discussion on 'general and complete disarmament' into a more realistic examination of security and stability. Stability was a concept familiar to all the neutral states which, for the first time, were forming a kind of 'jury' at the disarmament meetings. It gave them something tangible to hold onto after weeks spent listening to disarmament unrealism. But no sooner were we able to undermine Russian pretensions to being more general and more complete disarmers than the West than they called a recess.

Chapter 9

Nuclear Power Arrives

These diplomatic frolics and their technical follow-up were interesting diversions. Meanwhile, ordinary life continued. Literally so: we now had two children – Jeremy, born in 1951, and Nicola, who was three years younger. The prefab that had served as home for eight years was bursting at the seams and, early in 1956, we moved to a new house built on former glebe-land in the neighbouring village of Chilton. The design won a premier architectural prize. It was certainly attractive to the eye, but its engineering left much to be desired. As a friendly high-court judge had earlier warned me, with commendable prescience, 'Remember that a fool builds for a wise man to live in.'

Harwell was experiencing an explosion of new activity, as atomic energy advanced from distant aspiration to attainable reality. The Windscale reactors had made possible the first British atomic test explosion on the island of Monte Bello, on 3 October 1952. But there was a still unsatisfied desire to put gas-cooled reactor technology to civil use. This had its first expression in the Calder Hall reactors, built alongside the Windscale site. They were officially described as 'dual-purpose', a shorthand way of admitting that the value of their military plutonium output would provide a subsidy for electricity production. The first was completed in May 1956 and connected to the grid five months later on 17 October. It was still delivering 50 megawatts a third of a century later. That first reactor – eight were ordered – was built on a green-field site in three years from the decision to proceed.

Such energy and competence were characteristic of British engineering before the inflation of titles degraded the meaning of the term 'engineer'. The profession was still honoured by the public and had not yet been elbowed out of the way by accountants. It was a late and great flowering of the Brunel tradition. With regrettable irony, two weeks after the Queen formally opened the reactor, her government's deplorable instigation and handling of the Suez crisis called into question the political value of the nuclear weaponry for which the plutonium from Calder Hall had been earmarked.

So far as the reactors' potential for electricity production was concerned there was no trace of national self-doubt. The race was on to scale up Calder Hall. An initial programme was launched with a target of twelve stations by 1965, each several times the size of Calder Hall. In the belief that competition would provide the key to rapid innovation, four consortia were created. For a time there was even a fifth. Each brought together leading electrical, mechanical and civil engineering firms. Their task was to build a new generation of Magnox reactors, so called after the name of the alloy used to enclose the uranium.

Competition undoubtedly provided the expected spur. What was less obvious at the outset was that a variety of competing designs would create additional costs for training four – and for a time five – design teams; and, in the long term, extra maintenance costs would fall on the electrical utilities because of the multiplicity of spare parts needed. Furthermore, the reactors were physically so large as to be inherently unsuitable for series factory production: each was a major civil engineering project in its own right. The physically smaller, American (and later French), water-cooled, factory-built reactors soon mounted a formidable challenge. The overseas market dried up and hopes of a new export industry remained unfulfilled.

Nevertheless, most of the 36 gas-cooled reactors that were eventually built in the UK (plus one in Japan and one in Italy) performed well as engineering structures and their safety record includes no disasters like those at Chernobyl and Three Mile Island.

Harwell's contribution to these stimulating developments included setting up and running a reactor school, where the new engineers could be trained. My own modest task was to give occasional lectures on shielding. I still took an interest in the subject and was in the process of codifying a messy situation by the time-honoured but arduous process of writing a textbook, *Radiation Shielding.* I embarked on it thinking that a year's spare-time effort would see the job done. In the event, despite co-opting Cliff Horton and Ken Spinney as co-authors, it took four years, largely because of the explosive surge of new research that simply could not be disregarded. I knew that a competing book was nearing completion in America, so Robert Maxwell and Pergamon Press pulled out every stop. He may have been a rogue, but he was a splendid publisher. The finished copies were on sale in May 1957, only one month after the final corrections were complete. The book was a success and received the accolade of having a pirated Russian edition. My attempts to extract royalties from the USSR, however, met with a response which even with my rudimentary knowledge of the language, I found little difficulty in translating: 'Dear Sir, I greatly regret that owing to economic circumstances ... etc.'

Not only engineers but also the public in general needed to be informed about this new form of energy that had suddenly become such big news. All of us played our part in giving public lectures to lay audiences. We were always well received: the atom was a matter of pride and public esteem. Whether the message was always received in the form in which it left our lips is questionable. I remember being asked to frame a suitably polite reply to a letter sent to the establishment by a lady from Hounslow. Her epistle is a prized possession:

Dear Sir,

I listened last night to a talk on the radio, about the coming eclipse of the sun, and speculation about the green ray. I believe the following to be the truth:

Sun Spectrum

Red Ray (negative)   Blue Ray (positive)
Bring these two through a switch, controlled Atomic Energy

Yellow Ray (positive)   Mauve Ray (negative)
Bring these two through a switch, controlled Hydrogen Energy

Green Ray = Controlled COSMIC POWER.

Yours etc

She would have had much in common with a lady who wrote to *The Listener* after Sir William Penney had given a radio talk on the British atomic bomb tests in Australia. He had spoken in glowing terms about a wonderful camera that had been specially developed to observe the moment of detonation. The writer said that she was prepared to believe a good deal of what scientists claimed, but Penney's assertion that there was an interval of time as short as a millionth of a second was palpably absurd.

We also carried the banner abroad. I flew to Munich to give a lecture on the power programme at the Max Planck Institute. The talk was timed for 2.30 CT. I arrived early, but by 2.30 was still the only person in the room. At 2.40 people started arriving. At 2.45 the lecture theatre was comfortably full and Professor Heisenberg introduced me. I was baffled, and later asked for an explanation. It lay in those two letters, CT: '*Cum tempore*' – the academic quarter of an hour.

The Navy, meanwhile, was enviously viewing US developments in nuclear propulsion for submarines. In doing so it was following the Nelsonian tradition of seizing on whatever new things technology might have to offer. Five years before Trafalgar,

139

when Henry Bell submitted proposals for steam propulsion, Nelson wrote to the Board of Admiralty: 'My Lords and Gentlemen, if you do not adopt Mr Bell's scheme other nations will, and in the end vex every vein of this Empire.' Bell's *Comet* began operations on the Clyde in 1812, and was a success.

Now the Navy was looking across the Atlantic to a development of equal strategic significance. From the earliest days of nuclear energy the possibility of using nuclear power for submarine propulsion had been evident. Nuclear power needs no oxygen. Nuclear boats do not need to surface to recharge their batteries. Because they are submerged they do not waste energy making waves and can travel submerged as fast, or faster, than the surface ships that might try to attack them.

The US Navy had striven to make nuclear propulsion a reality. However, there is nothing easy about the technology. As is so often the case success came only after events had thrown up the right leader. He was the irascible, controversial and brilliantly competent Captain (later Admiral) Hyman Rickover. He drove through the development of a nuclear reactor small enough to be packed into a submarine hull. The reactor provided heat for raising steam. Ironically, this most modern of propulsion technologies had perforce to work with steam conditions that would not normally be tolerated today. Indeed, the steam was so wet that the US Navy had almost forgotten how to deal with it, and found it helpful to draw on British designs of steam gun-boats used fifty years earlier in World War I. *Nautilus* was launched at the beginning of 1955 and, a few days later, on 17 January, sent her epoch-making signal, 'Under way on nuclear power.' She quickly demonstrated her ability to stay submerged for weeks on end.

Almost from the outset there had been a small naval contingent at Harwell. In the early and mid-fifties it was considerably strengthened with engineers from the main naval contractors who, significantly, included Rolls-Royce. I became one of their links with the rest of the establishment, in particular for naval work on shielding – weight-saving being a major consideration.

A small reactor dedicated to shielding experiments was completed in 1956. I also had some responsibilities for studying the physics of the small water-cooled reactors that were used in submarines.

The Navy encouraged us by arranging a visit to the submarine base at Gosport. Before spending a few hours submerged in the English Channel we were shown the water-filled escape tower, where crews are taught how to escape from a depth of 130 feet without damaging their lungs. It was the time when Kellogg's Corn Flakes packets included small plastic submarines which could be made to surface with the aid of a pinch of baking powder. The submariners wrote to Kellogg's, saying that this had been successfully achieved from a depth of 130 feet. Kellogg's replied courteously, thanking them for the news and adding that Their Lordships (of the Admiralty) would doubtless sleep more soundly when they learned that Kellogg's had a fleet of no fewer than fourteen million. I told this story to a friend. A week later it appeared in print as part of an article by a mysterious, but extremely well-informed, science correspondent who wrote under the pseudonym Geminus. John Maddox's cover was blown.

Meanwhile, the British Navy was trying to persuade its American colleagues to receive and brief a technical mission, initially without success. Sir Alex Smith, in his autobiography, attributes the eventual change of heart to the favourable impressions Rickover received during a visit to Rolls-Royce at Derby. There he met Lord Hives who had known Henry Royce and who, by his own admission, was not the usual kind of feudal lord, but 'just a bloody plumber'. Rickover decided that here was a man and an organisation that could safely be entrusted with nuclear development. As a result the keel of the first British nuclear submarine was laid in June 1959.

In preparation for that event I was one of a twenty-strong technical party that crossed the Atlantic in the summer of 1957 to gather whatever advice was on offer. We were to spend a couple of weeks with Rickover and his team, and it was in a mood of high expectation that we had our first meeting in the old Main Navy Building in Washington. Rickover opened the proceedings by politely inviting the leader of our team to describe the British efforts. Rear-Admiral Wilson had been speaking for perhaps five minutes when Rickover brought his hand down with a crash on to the table. 'Wilson, you have the valour of ignorance.'

We were overwhelmed with embarrassment. But from that moment Rickover opened all his doors. We visited Westinghouse at Pittsburg, General Electric at Schenectady, the Idaho reactor test centre in its once-volcanic wilderness, and the east-coast submarine base at Groton. Rickover was aware that the British per diem allowance was meagre and kindly arranged for us to be accommodated in Quonset huts at a cost of one dollar a night. They were spartan, but the beds were comfortable. The younger members of the team were appreciative. A few senior officers, however, felt they were being patronised.

After days and nights of absorbing the generous outpouring of information, we assembled at the British Embassy on the evening before our final meeting with Rickover. The general consensus was that we had been extraordinarily well treated and that it would be a pity to spoil things by asking any more questions. When we met Rickover in the morning we said as much. 'Nonsense. The girls have gotten lunch for you. You will stay and work until twelve.' With that he walked out, while members of his team divided us into specialist groups. Promptly, at noon, he returned. 'Gentlemen, will you please stand.' In came his attractive secretary, Second Officer Sally Higgins, WAVES, who clasped her hands demurely and sang, without accompaniment, 'The Star-Spangled Banner' and 'God Save the Queen'. We sat down. The British looked at each other, and thought 'How nice!'

The girls brought in fried chicken in cardboard boxes, and soft drinks, and we settled down to a no-trimmings meal. We were nearing the end when Rickover came back into the long room and said, 'Sally, sing them your State song.' Sally sang the 'Song of Georgia'. She had an excellent soprano voice and, once again, the British looked pleased. Before long Rickover

142

said, 'Sing them some songs of England.' Sally sang 'D'you ken John Peel', and 'Drink to me only with thine eyes'. After another few minutes Rickover made a fresh request: 'Sing them that thing about the Lord is my Shepherd.' Sally sang a metrical paraphrase of the twenty-third psalm. By now the British were sitting to attention on the edge of their chairs, hardly daring to move a muscle lest offence might be caused. Then followed a memorable closing exchange:

Rickover (to us all): 'Sally's a good girl. Aren't you, Sally?'

'Yes sir.'

'And you go to church, don't you Sally?'

'Yes sir.'

'Do you pray?'

'Yes sir.'

'Whom do you pray for?'

'My father and mother, sir.'

'Don't you pray for me?'

'No sir.' After a moment's thought she added, with great emphasis, 'But in future I shall.'

The tension broke. We laughed. The meeting was quickly concluded and we left with feelings of extraordinary gratitude to our eccentric host. That evening I happened to run into Sally at a small party given by our Scientific Attaché, John Willis. I asked whether this sort of thing had happened before. 'Never,' she said.

As a follow-up to the mission Rickover arranged a day-long cruise in *Nautilus* in the English Channel. I drove to Plymouth in early October with John Dolphin, who had recently become Chief Engineer at Harwell. He already had some experience of submarines and, during World War II, had designed, built and tested a miniature submarine in the astonishingly short time of six weeks. During the journey he told me how, with such a tight timetable, improvisation had been needed at every turn. For instance, the fore and aft cruise trim control was a shower tap: 'hot' for dive, 'cold' for surface. The boat was taken to a large reservoir to the west of London to be demonstrated to

Mountbatten, who was Chief of Combined Operations. He asked whether he might operate it himself and, after being shown the controls, drove off. Dolphin became worried because something was clearly going wrong with the dive – the stern of the boat was remaining on the surface. He anticipated a reprimand, but was relieved when Mountbatten returned with his face wreathed in smiles. 'Marvellous. For the past twenty minutes I have been cruising around in perfect safety at a depth of 30 feet.' Dolphin said nothing, but when the great man had left he took a look inside to find out what had so fortunately misled the Admiral. He concluded that Mountbatten must have been reading the angle-of-dive indicator.

Nautilus was far bigger than our own boats – large enough, in fact, to play host to two visiting parties at the same time. We engineers and scientists never caught sight of the ministerial party during our cruise along the bottom of the Channel. The boat returned to Plymouth in the afternoon, and after I had gone ashore I heard the BBC news. The day, 11 October 1957, suddenly became doubly memorable: one of the Windscale reactors was on fire.

The fire had started during routine maintenance aimed at producing a controlled release of so-called Wigner energy. This is gradually and unavoidably locked up in the reactor structure during normal operation, owing to fast neutrons knocking atoms out of their proper places in the graphite crystal lattice. Left uncorrected, this would in time alter the geometry of the reactor core, making it unuseable. To avoid this there were periodical planned energy releases, a process which involved carefully warming the graphite core. However, on this occasion, the monitoring and control procedures had proved inadequate: the temperature had risen, the graphite became red hot, and eleven tons of uranium were now on fire. This left Tom Tuohy, the local manager who had helped me with the CIRCUS exercise, with the unenviable task of deciding how to bring a potentially disastrous situation under control.

History relates how he stood on the pile cap, wearing breathing apparatus, looking down through the inspection holes that had been my last-minute contribution to the design. Flames were coming from the reactor channels. Some of the staff were in favour of using carbon dioxide. Tuohy pointed out that this might exacerbate the conditions – as it did. Water was then the only recourse. But water reacts with red-hot graphite to form water-gas, an inflammable mixture of hydrogen and carbon monoxide. Would using water simply result in a catastrophic explosion that might blow away the filters at the top of the chimney and leave the Cumbrian landscape wide open to fission product pollution? Much would depend on how the water was used.

Tuohy decided he had no other option. By the time the hoses were ready the fire had been developing for 24 hours. He ordered everyone out of the plant except himself and the local fire chief before turning on the water. The drastic action worked, and the filters remained intact. They were too coarse to trap the finer particles and offered no barrier to gaseous fission products – like the iodine that contaminated local milk supplies for weeks afterwards, to the extent that the milk had to be thrown away. But much of the radioactivity was filtered out, and the time and energy spent ten years earlier in convincing the design team that the filters were necessary proved fully justified.

I should have loved to discuss the accident with the reactor's designer, my treasured friend, Jim Kendall. But he had died six weeks earlier from a heart attack, shortly after a sailing holiday with me in Brittany, when bad weather gave us a long and miserable passage back across the Channel. He was clearly overstrained by the effort – but at least he had had one final glorious day, sailing from Salcombe to Fowey.

Like the Navy, the merchant marine was also keeping an eye on nuclear propulsion. There was a small presence at Harwell from the British Shipbuilding Research Association (BSRA). But for merchant ships nuclear propulsion offers no competitive advantage unless it produces power as cheaply as conventional systems; or unless the nuclear ability to confer almost unlimited range, including range at high speed, could open up new uses. The Russians had indeed found one new application: ice-breaking. They had built the *Lenin*, which had the power and range to keep open a channel round the north of Siberia, something no oil-fuelled ice-breaker could match. But that market was self-evidently very small. The Japanese were interested in a nuclear merchant ship, possibly with a long-term eye to the emerging container trade. Some members of the Atomic Energy Authority felt that we should seize the moment and start work on a ship reactor of our own. Calder Hall had been a success. Why not a scaled-down version for shipborne use?

This was the background to a conference on marine propulsion that I helped BSRA to organise at Harwell in the autumn of 1956. It drew particular attention to economic factors. Safety also mattered, because to be useful nuclear ships would need to enter the crowded conurbations around the world's major ports. I looked at Lloyd's safety statistics, and found that we could not ignore the possibility of serious accidents in British coastal waters. The intensity of shipping in the Channel on its way to northern European ports, together with frequent bad weather, meant that this country would be unexpectedly vulnerable. If at some time in the future one hundred nuclear-propelled ships were afloat, Britain might be faced with a potentially dangerous marine accident every thirty years – quite apart from port safety. For land-based reactors we had been very careful about siting and operating standards. Could we be sure that marine reactors would be operated as carefully? And what about possible stranding at high water, when there might be no safe way of disposing of the considerable heat that a reactor emits even when shut down?

A nuclear reactor cannot be completely switched off – there is always some residual heating owing to long-lasting radioactivity in the reactor core. This heating is far from negligible: immediately after shutdown it is about 5% of the heat produced during normal operation. In this respect a reactor's behaviour somewhat resembles that of the earth's core. This planet is kept habitable by its long-lived radioactivity, without which it would have become a dead world long ago. The price we pay is the steady loss of life from vulcanism and earthquakes. One might say that nuclear energy in this entirely natural guise accounts for thousands of fatalities per year.

The enthusiasts for marine propulsion were dissatisfied with the 'not proven' verdict that seemed to be the majority view at the BSRA conference. One proponent of 'wait and see' suggested in a closing speech that 'we must learn to walk before we can run'. Whereupon, an ex-Navy officer jumped up and said, 'You must admit, sir, that walking is damned bad practice for running.'

Slightly disconcerted, the speaker responded, 'It's the way we take our first faltering footsteps.'

The gallant captain jumped on him triumphantly. 'And what happened then, sir? You fell over onto your ass.'

Although the way ahead was unclear, the Navy was willing to offer encouragement if a reasonable proposition could be produced for a nuclear-propelled Royal Fleet Auxiliary. By the spring of 1958 a ministerial committee, chaired by the Civil Lord of the Admiralty, Thomas Galbraith, was ready to consider the possibilities. However, my division head, John Dunworth, expressed private doubts about some of the more optimistic suggestions that were being made by our Authority colleagues, which he said 'smelt wrong'. He simply refused to believe that civil nuclear propulsion – unlike naval applications – would ever have sufficient economic advantages to outweigh the inevitable questions of safety and operational flexibility. He asked me to have a private rethink – no strings attached – and gave me two excellent assistants and three months to finish the job.

For a few weeks we pursued the standard approach, with which we were thoroughly familiar: choice of reactor system, sketch designs, rough costings, weights, and so on. We turned up nothing new and I began to feel doubtful about satisfying Dunworth. Fortunately, I realised while there was still some time left that we were too inbred – if any new light was to be shed on the problem it would come not from nuclear engineers but from the end-users. I shook the dust of Harwell off my feet and spent much of the next ten days travelling, visiting maritime experts up and down the country wherever they could be found.

It was a seminal period that strongly influenced my approach to policy-making in later years. By the end of the round of visits it was quite clear that there was no point whatever in proceeding with a nuclear merchant ship. It would have no economic advantages and there would be unavoidable safety problems. Moreover, the assumption of cheap financing that underlay the Atomic Energy Authority's interest in a nuclear propulsion project bore no relation to the economics of the real shipping world. If, instead of financing at 4% or 5%, a more realistic figure of 15% were used, capital cost considerations would overshadow all else. Moving to the higher capital charge would also invert the economic order of preference of the various types of reactor. 'Calder Hall in a ship' would come not at the top of the list, but at the bottom. The arguments were crystal clear. The report – 'Future Systems Group 70' – was written in ten days. It was printed for internal circulation in June 1958.

Dunworth was delighted; the proponents of a mobile Calder Hall, understandably, less so – no-one likes to lose an exciting project. They put up a fight and, three years later, were still advising a Ministerial committee that such a project was feasible. By then I had moved to Whitehall and had got to know Richard Chilver, who soon moved on to become the Deputy Secretary in charge of shipping policy. He rang me to ask whether I could shed light on this extraordinary proposition. I sent him FSG 70. Apart from a few death throes, that was the end.

Britain was not the only maritime nation anxious not to miss a trick. Norway was also interested. It was primarily because of her marine interest that Norway had built a small boiling-water reactor at Halden, south of Oslo. The money had been partly subscribed by the other countries of OECD so, naturally, they had a share in the management. I was the British representative, and had the enjoyable duty of visiting Norway every three months. I know of no other country where the seasons succeed each other more dramatically.

In October 1959 the Halden reactor was finally ready, and King Olav came for the formal opening ceremony. As with all reactors, start-up was visually unexciting. Indeed, if anything dramatic had happened something would have been seriously wrong. The King congratulated his engineers on the successful completion of the project and for having brought the reactor up to low power. 'At least, that is what I understand has happened. What I can say without fear of contradiction is that I saw a needle move across a dial.' He spoke in English, with wit and assurance. Those Norwegians who had not met him before were surprised – he was apparently not so effective in their own language. But then he had been born near Sandringham, to an English princess.

It was during one of my visits to Oslo that I had a long discussion with Lawyer Jens Hauge about the sense, or otherwise, of Norway starting a marine propulsion project. He was a man of immense distinction, still in his early forties. I mistakenly thought him older; he was certainly mature beyond his years. It was only later I learned that during World War II he had been head of MILORG, the military resistance organisation, and that following the coming of peace he had been successively the Prime Minister's secretary, the Minister of Defence, and the Minister of Justice. He clearly had some influence in matters nuclear. I gave him a résumé of the ship report, 'FSG 70'. It took some time to convince him that I was speaking in all sincerity and not merely wishing to head off a competitor nation. I think I persuaded him. At all events, Norway did not go down that road.

No sooner was the ship report out of the way than it was time to make final arrangements for a conference on shielding, to be held under the aegis of the European Atomic Energy Society. The venue was Caius College, Cambridge, whose original architect had made full use of symbolism. He intended the new student to enter through a gate marked 'Humilitatis'. The doorway to the second court carries the inscription, 'Virtutis'. From there candidates for graduation proceed to the Senate House through

149

the Gate of Honour: 'Honoris'. The formidably efficient lady bursar, the inappropriately named Miss Small, told me that a little before the conference an inscription had appeared above a fourth doorway: 'Necessitatis'. 'Those middens have been in use for centuries,' she added, clearly relishing the historical significance of that section of the College.

It was an international conference, with delegates from thirteen countries, so I took care to make the ambience unusually stylish. Being in Cambridge that was not difficult. Moreover, the weather was good – it was late August 1958 – which made it possible to include little touches like having sherry in the court before dinner. Lectures were held in the Regent House on King's Parade. On the one free afternoon punts were provided for the delegates to try their skill on the Cam, standing on the platform at what those raised at Oxford would regard as the wrong end of the boat (the Isis has sticky mud, the Cam a clean gravel bottom).

The need for detailed study of the physics of reactor shielding had arisen as a direct result of the discovery of the neutron in 1932. In the interim – a mere twenty-six years – warfare had been utterly transformed, and a new source of energy created. The man responsible for the neutron's discovery, the Nobel laureate Sir James Chadwick, happened by chance to be a Fellow of Caius. He agreed to reminisce about the discovery, and what had led up to it, in an informal talk from High Table during the concluding conference dinner. It was a *coup de théâtre*. One ecstatic American said that those fifteen minutes alone had justified the journey. We were all struck by Chadwick's modesty and matter-of-fact approach, but perhaps most of all by the way this, and so many other major discoveries, had been made at the Cavendish Laboratory at a time when it was operating with an annual budget of no more than £30,000.

A brilliant American mathematician, Herb Goldstein, took a leading role in the discussions; so it was a matter of general regret when he heard on the second day that his father had died. According to Jewish rites he had to be back in New York State within twenty-four hours, which meant he might have to forgo the special delight that he had promised himself: to see and handle the original copies of Pepys' diaries, which are lodged in Magdalene College. Indeed, as he told Jeanie during the conference dinner, this was one of the reasons why he had crossed the Atlantic. I had already made tentative arrangements on his behalf; now I endeavoured to change these at short notice. The librarian of the Pepys Library was off duty but the Master, Sir Henry Willinck, with infinite courtesy, offered to show Herb the diaries himself. I went along too and saw, for the first and only time, those miraculously tidy notebooks, with their nine-year record written in Shelton's system of shorthand (not, as is sometimes said, in a personal code). The symbols were placed with meticulous tidiness on a square graticule, their neatness telling us something of their author's personality.

Before he retired Pepys had been Secretary of the Navy Board and later of the Admiralty under Charles II and James II, and during that time had doubled the Navy's strength. Sir Henry showed us several beautifully executed sectional ship drawings, with overlays detailing how the various decks fitted together. Goldstein was enchanted – but there was no time for him to savour the experience. A car was waiting and he was driven to Heathrow in time to catch an evening flight, as filial duty demanded.

As the 1950s unfolded safety became an ever more important aspect of life in atomic energy. This went further than dealing with normal industrial hazards. There was a new kind of problem: how to make sure that fissionable material, during production, transportation or storage, did not unintentionally become the source of an uncontrolled nuclear chain reaction. There was, fortunately, no likelihood of accidentally producing an atomic bomb. That requires special engineering; it can hardly be the result of happenstance. But it is not difficult to imagine circumstances in which a store of plutonium or uranium-235 could, if mishandled, create a lethal source of radiation. For instance, the invasion of a dry store by water could do just that, unless the possibility had been previously considered and precautions taken.

The precautions were in themselves straightforward. What was less easy was to be sure that every possible eventuality had been considered; that the operators knew what had been decided, and why; and that their actions would remain disciplined and devoid of dangerous short cuts. The way in which safety information was published also needed some thought. Messages had to be sent in ways which guaranteed they would be read by busy men and not ignored. Maintaining mutual confidence between the workforce and management was also essential.

I was a member of a panel charged with studying the safety of the Capenhurst diffusion plant. This was a huge array of pipes, pumps and diffusion membranes round which circulated a gaseous compound of uranium. The purpose was to boost the concentration of the easily fissionable form of uranium, which in a naturally occurring sample forms less than one per cent of the whole. The panel sat under the chairmanship of Cyril Nicholls, a likeable and exceedingly competent chemical engineer. My task, in which I was helped by a mathematician skilled in reactor calculations, was to devise ways of demonstrating that a critical nuclear assembly could not be created within the plant accidentally. This was more easily said than done, because the geometry of the plant bore no relation to the ideal mathematical forms that make calculation easy.

After weeks of hard slogging the panel produced a lengthy set of recommendations and we were duly thanked. But acting on them required resources, and progress was at first slower than we would have wished. Then a serious accident in the US led to the death of a worker in circumstances that we had described as a possibility, but that had evidently strained the credulity of our readers. Thereafter our recommendations were given high priority.

A year or so later there was a need to modify the plant to produce a higher degree of enrichment, and the question arose as to whether it would still be safe. Again we worked through the cascade item by item and made further recommendations, underlining the absolute necessity of making it impossible for

152

cooling water to enter the gaseous uranium hexafluoride circuit. The danger was that this could cause the deposition of fissile material in quantities and in places that could not easily be guaranteed safe. We recognised that at one point water could, theoretically, enter the plant if a triple fault were to occur, but dismissed this as too improbable. One should never say 'never'. A few weeks later there was just such a fault. Some hundreds of litres of water did get into the circuit; fortunately, there were no dramatic consequences.

I was climbing the promotion ladder and acquiring more staff. We called ourselves the Reactor Development Branch, an all-embracing and deliberately ambiguous title chosen in the hope that it might offer flexibility at a time when much around us was changing. The gathering momentum of the power programme meant that the main action was moving away from research-based Harwell into the Industrial Group of the Atomic Energy Authority, based in Lancashire – and, of course, into industry itself. Even with promotion my Harwell salary was far from generous, and it was galling (though in retrospect hardly surprising) to see one's peer group being promoted and paid extra for working north of the Mersey. It was a simple case of market forces. I toyed with the idea of escaping – to a new professorship at Manchester, to one at MIT in the US, to the Moscow Embassy as Science Attaché, or to the then falsely-promising field of nuclear fusion. But this was more a recognition that change would overtake me before long than any considered intent.

Harwell itself was growing too large for its Berkshire site, and work on future reactors was about to be moved to a new establishment at Winfrith Heath in Dorset. The move was controversial: Winfrith was supposedly Hardy's 'Egdon Heath'. The senior staff immersed themselves in his novels. Never was so much literary erudition shown by a scientific organisation. Scholarly pros and cons apart, the task of convincing the public inquiry might well have been simplified by the fact that the Bovingdon tank range was almost next door. Hardy's Wessex had already been altered beyond recognition. The inquiry gave a favourable verdict, subject to constraints that were acceptable. The move to Dorset began in 1959, and the senior staff earmarked for the new establishment, myself included, began to plan for the expansion that this would make possible.

I was to have responsibility for an engineering laboratory, for shielding and, most interestingly, for surveying the many possible different kinds of reactor that looked promising in theory but had not yet been seriously investigated. Any nuclear reactor needs a nuclear fuel; most need a 'moderator' to slow down the neutrons produced in fission and make the chain reaction more efficient; all need a coolant to extract the energy. There were at least half a dozen families of nuclear fuel, four possible moderators and at least six coolants, to say nothing of many design variants. So there were literally hundreds of theoretically possible reactors. Most could be immediately ruled out on the grounds of incompatibility between components. But there were still several that warranted careful study, and they would provide our bread and butter.

My Branch grew into a Division. We were scheduled to move from Harwell to Winfrith early in 1960, and I made preparations. I started to put my house in order with an eye to selling it. I bought a much faster car, a Jaguar – there were not yet speed limits outside built-up areas – to ease the weekly journey in the interim. During the week I lodged at a Dorset pub, and started house hunting. But before I could complete the move chance events once again intervened and I was propelled swiftly down paths I hardly knew existed.

Chapter 10

With Zuckerman in Whitehall

What had deflected me, through a convoluted chain of circumstances, was my love of music. Soon after joining Harwell and getting to know Vernon Donnison, who lived nearby, we had organised a choir to sing at a wedding in his village, Hagbourne. This had grown into a madrigal group. It was not long before we tired of 'My bonny lass' and 'When going to my lonely bed' and opted instead for the greater satisfaction of the religious music of the Renaissance.

This was a completely new musical experience and challenge. Unlike those who came later, the composers of the time gave almost no indication of tempi or dynamics; one had to work out these things for oneself. Fortunately tape recorders were just becoming available. I spent long hours listening to our rehearsal efforts, gradually modifying the performance to bring out the significance of the words, until the effect was satisfying and, where necessary, dramatic. This meant marking every part separately, a method I later learned Beecham had used years earlier.

Our choice of works was guided by my accountant, Guy Severn, who was a church music enthusiast. We made him secretary of the group and, as Sabrina was the Roman name for the River Severn, we became the Sabrina Singers. We were about two dozen, including a former Kings' choral scholar who added much-needed tonal quality to the rest of the bass line.

One had only to listen to the other basses to know that there had been no auditions. But away from the choir stalls they were a particularly distinguished group. There was Vernon, an official war historian of such excellence that the Burmese dictator, Ne Win, instructed his cabinet to read Donnison on Burmese history. Vernon had been at Corpus Christi, Oxford, immediately after World War I with another bass, Ted Hale, who, after a distinguished Treasury career, was Secretary of the University Grants Committee. My solicitor Jack Hedges's family had lived in Wallingford for centuries; he was also my treasured partner for two-piano music. And (of most significance for this story) there was Basil Schonland, who had succeeded Cockcroft as Harwell's director, and who some years previously had been invited by Vernon to sing with us – an invitation I should never have dared to give. All these three had been knighted.

Friendship and love of music were the touchstones when recruiting new members. They conferred on our performances a degree of cohesion and sensitivity that still seem remarkable – there are recordings made in Dorchester Abbey to prove it. Singing there was a delight, and in that resonant chamber there was not the slightest difficulty over intonation. Palestrina's *Missa Brevis*, Byrd's four-part *Mass*, Thomas Tomkins' strange dronings, Orlando Gibbons' joyful six-part *Hosanna to the Son of David* – these were what brought us together once a fortnight on Fridays.

Voices age and jobs change. Unsurprisingly the Sabrinas did not survive long into the sixties. But the friendships that were their foundation remained for life – seven Sabrinas were present at our golden wedding forty years later, in 1997.

Basil Schonland first sang with us in the mid-fifties, when he was still Deputy Director of Harwell. As an undergraduate I had known his name as author of a monograph on thunderstorms. At Harwell he was so far in the organisational stratosphere that we did not see much of each other in the course of ordinary work. But we had already been thrown together in the context of the Lancaster House disarmament talks, and together had produced a dozen or more 'think-pieces', spelling out what might

156

be possible scientifically regarding the control of nuclear weapon materials. The underlying problem, however, remained unsolved: inspection was needed as a confidence-building measure, but without prior confidence it was unlikely to be effective. Schonland had commented: 'This is big stuff – but I can't see any of it actually happening.'

During the war Schonland had been Scientific Adviser to Montgomery. One afternoon I was invited to take tea with the Field Marshal, who was visiting Harwell. His ice-blue eyes flashed as he launched into a defence of his tactics in Normandy: how he had always planned to pivot on Caen while he delivered a 'right hook' further west. I later saw him more than once giving the same explanation on television. Was he, I wondered, guilty of slightly rewriting history? His difficulty in dealing with Caen must certainly have been compounded by the unexpected stubbornness of the German resistance and the high quality of their tanks and artillery.

Having Basil Schonland in the Sabrinas was a potentially delicate relationship. I took care to avoid over-familiarity, and at work never referred to our musical activities. He grew more and more appreciative of our repertoire of Renaissance music, and at a performance in Dorchester Abbey, when the choir was in unusually good voice, he turned to Vernon and whispered, 'This is the best thing I have ever done.'

By the beginning of 1960 I knew Basil well enough to mention that almost all my professional life had been spent in the depths of the country or abroad, and that if an opportunity arose I should welcome a chance of working in London. Some weeks later he told me that Sir Solly Zuckerman had asked whether the Atomic Energy Authority could nominate a scientist to fill an unspecified but senior post in the Ministry of Defence, where he had recently become Chief Scientific Adviser. 'As an "adviser" does Zuckerman carry much weight?' I asked.

'None more so,' was the reply.

I said I would be happy for my name to go forward. It was the most momentous decision of my life.

It was the second time I had heard Zuckerman's name. Three years earlier Jeanie and I had been taken by our best man, David Farrell, to Jacob Bronowski's house on Cleeve Hill, near Cheltenham. We had not previously met, but I knew of him through his public reputation as a polymath, someone who effortlessly straddled science and the arts. He was Director of the Coal Research Establishment, a somewhat odd niche for a mathematician who had not only written a book on William Blake, but had also been on the Chiefs of Staff Mission to examine the effects of bombing in Japan in 1945. It was clear from what Bronowski told me that his relations with Zuckerman were far from cordial.

Some weeks after my conversation with Schonland I was called for an interview at Zuckerman's house at Burnham Thorpe, near King's Lynn – the village where Nelson was born. I cleaned and polished the aging Jaguar, prayed that it would not have another of its bouts of unreliability, and managed to arrive on time. I immediately felt under scrutiny, but Zuckerman's face was essentially kind. In his gravelly voice he set out the problem.

'I need help. The Scientific Civil Service doesn't seem able to provide the kind of people I need. The Atomic Energy Authority has a better reputation. Bill Penny has given you good marks. Tell me something about yourself.'

I did so. It was summer, and he suggested we might drive a couple of miles to Burnham Staithe and stretch our legs. We wandered across a dyke, discussing how to stop the harbour silting up. I told him my friend from Wallingford, Fergus Allen, was the best man to consult. He was head of the Hydraulics Research Station; I knew him because he was married to a Sabrina singer. I took Sir Solly back. As he got out of the car he said, 'I'll tell the Permanent Secretary you can have the job. It's at two-star level – ranking with Major-Generals and Under-Secretaries.'

It had been the easiest interview of my life. I drove lightheartedly down almost empty roads to a dinner in London, and returned home to tell Jeanie that life was about to change.

I also told David Garstin, my sailing, motor-rallying and erstwhile bridge partner. He was now a Commander in the Navy and 'Chief' (engineer) of the new aircraft carrier *Hermes*. He immediately invited me to join the ship for her commissioning cruise, saying that if I was going to Defence I ought to know something about the modern Navy. In early November I travelled to Portsmouth and, on the following day, we sailed with the ship dressed overall, the ship's company manning the flight deck, the Marine band playing and counter-marching, and six helicopters hovering overhead, keeping station until we were well out into Spithead. By the morning we were off St Bride's Bay, at the south-west corner of Wales, where a squadron of fixed-wing aircraft was due to fly in for practice deck landings. There was tension just before nightfall – one aircraft had already made two missed approaches, and had only sufficient fuel for one more attempt. Luckily, this was successful.

David used this incident as a peg for discussing the difficulties of operating modern high performance aircraft from carriers that were really too small. His words stuck in my memory and I drew on them a couple of years later, when the future of naval aviation was reaching a crunch. In the morning I was helicoptered ashore to the naval air station at Brawdy and joined Jeanie for a short holiday in the Wye Valley.

I left Winfrith on 2 December 1960 with an armful of appropriate presents from my division: a large globe and a *Times* atlas, to instruct me in matters strategic; a bin for the waste paper that I would unfailingly generate; and a copy of that day's *Times*, tied with red tape. Three days later I joined the Ministry of Defence.

My new secretary, Louise, was a grey-haired lady whose savoir faire and knowledge of the Defence Department I soon came to treasure. She advanced on me with a tray of papers that had been accumulating since 'Bill' Williams, my predecessor, had moved to a NATO appointment. They were stacked more than a foot high and every day she brought another fifty pages.

'How on earth am I to deal with all this paper?' I asked Zuckerman.

'Skim it if you have time. The priorities will settle themselves.'

And so it proved.

Zuckerman – Sir Solly as he was universally known – had me installed in a magnificent corner office on the second floor of the Treasury building, looking out over St James's Park and down Birdcage Walk. As a two-star official I was entitled to some pictures from the Ministry of Works collection – originals, not prints. One that caught my eye was 'The Boatbuilders', a Stanley Spencerish painting that I remembered seeing in the lounge of the Harwell staff mess on the day of Fuchs' arrest. Another was a portrait by the academician, Carel Weight, of a lady in the Isle of Wight. John Julius Norwich, who was then still a diplomat, noticed it a couple of years later and introduced me to the painter. Weight told me that the lady had the thinnest face, seen from the front, that he had ever encountered, so he had painted her in profile. He also expressed surprise, as he had believed that the painting was in the Athens embassy. An unavoidable sadness of being a painter is that one may not know where many of one's best-loved creations are to be found.

By the time the pictures had been hung my office was all that I could wish for; indeed, it was later occupied by a Treasury knight. Mountbatten had the mirror-image room at the other end of the corridor. In between were the Minister of Defence, Harold Watkinson; the Permanent Secretary, Sir Edward Playfair; Zuckerman; and Richard Chilver, who was to be my mentor.

The Defence Department faced strategic and political dilemmas that were as fascinating as they were baffling. In Europe NATO confronted the Russians in an uneasy state of deterrence. No-one could be confident how secure that equilibrium would remain. The very nature of major war on land was increasingly obscure, as weapons technology carried its potentialities far outside the professional experience of any commander. At sea we faced the huge Russian navy and, understandably, our own was forever complaining of inadequate resources, particularly as regards sea-borne air cover and ship maintenance. The Army of the Rhine was draining our economy and further undermining our position, while boosting that of Germany. We were withdrawing from Empire, but still faced the likelihood of limited wars – or at least skirmishes. We were knowledgeable and skilled in that kind of engagement, having dealt with over fifty incidents since World War II. But maintaining the necessary intervention forces was a strain on the economy. There were also major decisions to be taken about the RAF's future mix of aircraft.

In support we had a highly inventive weapons industry, but the expense of new weaponry was outstripping our ability to pay. The balance between quantity and quality was becoming ever more difficult to maintain. We no longer carried sufficient clout for overseas arms sales to provide more than a palliative, and were not helped economically by our political separation from Europe. For all these reasons we faced the possibility of a seemingly endless string of expensive cancellations. The Treasury was making carping noises, which foreshadowed large-scale defence cuts. Altogether we had more policies than resources. In Zuckerman's words, we were down to our last dollar, our last bottle of whisky!

These problems would soon force a major defence reorganisation. Before that took effect in 1964 the best that could be said for the existing arrangement was that it promoted debate. This was fostered not only by the multiplicity of other Defence departments – Admiralty, War Office, Air Ministry and Ministry of Supply – but also by the internal structure of our own small central ministry. Alone in Whitehall it was managed, under the Minister of Defence, by a triumvirate.

The military triumvir was Mountbatten, who still basked in the glory of the role he had played in the Far East. He liked to recall the incongruous words of his appointment: 'Rear-Admiral Mountbatten to HMS *Vernon* for Senior Officers' Training Course, then to Government of India as Viceroy.' He was an immensely arrogant man, who could fly into a raging temper without warning. Yet, when Mountbatten returned unexpectedly to his office while my eleven-year-old son Jeremy was being shown war trophies by his secretary, the Admiral could not have been more welcoming to the boy.

Mountbatten was now Chief of Defence Staff – CDS – and had pressed Zuckerman to take the job. Without his unstinted support Sir Solly might not have survived. Mountbatten's experience during the war, following the Dieppe disaster, had convinced him of the need for the closest collaboration between scientists and the military. What he wanted from them – and what Zuckerman had provided prior to the Normandy invasion – was objective analysis of policy, rather than scientific advice in any normal sense.

To illustrate how useful scientists could be Mountbatten liked to tell a story about Bernal, the brilliant but controversial crystallographer, who was attached to Combined Operations HQ. Shortly before the Normandy battle Bernal went to Mountbatten complaining that he had been asked for advice on the feasibility of a lightweight echo-sounder, without being told its purpose. Mountbatten gave instructions for him to be informed. On being told it was intended for use in commando canoes operating close inshore just before D-day in an attempt to plot submarine contours, Bernal is said to have responded: 'There is another approach. Due to the earth's rotation there is an unusually large rise and fall of the tides along the French coast. We have command of the air. Vertical photographs of the shore-line taken at different states of the tide will plot your contours automatically.' After this brilliant piece of lateral thinking there were no more problems of communication between scientists and the Armed Services at Combined Operations, where Mountbatten actively cultivated what he called 'the spirit of the hive'.

Regarding peace-time defence policy analysis Mountbatten probably expected too much from scientists. But as long as he was Chief of Defence Staff Zuckerman could walk on water. Provided he did not overplay his hand (and no-one had more sensitive antennae) he was free to give his views on the most central issues – most notably on nuclear weapons policy. This mutual admiration between the two men was to have a significant influence on my own career.

The administrative triumvir was Sir Edward Playfair, the Permanent Secretary, who had a quicksilver mind that meshed well with Zuckerman's. Earlier, while still in the Treasury, he had been a protégé of Sir Edward Hale, one of the Sabrina basses, who gave him top marks. He did not stay long, and left to run the new computer company, ICL. His successor, Sir Rob Scott – described by a colleague as 'dripping with sanity' – seemed less close to the scientists, though he always gave us a fair hearing. By the time he too departed in 1963 the incoming Permanent Secretary, Sir Henry Hardman, had as his main task the integration of the whole defence administration into one mammoth Department. Hardman naturally aimed for maximum administrative tidiness – anything less and the job would have been all but impossible. Zuckerman felt that Hardman was in some way challenging the intellectual independence of his scientists. It was certainly something that had to be argued and fought for more vigorously than in the easy-going Playfair days. Zuckerman's memoirs make clear that his refusal to regard scientific policy advice as just another input, to be coordinated like all others by the Permanent Secretary's staff, was one of the factors that eventually led to his departure from the MOD in 1966. There was, fortunately, no loss to Whitehall: Zuckerman became Scientific Adviser to the whole Government instead of to just one department, eventually receiving a peerage. But while the tensions existed they complicated life for his underlings.

Playfair saw me at the first opportunity, and spent some time advising me on how to survive in the Whitehall jungle: how life at this level was a struggle for influence; how a frontal attack on a well-defended position might not be the best course, no matter how right one might be.

'Remember ju-jitsu. Try to make your opponent fall by his own weight.'

I mentioned that I might need some staff, and added, 'I suppose we shall have to trawl' (i.e. advertise within the Service).

'Or winkle,' said Playfair. 'Remember the other kind of fishing.'

He called in Richard Chilver, the Deputy Secretary whose office was next to mine, and asked him to guide me in the coming months. It was a most agreeable master-pupil relationship. He liked looking at problems in the round. 'What is the *gestalt*' he would ask. He elevated scepticism to an art form, and encouraged me to do the same. He had an insatiable curiosity and, although not a scientist, kept himself up to date with the implications of science. He was married to the equally brilliant Sally, Principal of Bedford College and later of Lady Margaret Hall. Over dinner at their house one could be sure of finding intellectual challenge, without the remotest hint of artificiality. One night Stevie Smith, the poetess, was there, memorably declaiming: 'God the incomprehensible, the Son the incomprehensible, the Holy Spirit the incomprehensible.' Another time Jeanie was invited to use Richard's clay and potter's wheel, and throw a pot in her party dress at midnight. Some thought him excessively austere. To me he was a delightful colleague. He was moved all too soon to the Ministry of Transport to look after shipping. There he helped to give the nuclear merchant ship its well-deserved *coup de grâce*.

I quickly learned more of my new master. When the war began he was in his mid-thirties, full of energy and already with an impressive circle of friends who were politically and scientifically influential. He was of exactly the right age to make an important contribution and, unsurprisingly, had enjoyed what was known as a 'good war'.

Being an anatomist he had initially been asked to work on the physiological effects of bomb blast. That in turn had led to an interest in bombing and how to maximise the destructive effects of air power. He came to oppose Bomber Command's policy of mass air raids on strategic targets, not on moral grounds, but because it was vastly expensive in men and matériel for what it was able to achieve. His own preference was for more surgical attacks. His policy of 'taking out' transport links to isolate Normandy prior to the invasion was so successful that enemy intelligence commented that a new mind must be at work. The surgery was, of course, done far from the beachheads, so that the invasion plans were not compromised. Albert Speer wrote to Hitler saying that the attacks on the rail network 'throttled traffic and made transport the greatest bottleneck in our war economy'.

All such operational research needs a patron, and Zuckerman was particularly fortunate with the Deputy Supreme Allied Commander, Air Marshal Tedder, whom he revered. 'There goes the only military man who was invariably objective and intellectually honest,' he once said to me, pointing out an old man hobbling up the grand staircase of the Athenaeum.

In 1932 Zuckerman had helped to set up a brilliant group known as the Tots and Quots – *quot homines tot sententiae* (as many opinions as there are men). Although young, the group was sufficiently influential to be able to welcome cabinet ministers to its discussions. Zuckerman liked to tell the story of how in May 1940 Allan Lane, publisher of Penguin Books, listened to a discussion on how science was contributing to the national war effort. He was fascinated, and regretted that no record had been taken. Zuckerman issued a challenge. 'If we give you the script in a fortnight, will you publish it in a fortnight?' The challenge was accepted and, when the Tots and Quots met four weeks later, a copy of the new Penguin paperback, *Science in War*, was at every place setting.

Zuckerman was the honorary secretary of that pillar of the Establishment, the Zoological Society of London. Given his social and professional contacts it was hardly surprising that with the coming of peace his links with government steadily strengthened. Throughout the 1950s he was constantly in demand in Whitehall as an expert adviser and committee man, particularly, though not exclusively, in defence. In 1956 he was knighted for his services. Meanwhile, he retained his chair in anatomy at Birmingham. When Sir Frederick Brundrett retired Zuckerman was the obvious choice as the next Chief Scientific Adviser in

Defence. The Air Force may have hoped that he would be their placeman, but they overlooked his fierce independence. From the beginning, Mountbatten acted as his patron and protector.

I joined Zuckerman a year after his arrival and soon formed the impression that he was at war with the administrators, whom he called 'the interpreters': people whose expertise lay not in doing for themselves, but in interpreting and relaying the expertise of others. Once he exploded in my hearing: 'God knows I'm arrogant, but (he mentioned an Undersecretary), he KNOWS.' He spat out the last word with much feeling. At the outset Sir Solly also distrusted the Scientific Civil Service, believing them to be too ready to create new technological marvels without paying sufficient attention to their purpose and utility. In sharp contrast he was interested only in what he personally judged to be important – a luxury not available to lesser men. That, in turn, affected the way he dealt with the basketful of paper that, as one of the directing triumvirate, he received every day. He read fast, but made no attempt to read everything, relying instead on his committee chairmanships, his small staff and his ever-effective grapevine (which operated on both sides of the Atlantic) to alert him to the important issues.

He was dazzlingly quick to grasp a point – so much so that he avoided as far as possible the painstaking and time-consuming preparations for important occasions that others found necessary. Many times I saw him arrive, five minutes late, to chair the Defence Research Policy Committee, a bunch of papers in his hand, still reading as he raced down the corridor. Within ten minutes he was fully in command, taking his cue from what was being said by the few committee members whom he specially trusted.

Organisationally, he fully deserved the epithet 'chaotic' that was hurled at him more than once by both the military and the administrators. Once he quarrelled with the message of a paper already circulating in the Department. 'But he had cleared the text himself,' complained the exasperated Lawrence-Wilson, whose view of Zuckerman was that self-preservation came first.

On another occasion Zuckerman signed an agreement on research with the Americans without remembering – accidentally or deliberately – to tell the senior British administrator who was accompanying him. This was a Deputy Secretary who had once said of him, 'We must contain this man'. After evident failure to do so, and a number of comparable frustrations, he exploded in my hearing with a torrent of epithets so colourful that, as I noted in my diary, the occasion must have been unique in the annals of the Higher Civil Service. Sir Rob Scott, who succeeded Playfair as Permanent Secretary, was kinder than most: 'His heart's in the right place, but he's a muddler.'

Zuckerman's inability to win over the administrators as willing allies, despite his undoubted ability to charm, did not help those of us on his staff. Being more interested in ends than means, he either did not sense instinctively what was needed to lubricate an organisation as complex as the defence machine, or did not care. For instance, one of our scientific staff, Ian Shaw, had impressed the chairman of the Joint Planning Staff – a key military group – who paid him the considerable compliment of inviting him to sit in at their meetings. Zuckerman's reaction was not, as I had expected, one of pleasure, but a brusque assertion that he would not be bound by anything that Shaw said. That was as unhelpful as it was unnecessary.

Zuckerman unquestionably had a reputation for deviousness. When Dick Crossman wrote in 1963 asking whether he might meet me informally to try out some ideas on defence I naturally felt flattered and wished to accept but, as a civil servant, first had to seek permission. Zuckerman refused, since Crossman was a front-bench member of the Opposition and defence 'shadow'.

'Say it's the administrators.'

I made my apologies accordingly.

'Administrators?' snorted Crossman. 'Nonsense. It's Solly, isn't it?'

However, in Whitehall deviousness has the effect of stimulating a powerful opposing force, the grapevine. It was rare for us not to know exactly what he was up to.

Secrecy was for him more than an obsession: it was a way of life. On more than one occasion Zuckerman borrowed the whole of my small staff (of two) without telling me, and swore them to secrecy over the tasks he had given them: 'Don't tell Price.' But they had a duty to me also; inevitably, the news leaked out. Against his instructions I checked one paper Zuckerman had almost finished with the help of my colleague, John Wright, on collaboration with the French on research and development. I noticed that the important American right of pursuit of anything derived from Anglo-American collaboration had been overlooked. Wright had to go through an elaborate charade to get the paper corrected without embarrassing Zuckerman by admitting I had seen it.

He was obsessively preoccupied with nurturing his own influence. Michael Cary, when Deputy Secretary of the Cabinet, used to say: 'Solly doesn't like rivals too near the throne.' While he would open doors for colleagues of whom he approved – particularly those he called his 'équipe' – there were limits to his generosity. It was up to us to cope: we could not rely on his help if we floundered. He did not like to be associated with failure.

He could be as brutal to his colleagues as he was in his memoirs to Bronowski. He dismissed a junior who proudly offered up a carefully drafted paper on disarmament with the remark: 'I'm surprised you waste your time on these platitudes.' I never heard him apologise. The nearest he came to doing so with me was to open a discussion with the query: 'Now what have I done wrong?' The economist, Thomas Balogh, himself a noted controversialist, told me that he was used to being stabbed in the back. 'But with Solly it may happen when you are face to face.'

Until he knew you well there was something about his manner that inhibited free discussion. It was many weeks before I dared to disagree with him for the first time, and when the day came I felt I had survived a dangerous passage. One of my scientific colleagues, Clifford Cornford, who was later knighted after a distinguished career in defence and aviation, felt the same way. 'Solly mesmerises me. I can't say anything in his presence.'

He hated criticism, and no-one could move faster to deflect it by changing the subject. This fault – if fault it was – was tempered by a healthy respect for facts, and by a willingness to listen to new information, whatever its implications. For him scientific truth, and truthfulness in presenting arguments, were inviolate. 'Trimming' was frowned on as unhelpful, even cowardly. Very occasionally he showed a disarming willingness to hold up a mirror to himself. Once, when I was standing in front of his desk, I happened to comment on his very distinctive signature – 'the easiest in the world to read upside down.' He was unexpectedly silent for perhaps fifteen seconds. Then he got up, and started pacing up and down, looking out at St James's Park. I heard him slowly murmuring his name: 'Solly Zuckerman ... Solly Zuckerman.' His face lit up. 'You know, with a name like that I couldn't miss!'

It was his self-chosen and commendable mission to jolt the Department into fresh thinking. When a journalist asked whether he thought of himself as a scientist or as a defence expert, he replied, 'Neither. A policy-maker.' A favourite approach was to propound a number of 'propositions', which in early drafts were often turgid and not always models of clarity. But his anxiety to be the Departmental tutor sometimes led him into dangerously exposed positions. He once contradicted the Chief of the Air Staff on a matter concerning the RAF – and was wrong.

Life with this complex man, to whom I owe so much, was frequently difficult but never dull. His conversation drew on the whole of his experience, often with great brilliance. At the 1962 Geneva Disarmament Conference he was the man of the world: 'What we have to do is to find the table where the Russians are not so heavily engaged. But this is an extensive casino. There's Boules in the courtyard, Baccarat in the entrance hall, Chemin de Fer upstairs.' Sometimes he was the anatomist: 'There is no correlation between the descent of the testes into the scrotum and the beginning of wisdom.' On rare occasions, when he was on his best behaviour, he could be the kind and experienced master advising younger colleagues how to handle

169

delicate negotiations: 'Such things are best done by word of mouth.'

The fact that Zuckerman, until his departure from MOD, could continue with his own fiercely independent approach was due in no small measure to his success in getting his colleagues to think more deeply about nuclear weapons. He knew a great deal about war and weaponry – more, indeed, than many serving officers. In World War II he had planned the bombardment of Pantellaria, and later of Calais. His abiding impression was that, however carefully one did such planning, what happened thereafter was always fundamentally unpredictable. The fact that he had come from the complexities of the life-sciences, rather than from the more deterministic world of physics, may have helped to shape his view.

Unlike some Generals and Air Marshals, he held that nuclear weapons were altogether too powerful to be used as armaments. They were not just 'bigger bangs' but devices that would sweep away the political purposes for which a conflict had been launched. He was reinforced in this view by the war-gaming work of the Army operational research team (which I later inherited). Their games showed consistently that against a well-prepared army a nuclear attack would be surprisingly ineffective. On average only about one hundred men would be 'taken out' per nuclear explosion. So to mount an effective defence, if it ever came to war, it had become accepted doctrine that it would be necessary to use a substantial number of nuclear warheads – perhaps as many as twenty in the course of a single afternoon on an Army Corps front along the River Weser. Zuckerman asked in what sense 'twenty Hiroshimas between lunch and tea' could be regarded as a meaningful 'defence' of Germany: the damage to the country and people would destroy the political purpose of the operation. He also pointed out the virtual impossibility of retaining control, radio communications being amongst the softest targets. By the destruction of command and control systems on both sides, strategic 'planning' would be rendered futile. He said as much in a courageous speech to

170

NATO's annual conference in the summer of 1961. Questions were asked in Parliament about what some mistakenly regarded as defeatism in high places, but he was staunchly supported by the Prime Minister, Harold Macmillan, and from that time his views had to be taken with the seriousness they deserved. Understandably, Zuckerman was not popular with those for whom nuclear weapons were just another form of high explosive. But he had Mountbatten's backing, and was untouchable.

His views could not have been more at odds with those of Sir Henry Tizard, one of his predecessors as chairman of the Defence Research Policy Committee. Only ten years earlier Tizard had written in *Science and Strategy*, seemingly with considerable confidence: 'A few atomic bombs are not going to have a destructive effect on any nation, provided morale is high. Numbers count as in any other branch of war.' It was a false conclusion that developments in nuclear weaponry quickly made obsolete.

Zuckerman's views prevailed. At a dinner on the occasion of his retirement from the Ministry of Defence in 1966 the usual Whitehall tradition was maintained of slightly teasing, but fundamentally complimentary, reminiscences from colleagues, over the port. Denis Healey, who by then was Secretary of State for Defence, remarked with a straight face: 'Sir Solly now no longer has any right to lecture the Defence Council – because' (and Healey began to smile just as Zuckerman began to bridle) 'the fact is that we have all accepted his views on nuclear weapons.' That compliment had a strong element of truth – witness Field Marshal Lord Carver's public opposition to the use of nuclear weapons as actual weapons of war. But not all were willing to be persuaded as regards Zuckerman's fundamental point: that under nuclear attack no-one could count on retaining effective control.

Zuckerman's relationships with the defence industries, and their sponsors in the Services, were often fraught. He had arrived at a time when our military commitments were outrunning our ability to fund them. The result was a king's ransom lost in

171

cancelled orders. It would have happened anyway, but he was regarded by many as personally responsible for the abandonment of several weapons systems. When, in 1964, the Labour government came in, Wilson had already made political capital out of his intention to cancel the TSR2 aircraft. Zuckerman found that decision not too difficult to accept in the context of an Atlantic alliance. He still enjoyed close relations with the high-ranking Americans with whom he had worked during the War. He was dazzled by the scale of their resources and perhaps relied too readily on their assurances of support – provided we cancelled competing weapons. The difficulty of making sound policy decisions was that in the early stages of any development of aircraft or weaponry the initial capability is often far smaller than what can eventually be obtained through steady development. British projects risked cancellation on the basis of comparing their prototype performance with the glossy, longer-term predictions of their American allies. For instance, at the outset the Hawker P1127, which eventually grew into the vertical take-off Harrier, was an aircraft of extremely limited capability – so limited that the more powerful P1154 was not pursued. But with the passage of time the Harrier showed that it could fulfil a useful role: its Falklands record speaks for itself. It was adopted by the US Marines with every prospect of still further development. There are those who feel that several of the cancelled weapons systems could similarly have been brought to fruition, given time and effort. But because Zuckerman was fundamentally sceptical about our military-industrial capabilities he came to be regarded by some as an American apologist, rather than as a defender of British industry.

Certainly the policies to which he contributed were sharply different from those of France, which retained its technical self-confidence and, in the end, outstripped the UK in space technology. We can never know whether a policy of greater independence, or possibly of active collaboration with the French, would have turned out better in the long term. Given the political climate of the day our policy of relying on the Americans could hardly have been otherwise. And given that we had to rely on them in several major respects, the fact that Zuckerman could move effortlessly in Washington circles, up to the White House itself, was of some importance in defence policy-making in the early 1960s. The Kennedy assassination, and the Americans' ever-growing concentration on Vietnam, weakened these political links; but he maintained his close association with the US scientific elite, who tended to be more closely involved in defence matters than their British counterparts. He tried to create a nucleus of British academics with the brilliance and intellectual independence of the President's Scientific Advisory Committee (PSAC), but found it difficult to recruit a group with relevant experience and to graft it onto the Whitehall machine.

Richard Chilver, who once occupied an office next to Zuckerman's, summed him up in terms that came naturally to an amateur potter: 'You can say many things about Solly, but you cannot say that he was made of common clay'. The reaction of Edward Heath must have been similar. Why else, when Prime Minister, should he have accorded Zuckerman the unique honour of an office and secretary in the Cabinet Office, from his final retirement from the public service in 1971 for as long as he found it useful? The last word lies with Robert McNamara, US Secretary for Defense and later President of the World Bank. In his biography, *Solly Zuckerman*, John Peyton quotes McNamara as saying: 'He was huge. He has no counterpart in your country or in mine today'.

Chapter 11

Settling in at Defence

A major delight of working for central government was the rapid learning that followed transfer to a new field. The canvas was vast, the resources huge, the welcome shown to a newcomer heartwarming. At least, this was so before the Civil Service was dissected, after my time, into 'agencies'.

The diary I inherited from my predecessor was heavy with engagements. Most arose directly from the triumvirate system at the head of the Ministry of Defence. If a policy was to prevail it would need support from the military, the administrators, and the scientists – all three. The easiest way of ensuring this was to involve people from each of the constituent elements in the drafting of any reports that were likely to be sensitive – and most were. The hope was that their masters would then feel committed, or would at least be briefed to support what was being recommended. So far as Zuckerman was concerned this certainly did not follow automatically. However, in this over-optimistic expectation I was routinely invited to take part, as his representative, in much of the regular machinery of the Department.

Although this took up a good deal of time, it had the positive advantage that it did not take long to get to know the broad outlines of defence policy. There were weekly meetings of the Joint Planning Staff, Mountbatten's briefings prior to Chiefs of Staff meetings, and seemingly endless ad hoc discussions. I was also a member of the Defence Research Policy Committee, at which new weaponry projects were examined. I had no direct responsibility for hardware, though longer-term research was my concern. So I took every opportunity of visiting defence research establishments and the specialised thinking groups working in obscure offices off Whitehall.

Zuckerman had brought me in to help with some of the more intangible issues, notably the rôle – but not the technology – of nuclear weapons, on which his views were still only half-formed. The only post he had at his disposal was the one vacated some weeks earlier by Eric Williams, whose official title had been Scientific Adviser (Intelligence). Nothing had been said about this at my interview. During the war I had been distantly connected with the electronic gathering of intelligence, and knew that this was becoming ever more important. About the whole complex machinery of analysis and dissemination of the 'product' I knew nothing.

Nevertheless, I was now scientific adviser to, and a member of, the Joint Intelligence Committee. At my first meeting the chairman walked me courteously round the table, making introductions. Here were the people I had read about only in guarded references in newspapers. I was soon to find how sharply their professionalism contrasted with my own amateur status. I contributed what I could to their meetings but, as I had no staff back-up or other direct involvement, they must have thought it a meagre offering.

It was early in 1961, the time of the troubles in Laos, and I remember being struck by the contrast between the vivid immediacy of television news pictures of the Plain of Jarres, even in black and white, and the difficulty of extracting anything like a realistic picture of places I had never seen simply from intelligence reports, no matter how well drafted. Electronic news-gathering has made the world altogether better informed.

From time to time the JIC busied itself with the situation in Europe: what might happen if the Russians were to invade the territory held by the West. Here the Committee's staff was at its most brilliant. One paper carried total conviction, ending with a warning that in the event of any serious Russian incursion time would be desperately short before the situation became uncontrollable – just as Zuckerman was beginning to preach.

At one meeting that I shall not forget, in the spring of 1963, Sir Roger Hollis, head of MI5, told us of the background to the arrest that morning of Guido Martelli. I was jolted. I knew about Martelli, though I had never met him. He was a physicist and the partner of Pam Rothwell, who had been my colleague at Harwell and at the Aiguille du Midi a dozen years earlier. At that time we were both working for Bruno Pontecorvo, before he decamped to Russia. Subsequently Pam moved to an Italian laboratory. Martelli was brought to trial at the Old Bailey, but acquitted. I made no contact with her, but felt torn between conflicting duties – to a friend and former colleague, and to the Defence organisation and myself. Some years later I went to a party given in honour of John Whitehouse's seventieth birthday by past members of his staff. John had taken Pontecorvo's place at Harwell and, for a short time, had been my boss. I went, hoping to have a frank conversation with Pam about the affair. She was there, but so was Martelli, and I never managed to speak to her out of his hearing.

Other duties as Zuckerman's representative began to take more time. Eventually I concluded that if Intelligence was truly an important national activity, as it could hardly fail to be, it deserved its own full-time scientific guru. Perhaps my best service to the intelligence community was my final act of helping to make the case for the appointment of a full-time senior scientist. As much of my time was by then spent helping Zuckerman with the more philosophical aspects of defence thinking my title was changed to Assistant Chief Scientific Adviser (Studies) – which combined the twin virtues of giving nothing away while being infinitely accommodating.

Soon after going to Whitehall I joined a working party under Frank Mottershead, a Deputy Secretary, which was beginning to examine whether nuclear weapons could ever be used selectively and with discrimination without provoking a global conflict. It was an extraordinarily woolly remit; yet it was essential to clear our minds as far as possible because the stakes were so high. The Foreign Office representative was Peter Ramsbotham, who often referred with obvious respect to the latest musings of a young Harvard professor called Kissinger. After several meetings agonising over the issues I became convinced of the importance of two propositions.

First, the more accurately a weapon could be delivered the smaller the 'bang' that would be needed to achieve a given degree of damage. In the early 1960s the accuracy of delivery of nuclear weapons was poor, and against military targets they therefore had to have huge explosive strength, or (in the jargon) 'yield'. By developing 'smart' weapons, with television on the warheads for homing onto the target, the same job could be done with strikingly reduced explosive strength. Indeed, for many battlefield purposes nuclear weapons would be quite unnecessary. Cruise missiles armed with ordinary high explosive could do the job better.

The second proposition was one that had been advanced by another young American, Tom Schelling, in his book, *The Strategy of Conflict*. I read it in response to Zuckerman's perception that Civil Service scientists were deplorably inbred in their thinking, and to his insistence that at least his own staff should 'get outbred.' Zuckerman commented disdainfully on the way in which fashions could develop in Defence, with oft-repeated dogmas all too easily developing a spurious patina of truth.

He was particularly critical of the policy of deploying tactical nuclear weapons behind the front; but here, after reading Schelling, I found myself in disagreement. Schelling's uncomfortable main proposition was that deterrence rested essentially on uncertainty. In many conflict situations deterrence is created by putting oneself in a position such that if an adversary moves beyond a very limited threshold of aggression, then neither party will be able to guarantee to avoid disaster for both sides. Under such

177

conditions a rational adversary will be deterred. It is not a doctrine that is of much relevance when dealing with suicidal religious fanatics. But in the Europe of the early 1960s the Russians still exercised tight control over their forces and their warheads, and gave every sign of behaving rationally. It therefore seemed plausible that by deploying 'tactical' nuclear weapons perhaps seventy miles behind the front, the East could be made to realise that if they pressed an incursion too far a beleagured defender might all too easily, as a last resort, use his nuclear weapons, whatever the instructions on command and control might say to the contrary. If that ever happened no-one would be able to predict the outcome. Put differently, there should be no obvious firebreak between a minor incursion and an exchange of strategic weapons. For once the fog and chaos of war that Zuckerman had so clinically observed during the wartime planned bombardment of Calais seemed to be on the side of the defenders – and, indeed, of peace.

Coexisting with this need for uncertainty throughout the potential battlefield there was an equally important need for absolute certainty at the East-West frontier itself. When I was staying a few years later with a divisional commander in Germany, and dinner for his house party was in progress, he excused himself, pleading urgent duty. Returning hours later, he explained that the Russians had tried to move a frontier marker, part of the Iron Curtain, a yard or two into our territory. 'So we had to blacken our faces and stand around looking tough and holding machine-guns until they moved it back.'

This inescapable dichotomy led to some confusion in press comments on NATO strategy. Moreover, the Schelling type of uncertainty did not fit easily with the need to draft daily orders for the British Army of the Rhine. Army morale had to be maintained by the classical devices of clear objectives and carefully practised tactics. The other armed services had similar needs. But in the small, central Ministry of Defence – the Whitehall equivalent of All Souls – we had the duty, and were given the intellectual freedom, to form our own conclusions about the danger from the East. There could be no certainty, but we were reasonably confident that stability would not break down. So it proved. I should not have had the same confidence that a nuclear conflagration could have been avoided had there been a Sino-Soviet nuclear confrontation along a less well-defined frontier 3000 miles long – ten times greater than in Europe.

I generally saw eye to eye with Zuckerman, but once disagreed strongly, when I heard him say that if the Russians made a particular move 'then SAC would be released' (SAC was the American Strategic Air Command). Had that happened there could well have been an exchange of nuclear weapons, with the devastating consequences for Europe that Hermann Kahn had described when he asked: 'Would the living envy the dead?' I told Zuckerman that I did not believe that SAC would ever be ordered to attack.

'Why do you say that? You are undermining the whole of NATO strategy.'

My reply was to ask him to think about the headlines he would read in the broadsheets immediately before any such decision was taken. There would be an infinity of political moves afoot to head off the impending disaster. Russian self-interest was our best guarantee. It would prevent them from pressing us too hard, though they might wish to appear willing to go to the brink. Chess was their national game; Russian roulette was not.

We frequently discussed these issues with our American opposite numbers. I had breakfast with Kissinger in Paris. And there were meetings in London with an influential group of analysts from the Pentagon, led by Alain Enthoven, an Assistant Secretary of Defense. In February 1962 he harangued us on the absolute necessity of leaving strategic questions to economists. We had not previously met, and perhaps he thought that I too was from his own profession. I could not help asking whether, in the absence of suitable economists, other numerate and intelligent professionals might do just as well – a physicist, perhaps. Enthoven was flat-footedly insistent: 'He wouldn't ask the right questions.' The twinkling eyes of my British colleagues betrayed their amusement at such overweening self-assurance.

Meanwhile, Zuckerman was pushing hard for greater understanding of the amount of damage nuclear weapons would cause if dropped on cities. With Mountbatten's help he sponsored a small group called JIGSAW – the Joint Inter-Service Group for the Study of All-out Warfare (it was rumoured that Mountbatten felt a good day's work had been done when this acronym first saw the light of day). Its director was Captain Jewell, a man who carried his wartime honours lightly. As a submariner commanding *Seraph* he had put General Mark Clark ashore in North Africa in 1942 to prepare for the 'Torch' landings and had picked up from the Riviera the audacious French General Giraud and his two sons. He had also carried out 'the man who never was' deception mission, in which a corpse was left floating off the Spanish coast holding purportedly secret papers, in the hope of confusing the Germans about our intentions prior to the Sicily landings. Running a contemplative group like JIGSAW seemed an odd rôle for someone so geared to action, but I heard no word of complaint.

Also involved part-time was the distinguished molecular biologist, John Kendrew, whom Zuckerman hoped to draw in to defence work full-time. Things worked out differently. In 1962 Kendrew shared the Nobel Prize for chemistry and, understandably, preferred to remain as a leader in one of the human race's most extraordinary intellectual triumphs: the discovery of DNA, and all that has since flowed from it.

I was asked to take a close interest in JIGSAW's work and to help publicise its conclusions within the Ministry. Its first study examined in great detail what would be suffered by Birmingham – where Zuckerman had his house – should it be hit by a one-megaton bomb. A similarly detailed study examined a 'tactical' fifty-kiloton attack on a railway junction, Carlisle. Interestingly, both studies confirmed a war-time rule of thumb: that three times more people would be effectively 'knocked out of the war' through general disruption than the number of direct casualties. JIGSAW later turned its attention to the strategic East-West conflict: how many weapons would be needed to guarantee to knock out Russia or the US? It came up with numbers far smaller than those being advanced by US air-power lobbyists – an absolute maximum of two hundred or so.

Towards the end of my first year JIGSAW felt sufficiently sure of its ground to give a presentation to a high-level audience – the Minister and Defence Council, and the Secretary to the Cabinet. Soon afterwards I went with Zuckerman to Washington to discuss these findings with Wiesner and his staff. Wiesner was Kennedy's Special Assistant for Science and Technology, with an office in the White House executive block. He was supported by PSAC, the President's Scientific Advisory Committee. It was a dazzling array of Nobel laureates and other scientists, several of whom had made vital contributions to winning World War II. Wiesner was inclined to accept the validity of the JIGSAW analysis, even though it was in direct conflict with pressures from the US military-industrial complex. While Kennedy was alive there was some chance that a curb might be applied to the nuclear arms race. Once he was assassinated, in November 1963, our influence diminished, and was further reduced by Wiesner's decision, made shortly before Kennedy's death, to return to academic life at MIT. It was a move that he subsequently regretted, since it destroyed the continuity of the intellectual battle over the role of nuclear armaments.

The full irony of the situation can only be fully appreciated in the perspective of history. There can be little doubt that it was the enormous cost of the arms race that eventually led to the collapse of the USSR, thus providing the world with respite from major conflict at no cost to life. In this sense deterrence may be said to have succeeded. Whether this chain of causation was ever thought through in advance is in the highest degree unlikely. Indeed, one bright denizen of the RAND (Research and Development) Corporation, Amron Katz, used to amuse himself by demonstrating how little some of the American military knew about the nuclear weaponry they valued so highly.

He would innocently ask a General how big a warhead would be needed to 'take out' Washington, D.C. The General would typically reply that perhaps it would take ten megatons. Then Katz would ask whether the General knew how deep a pile would have existed if the ten megatons had consisted instead of high explosive spread uniformly over a circle of one-mile radius around the White House. When the General confessed that he had no idea Katz would tell him, with relish, that he would be 'up to his ass in high explosive.' 'Goodness!' would come the reply, 'I didn't know it was that much.'

Another of the tasks forcing me to leave my Intelligence work to others was liaison with the scientific side of NATO. The Americans regarded NATO as something more than a purely military alliance. Isidor Rabi, the influential Nobel laureate physicist, believed that it should also have a cultural side, and vigorously supported the NATO Science Committee. Whether this interest was purely altruistic is impossible to know. The US was benefiting greatly from the brain drain. How better to foster this and guarantee its continuance than through an institutionalised survey of the high technology that characterises defence science? It was not long before Rabi complained to Zuckerman about my sceptical attitude. I should have been more willing to sympathise had the American defence scientists at NATO Headquarters – then in Paris – been generally more impressive. As it was, making scientific liaison work effectively within the Alliance depended heavily on a strong input from the member governments.

No-one could deny that defence scientists had a duty to help their military colleagues understand how technology might reshape future warfare. Using the combined resources of NATO to do this seemed attractive. National security might exclude discussion of some subjects, but that still left a broad and important field. The US used its influence to institute a NATO Long-Term Planning Group, under the chairmanship of Theodore von Kármán.

Von Kármán had been born in Hungary in 1881. As a child

he had been a mathematical prodigy, by the age of thirty an internationally celebrated aerodynamicist. He moved to California in 1929 and, in 1936, became director of the renowned Jet Propulsion Laboratory in California. He played such a leading part in revitalising the previously torpid American aeronautical industry that the US Air Force chose him in 1944 as chairman of its principal scientific advisory board. One of his first tasks was to draw up a master plan for the post-war development of the Air Force. He was, therefore, an obvious choice to assist NATO in similarly attempting to prophesy the future, though he was always careful to insist that 'prophesy is not a scientific activity'. Zuckerman was captivated by the exuberant *joie de vivre* of this man twenty years his senior, who still enjoyed the good things of life – not least fine wines and cigars – even perhaps to the extent of regarding him as a rôle-model.

But von Kármán was eighty years old. His powers of chairmanship and organisation were ebbing. Though his name and reputation meant that he could still act as figurehead, success for his NATO study would clearly depend on strong support from the national delegations. Over the next few months some of the hard work fell to me. I regret that in getting through the mountains of paperwork I did not always have time to treat him with the ceremony that was his due. When he died in 1963 conscience overcame me and I spent a long day researching and writing an obituary for the *Times*. Zuckerman topped and tailed it, and I took it to Printing House Square one minute before the seven o'clock deadline.

The 'von Kármán Exercise' brought together well over a hundred defence scientists from the NATO countries, covering around twenty aspects of warfare. The Italians sent, as their chemical warfare expert, Dr A. Borgia – a hereditary appointment perhaps! I was the British team leader. Whether it was with von Kármán's approval or not I do not know, but the NATO Secretariat appeared to be assuming that the way forward would be for specialist teams to prepare reports, which would then be collated and eventually brought together into one massive document.

That was logical but time-consuming. With so many participants, not to mention the language problem, completion seemed scarcely possible in the two weeks that had been allotted. Some other approach was needed. I told the French leader, an Admiral, that I was going away with a couple of British colleagues to write a draft report, taking not more than three days over the job. He objected that, on Cartesian principles, I could not possibly start writing until I had seen the working party reports. I knew that they would contain nothing that was not already familiar, if only because the conference was not authorised to deal with the most secret topics, so I got on with the job. Things turned out as expected, and our comments on individual subjects – navigation, data processing, logistics, telecommunications, reconnaissance and so on – needed only minor adjustments in the light of the section reports. The Admiral said, 'I do not pretend to understand your method, but it seems to work well.'

Early in the 1960s Britain was being affected by the steadily increasing cost of weaponry. International cooperation offered a possible way of reducing costs, by sharing development. France had industrial capabilities similar to our own and was an obvious potential partner. But whereas we approached cooperation in a classically British spirit of give and take, the French were more hard-headed. Whatever was in France's interests would be favourably considered, but only on a strictly case-by-case basis. In later years they drove the hardest of bargains over helicopters, and I was glad not to have been involved.

Zuckerman arranged that my own links with France should be concerned with longer-term research. My contact was to be Pierre Aigrain. His brilliance was recognised by de Gaulle, who invited him to the Elysée one evening to explain how lasers work. The word is an acronym, derived from 'light amplification by the stimulated emission of radiation'. As he was waiting in the anteroom, only moments before being ushered into the presence, the secretary mentioned in passing that 'le Président déteste les Anglo-Saxonismes.' In the thirty seconds that remained Aigrain successfully invented a French equivalent. Zuckerman was heard regretting that he did not have several such young men on his staff.

Later, in 1963, I found myself involved with Aigrain in drafting a report to the Secretary-General on how scientific advice should be provided for NATO – 'science' in this context being mainly concerned with defence technology. Our small 'exploratory group' met several times in Paris, but each time he was summoned back to his office. Finally, I told him that we would meet him anywhere in the world except Paris. He arranged a meeting in the Landes at Biscarosse, the still embryonic French space development station. On arrival there we were told that we would work from 8.00a.m. to midnight, with the afternoons off: 'We have arranged a car, a boat, and a helicopter for your amusement. And a cordon-bleu cook.' The job was done in three days. More than thirty years later I learned why French hospitality had been so lavish on this occasion – someone in defence headquarters had mixed up old and new francs when issuing the authorisation.

The Italian member of the team was the elderly Marchese Catalano Gonzaga. At the time I knew almost nothing of Italy and, to my shame, failed utterly to connect him with the princely family of the Renaissance – rulers of Mantua for four centuries and patrons of Mantegna, Titian, and Monteverdi. I missed a great opportunity by pleading pressure of work as an excuse to decline his invitation to visit him in Rome and examine his, doubtless outstanding, collection of Georgian manuscripts.

The Aigrain meetings left me with two legacies. One has been a guaranteed welcome at Beoty's splendid restaurant in St Martin's Lane. My secretary, Louise, had arranged lunch there for a party of four. When we left the office for lunch two Rolls-Royces were waiting at the door. I was assured they were ours. After lunch I asked Louise how she had arranged it. 'Ask no questions. They were for the Minister's party.' Maybe so, but Beoty's have never forgotten. The second legacy is a continued friendship with Aigrain's assistant Jacques Haas, who became an Air Force General. He invited me to lecture on British military science at the École Militaire. More than thirty years later I had the pleasure of introducing him and his pianist wife to the delights of Glyndebourne.

Working in Defence was very different from anything I had done in the recent past. In atomic energy strong teams had backed me up. Now I was almost on my own, with only my secretary, a registry clerk, and one young scientific assistant. So when, a few months after I joined MOD, my economist friend, John Wright, telephoned out of the blue asking to be 'rescued' from the Atomic Energy Authority, I willingly responded. He said he could no longer stand the claustrophobic, inward-looking atmosphere of the headquarters economic unit. Wright had read history and economics at Cambridge, where he had won the Gladstone Memorial Prize, before going to Yale. He had worked at OECD and had a pan-European view of politics. I knew he could contribute to the 'studies' side of Zuckerman's work. In addition he was no mean artist, having been 'hung on the line' at the Royal Academy. It was just the combination that would appeal to Zuckerman who prided himself, with good reason, on his all-round cultural knowledge. Things turned out as expected and, in spite of difficulties over negotiating a suitably ranked slot, John Wright joined the Defence Department in December 1961. What I could not then know was that precisely the same difficulties he had faced would confront me a few years later.

Outside work, life as an official was extraordinarily agreeable, with many invitations to interesting, and sometimes colourful, events, including Trooping the Colour and the Royal Tournament – where Jean and I once shared the Royal Box with the Defence Minister, who was taking the salute. But the family base was fifty miles outside London and I had nowhere near at hand to return hospitality. I sought Zuckerman's advice. His response was: 'The Athenaeum: the Civil Servant's essential axe-grinding machine.' He put me up; other friends gave their support; and, in due course, I was elected. The club has proved even more valuable after retirement. It is a place where the 'dumbing-down' that has affected so much of our national life is not apparent. It may have lost the political clout it possessed in Victorian times, but culture, argument and good conversation are still cherished, as they were in the days of Dickens, Trollope and Sydney Smith. The clubhouse, built by the young Decimus Burton, manages to combine classical elegance with a welcoming warmth.

Six months after I joined MOD, work was still leaving little time for attending to my own affairs. I was living out of a suitcase, returning home only at weekends to the family house near Harwell. Jeanie was fretting at her isolation. Jeremy, now ten, and Nicola, who was seven, needed stability. Clearly we had to move closer to London. In the summer of 1961 Jeanie and I took a car each and circled the capital for a week's house hunting. We were looking for somewhere in the country, within commuting distance, and with a room large enough to house two pianos so that I could continue to play duets with our friends. The first expedition was unsuccessful; but we finally found somewhere suitable in a Buckinghamshire village, Jordans, of which I knew nothing. On 19 October 1961 the family moved in. It had been a long day. There was a knock on the door and outside was a smiling young woman carrying a tray with a three-course meal on it. 'I am your new next-door neighbour,' she said. 'Here is your supper – you must be tired.'

In the days that followed it soon became evident that Jordans was no ordinary village. Before 1919 it had been the merest hamlet, with just a few scattered farm buildings. Quakers from London had been welcomed at nearby Jordans Farm in the seventeenth century, when they were a proscribed sect. Two years after the Declaration of Indulgence of 1687 the Jordans Meeting House was completed to provide a permanent place of worship for local Friends. William Penn is buried in its grounds. It is so much a national treasure that in 1928 a proposal to build a major new road immediately outside was abandoned after examination by Parliament. The *Spectator* commented approvingly: 'Jordans is a well where men come to draw the waters of peace'. While World War I was still at its height funds were established to construct a village nearby, dedicated to high moral values. There have been many changes since the first villagers moved in, in June 1919, but the high moral tone of the early days has not disappeared. The kindness shown on our first evening by Sheila Sparkes proved to be entirely typical of our new neighbours. My search for a new music room had led me, by the greatest good fortune, to one of England's havens.

Chapter 12

Disarmament Again

Towards the end of 1961 there were stirrings in Whitehall regarding disarmament, a subject that had been dormant for half a decade. The Prime Minister, Harold Macmillan, wished to push it forward if at all possible. With memories of business unfinished from my atomic energy days I asked Zuckerman if I might be one of two Ministry of Defence representatives at whatever forum was finally decided upon; this met with his approval. John Wright would be my alternate.

I was curious to know whether any progress had been made since the sterile exchanges in the London conferences of 1954 and 1955 and, in particular, whether anything could be done to terminate the ritual dance round the altar of 'general and complete disarmament' (GCD) and move the discussion towards more realistic issues, like world stability. It was encouraging that the Minister of State at the Foreign Office, Joseph Godber, seemed to have his feet firmly on the ground.

An Eighteen Nations Disarmament Committee was arranged for the spring of 1962. It would take place in the Palais des Nations at Geneva. As an experiment, besides delegates from East and West there would also be a kind of jury, drawn from eight neutral countries. France slightly upset the East-West balance by indulging in the politics of the empty chair. The conference and all that went with it was to provide one of the most crowded and exciting periods of my life.

By chance, a few days before my departure for Geneva the leader of the Campaign for Nuclear Disarmament, Canon Collins, was to speak at the Jordans Meeting House. Being a professional insider I went along to hear him, wondering what insights a professional outsider might provide. He spoke fluently and to the point for about fifteen minutes, and I began to take a more favourable view of the people from his ministry who sat on pavements outside my own. But he ran out of steam just as he was coming to the interesting bit: what should actually be done? He seemed to have nothing negotiable to say. As the *Observer* remarked of one of his CND colleagues, Philip Noel-Baker, '...disarmament is not a subject for idealists.'

The chairman invited questions. A bearded gentleman stood up, pointed an accusing finger at Canon Collins and launched into a tirade. 'I have been listening to our distinguished speaker with increasing disquiet. What he says is contrary to the teaching of Christ. In the Gospel according to Saint Matthew, Chapter twenty-four, it is written: "Ye shall hear of wars and rumours of wars ... nation shall rise against nation, and kingdom against kingdom ... then they shall see the Son of man coming with power and great glory".' He raised his voice. 'Our speaker would be better occupied preaching the second coming of Christ, instead of wasting his time on irrelevancies such as nuclear disarmament.'

The Canon was caught off guard, but he pulled himself together and, in a few minutes, was back in business. He began a discourse on the subject of faith. The West as a whole had too little faith. In the Korean War our prisoners had been notoriously susceptible to brain-washing – unlike the Turks. They had faith. He paused. Another man rose and said diffidently, 'Might it not have been due to a shortage of Chinese-Turkish interpreters?'

Three days later I set off for Geneva, arriving just in time to be bundled off to the airport to swell the delegation that was meeting the Foreign Secretary, the Earl of Home. On the Ides of March Gromyko tabled a Russian 'draft treaty' on general and complete disarmament. To use such a phrase betokened an approach that was either purely political and tongue-in-cheek, or blind to military realities. Dean Rusk followed for the USA with a proposal for a virtually non-negotiable 30% cut across the board. We were back to a competition for the hearts and minds of the listening world, rather than the serious search for world stability that was our daily preoccupation in Whitehall.

In the course of a short meeting with Lord Home and his private secretary I was able to put a defence gloss on the business. It was already evident that the principal players would be the USA and the USSR, who would meet *à deux* whenever it suited them. But at least the UK could ensure that key issues like verification were not neglected. I drew his attention to a newspaper report that there had been an earthquake and, apparently, an under-water volcanic explosion in South Georgia, a British Antarctic possession – a ship's water intake had been blocked with clinker. We might ask the conference to consider how we might distinguish between such seismic events and new bomb tests. And might it be possible in his opening speech to link this incident, for light relief, with the Georgias of the USA and the USSR?

On the military aspects of the Russian and US plans I felt duty bound to alert the Foreign Secretary to the dangers such unrealistic proposals could pose to the world's strategic balance. As we had concluded almost a decade earlier at Harwell, there should be 'no critical risk' during any nuclear weapons rundown. He was easy to talk to and receptive. He placed his pencil behind his ear – as only a fourteenth earl can do without loss of dignity – and asked: 'Why did we propose this conference?'

His technique for giving speeches was highly effective. He would boil all the points down to mere keywords, write them on a single small sheet of paper, about the size of his hand, and speak extempore. In his opening speech he underlined the importance of verification of whatever was agreed. 'For instance, the other day we heard a noise in South Georgia. Not your South Georgia, Mr Rusk; nor yours, Mr Gromyko; but ours, in the Antarctic. A kind of innocent *troika*.' The conference enjoyed this teasing reference to the arrangement whereby Russia had recently been ruled by a triumvirate.

A couple of days later Gromyko entertained the British delegation, and Lord Home took the opportunity of re-stating the point about seismic verification of nuclear bomb tests. 'If you hear anything,' replied Gromyko, 'it will be Mr Rusk falling downstairs.' He spoke good English and could be quite engaging. The same could not be said of his number two, Zorin, the wartime prosecutor of Warsaw. As the time drew near for us to depart, Home broached the question of access to Berlin, where people trying to escape from the East were still being shot. Gromyko remained impassive. Home rose to go. 'All the same, don't think you can winkle us out, because you can't.' It was the informality of the warning that was most striking. As we left there were jocular remarks about not putting horses before carts. Someone observed: 'You can lead a horse to water, but can't make it drink.'

'It must have been salt water,' said Gromyko. And on that light-hearted note we took our leave.

During the dinner we had asked whether it might be possible to meet some of the Russian officials informally, to see whether any progress might be made, and this was agreed. A few days later, Griniewski, one of the youngest members of the Russian delegation, took me to lunch at a splendid restaurant at Cotigny. Both of us were expected by our masters to gain an insight into the other side's thinking, but it was not long before it became clear that neither of us was likely to succeed. By tacit consent we switched to safer things. Griniewski asked if I had any children. 'In Russia we like to send our sons in summer to explore the white areas – they are still white on the map. When your son is older perhaps he could come to Russia and help mine explore some of those areas.' He warmed to his theme. 'In some areas there may still be monsters. Yetis.' A new thought struck him. 'The United Kingdom has a monster.' He searched his memory. 'The Holy Loch monster.' It was a delicious moment when he realised what he had said – Holy Loch was the American

Polaris submarine base. Griniewski remained involved with disarmament questions and, thirty years later, was still the peripatetic Russian ambassador who dealt with nuclear non-proliferation issues.

For the benefit of our delegation our ambassador, Sir Michael Wright, summarised our rôle in the conference. It was limited, he said, to acting as a lightning conductor – or to casting flies over the Russians. If we really wished to exert influence our first hurdle would be to convince our principal ally. Within a few days of arriving in Geneva the British prepared a plan for discussion in private with the Americans, who seemed to like it, so we asked whether we should table it. They seemed surprised, and demurred. We were naturally disappointed. A few days later they asked why we had not used the paper. 'We asked whether we should table it, and you said "no".'

'That's right,' said the Americans, and we withdrew, once again discomfited.

It took several days for the two delegations to realise that they had been talking at cross-purposes, and that on the two sides of the Atlantic the phrase 'to table a paper' conveys exactly contrary intentions. Both usages derive from a British parliamentary practice of placing a paper on a table for examination. In Britain the implication is that the paper will be used; to Americans it means the opposite.

The Foreign Secretaries, their work of launching the conference done, returned home and their deputies took over. Zorin relentlessly read the Russian draft treaty into the record. He was a skilled debater, with a penchant for inquisitorial confrontation. It was rare for him to show warmth or to meet us halfway. Once I found myself at the table, the sole British representative, when Zorin was attacking a technical paper on disarmament mechanisms that, for tactical reasons, we had felt compelled to table (in the British sense) before it was really ready. He did not let the opportunity slide. Sitting there uncomfortably, half agreeing with his criticisms, I was glad I had not been in his sights at Warsaw towards the end of World War II.

193

For the Americans Arthur Dean took over from Dean Rusk. He argued cogently that the Russians were putting the cart before the horse; that it was necessary to agree on substance before producing treaty language. His own language verged on the homely. 'The Soviet draft is something and nothing. It's like the song:

> Mother dear, can I go and swim?
> Yes, my darling daughter.
> Hang your clothes on a hickory limb,
> But don't go near the water.'

This brought the conference to a standstill for several minutes, while the interpreters wrestled with the problem of rendering his remarks faithfully into Russian. He was, of course, right. The Russian text did indeed gloss over countless matters which deserved the closest attention: inspection, peace-keeping forces, reduction of weapon delivery vehicles in Stage I, nuclear test bans, nuclear accounting – the list was long.

For my part, although from the Ministry of Defence, I felt insufficiently expert and dangerously unsupported. Only on nuclear topics did I personally have much expertise, based on our work five years earlier at Windscale. Our 1956 study of nuclear materials accounting in exercise CIRCUS might conceivably be used to show up the Soviet advocacy for general and complete disarmament for what it was – mere propaganda. But the West was also in some danger of placing itself in a propagandist trap by speaking of General and Complete Disarmament – 'GCD' – as though it might be an attainable goal. If progress was to be made, London would need to take Geneva more seriously, and start tackling the real issue more effectively: how to avoid dangerous instability. I said as much on my next brief visit home. Duncan Wilson at the Foreign Office replied sadly, 'You can't have a line without a policy. And you can't have a policy without resources.' All we could do was improvise. The JIGSAW team from Defence was pressed into service. Sometimes their papers were useful, sometimes unconvincing through being short on supporting detail.

The neutrals who comprised the 'jury' took turns at speech-making, irrespective of their ability to contribute effectively. During one session that was conspicuous for its longeurs, even by Geneva standards, I produced a scurrilous cartoon showing a future greatly enlarged conference, whose Chairman was saying, in authentic conference jargon:

'Continuing our procedural discussion, we now come to the inter-esting and important proposal of the Distinguished Representative of Zanzibar, which is supported by the Distinguished Representatives of the Maldives and Basutoland, that we abandon our present arrangement whereby the Chair rotates according to the English language alphabetical order and, instead, adopt rotation of both Chairmanship and the language whose order determines the Chairmanship.'

As things stood, it was the English-language order that determined seating. So we from the United Kingdom found ourselves next to the United Arab Republic, that transient confederation of Egypt and Syria. Their Minister, Samir Ahmed, was sympathetic to what we had to say and, on more than one occasion, a surreptitious note passed to him resulted in a helpful comment that, if it had not been made by a non-aligned country, would have resulted in immediate rejection by the USSR. In such small ways the neutrals introduced a modicum of balance into what was being said.

There were a couple of neutral delegates who were, frankly, passengers. But that was assuredly not true of the Swedish representative, Mrs Alva Myrdal. She brought a mind of unusual distinction to the task of pushing forward the cause of disarmament. She complained that she got insufficient help from the Americans. 'They speak up to the gallery and down to us, as though we were a bunch of ignorant Congressmen!'

As the conference wore on it became tactically important to

recall points made by the other side that might be used against them. That was made difficult by the sheer mass of verbiage. There might be thirty pages of transcript per day, the United Nations provided no index, and our own resources in the delegation were limited. It was here that the other Ministry of Defence representative, Major-General Riddell, made an invaluable contribution. He had a photographic memory. Given the merest hint of a remark by Zorin or Tsarapkin that might be useful he would close his eyes and recall, typically, that it was on a Wednesday, during the late afternoon, about half-way down a right-hand page. In five minutes he would run it to earth. His extraordinary memory had been put to good use prior to D Day, when he had been responsible for logistics. Asked what he did on the actual day, he said, 'There was nothing more that could be done. I went home and dug my garden.' His initials were R.A., but he accepted with good grace the inevitable nick-name of 'Jimmy'.

Our speech writer was John Julius Norwich, whose quick mind did not gladly suffer boredom. The anthology of risqué limericks owes much to his having lived through the ennui of many speeches. Once, referring to the five gigantic allegorical undraped figures that grace the ceiling of the Council Chamber, John Julius remarked, 'So these are the five continents.' He looked at the ceiling apprehensively and added, 'But can we be sure?' He chafed at his job and was thinking of resigning from the Foreign Office to have time for his own writing. We spoke about it at some length one afternoon. I made the obvious comment that with his remarkable talents he would quickly win promotion if he stayed in the diplomatic service. I had missed the point. He did not wish to act merely as a conduit for other people's ideas and decisions. I should have understood, since his thoughts paralleled mine in my closing days at the BBC. He gave my advice the treatment it deserved.

Sir Michael and Lady Wright could not have been more helpful in introducing me to the diplomatic scene. But, although he was one of our most senior ambassadors, he was strangely reticent about making suggestions that were not entirely in line with already established policy, even when that seemed likely to be unproductive. His colleagues concluded that the violent end to the Iraqi royal family and its government during the 1958 revolution which, as our representative in Baghdad, he had failed to foresee, must have been responsible for a certain loss of self-confidence. At the conference table he was still a skilful debater and marshaller of facts, but he took no risks. That, coupled with his view that in the opening weeks of the conference we were mainly there to support the Americans, meant that we cut less ice than we might have done.

By the end of two months I was finding this deeply unsatisfying and tried my hand at drafting a speech centred on the alternative line of seeking stability in the real world, where there was zero chance of abolishing nuclear weapons and strategic delivery vehicles – particularly in Stage One, as required by the Russian draft treaty. To argue otherwise was simply pandering to the disarmament lobby in the hope of winning a propaganda war. The effort of pretending that the Americans had anything convincing to put in its place was equally wearing. The reality that I believed should be our starting point remained as it had been in the Harwell discussions of a decade earlier. Since no-one could give a guarantee that every piece of fissile material or every bomb had been identified and dealt with, the world should take 'no critical risk'.

Sir Michael, who was due to go on leave, appeared unwilling to adopt this line on his own responsibility, but he did send a copy of my text to London. Almost at once the Foreign Office sent a welcoming telegram. The Minister of State, Joseph Godber, who had arrived to take Sir Michael's place while he was on leave, seized the first opportunity to make a speech centred on the need for stability. He emphasised that our studies had shown that 100% verification of fissile material might not always be possible. I was sitting beside him and noticed Usachev, the intellectual of the Russian delegation, looking at me enquiringly. A day later the Brazilian ambassador congratulated the Minister, gave his support, and suggested that it would be helpful to circulate our work on verification. Soon afterwards there was a strongly encouraging speech from Egypt. At last the conference was speaking a language that the uncommitted nations could understand. Godber worried a little about what kind of reception he might get from unilateral disarmers at question time in the Commons, but brightened when I told him he had the perfect answer: not one of the neutral 'jury' at Geneva had advocated unilateral disarmament. Within ten days of the Minister's speech the conference was moving at a tremendous pace, with peace-keeping coming under active discussion months earlier than expected.

It was most exhilarating, but it could not last. The Russians were simply not yet ready to play at that particular table. Their discouraging response was that, before discussing any such thing, we should first work through the entire text of the Russian draft treaty. But Godber kept the stability point in mind and returned to it in May 1963, when he judged the time was more propitious. Eventually, in June 1964, Zorin made a significant speech in which he analysed a possible future arrangement that retained some kind of minimal nuclear deterrent. Progress!

There was one contemporary issue of major importance that fell outside the competence of the Geneva Conference. In November 1962, following the Cuban missile crisis, while the spectre of narrowly averted nuclear disaster was still fresh in everyone's mind, the United Nations General Assembly passed a resolution demanding that all nuclear tests should cease. By July 1963, in a surprisingly short time, this led, through separate negotiations, to the Partial Test Ban Treaty. It pledged the participants, for an 'unlimited period', to conduct no more weapon tests in the atmosphere, under water, or in outer space; underground tests were, however, still to be permitted. Zuckerman and my Defence colleague, Bob Press, were two of the British delegates at the negotiations, which took place in Moscow. Congratulations flooded in from countries all over the world. I particularly relished a courteous exchange of telegrams between the Prime Minister and the Captain Regent of microscopic San Marino.

The conference sessions at Geneva allowed few opportunities for finding out what the Russians really thought, let alone for influencing them – all was predetermined from Moscow. There was one other forum where some progress might still be possible. It was a series of meetings of scientists from East and West, supposedly acting as individuals. It was called 'Pugwash', after the village in Nova Scotia where, after two years of persuasion and preparation, the first encounter took place in 1957. No-one really believed that the Russians who attended were free in the same sense as our own people, who were there in a truly personal capacity as distinguished scientists. Nevertheless, messages could be sent and received in the relatively uninhibited atmosphere of the conference, particularly over dinner. The Russians could even be heard occasionally disagreeing with each other – something unthinkable elsewhere.

The ninth and tenth Pugwash meetings were to take place in Cambridge and London in August 1962. I asked for permission to attend and was encouraged to do so. As a government official I was, formally, an observer rather than a delegate. But, in practice, this distinction had very little effect and I was given a degree of intellectual freedom that, in retrospect, can only be regarded as astonishing.

The Russian delegation included not only scientists but some military – in particular Andrei Nikolaevitch Tupolev, the distinguished aircraft designer. I was driving an American friend to the Cambridge meeting one morning when we overtook Tupolev walking. I offered him a lift and he climbed into the back of the car. Almost as soon as I drove off, however, he asked me to stop. Pointing to the front seat, where Amron Katz was sitting, he said, 'I always sit there'. So they changed places and I completed the remaining few hundred yards of the journey. In this and many other ways we were reminded that there were real human beings on both sides of the Iron Curtain. We were pleasantly surprised and relieved to find that the Russians had a sense of humour. 'What is the difference between Capitalism and Communism?' Answer: 'Under Capitalism man exploits man; under Communism vice-versa.' What could be better than Lev Artsimovitch's comment that 'science is the best way of satisfying one's curiosity at someone else's expense'? If there was a danger it was in the easily-made, but naïve, assumption that people of high distinction automatically had the power to influence the political evolution of a communist state to any significant degree.

At the farewell banquet we followed the Russian tradition of having impromptu speeches throughout the meal. The American Nobel Prize winner, Rabi – the man who had led the 'Little Geneva' talks in 1955 – climbed on the table and implored us 'not to waste Pugwash'. Then it was Artsimovitch's turn. He was head of the Russian atomic energy commission and one of the fathers of their hydrogen bomb. He had the physique of a village blacksmith, and added to the impression of physical power by his habit of working with his sleeves rolled up. He said he wanted to tell a story. The mathematical physicist and Nobel prizewinner, Igor Tamm, author of one of my Cambridge text-books, offered to act as interpreter.

The story was of a very old man who had married a young and beautiful woman. After a brief honeymoon he began to worry whether she was being faithful. So he went to a soothsayer (Tamm struggled a little before he found the right word). The soothsayer, having heard his problem, said, 'It's really quite simple. You must spin a coin. If she's being unfaithful to you while you're away and she's at home the coin will come down heads. If you're at home and she's away it will come down tails.' Crestfallen, the old man asked, 'What if she's being faithful?' 'Then the coin will hang in the air.' When the laughter had subsided Artsimovitch said, more seriously, 'Disarmament is like that. If the coin comes down heads the Americans will make a proposal that the Russians will reject. If it comes down tails the reverse will be true. As for "general and complete disarmament", that corresponds to the coin hanging in the air.

But there is one further possibility – that the coin lands on its edge – which I intepret as some kind of accommodation between the two sides. We need to become so practised that we can make the coin land on its edge every time.'

I saw Artsimovitch once more at a Pugwash meeting in Dubrovnik in the following year. Towards the end some kind of argument broke out among members of the Soviet delegation. Artsimovitch was shouting at Pavlichenko, the 'politically correct' Russian 'commissar', who had been trying to tinker with the wording of the 'protocol' – the piece of paper without which no Russian delegation dared to return home. The western delegates, most of whom were academics, found themselves forced to accept these tactics if they wanted Pugwash meetings to continue. On this occasion there had been a long afternoon discussion about access to Berlin, at the end of which at least a partial meeting of minds had been achieved. This was reflected in the draft protocol that Pavlichenko was now trying to modify. My heart went out to Artsimovitch – the interpreter told me he was saying, 'We've given our word. Why can't we behave like men?' A little later I had a brief word with him, regretting that the spirit of the conference had been upset in this way. He laid his hand on my arm: 'Mr Price, every country has its Pavlichenkos.'

From the beginning of 1963 my other duties began to crowd out disarmament. But there are four final memories. The first began at home one evening, a week after the 1964 defence reorganisation had moved me from my delightful office overlooking St James's Park to an 'egg-box' looking out over Whitehall. Sheila Sparkes, the next-door neighbour who had been so kind on our first evening in Jordans, rang with an invitation to join an after-dinner gathering. Her sitting-room was packed with friends waiting to hear from an American woman who was on her way back to the US, having joined nuclear-weapon protesters in sitting on Dutch pavements. It had all been very respectable – a member of the Dutch royal family had taken part. There was little new thinking in what she had to say, but I was struck by her claim to have an appointment with the Minister of Defence the following morning. I asked how she had arranged it. That, she said, was her affair.

In the morning I rang the Minister's office as soon as I could. The diary secretary agreed that a request for a meeting had indeed been received, but the Minister was too busy. I went about my business. At 11.00a.m. the guard rang from the North Door to say that two hundred women were outside, asking for me by name. I went down to see them, received them courteously, and took a small delegation back to my room. With John Wright's help I spoke to them for about half an hour; they seemed surprised and encouraged to find how thoroughly we had studied the problems that were exercising them. To all their questions there were reasoned answers. They said farewell with considerable goodwill. But a couple of weeks later I had a call from a colleague who was looking after security matters. 'This is an embarrassing question I know, but why exactly did those women at the North Door ask for you?' Fortunately, 'Big Brother' seemed satisfied with my answer.

The second memory, from the autumn of 1964, concerns the Multilateral Nuclear Force (MLF). This was a proposal, first mooted by the Americans in December 1960 and firmed up in 1962, that was intended by its sponsors to head off pressures for nuclear proliferation from America's allies. The Germans in particular wished to participate, arguing that it would strengthen NATO as a political entity. This was sufficient reason for the Russians to be implacably opposed. They made it plain that there would be no reconciliation so long as the US contemplated any kind of nuclear sharing within NATO.

As American thinking developed the MLF proposal began to verge on the grandiose. A fleet of 25 ships, each of about 20,000 tons and carrying eight missiles, was mentioned at an Anglo-American conference held at Ditchley, Oxfordshire, in September 1963. The conference was graced by the presence of Dean Acheson who, over breakfast, told how he had travelled secretly to Paris to tell de Gaulle about the Cuban missile crisis and to show him photographs taken by a U2 spy-plane. 'Tell me,' the

General had said, 'are you here to inform me or to seek my advice?'

'Monsieur le Président, I'm afraid it's the former.'

'Quite right,' replied de Gaulle. He said goodnight to Acheson in English.

As became clear at Ditchley, there were mixed views about the MLF. Proliferation would be a worry, since the largely non-American crews could hardly fail to learn something about nuclear weaponry. Realistically, it was improbable that the Americans would surrender any control over the actual firing, so the proposal smacked of a confidence trick. Those who were supposed to be deterred would regard it as a relatively small addition to the already huge American deterrent. Henry Kissinger, who though still young was already influential, believed that few Europeans wanted the MLF, and that those who had agreed to it had done so by sacrificing their better judgment to their understanding of what they thought the US wanted. He said that to say that American policy was following a European consensus seemed a delusion ... the MLF might magnify, rather than reduce, the German problem. All in all, he believed the case for the MLF was not proven and that there were strong arguments against it.

Despite these misgivings the Foreign Office's view seemed to be that Anglo-American solidarity should prevail. However reluctantly, we would, for political reasons, have to go along with the proposal. Although unconvinced by the American arguments, Ministry of Defence officials had to take the proposal seriously. I saw Mountbatten interrupt a meeting Zuckerman was chairing, dragging him off to discuss the MLF – 'the most important issue facing the Alliance today'.

This was the position when Zuckerman took me to Washington in November 1964 for a variety of meetings, including two with the Arms Control and Disarmament Agency. During previous visits I had formed a friendship with Mark Raskin, who had been on the White House staff in the early Kennedy days. He had subsequently resigned, having developed the gravest doubts about the Vietnam war, and had become one of the leaders of the intellectual opposition. When I saw him this time he listed five points against the MLF and added, 'The people in your Embassy don't seem to realise there are two governments in this country – one in the White House and one in Congress. Congress is not happy with the MLF and is looking for a way out. If Prime Minister Wilson signs on the dotted line (he was due to visit Washington in a few days) they will reluctantly agree. If he does not, the idea is dead. He must not sign.'

I asked how he knew this.

'I've just written a speech that the Majority Leader in the Senate will give in a few days' time.'

That same evening I was at the house of General Sir Michael West for dinner. He was the exact opposite of the Blimp of popular caricature – engaging, informal, and extremely well informed. He had recently moved from the Northern Command at York to the Pentagon, where he was chairman of the NATO Standing Committee. One wall of his office was already adorned with newspaper headlines: KRUSCHEV ATTACKS WEST. WEST REPLIES TO KRUSCHEV. The other guests included the French ambassador, Hervé Alphand, and Walt Rostow, Chairman of the Department of State's Policy Planning Council. We argued the pros and cons of the MLF for an hour, and I deployed Raskin's five points. Rostow countered with all the zeal of a missionary. Alphand was listening intently, as became evident a couple of days later when the French made it quite clear they were not interested. As I left the party early to prepare for the following day's meetings Sir Michael was performing an astonishing apache dance with one of his lady guests.

One of those meetings was on remote area conflict – Vietnam in all but name. The Americans were seeking to draw on our own experience of fifty or so minor skirmishes since World War II. David Bayley-Pike, a British Army operational researcher, was there. He had studied such conflicts in detail and soon had the Americans eating out of his hand. It was the precision of his information that intrigued them – as, for example, when he remarked that some of the interpreters the Americans were using in South Vietnam spoke with a North Vietnamese accent.

Twenty-four hours after the dinner at the Wests' house Zuckerman and his party were guests of Harold Brown, the young and incisive Director of Defense Research and Engineering, for dinner aboard the *Sequoia*. It says a great deal for Zuckerman's standing with the White House that the venue for the evening should be the presidential motor yacht. Roosevelt had commissioned her in 1933, and she remained in presidential service, manned by the US Navy, until President Carter decided in 1977 that she was an extravagance. We cruised down the Potomac as far as the Woodrow Wilson Bridge before returning. Driving back from the Navy Yard in Zuckerman's car I told him about Raskin's views on the MLF.

Zuckerman knew about him. 'He's very controversial.'

'I know, but that is what the Senate Majority Leader is going to say.'

We drove slowly round and round The Ellipse near the White House for perhaps twenty minutes, arguing the pros and cons. Finally, Zuckerman was convinced.

'What you've got is immensely valuable,' he said, and we drove back to the Residence, where he was the guest of the ambassador.

Over the next few days I found confirmation that Raskin was not exaggerating when he implored us to realise that a large number of people in the US government were unhappy about the MLF. In the event, Wilson did not sign. Eventually, the Russians were persuaded that the idea had been dropped and, by 1966, the way was clear for President Johnson and Andrei Gromyko to have private talks on how to achieve a significant reduction in armaments.

Two years earlier Raskin had introduced me to Leo Szilard, a Hungarian expatriate scientist. He was a passionate advocate of the need for humanity to find some way of curbing nuclear weapons. It was the message underlying his short story, *The Voice of the Dolphins*. Szilard had more reason than most to be concerned, for it was he, along with Einstein and Wigner, who in 1939 had alerted Roosevelt to the possibility that an atomic bomb was feasible. He invited John Wright and me to dinner. We accepted with alacrity – he was an important piece in the jigsaw – but were disappointed when the conversation was all but sabotaged by an accordion player who spent the evening pestering us with his over-loud efforts. Later, in his hotel, Szilard implored me to go to Moscow to act as a kind of intermediary or educator – someone who could bring the USSR and the USA closer together. It was flattering, but a one-man expedition by an official of a third government had as much chance of success as someone using a water-pistol to put out a forest fire.

The MLF evening was not the only memorable encounter at General West's house. It was there, on a previous visit in June 1963, that I had been given a fascinating insight into the beginnings of nuclear warfare. Becky Spaatz – the pianist daughter of General Spaatz, who had commanded the US air forces in the later stages of World War II – spoke with great affection of her father. She related how, as he was about to fly to Europe in 1942 to take charge of the American effort in the air, he had been found alone at the top of the house in sombre mood, contemplating the carnage that would be an inevitable accompaniment to the air campaign. Charles Murphy, an editor with *Time-Life*, once described him as the only general he had met who was actively against killing people. So it was one of war's ironies that Spaatz should be chosen to command the air forces in the Pacific that bombed Hiroshima. On being told to organise the attack he asked that the order should be put in writing. For better security he kept the paper in the safest place he knew – his trouser pocket. However, while he was having a shower his orderly sent his trousers to the cleaners. The base at Guam was turned upside-down until they were recovered. Immediately after the attack Robert Lovett, Assistant Secretary of the Air Force, sent him a congratulatory signal, referring to the 'high ground' of victory. Spaatz replied, with remarkable insight, 'Have looked at good photos of Hiroshima. The atomic bomb disposes of all High Ground. Hope there is never an occasion to use another.' He argued against a second attack and won some delay – but was over-ruled.

Another memory is of a meeting in London in the late autumn of 1964, a few days after the Washingon MLF visit. It was the intention of the new government under Harold Wilson to elevate disarmament to the status of a major plank in British policy. A few weeks earlier Zuckerman had been invited to become Minister of Disarmament, but had refused. The job eventually went to the journalist, Alun Gwynne-Jones, who took the title Lord Chalfont.

As part of the Wilson policy the new Foreign Secretary, Patrick Gordon-Walker, wished to lower the level of armaments in Europe. This I learned at first hand when Zuckerman telephoned me.

'Meet me at the North Door in two minutes.'

I did so. 'Where are we going?'

'To see the Foreign Secretary.'

'Are there any papers?'

'No.'

We were shown into his room. The new Minister for Disarmament was there, a few Foreign Office officials, Zuckerman and I. There was some discussion about a 'scientific' approach. I had the distinct impression that Zuckerman had been guilty of overselling it. The Foreign Secretary started to outline a plan for major troop reductions in Germany. I heard him with some surprise. When he stopped speaking Zuckerman said nothing and looked at me. He was keeping his powder dry.

I took a deep breath. 'Secretary of State, have you discussed these ideas with the Chiefs of Staff, or with the Secretary of State for Defence?'

He had not. So I spoke about the overwhelming importance of doing nothing that might destabilise the European front – there was simply too much at stake. Gordon-Walker seemed surprised. For my part I was astonished that such well-intentioned naïvety could exist just across Whitehall, only a stone's throw from the Ministry of Defence. On my way out of the meeting a Foreign Office official attacked me for 'interfering with the internal affairs of the F.O.'. The exact bone of contention was not clear. It may have been my scepticism about precipitate troop reductions, or it may have been the MLF. Fortunately, I was still in a Civil Service that had yet to feel the effects of Thatcher's 'is-he-one-of-us' doctrine, or Blair's 'on-message' conformism. Any worries I might have had were short-lived. Gordon-Walker stayed in post for only three more months, resigning the day after he lost a by-election.

The final disarmament memory is of a Pugwash conference that took place in the summer of 1970, after I had moved from Defence to Transport. Out of the blue I received an invitation from Frank Long, then a professor at Cornell, to take part in a meeting at Racine, Wisconsin. Frank had been the first Director of the US Arms Control and Disarmament Agency at the time Zuckerman was closest to the US administration and I had a high regard for him. The subject was to be the arms balance between East and West. It was no longer my official field, which made me doubly pleased, and a little surprised to have been invited. Through a happy conjunction of dates I was able to accept, as I would already be in the United States for another conference – on tunnelling. However, I felt unable to respond to his invitation to give a paper. Anything I had been able to contribute in earlier years had come from the precise knowledge that stemmed from immersion in defence problems each and every day. There were enough woolly generalists pontificating on disarmament elsewhere.

The conference took place at Wingspread, one of the architect Frank Lloyd Wright's celebrated 'prairie' houses, whose inspiration had been the Indian tepee. An atrium provided a centre-piece from which three long wings stretched out into the countryside. One was the service wing, in which the architect had given his ingenuity full rein. To avoid having servants intruding into the Johnson family's conversations, the whole dining table was designed to retract between courses through a hatchway into the kitchen. Wright had not realised that the diners might then feel a little odd, sitting in well-marshalled rows facing each other. It was not an arrangement that lasted long.

One of the Pugwash delegates was the same Isidor Rabi who had led the US delegation at 'Little Geneva' fifteen years earlier. He had then proposed a somewhat specious scheme of 'tagging' nuclear fuel with a radioactive isotope. I asked him whether he had put this forward as a smoke-screen, to hide from career diplomats the fact that science did not have a ready-made, leak-proof method of keeping fissile material under control. He gave one of his throaty chuckles. 'Someone had to do something.'

Wingspread was encouraging in one important respect: the quality of the new Russians supporting their leader Emilianov was striking. Such men gave hope for the future. It was a happy ending to my work on disarmament as an official. I had closely observed its intractable problems for a decade without seeing any significant progress in the field of conventional armaments. I had taken no part in the preparations for the partial nuclear test ban. All that I could reasonably claim was to have kept my feet on the ground and to have helped to foster understanding with the East whenever opportunity afforded. I sympathised with the Campaign for Nuclear Disarmament, but regretted its lack of realism. I did not feel any need to apologise to my pacifist friends in Jordans, nor do I now.

Chapter 13

Defence Reorganisation

In 1961, not long after joining the Ministry of Defence, I acted as the scientific secretary of the British Nuclear Deterrent Study Group – irreverently known as 'BENDERS'. The current deterrent was the responsibility of the RAF and its V-force bombers. To be effective it needed to be deliverable. I sought the advice of operational research scientists working with the RAF. 'Can we rely,' I asked, 'on being able to penetrate Russian air defences and guarantee "assured destruction" on a decisive scale?' My enquiries, however, were rebuffed. I was told, politely but firmly, that the Air Force, while duty bound to advise the Minister of Defence directly, was reluctant to take the central staffs into its confidence. It was not, in the Air Force's view, our concern. This seemed bizarre, given the efforts we were expending to try to understand the circumstances in which war might be unleashed and what might happen thereafter. We were not the only ones asking questions. A year later I heard of an internal War Office (i.e. Army) report that gave our low-level V-bombers no more than a small chance of reaching Moscow.

This was an example of the clash of responsibilities the small central Defence Ministry could sometimes face in its dealings with the four other government Departments that also had a direct interest in defence. Even within the restricted circle of the Cabinet our own Minister, Harold Watkinson, was not the only defence spokesman – the Minister of Aviation sat alongside him. Moreover, the political heads of the three Armed Services also held Cabinet rank, though they were not regular Cabinet attenders.

The replacement of Watkinson in July 1962 by Peter Thorneycroft, who had moved from the Ministry of Aviation, provided the trigger for much-needed change. Almost his first act was to write to the Prime Minister, Harold Macmillan, saying that the system was difficult to operate. While his small Ministry nominally had overall responsibility for policy, it had no direct authority over weapon procurement or deployment. Nor, as I had discovered, did it have automatic and direct access to sources of operational information. It was not long before Thorneycroft set in train a study that resulted first in the Jacob-Ismay report of February 1963, then in the reorganisation White Paper of July of the same year, and finally in the April 1964 amalgamation of the Ministry of Defence and the three Armed Services, and the move across Whitehall to 'the Quadragon' – as some jokingly dubbed the British equivalent of the American Pentagon.

Zuckerman made it his immediate personal duty to ensure that the new Minister was fully aware of the supreme importance of accepting that nuclear weapons were instruments of deterrence rather than armaments that could be used and controlled in active warfare between two nuclear powers. He prepared twenty 'propositions' summarising his own thinking for Thorneycroft's benefit. The first attempt was overlong. I spent the best part of a weekend in the office working quietly on a redraft, expecting to be undisturbed. But the door opened and in came the Permanent Secretary, Sir Rob Scott, proconsular to the fingertips. He looked at my rolled-up sleeves, raised his eyebrows, said, 'I should take off my trousers if I were you.' and left, smiling.

For several weeks further redrafts shuttled backwards and forwards, gradually becoming less turgid. Once, finding myself in disagreement on a particularly vital point, I thought it wise to resort to 'soft soap' when submitting my suggested rewording to Zuckerman:

211

You may feel at times that I am no longer on the side of the angels. I have suggested toning down what you say because of my feeling that this is such an important document that it would be a great pity if the forces of darkness could point to even one statement which if quoted out of context would appear unfair or exaggerated.

Somewhat to my surprise he quotes this passage in his autobiography.

Planning for the impending Defence reorganisation took place against a background of inter-Service competition for a diminishing pot of gold. Given stalemate in Europe the Treasury was determined to reduce the proportion of GDP taken by Defence to well below the figure of 8% that had applied when I first joined the Department. Reviews to seek possible economies became part of the fabric of life. It did not take the Armed Services long to realise that their real and immediate opponents were not so much the Russians as those British colleagues who wore uniforms of a different colour.

Deciding on the best way of using military force in support of our remaining colonial responsibilities brought all three Services into contentious debate. The Army could provide garrisons. When there was trouble in coastal areas the Navy could hold a force poised just beyond the horizon, for weeks if need be. The Air Force claimed to be able to mount a major deployment almost worldwide within a very few days by means of an island-hopping strategy. If the RAF were to be believed, and were given the wherewithal, the other two Services would inevitably suffer cuts. Much, therefore, depended on the debating skill of the chosen advocates.

The RAF was particularly well served by Peter Fletcher, who had been trained as a lawyer before joining the Rhodesian Air Force at the beginning of World War II. He was now an Air Vice-Marshal. At one meeting he was running rings round his naval opposite number regarding our ability to stand up to Indonesia. According to his scenario the Cocos Islands – the

Jean Vidal, Colombo, 1945.   (Plâté)

Dr Herbert Sumsion,
Gloucester cathedral
organist.

The author: BBC Music Programme Engineer, 1946-7.

Starting up the Harwell reactor, 3 July 1948. Cockcroft is leaning on the control desk, with John Dunworth on his right and Egon Bretscher on Dunworth's right. The author is at the extreme left of the picture.

(AERE Harwell)

Vernon
Donnison,
1948.

The upper téléférique station serving the Cosmiques laboratory at a height of 12,000 feet.
David West and Pamela Rothwell, both from Harwell, are on the platform.

The laboratoire de l'Aiguille du Midi, on its rocky ledge above the Vallée Blanche.

Paul Chanson and Field-Marshal Montgomery during the latter's visit to Les Cosmiques.

The author with Dr. Egon Bretscher on the platform of Les Cosmiques, 1950.

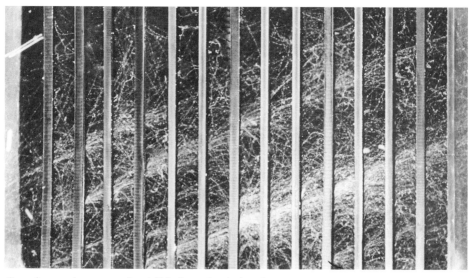

Cosmic ray shower made visible in a cloud chamber.

Baron Zuckerman of Burnham Thorpe, OM, KCB, FRS.   (Schwartz)

Wecoming party for Lord Shackleton, Minister of Defence for the RAF, at DOAE, Byfleet, 1965. The Armed Services are represented by Brigadier Paul Ward, Deputy Director, and Group Captain (later Air Commodore) John Ellacombe.

The Uranium Institute's inaugural day, 12 June 1975. The author with John Kostuik, the Canadian first chairman, who is holding the Certificate of Incorporation.

The Institute's Annual Conference and Reception, 1977. Jean greets Dr. Heinrich Mandel, of RWE, Germany, the first Institute chairman from the electrical generating industry.

The author speaking at the Arab Energy Conference, Amman, 1981.

With Wallace Mays at an in-situ leach uranium extraction plant, Corpus Christi, Texas, 1985.

Jean Féron, Inspecteur-Général of Electricité de France, Institute chairman 1981-1983.

Unmissable photo-opportunity: the author during the Uranium Institute's visit to the Lodève uranium mine, Hérault, France, 1983.

The author with Jan Murray, his successor as Secretary-General, at a rodeo, Saskatchewan, 1984.

On Ayer's Rock before breakfast during the Institute's Australian tour, 1985.

Juliet November, reliable antidote to depression during difficult periods, c.1975.

Near Cape Cornwall: Jean's unquenchable joie de vivre, c.1990.

Laszlo Gombos, distinguished specialist in energy law.

Dr. Theo Williamson, FRS, engineer, designer of the automated production System 24.

(Argent)

Before Margaret Thatcher came to power in 1979 John Hoskyns and Norman Strauss (reading in the lower picture) had frequent evening discussions in the Uranium Institute's offices, arguing over policy objectives of an incoming government. Williamson sometimes joined them.

Dr. Sebastian Pease, FRS, physicist, pianist and clarinettist.

The author at the console of his practice organ, Jordans, 2003.   (David Farrell)

Indian Ocean atoll where, by chance, I had spent the last night of the war – would, within a few days from the start of an alert, witness a level of activity reminiscent of Heathrow on a summer afternoon. I knew that the only island in the atoll suitable for an airstrip was narrow and slightly curved – full throttle could not be used until the corner had been passed. My questions – 'Can you in reality operate one hundred aircraft from Cocos? Will there be enough room for hard standings for aircraft and equipment?' – produced an embarrassed silence.

The Navy, for its part, was fighting to retain its air power. As David Garstin had explained during *Hermes'* commissioning cruise in 1960, aircraft were getting heavier and approach speeds higher. The landing problem was becoming intractable, unless carriers could be increased in size. So the Navy was pressing for a new ship, the CVA 01. At around 65,000 tons she would be twice the tonnage of *Hermes*. The holders of the money-bags were doubtful. Zuckerman became involved in an aircraft-carrier study. I wondered whether new technology might offer a way out of the difficulties and sent him a memorandum drawing attention to the promise held out by the new generation of vertical take-off aircraft – the P1127 that later became the Harrier. True, its payload when using vertical take-off was so far minimal but, unlike a land airfield, a carrier could steam into wind; it also had catapults. Both would improve the payload. Moreover, after weapons had been jettisoned and fuel burnt off the aircraft could land vertically, thus breaking the 'ton of carrier per pound of aircraft' constraint that Garstin had propounded.

My efforts were not appreciated. The First Sea Lord, Admiral Sir Caspar John, himself a pilot, called on Zuckerman to protest personally about my 'well-known anti-naval tendencies'. I reminded Zuckerman that during the war I had been in the RNVR – albeit briefly and far from actual combat, that my brother had been a regular straight-stripe naval officer, and that I had married a Wren. However, before long the Navy accepted that economic constraints and past ministerial statements meant that they could no longer build any ship that was described as

213

an aircraft carrier. Instead, with commendable finesse, they invented a new description: the 'through-deck cruiser' – a mini aircraft-carrier by another name – which they would be permitted to build. The Harriers from *Invincible* were to prove invaluable during the Falklands conflict twenty years later. By then ingenuity had added a fourth innovation – the 'ski-jump' take-off ramp – to the trio of other British inventions that had progressively transformed carrier operations: the angled deck, the mirror landing sight, and the steam catapult.

While these struggles for resources were taking place General Sir Ian Jacob and General Lord Ismay were preparing the reorganisation report that Thorneycroft had commissioned. Its arrival was the signal for action. The Department was engaged in trying to foresee and deal with the many problems that would inevitably arise and in propounding its solutions in the form of a White Paper. Two issues in particular exercised Zuckerman. One was the role of operational research, of which more later. The other was what to do about the three Chief Scientists who worked respectively for the Army, Navy and Air Force.

Their position was perhaps a little better than that of Harold Agnew, the distinguished scientific adviser to General Norstad, who commanded NATO in the early 1960s. I once asked Agnew how often the General asked for scientific advice. 'When he has a visitor he will call me in. As usual he will be swinging a golf club. He will say, "Scientific Adviser, give me some scientific advice." And I will say something like, "E = mc^2, Sir," and click my heels. He will turn to his visitor and say, "There, you see I do have scientific advice. Thank you, Scientific Adviser."'

The underlying problem that any scientific adviser faces is that science operates on a time-scale far longer than that of any normal administrative issue. And when advice is to be given it often cannot be clearcut, but must be based on a balance of probabilities. Yet science is one of the greatest forces for change that the world has seen. For that reason, and despite the difficulties, Zuckerman fought a hard battle for defence scientists to be represented on the newly reconstituted Boards of the three Armed

Services. There was the inevitable opposition from those who thought scientists should remain in their traditional position: on tap rather than on top. But Zuckerman was supported by Thorneycroft and Mountbatten, and succeeded. He had actually hoped for more. He wanted them to be free to give advice that was truly independent and personal, and not merely one of several inputs to be coordinated by non-scientific administrators. However, although the Services' Chief Scientists were worthy men and, in their own way, highly professional, they did not share his unique free-booting mould. Moreover, they were not there primarily to provide a new and inspirational approach to defence thinking, but to help create effective weapons systems. Too great an assertion of independence would have risked jeopardising personal relations with their uniformed colleagues. I minuted him: 'It really does come back to the chaps. Rather than continuing the argument on theological grounds perhaps we ought now to concentrate on finding the new Messiah.'

Even Zuckerman himself found, before long, that it was possible to seek too much freedom. As he records in his memoirs, a manifesto he wrote in favour of free speech in the end brought about his departure from Defence. He adds that he wrote it after discussing the problem with me, but at the time I did not know his future was in the balance. What I did know was that a disagreement seemed to be brewing with the new Permanent Secretary, Sir Henry Hardman. Zuckerman asked for my views, and I responded with a two-page minute that told him some home truths. 'You do operate fast, and to some extent it is because your timetable is so tight ... you have often pushed things out without the routine checks that the administrators, with their larger resources, can normally undertake.' I went on to examine what should be done. 'It seems to me that the Secretary is trying himself to decide whether assessments are, or are not, predominantly scientific... Issues will inevitably arise which you think ought to be handled by the scientists, while he believes the opposite. The only possible way of dealing with this situation is close working between you and Lawrence-

215

Wilson.' (He was the administrative Under-Secretary assigned to work with him.). I added, 'I should deplore a system which fed to the Minister of Defence a single, coordinated, piece of advice on every subject. The whole essence of policy-making is that there is no single, ideal solution. The Minister must be exposed to this debate. He may not like it, but it would be a disservice to the country to shield him from it.'

As I took this minute along to Zuckerman's office I saw Hardman also arriving. I pushed past him with a murmured apology and handed the paper to Glyn Owen, Zuckerman's young Welsh secretary, with the instruction that by no means should the two men be allowed to meet until Zuckerman had read what I had written. Owen handled the situation with admirable tact. A week later Zuckerman asked me in for a drink to talk things over. Over the second whisky he said, 'Why are you one of the few men of your generation who stands up for his views, as any man of culture should?' For all the, no doubt, whisky-induced exaggeration, such moments made all the hard work worthwhile.

On another occasion Zuckerman remarked that while some administrators understood, others were confused at finding themselves mixed up with twentieth-century science. 'It keeps blowing puffs of smoke in their face.' He added, 'What we are doing will outlast me – and you.' In this he was over-optimistic. After his departure to the Cabinet Office in 1966 the standing of scientific civil servants noticeably declined.

As part of the recasting of scientific support to the Armed Forces a Defence Research Committee was established to ensure that long-term possibilities were not crowded out by more immediate project weapon development. I remarked, once the DRC's procedures had been agreed, that it had been a difficult birth. Zuckerman responded, 'Birth? It's not finished yet. Only one leg's sticking out.' He slightly spoilt one of the Committee's first meetings, which he was chairing, by leaving early. As ever, he was doing too much. At times the only way of having ten minutes with him was in his car on the way to the Zoo or to London Airport.

216

The other important element in the scientific side of the defence reorganisation was what to do about operational research (or operational analysis, as it came to be called to avoid confusion with operational requirements in abbreviations). Its potential importance went wider than the systematic observation and analysis of actual operations that had proved so successful during World War II, and on which Zuckerman had built his reputation. Now, in peacetime, there were relatively few events to observe, while at the same time weapons effectiveness was developing with extraordinary speed. Analysis of what might lie ahead when all sides had new equipment was becoming more and more central to long-term defence policy-making. This was why Zuckerman wished to get his hands on Operational Analysis (OA) – without in any way wishing to prejudice its usefulness for lower-level and more immediate matters.

Mindful of the RAF's reluctance to show its hand, he and I had first discussed the possibilities of centralising the running of operational analysis in 1962. I had expressed a personal interest in being given some responsibility, but was told that the Chiefs of Staff would never agree.

I said, 'That is hard to bear.'

Zuckerman responded, 'Do not make the mistake of thinking that grown men are necessarily adult in their behaviour.'

Action had to wait until Peter Thorneycroft's arrival. Thereafter, it was he as much as Zuckerman who brought ultimate responsibility for OA into the centre. When the White Paper on reorganisation appeared it stated: 'Operational research must be more closely coordinated. A ... committee, chaired by a member of the Chief Scientific Adviser's staff ... will coordinate operational research activities.' A small first step had been taken.

For a time Mountbatten, Chief of the Defence Staff, seemed to have ambitions for any new OA organisation to report to him, though it was always more likely that it would finish up under Zuckerman. Nevertheless, it was to Mountbatten that the Minister wrote in February 1964 telling him to organise a 'defence operational research establishment'. By the time Vesting

Day for the new integrated Ministry arrived on 1 April 1964, ambitions for the future of OR (or OA) had grown far beyond the weak and conciliatory statement of the White Paper. It had become clear that an expanded organisation could most easily be built on the foundations of the existing Army Operational Research Group at Byfleet. By chance, this had once been run by Basil Schonland, the man who had originally suggested that I should leave atomic energy to join Zuckerman. I paid Byfleet a visit, noting in my diary that it seemed to be a bottom-heavy establishment, not obviously geared to policy work. Little attention was being paid to several issues of major importance to defence.

Not all in the newly-integrated Ministry were convinced that we needed a 'super-Byfleet'. The Service Chief Scientists, in particular, were far from happy. At one meeting they remarked that 'the Minister has been wrongly advised' – and from their expressions it was quite clear whom they regarded as the culprit. Their opposition collapsed after Mountbatten took it as a personal affront that they were being obstructive, especially after he had argued so strongly with his military colleagues, in support of Zuckerman, that these same scientists should become members of their Service Boards. He told Thorneycroft that any opponent could forget about subsequent honours. An administrator who had been present told Zuckerman, 'He doesn't mean it.'

He replied, 'He does. He's brought down bigger men.'

Time being a great healer, the new arrangements soon came to be accepted. The main dissenter was eventually knighted and the story serves only to emphasise that, right from the start, centralised operational analysis excited high passions.

Thorneycroft was under no illusions about the formidable unpopularity of the move or, indeed, of the whole amalgamation. He told Zuckerman in January 1964, 'Only you, Mountbatten and I believe in this reorganisation. The rest simply don't understand what's going to happen in April.' He did not have long to enjoy the fruits of the changes he had brought about. At the election on 15 October 1964 the Conservatives were defeated by the narrowest of margins, and Denis Healey took over as

Secretary of State for Defence (the amalgamation had brought with it a new and longer title). Glyn Owen rang me early on the morning of Saturday 17 October and said that Zuckerman needed the complete paper on operational analysis reorganisation by that evening. It was still only in an early draft, so I drove to the office, somehow found a typist, and worked through until 10.45p.m. I then drove round to Zuckerman's pied-à-terre in Kensington. He was due to see Healey at 9.00a.m. on the Sunday morning.

On the Monday evening Thorneycroft, in a charming gesture, threw a cocktail party for his successor in the King Henry VIII Wine Cellar – a relic of the old Whitehall Palace that is built into the foundations of the 'Quadragon'. Thorneycroft introduced him to the senior officials and, after saying, 'You have a good team – good luck!' withdrew, leaving Healey as host.

Healey had made a serious study of defence issues. He had been a soldier in World War II and had served with distinction. Right from the start he looked and acted the part. This was a relief after some of the pre-election pronouncements of his Prime Minister, Harold Wilson. A year previously Wilson had been making doctrinaire statements about defence, the air component in particular. Since he was clearly coming to power what he was saying might soon matter. It was a prospect that had begun to worry some of us. I said as much to Wayland Kennet, a Labour peer whom I knew from meetings at the Institute for Strategic Studies and as a sailing companion. So, in May 1963, he had organised a dinner at his house for Wilson. From the scientific side there were John Kendrew, who was still part-time with Zuckerman, Brian Flowers, Patrick Blackett, John Cockcroft – all Fellows of the Royal Society with some knowledge of weapons and war. Military history was covered by Michael Howard and Robert Neild. Philip Noel-Baker and Joe Rotblat provided the anti-war element, Lady Kennet her usual blend of expert defence knowledge and common sense. Outside Whitehall it was as experienced a group as one could hope to assemble – and we were ready to answer any defence questions that Wilson might wish to ask, provided we were not prohibited by the Official Secrets Act from answering.

In the event, the provisions of the Act were in no way threatened. The conversation started by focusing on science, but Wilson was more interested in personalities than substance. Wayland moved us on to defence. I gave a résumé of disarmament progress at Geneva – which I claimed was promising. Wilson kept remarking, semi-automatically, that he agreed with everything I was saying. He soon grew tired, and was also distracted by telephone calls about a possible railway strike. He started to argue about defence on party lines, but was reminded that it was not that kind of evening. I left feeling grateful to Wayland for having tried – but little had been achieved.

Healey was a breath of fresh air – as I had expected he would be, having seen him in action at a number of outside meetings on defence issues. He took an immediate interest in OA. He needed any help we could give him, particularly in the air, where there were great difficulties. Should the P1154 (the uprated version of the P1127, which became the Harrier) go ahead? How many Phantoms should be purchased? Should the TSR2 strike aircraft be cancelled? I had to confess that we were not ready to answer such questions and, moreover, that it was impossible to settle some of these issues on the basis of operational analysis alone. He reminded me with a smile that he was 'an old man in a hurry'. Later, after the new organisation had got into its stride, he asked whether it would make sense to continue to use Commando (i.e. helicopter) carriers as a means of projecting our military strength overseas. By then a powerful team had been assembled, which was able to do a useful major study that shed light on the whole question of military intervention, and also identified some hitherto unrecognised logistic problems in NATO.

The Permanent Secretary, Sir Henry Hardman, had been watching these developments with interest. He knew that an enlarged operational analysis organisation would be more than just another piece of defence reshaping. It would alter the flow of information, which in Whitehall equates with influence. His responsibility was to see that the new organisation came into existence without too much spilling of blood. He had concluded that it should have an appropriate mix of professionals, including economists, military and administrators, in addition to scientists. I had no quarrel with this and welcomed his constructive approach. We had several long discussions, which were the more enjoyable because of his willingness to listen and to debate with an open mind.

However, as I was soon to find out, there was one point on which he would brook no argument: where ultimate financial responsibility for the new OA organisation should lie. Given the sensitivity of the information it would be handling, there naturally had to be a senior controlling committee. It was to be under the chairmanship of Alan Cottrell, a distinguished metallurgist and former Harwell colleague, whom Zuckerman had recently brought in as his deputy. Cottrell tried to persuade Hardman that financial control would be safe in the hands of this Operational Analysis Committee. Hardman brushed his argument aside and insisted on giving that responsibility to one of his own administrators.

By then – late 1964 – I was becoming involved personally as one of several possible candidates for the directorship of the newly-integrated tri-Service OA organisation. Wishing to increase his options, Zuckerman asked me to introduce him to some of the younger up-and-coming men – it being notoriously difficult for someone so senior to know much about the younger generation, especially those from a different discipline – 'but secretly'. One such introduction failed when a Harwell friend left his office with the comment: 'No-one with that number of telephones can possibly be honest!' The encounter with Fergus Allen went more smoothly. His wife, Joan, had been one of the Sabrina Singers, the same choir that had fortuitously helped me to meet Zuckerman in the first place. He was a civil engineer, Director of the Hydraulics Research Station at Wallingford, a poet, a splendid conversationalist, and generally someone of considerable culture. For a time Zuckerman was undecided which of us should handle operational analysis but, eventually, Fergus went to the Cabinet Office to help generally with broad policy for government science.

Before I could be formally appointed as Director there was still the question of financial control to be settled. I was of the view that directors are best kept to the paths of administrative rectitude by head-on-the-platter responsibility for everything, including finance. Hardman would have none of it. I told him that his wish to control finance through a member of his Secretariat was hardly an acceptable arrangement. 'If it's not acceptable,' said Hardman, 'that's the end of the matter.' And he rose from the table. In ten seconds this peach of a job seemed in danger of slipping from my grasp. Fortunately the Establishments Officer acted as peacemaker and, within a few days, we met again. Hardman advised me to regard half a loaf as better than no bread. I had no other option, and did so.

The arrangement actually worked extremely well at the personal level. The Assistant Secretary appointed to Byfleet, Geoffrey Ashcroft, went out of his way to be helpful. He had been picked personally by Hardman as being temperamentally suited to the role. He was the unstuffiest of people, with a razor-sharp mind. On many occasions when we were under challenge it was a comfort to know that the Permanent Secretary's representative was, quite independently, on our side. Given the tensions within the Department, and the ways the Civil Service worked in those days, I do not think Hardman could realistically have acted more helpfully. Shortly after the 'half-a-loaf' meeting I was confirmed as the Director-Designate of the new OA organisation.

The appointment put an end to all thought of looking for jobs outside the central Ministry of Defence. During the previous year there had been a number of unsolicited suggestions that seemed interesting. I was not seriously dissatisfied with my lot and did not mind hard work, even when it meant starting a meeting with Zuckerman at 9.00p.m. – or even on one occasion 11.30p.m. The family was used to taking second place when the pressures were on. But there were certainly tensions inseparable from serving my controversial master, while trying to ensure that his many positive contributions were not dismissed by colleagues who had been irritated by his deviousness. From time to time things reached a pitch at which I was ready to consider other ways of spending my life. Running a major electronics firm was one prospect for which I was head-hunted but, although I visited the factory, I knew in my heart that this was not what I was meant for. A suggestion that I might be invited to become Chief Scientist at the Australian Ministry of Defence was immensely flattering, but my roots were too firmly planted in English soil. I was invited to become Deputy Director at the Fort Halstead Armaments Research Establishment, with a view to early succession, but I did not want to move to the periphery from my central niche, least of all as a deputy. None of the other possibilities could hold a candle to the Byfleet job. I put all thought of moving out of my mind for the time being.

Meanwhile, behind the absorbing problems of reorganisation and personal career planning, defence policy was becoming ever more complex. Zuckerman's emphatic assertion, in his NATO lecture of 1961, of the disutility of nuclear weapons – as weapons of war – stemmed principally from the impossibility of controlling the outcome once they were used. Conventional weaponry was also far from static, as I was reminded every few weeks by visits to research establishments, airfields, submarine bases, and firepower demonstrations. Warfare was becoming more and more complicated and ever more remote from previous combat experience. Nowhere was this felt more acutely than in the Defence Department itself. If its policies turned out to be wrong the people who would suffer first would be its own members in the Armed Forces. There was thus a compelling and directly personal incentive to get policies right.

It was no accident, therefore, that Hardman had become interested in how to prevent Departmental myopia. To this end he set up an informal committee, which he chaired, and on which I was Zuckerman's representative. I already knew from talking with him about my new organisation that he had a lively interest in what systematic analysis could achieve. There might

223

also be useful lessons to be drawn from historical and political analysis, as practised in universities and a few non-governmental research organisations. He encouraged the committee to meet and argue with the main independent defence thinkers. In these meetings the comments of the outsiders were not always as complimentary as we might have wished, but a meeting of minds was usually achieved. My colleagues on the committee from the Armed Forces held surprisingly liberal views, which made it easy to discuss possible shortcomings and areas of uncertainty.

The outcome was the creation of a number of Defence Fellowships, tenable at any universities that would accept them. Fellows were to be given the freedom to write as they found, provided their studies were in some way likely to be relevant to defence policy. In addition, strong support was offered to bodies like the Institute of Strategic Studies (ISS) which a few years earlier had been set up in London under the careful guidance of Alastair Buchan – though only after Buchan had vigorously protested against the unnecessary secrecy that had dogged his dealings with the Defence Department. The fellowship scheme was successful and offered some protection against intellectual inbreeding. The country would arguably be better governed if every government department had, over the years, encouraged a similar degree of open debate on difficult policy issues.

The confirmation of my Byfleet appointment was like a coming of age. Almost immediately, Zuckerman wrote to the Medical Research Council putting forward my name for membership of a committee that was then being formed to advise on the future programme of experimental and applied research in psychology. The fact that he was consulted bore witness to his towering reputation; any scientific enquiry carried more weight if he was involved. But as his time was heavily mortgaged some jobs were passed down to his staff. Very interesting they often turned out to be.

The background to the committee's work was familiar. Machines of all kinds were taking over from human beings, not only to replace muscle-power but, even more significantly to process and act on large volumes of information. The problem was how to maximise efficiency. As a subject it was closer to Defence than might at first sight appear. In aviation the way in which information is presented to pilots, and how this affects their reactions, could make the difference between an Air Force that was on top of its job and one that would be at a fatal disadvantage in combat. And not only in wartime; similar problems arise when flying in difficult conditions. The Army and Navy were interested in the control of guided missiles and radar systems. Similar problems were to be found throughout industry. We even heard of a study of dental efficiency. Altogether, the importance of the man-machine interface was not in dispute. The question was whether it should properly be a concern of the Medical Research Council. The Council had a number of small units and a larger establishment at Cambridge. Should they be retained or hived off to some other organisation?

After two years of sporadic deliberation we concluded, unsurprisingly, that the work should indeed remain under the MRC's wing – but not before there was some heart-searching regarding the reliability of some of the work. The experimentalists can be excused; it is an inherently woolly subject. But that makes it all the more necessary for their results to be examined with at least the normal degree of scientific scepticism.

During our visit to the Cambridge establishment we were told about the derivation of the British alpha-numeric postal code. This had been chosen after the laboratory had concluded that it was easier to remember than the American all-numerical 'zip code'. My personal experience suggested the contrary.

The most memorable conflict with reality concerned studies of driver efficiency and fatigue. In designing such experiments the main problem was how to define and measure 'efficiency'. It was posited that one possible measure could be the number of reversals of the steering wheel that a driver made over a triangular course. A specially instrumented vehicle was prepared and subjects were given progressively more and more mental tasks while driving, as a way of simulating stress. The experimentalist announced, with impressive seriousness, the fascinating conclusion that the more the driver was stressed the better he drove – as measured by a declining number of reversals. One possible explanation, he suggested, was that more stress led to greater alertness. We nodded appreciatively. It was a glorious day and, on my way home from Cambridge, I drove fast along country roads, with the roof open. I was listening to Beethoven's Seventh Symphony, but because of the wind noise could hear it only by having the volume high and concentrating hard. I was acoustically stressing myself. My driving became better and better, according to the Cambridge criterion. Eventually it was so good that when I came to a sharp bend I did not move the steering wheel at all, but went straight on into a field through a gate that was fortunately open. I burst out laughing as the fallacy of what we had been told suddenly became obvious.

One unavoidable consequence of the defence reorganisation was that in the summer of 1964 the central Defence staffs had to leave their spacious and elegant offices in Great George Street and move in with the rest of the Department on the other side of Whitehall. That meant losing the cosy luncheon club with its worldwide maps and the chance it gave of mulling over difficult issues with senior colleagues. I also regretted losing my view down Birdcage Walk, the annual sight of the Guards rehearsing for Trooping the Colour, and their Old Comrades' annual parade in May in their uniform of bowler hats and immaculately furled umbrellas. Fortunately, St James's Park was still close at hand. Before Irish troubles forced the installation of iron gates one could still walk down Downing Street and show visitors the seat of government. In those peaceful days protection came from above: a man could often be seen kneeling in front of Number Ten, counting off his beads as he prayed for good governance.

There was one privilege that I did miss – one that had never failed to impress foreign visitors. The 'new government offices' that we were leaving had a deep basement, which had been Churchill's war headquarters only nineteen years previously. If one spoke kindly to the janitor one could visit for as long as one liked. It was all deliciously improvised and quintessentially British. Everything had been left exactly as it had been on the day war ended. I looked in vain through the War Diary, open on the desk, to find any reference to Hiroshima and Nagasaki. It was as though these events, by their very magnitude, had somehow escaped the need to be recorded. Visiting the same rooms today the visitor is corralled and limited by the plastic screens of a 'heritage museum'. They may be unavoidable if anything is to survive, but the sense of immediate and intimate contact with history has gone. And no lingering is allowed.

Although my new office had no architectural merit it did have the advantage of a small balcony overlooking Whitehall. In January 1965 Jeanie and I looked down on Churchill's funeral procession. The troops were drawn up in companies, spaced perhaps a hundred yards apart. All were standing to attention. The cortège could be heard in the distance moving in slow time up Whitehall from the Abbey, the band playing a funeral march. The gun-carriage bearing the coffin was preceded by a column of troops. As the procession moved forward the still-stationary troops ahead stood fast. No-one moved a muscle until the separation was exactly one pace. Then, perfectly in step, and apparently without any order being given, the new company miraculously took up the march, swelling the column. The same thing happened as the next gap was closed. It was a breathtaking spectacle, which could only properly be appreciated from above – a disastrous collision many times avoided with a skill and majesty that would have graced the Royal Ballet.

Chapter 14

Operational Analysis

On 1 April 1965 I took my ancient Jaguar to Broadoaks, a red-brick mansion in forty acres of parkland at West Byfleet. It was the first day of the new Defence Operational Analysis Establishment (DOAE). Yet another period of rapid learning lay ahead – not only a new branch of applied science, but also how to maintain good relations with officers from the three Armed Services, whose professionalism normally lay in efficiently carrying out orders rather than questioning policy.

We were not the first to try marrying science and soldiering. F.W. Lanchester, the engineer who later gave his name to one of the first cars with automatic transmission, did seminal work in the first World War. That was a war of attrition, in which the rate at which the enemy was killed was proportional to our own fire-power, and vice versa. Lanchester pointed out that it was easy to show mathematically that 'victory' depended on the *square* of the force ratios. His mathematical approach validated a long-established military rule of thumb: that in attack a three-fold local superiority can be decisive.

In World War II there had been a few spectacular operational research successes at the policy level, like the Zuckerman-inspired surgical attacks on the French railway system prior to D-day. But most operational research had been directed towards maximising efficiency at the 'micro' level. For instance, one RAF scientist noticed that there were more sightings of enemy submarines on the port side of Coastal Command aircraft than on the starboard side – which, at first sight, was surprising since aircraft are symmetrical. But internally there was no symmetry. On patrol the aircraft flew mainly on automatic pilot. The captain – who occupied the left seat – could spend a good deal of the time looking out of the window. The navigator on the right side kept a plot, which meant working with charts, eyes down. By bringing in another crew member, and giving him his own window, the number of starboard-side sightings rose to equal those on the port side.

There were still occasions when pure thought was sufficient. Patrick Blackett, Nobel prize-winning physicist and, incidentally, a survivor of the Battle of Jutland, worked for a time on naval operational research. Our shipping losses in 1940 were great and growing, and we had only a limited number of escorts as protection against submarine attack. The crucial issue was the optimum size of convoy: how many eggs should there be in one basket? Blackett argued – in those days before the advent of fast nuclear submarines – in favour of the largest possible convoy. He reasoned that the number of ships protected depended on the convoy's area – on the square of its diameter. Doubling the diameter would increase four-fold the number of ships in the convoy, whereas the vulnerable periphery that needed patrolling would be only doubled. Each escort could, therefore, protect twice as many ships. The argument was simple and direct; but before finally recommending large convoys Blackett asked himself whether he would still believe his conclusion if his own son were in such a convoy. He decided that he would. His policy was adopted, and played an important part in defeating the U-boat blockade.

On being given my new job I sought his guidance. He underlined, in particular, how misleading elaborate computer simulations could be. Although simulation may sometimes be the only available tool, the data needed for modelling may be, at best, imperfectly known. Moreover, the more complicated the simulation the easier it is to lose one's sense of intuition and

229

the harder to judge the reliability of the result. I had reason to be grateful for his warning.

The mixed military-scientific team that was already at Broadoaks was largely concerned with the Army, but Navy and Air Force additions were on their way. Within two years the team grew to 60 civilian professionals – scientists, engineers and economists – plus 36 serving officers. Together with the support staff we made a close-knit family of around three hundred.

On that first morning I was greeted by my two deputies, Ken James and Paul Ward. Ken had been running the establishment during the three months since it had been relinquished by the Army. He was a chemical engineer from the Porton Chemical Warfare Establishment, with striking practical abilities that included cordon-bleu cooking and home film-making; he was also skilled at metal and woodwork. Since he had been temporarily in command pending my appointment his new role was personally awkward, but he discharged it with admirable loyalty. As the awareness of what operational analysis might achieve spread through the Civil Service, new opportunities opened up. Eventually, he found exactly the right slot and moved on promotion to the Treasury as their operational research specialist – but not before he had given me one small piece of advice that transformed the way I handled the establishment. Early on I had been thinking aloud about what should be done, with a good deal of emphasis on the 'vertical pronoun', when Ken interrupted me.

'Not "I", Terry, "we".'

I accepted his gentle reproof and resolved to become more of a team player. A year later, a Whitehall colleague commented with scarcely veiled surprise that my approach had changed.

The military were under Brigadier Paul Ward, a genial and portly bachelor. Byfleet was not his first unusual appointment, nor was it to be his last. I had met him three years earlier at a Northern Command study conference, where he had spoken of his duties as commander of the Nigerian Brigade in the 1960 United Nations operations in the Congo. There he had had to deal with an enemy who shot poisoned darts from behind trees

– 'they never taught us about that at Sandhurst' – and had 'learned how to meet people that eat people'.

Since I was unversed in military operations, despite four years at Defence headquarters, he quickly arranged a number of visits, beginning with the Far East where a confrontation with Indonesia was brewing. We both spent a day at the Jungle Warfare School in Malaysia, where my worst fears about tropical creepy-crawlies were confirmed.

On the way home I called at Aden, where there was trouble up-country. I stayed with Group Captain Le Bas, who had been one of the fighter pilots who flew the three Gloster Gladiator biplanes – Faith, Hope and Charity – that for a time during World War II had been Malta's only air defence. I was helicoptered a hundred miles north of Aden into the wild desert of the Radfan, on the border with Yemen, and saw the difficulties of maintaining land communications over territory controlled at night by hostile guerillas. I also dined with the area commander, General Sir Charles Harington, who mentioned a recent intervention in East Africa. My mind went back to one of Mountbatten's briefing meetings, when he had flown into a towering rage over a signal relating to what must have been the same incident.

'The trouble,' said the General, 'is that Whitehall is so enchanted with modern communications that it thinks it can conduct platoon operations itself from a distance of two thousand miles. I had an inkling that trouble was brewing, but did not know precisely when and where. As things turned out, when it came we were ashore immediately, and the whole thing was dealt with in hours.'

After dinner we chatted on his terrace overlooking the harbour, while he stroked a pet bush-baby on his shoulder. It became clear that his efficiency was matched by his refreshingly clear-headed scepticism regarding conventional doctrine: 'Army "policy" and "history" are based on a random collection of accidents.'

Later, Paul Ward took me to the British Army of the Rhine. To make sure that I arrived safely he prepared a huge luggage label carrying my travel instructions – 13 inches by 8 – with long red streamers to fasten it round my neck. It read: 'My name is Terry Price. When I arrive at the Hook of Holland I have to catch the Rheingold Express. At Bonn I shall meet my dear friend Paul Ward, who will look after me...' The visit was certainly educative. From the headquarters in München-Gladbach I was helicoptered around the divisional headquarters, lunched in the art-deco house that had been the home of Göring's lady-friend, force-landed later in bad visibility, arrived a couple of hours after the baggage car, and spent the night at the home of the General commanding the First Division. It was then, during dinner, that the incident of the Iron Curtain command post occurred.* It taught me how precisely spheres of influence in Europe needed to be defined if nuclear war by accident were to be avoided.

In planning the development of the Byfleet establishment an over-riding need was to win and retain the confidence of the top echelons of the Ministry of Defence. We would be acting as internal consultants – purveyors of information and, therefore, potentially influential. Two committees were appointed to keep that influence within bounds. One was the Operational Analysis Committee, chaired by Zuckerman's deputy, Alan Cottrell, who had been a colleague ten years earlier at Harwell. It included the Service Chief Scientists and the Assistant Chief of Defence Staff for Operational Requirements. Below that was a Military Priorities Subcommittee, chaired by the same Assistant Chief. Through it we agreed the assumptions underlying our studies, helped to maintain links with the Services, and generally tried to create the confidence without which we would have failed.

What I was seeking was 'bureaucratic respectability' – not latter-day political correctness, but in the sense the term was used by Bob Sutherland, my percipient and tragically short-lived Canadian opposite number. He was referring to the need to approach a controlling bureaucracy – Whitehall in this case, but it might be anywhere – in a way that enlists it as an ally.

---

*See page 178.

Fortunately, the Ministry of Defence was probably the most welcoming of all government departments to new ideas – not surprisingly as, for some of its members, there was a life-or-death price tag on getting things right.

As further protection against possible criticism from Whitehall I negotiated, with some difficulty, three new Service posts at four-stripe naval captain or full colonel level. The duty of these officers was to maintain contact with their Service headquarters. They were to be privy to everything that went on at Byfleet and were free to carry reports back as they wished to their Service colleagues. All I asked in return was that they should report on us fairly and feed us a fair share of Service grapevine.

They were not only marking what the scientists and economists were doing. More important from their own viewpoint, they were keeping an eye on the other Services. The Treasury was applying strict financial limits to Defence. So, if the Air Force had a new aeroplane, the Navy became anxious about its next frigate. In that sense the RAF had become the Navy's opponent now that real enemies were becoming harder to find.

It must have been this struggle for resources that lay behind a dispute which erupted unexpectedly with the Vice-Chief of Defence Staff (VCDS), at that time a soldier. It followed a request from Denis Healey for advice on whether to replace an ageing Commando carrier – a major unit of the Fleet that could carry assault helicopters and Royal Marines to any seaboard trouble spot. In the mid-1960s we still exerted military influence in the Middle East. This we could do through garrisons, through Marines pre-positioned in ships just over the horizon, or at short notice via rapid air build-up. Apart from cost, a rational choice would turn on the kind of incidents we foresaw and the likely warning time. In casting the Secretary of State's inquiry into researchable terms – always the first and most important step in any major study – we sought two kinds of information. The military planners were asked to draw up a number of plausible scenarios, covering the likely range of possibilities. Most scenarios were in some way related to the coastline in the Middle or Far East, or in Africa – reflecting the way the British Empire had developed. We also asked the intelligence staff to examine the 60-plus incidents that had involved our military intervention since World War II, to see how often there had been enough warning time to position the Navy over the horizon. It was found there had been sufficient time in all but a handful of incidents.

It was at this point that we ran into opposition from VCDS, and it took me a little time to understand why. The intelligence information pointed to a naval solution, which implied using Royal Marines and providing ships to carry them. But as the Army might then be forced by a parsimonious Treasury to lose a battalion, VCDS insisted on having the intelligence review checked. It had been well done and the conclusion stood.

Given these basic pieces of information the rest of the study, though complex, was relatively straightforward. The various military capabilities and costs were expressed in more than seven hundred simultaneous equations, and a solution found via mixed-integer linear programming – the largest computation of its kind yet attempted in the UK. The conclusion was that, given the political objectives reflected in the scenarios, a replacement Commando carrier would indeed be needed.

Interestingly, it also turned out that the resulting force mix would not differ greatly from what classical horse-trading between the Services had already produced, and might well have produced in the future. But the study did offer a new tool for evaluating the effect of any future cuts. It also provided a foundation for a whole new programme of work on logistics. The same approach, when applied to NATO reinforcement, later showed up bottlenecks that had not previously been identified.

At the time I held two appointments, one at DOAE Byfleet and one in London working directly for Zuckerman. I was in effect my own headquarters boss – an arrangement that can be thoroughly recommended for its convenience and easy lines of communication. For a time the VCDS tried not only to gain control of the Byfleet committee structure but also to deprive me of my headquarters 'hat'. This personal problem was resolved when he unexpectedly resigned. Rumour had it that he had deployed a major ship of the fleet without prior agreement by the Chief of Naval Staff.

A couple of Byfleet's medium-sized outbuildings had windows placed so high that looking in from the outside was impossible without a ladder. This was a security precaution, as they housed the war-gaming tables on which Army commanders 'fought' imaginary nuclear battles in Germany. It was the way these battles had almost invariably evolved that had so disturbed Zuckerman.* To mount an effective defence, if it ever came to war, it had become accepted doctrine that it would be necessary to use a substantial number of 'tactical' nuclear warheads – perhaps as many as twenty in the course of a single day. The Russians had, presumably, come to the same conclusion. In Byfleet's cosy surroundings it was difficult to visualise just how quickly such a nuclear combat would destroy any possibility of command and control and, moreover, sweep away any political purpose there may have been in continuing the 'defence' of German territory. Zuckerman's argument was that the prospect implied by these war-games was both unacceptable and wholly unreal. He insisted that an alternative way forward be found. His intellectual victory on this central issue was arguably his greatest single contribution to policy-making, in a lifetime crammed with high-level action.

Manual games were slow and expensive in staffing, so it was a natural development to turn to computer simulation as an alternative. Alan Goode, one of our Superintendents, pointed out that many of the numbers used in such simulations were 'guesstimates' that might, or might not, be correct. For instance, in the developing conflict between guided-weapon helicopters and tanks, much depends on the ability of each to 'acquire' the other visually. Modern weapons have a very high first-round hit

---

* See pages 170–171.

probability, so that once an opponent has been sighted he is as good as dead. But there were no reliable data for visual acquisition capabilities in the European theatre, where tanks, and helicopters flying tactically at very low level, could both count on finding cover. Goode organised trials to explore this important point, deliberately using two easily distinguishable helicopter types to represent the two sides. The trials were quite different from normal field exercises – more like the clean experiments of physics, concentrating on what Goode called the 'essence' of the problem. The results made sober reading:

> There were many engagements of friendly aircraft...the helicopters exposed themselves frequently and for significant lengths of time to enemy weapons, particularly the long-range guided weapons, yet the reconnaissance information they obtained was poor.

There was more of a similar nature. We concluded it was essential to maintain this kind of field-trial capability, even though it might take effort away from studies that Whitehall thought more immediately interesting. It was the nearest approximation to wartime operational research we could devise.

Goode was, in effect, tackling part of the difficulty that I had been warned of by Blackett – that large-scale simulations make it easy to lose all sense of intuition. Wrong parameters can lead without warning to wrong results (just as with economic modelling). We did not always remember to take Blackett's advice. Once we were studying how quickly RAF Transport Command, in an emergency, could be brought together from its peacetime deployment and placed on a war footing – in the jargon of the Service, 'generated'. A large computer simulation was begun, correct down to the level of individual crews. It grew and grew, until estimated programming costs reached £250,000 – and they were 1965 £s. Fortunately, we had recently recruited Gerry Lorimer, who had been in charge of operational research at RAF Transport Command itself. He had the intuition that others lacked and, within three weeks, solved the problem by simple and direct simulations of component parts of the study.

There are two other problems with computer simulations that are easily overlooked. After I had been advertising Byfleet's wares to a Commonwealth military conference Denis Healey commented: 'Remember that not all facts can be expressed in numbers: some can only be expressed in words.'

A second equally important warning comes from a remark of Hermann Bondi, war-time naval scientist, co-author of the theory of continuous creation and one-time Master of Churchill College: 'Most professionals can be trusted to do algebra and arithmetic correctly. If they reach a conclusion that seems odd, even absurd, one should look for the reason *before* Equation One, amongst the underlying assumptions.' It did not take long after DOAE's creation for the three Services to become adept at questioning our assumptions. The elaborate liaison arrangements then became even more necessary. Without them we risked having to throw away weeks of work based on assumptions that the rest of the Defence Department might not support.

We usually had half-a-dozen policy-related studies in hand and a great deal of war-gaming. Most of this work posed few organisational problems. The relatively few major studies, like the Commando carrier investigation that Denis Healey had commissioned, were a different matter, not least because they might well influence major decisions on expenditure. They brought together huge amounts of information that otherwise might not have been assembled. Weaknesses in the argument had to be eliminated because they would assuredly be unearthed later on in Whitehall. The only way I knew of ensuring the necessary quality control was for one of the three senior people at DOAE to take several weeks off from his normal administrative duties and concentrate full-time on welding the study together for as long as it took, while others ran the shop. Similarly, the main professional divisions of work needed to be headed by men of experience and quality – which meant more senior appointments. It was not a conclusion that was popular with

237

personnel managers in the Whitehall Establishments Division, but we won our case. Byfleet rapidly acquired a name as a place where young men in a hurry could get a 'leg up'. Consequently, recruitment proved no problem. But, of course, they remained in a hurry and soon moved on to their next appointments. We were always in a state of flux, but no-one could say that the establishment was moribund.

There was a quick pay-off for the extra expense of first-rate staff. A Treasury Under-Secretary, outposted temporarily to the Ministry of Defence, commented on our study of helicopter policy: 'Everything set out and argued... A revolution in our way of doing business.' A colleague added, 'I wouldn't have thought work of such quality could have come out of such a young organisation.'

Our new and closer organisational links with the Service's worldwide operational research community proved of the greatest value. The RAF in particular had resisted transferring their operational researchers to the central staffs. They were now formally on our books but, except when we needed their advice, they worked exclusively for their local Service chiefs. In practice there were no problems over such divided loyalties because there were hidden built-in safety mechanisms. One was that when it came to such 'bedded-out' appointments we were under an obligation to provide the best people we could find, or risk damage to our reputation. For their part the outposted staff knew very well that their careers were made centrally by Byfleet, so they took care to remove unnecessary barriers to the flow of information. Career movements meant that after three years almost all the senior outposted staff were in their jobs thanks to boards conducted at DOAE. From then on there were no problems. It was all very British in the way it depended on give and take, but it worked.

Being at the interface between civilian science and military operations, Byfleet was an object of some curiosity to the rest of the MOD. I received many invitations, which provided some escape from the tensions of never-ending Defence Reviews.

These were supposed to lead to White Papers, but it became progressively harder to find new and arresting things to say. One Under-Secretary drily suggested that they should be filled with irrelevant statistics, 'like the number of teeth extracted in Aden in the previous financial year'.

On Salisbury Plain a demonstration of firepower and high-level bombing left me chastened, wondering how I might personally have stood up to such a battering. I was also glad that those putting down the fire had been accurate with their targetting – during World War II a high-level delegation had been severely mauled at a similar demonstration when something went wrong.

Just how easily that could happen was illustrated at the RAF Staff College at Cranwell, where the RAF gave a demonstration of logistic support. First there was a low-level drop from a cargo aircraft flying at about 100 feet. The load, weighing some tons, was pulled out by parachutes, the intention being that it should skid quickly to a standstill. But it had been raining, and the water acted as a lubricant, causing the heavy load to aquaplane at high speed until it was out of sight. Later that afternoon there was a ten ton drop, using very large parachutes. We watched fascinated as the load came down half a mile from the appointed place, in the middle of a small wood. Trees broke like matchsticks. The RAF held a post mortem. I was told apologetically, 'To make matters absolutely certain we didn't leave the crew to work out their own surface wind, but gave it to them. However, the wind direction, 030 degrees, was mistakenly entered into the computer controlling the drop as 300 degrees.' This was all of a piece with Zuckerman's comment on an air attack on Calais in World War II, which he had helped to plan and whose progress he had clinically monitored: 'In war nothing is predictable.'

I was invited to a Guards' mess to lecture and stay to dinner. Over the port my host asked if there was any particular piece that I should like the band to play. Knowing nothing of the military band repertoire, I apologised and, like a novice asking an experienced wine waiter what to drink, threw myself on the mercy of the Bandmaster. He responded with the Post-Horn Galop, with trumpet obbligato. For good measure, the same obbligato was then played on a rifle, and finally on a length of garden hose! The only modification needed to convert these unlikely artifacts into musical instruments was the insertion of a trumpet mouthpiece.

Byfleet had a steady stream of visitors. Denis Healey came before we were properly up to speed, and was somewhat disappointed that we could not provide as much help as he needed in the immediate future. He reminded me that in the long term we are all dead. But back in London he was reported as saying, 'I had the impression that there was something there, and that we could learn a lot by analysing the information available to the three Services.'

Lord Shackleton, Minister for the Air Force, arrived by helicopter after a short journey from London. The approach to our lawn was cluttered with trees and, to ensure a safe landing, the pilot drove over the previous day for an inspection. Expensive – but the staff were impressed.

Hardman, the Permanent Secretary, and Zuckerman each paid separate visits before leaving the Ministry of Defence. Hardman was 'enormously stimulated and encouraged'. Zuckerman, though he enjoyed seeing how DOAE was shaping seemed, when we spoke privately, to be in a more sombre mood. He was not specific, but clearly his relations with the Permanent Secretary – and, it seems likely from Healey's autobiography, with the Secretary of State himself – were causing problems. 'My record has been five years of unrelieved failure.' I assured him that no-one else thought so. Soon afterwards, Healey made generous amends at Zuckerman's farewell dinner, laying stress on his seminal contributions to defence thinking.

Peter Vinter, a Deputy Secretary, came from the Treasury. I tried to persuade him that Government should be treated more often as a research activity; issues that were straightforward should already have been solved lower down. The approach that was working so successfully in Defence could, and should, equally well be applied to other departments of state. And as departmental interests often overlapped, co-habitation of their various analysis teams in a kind of Whitehall research annexe might well improve the quality of Government decisions. There was plenty of room for such a campus on our 43 acres. Vinter did not dissent, but clearly thought my proposition non-negotiable in a Whitehall where the political heads of Departments were in fierce and continuous competition for resources, despite all that might be said about collective responsibility and 'joined-up government'. Nothing came of it and, thirty years later, Byfleet remained one of a mere handful of attempts to bring a critical mass (in both senses!) of interdisciplinary skills to bear on the problems of Government.

The least successful, and in a way quite disturbing, visit was that of Enoch Powell in December 1966. At the time the Tories were in opposition, but Denis Healey had agreed that, as defence 'shadow', Mr Powell could be given a briefing on a variety of defence subjects. We were aware of his brilliant record as a wartime soldier: private in the Warwickshires to Brigadier in less than five years. So we spent the morning doing our best to set out current thinking for his benefit. Amongst other items this involved demonstrating that, while 'brush-fire' wars and skirmishes would remain our lot until our imperial obligations were liquidated, a major war with Russia over Europe was most unlikely, provided we remained alert and prudent. This was not simply a matter of nuclear deterrence; a variety of other dispositions had been made consciously and with care. Moreover there was tacit agreement regarding zones of influence. We then stood him lunch (out of our own pockets, since there was no entertainment allowance) and over coffee asked for his impressions. We pricked up our ears when he said that he still felt we should concentrate on the most likely war.

'And what is that?' I asked.

'A major war in Europe,' he replied.

I kept a straight face with difficulty and noticed signs of

disbelief on the faces of several of my younger colleagues.

Nearly three years after he had retired from the Ministry of Defence Mountbatten came to see what we had made of the new organisation that he had sponsored in the face of considerable opposition. Precisely to the second his car entered the curving drive, wearing on its radiator grille miniature naval signal flags denoting 'I have a dangerous cargo on board'. I asked how he managed the timing so miraculously. 'One thing worse than arriving too late is arriving too early, before your hosts are ready. I parked round the corner and waited.' The visit was an undoubted success. He was in genial mood, and predisposed to think well of us. Our young men gave him a dazzling presentation, and in return he told the anecdote about Bernal* that had helped to shape his approach to operational research. As he left he showered compliments on our work. If, long after his death in 1979 at the hands of an IRA executioner, he had been able to look down from some naval Valhalla, he would have been delighted to see how useful a contribution the establishment was still able to make, thirty years after its inception, to the evolution of military strategy.

A think-tank cannot work effectively without good personal relationships. I was singularly fortunate in having so many congenial and clever colleagues, particularly Geoffrey Ashcroft. He was the Assistant Secretary whom Hardman had insisted on appointing as his personal Byfleet representative. As such he was an essential guarantor of our 'bureaucratic respectability' and a considerable asset in other ways. Once, after giving a morning lecture at the Royal Air Force College at Bracknell, I returned to Byfleet to find there had been some excitement in my absence. A letter about our staffing requests had come in from Establishments at Defence headquarters, couched in such inflammatory language that Ashcroft and James had deemed it inexpedient to let me see it before I gave my performance. Ashcroft had immediately taken the train to London. Standing

---

*See page 162.

in front of the Establishments Officer, who was considerably senior to him, he had torn up the letter and given him a lesson on how to be more tactful – a lesson which it later became clear had been well understood. With such loyalty it mattered not a jot that Ashcroft was not formally a member of the Byfleet staff.

Ken Bowen, who specialised in naval matters, revelled in problem-solving. He played a leading role in the Commando carrier study that did so much to consolidate Byfleet's reputation in the early days. This contribution was recognised by his appointment to the first 'special merit' post to be awarded to an operational researcher. On retirement he took up a second career as a professor at London University's Royal Holloway College. Among his more esoteric accomplishments were a wide repertoire of string games, and knowing how to win at Nim, a game played with matchsticks.

Several of the cleverer members of the staff liked to play croquet on the lawn after work, thus keeping their gamesmanship well honed. Prominent among them was Nigel Beard, who had also taken part in the Commando carrier study. When he left Byfleet he went to the Greater London Council, where he carried out the first exploratory study of what might be done with Docklands. Eventually, he achieved a lifetime's ambition by entering Parliament at the 1997 General Election as Member for Bexleyheath and Crayford.

Not all the uniformed officers were so happy. They found themselves somewhat torn between old doctrines and new and seemingly subversive thinking. My military deputy, Paul Ward, in particular did not always find the tensions easy to bear, especially when we differed over responses to Whitehall's questions. To his delight he was rewarded for his forbearance by a military CBE. On leaving Byfleet he went to Washington to take part in a disarmament study, which he tackled with his usual loyalty while deploring having to fend for himself with no support in a foreign land – and on such a strange assignment. His final appointment was a fitting compensation for the tribulations

243

of Byfleet and Washington: he was the last commander of the Malta army garrison, a posting whose trappings of Empire he must have greatly enjoyed.

John Templeton-Cottill who, for a time, was our Naval liaison captain, had all the social graces. His career had flowed effortlessly in the fast stream. In matters of command he believed, like Mountbatten – whom he had been close to – in making use of 'theatre'. As Commander in charge of a Portsmouth barracks which took in raw recruits he had felt it would improve personal relationships if at their very first parade the officers knew all the recruits' names. New entrants were photographed on arrival, and T-C and his officers spent hours memorising a hundred faces.

He did not greatly enjoy his Byfleet posting – there was no 'theatre' and certainly 'no cream on the cake'. To his relief, on leaving he was appointed to command *Bulwark*, a large Commando carrier. She returned to Portsmouth for a refit and, while there, he invited me to dinner. I caught the appointed train from Waterloo and was reading the *Times* when two young men opposite began to talk about what was clearly the same dinner. 'There'll be a scientist there... Where are we supposed to meet?' They could not remember. I put down the paper and told them. Jonathan Aitken looked at me and said, 'You're not...? It's not fair!' The dinner was a success. T-C took his eating seriously and had instructed the Chinese cook to perform miracles. (I was astonished to find that the British Navy still used self-employed Chinese, who were not themselves members of the Service.) John T-C gained his admiral's flag not long afterwards and retired as the last Joint-Services commander of the British Forces in Malta, where it fell to him to haul down the flag, as he had already done in Singapore. His subordinate commanding the Army garrison was Paul Ward.

My stay at Byfleet gave me an insight into the different ways the three Services handled their officers' careers. I had to countersign the annual confidential reports on the soldiers, sailors and airmen who provided the military contribution to our work.

These forms reflected in an interesting way the differences between the Services. The Army concentrated on the qualities that bind men together. The officer being reported on had to read and countersign the assessment. This inhibited extremes of criticism, but when facing the enemy at close quarters everyone knew exactly where he stood. The forms for the RAF and Navy did not dwell on aspects of mutual trust. In these Services men fight in their vehicles, so support from other crew members can be taken for granted. The RAF's form was better developed than the Navy's. A series of boxes, each with a few words of description, left the assessor in no doubt as to which to tick; cheating or favouritism was all but impossible. The Navy's form was based on a scoring system, with marks from one to nine for qualities such as intelligence, seamanship, competence in command, and so on. What a non-naval assessor could not know without being told was that all naval officers were, by definition, well above average, so the only acceptable markings were six, seven, eight or nine. In a tri-Service establishment like Byfleet that could, and did, lead to difficulties when the reporting officer was from a different Service and unacquainted with this aspect of naval superiority.

Despite the tensions, running Byfleet was a peach of a job. Nevertheless, by mid-1967 I had an uncomfortable feeling that just above my head was a glass ceiling. Having been parachuted in from Atomic Energy I did not have the career profile of an orthodox civil servant and knew this would count against me. Moreover, under Zuckerman's influence top scientific posts seemed to be going to distinguished academics from outside the Service. The Fulton inquiry, whose report could not be long delayed, would probably make a bow in the direction of opening up the higher reaches of the Service to career professionals like me – but foot-dragging was equally probable when the time came for its actual implementation. Reform, if it occurred at all, seemed unlikely to get very far during my remaining time in the Service.

I began to look around, and discussed the outlook with an old friend from Harwell, Monty Finniston, who was then Deputy

Chairman of the nationalised British Steel Corporation. He had a possible opening, so I met Lord Melchett, the chairman. What was on offer was a new planning job, whose purpose would be to reshape the Corporation so that its abysmally low productivity would be a thing of the past. The principal difficulty was not any backwardness on the part of the Board – quite the reverse – but their evident inability, under a Labour government, to tame the trades unions. That was a deterrent, but so was the glass ceiling. I liked Monty and what I had seen of Melchett, and was beginning to think seriously of a move when, at the end of November 1967, a letter arrived asking whether I should like to be considered for an appointment as Chief Scientific Adviser at the Ministry of Transport.

This was unexpected and immediately threw a different light on the future. The magic letters, CSA, were a career goal. They would mark my arrival near the top, if not of the Civil Service, at least of its scientific element. A CSA had direct access to his Minister. The appointment conferred automatic membership of the Official Committee on Science and Technology, which met frequently in the Cabinet Office under Zuckerman's chairmanship to establish priorities and examine a huge variety of intractable problems, from Concorde to the culling of seals (on one occasion these were placed on the same agenda!). Membership of the ST(O) Committee would open the door to the Cabinet Office mess, the hub of lunch-time gossip amongst policy makers. There could be only one answer.

Soon afterwards I found myself in Southwark, in a dingy waiting room in the equally dingy St Christopher House. This speculative building, constructed as cheaply as possible and with matching architectural qualities, was the Ministry's home. It was a good twenty minutes' brisk walk from Whitehall, and was not a popular location. I arrived having done no preparation whatsoever for the interview: life at Byfleet had been too frantic. A table was piled high with transport magazines and I set to, skimming and reading faster than ever before. Fortunately, the interviews were running late. By the time my turn came I had concluded that the country had no coherent transport policy. I said as much to the Permanent Secretary, Sir Thomas Padmore, and to Zuckerman, who was there as the senior government scientist. The Secretary smiled and said he thought I might be right. 'Perhaps you should join us.'

The interview was successful, but that made it necessary to choose between Transport and Steel. I naturally turned to Zuckerman, who argued strongly that I should stay in the Civil Service. At that time he still had faith in the Fulton review and assured me that career prospects for scientists would soon be much better.

'At Transport it's the whole infrastructure of the country that's up for examination.'

I heard on the ever-efficient grapevine that Padmore was less than pleased that I had not yet ruled out Steel as a possibility. 'If that's the sort of chap he is...'

Time for decision was running out. I wrote to Finniston apologising for having taken his time, and opted for Transport. I did so with some embarrassment, having years before almost made a transfer into his Metallurgy Division when we were both at Harwell, before having second thoughts – wisely as it turned out. He courteously forgave me. When I next saw Zuckerman he patted my arm and said, 'You won't regret it.' He spoke in glowing terms of my new Minister, Barbara Castle. 'Quite one of the most intriguing and exciting animals I know.' I was not to have the pleasure of discovering that for myself because by the time I took up my new appointment she had moved to the Department of Employment as part of a ministerial reshuffle. After a brief interview with the lady herself my appointment was confirmed. *Nature* carried the announcement, with a photograph. Letters of congratulation flooded in.

I was impatient for the transfer, which would not take place until April, and in the intervening eight weeks it was difficult to settle back into the routine of running Byfleet. Fortunately, there were some enjoyable distractions.

A trip to Rome to lecture to the NATO Defense College (the

spelling acknowledges American leadership) provided respite from the hard slogging of major cost-benefit studies. And a meeting of the Cambridge University International Affairs Study Group took me to Eltham Palace, in south-east London, where the Army Education Corps had its headquarters. I was given, memorably, the Venetian bedroom. The University had been invited by the Defence Ministry to consider what the political content of our future defence problems might be. The hours of discussion between modern historians and defence planners were fascinating – not least for the reassurance they gave us within the Ministry, helped as we were by a highly professional Foreign Office, that there was not a great deal that had escaped our attention. One assertion by Harry Hinsley, at that time reader in the History of International Relations, and later Master of St John's College, sticks in the memory: 'Great powers do not have policies; they have interests.' The remark came to mind as the Kosovo War of 1999 ran its course, and again when the Iraq war of 2003 unfolded.

Throughout these three years Jeanie had been helping me with the 'family' side of the Byfleet establishment: arrival and farewell parties, dances and bonfire nights. She had watched with astonishment equalled only by my own when I made a small score (five, not out) for the Director's cricket team – which, in strict accordance with the Ministry's non-discrimination rules, included two of our ladies. The extent of these family duties was a source of surprise to some administrators at headquarters, who needed reminding that, in a place where the main activity is thinking, it is as well to ensure that the work-force is contented.

At home Jeanie had been happily engaged in becoming an outstanding studio potter. Two small rooms had been converted for her kilns and wheel, and she was throwing and firing every minute of the day that could be spared or stolen from more mundane duties. Her throwing had extraordinary delicacy and her decoration was gloriously free; her pots were already sought after. So when we went with the Garstins to ski at Andermatt about a month before leaving Byfleet I was expecting that her excellent coordination would mean she would do well. She was, however, surprisingly clumsy and slow to make progress. What neither of us knew at the time was that her difficulties with her legs were the first signs of a deteriorating condition that, slowly but ineluctably, and despite her extraordinary resilience and courage, would cast an abiding shadow over both our lives.

A couple of days before leaving Defence I took part in a meeting called to consider possible events in the first forty-eight hours of a conflict in Europe, should another ever take place. The papers to be discussed were disappointingly vague. I was the only person present who had been around long enough to recall a far more brilliant paper on the same subject written six years earlier by the Intelligence staff. What was happening was that the policy of moving people around in the interests of career planning was destroying the Department's corporate memory. The problem, which is widespread in large organisations, can lead to unintentional waste of resources. I remember hearing from an American defence research director how he had instituted a rule requiring a mandatory review of previous literature before any new project could be approved, only to find himself facing a new and unexpected difficulty: so much had already been thought of, dealt with, and forgotten, that he now had problems in spending his budget!

Looking back on those three years at Byfleet, with their extraordinary and unending stimulation, perhaps the most important lesson I learned was the need for intellectual humility – not to assume that one's view of the world is necessarily complete. When the Falklands war erupted I naturally took a close interest in what was happening. On the whole, events were unsurprising, with one major exception: the Exocet attacks. During the whole of my stay at Byfleet, which had ended only fourteen years earlier, I do not recall a proper discussion of sea-skimming missiles. Yet this new technology was about to transform naval warfare.

Sixteen years after leaving Byfleet, in December 1984, at a Cambridge conference on Analysing Conflict and its Resolution,

I tried to warn a new generation of operational researchers against their evident belief that the growing power of modern computers would enable them to predict the future. Of course, computer power has its uses. It can offer support for decisions reached by other means. It may generate fresh insights. The need to recast a problem in researchable terms will always be a powerful step towards identifying the essence of a problem. The explicit nature of mathematical analysis will focus attention on assumptions, parameters, criteria – things that might otherwise be taken for granted. But, as I told an audience that was clearly reluctant to agree, the trap is to imagine that casting knowledge and facts into numerical form thereby adds precision and encompasses the whole truth. Denis Healey's reminder that there are facts that can only be expressed in words should be engraved on every defence analyst's computer.

Chapter 15

Ministry of Transport

One of the delights of the old-style civil service, before it was fragmented into 'agencies', was the possibility of transferring with little difficulty from one Ministry to another. The arguments against such transfers are self-evident: loss of continuity, an apparent cult of the amateur, failure to see major projects through to completion. These set limits on the extent to which such transfers can be regarded as sensible. The arguments in favour, for those fortunate enough to benefit, are equally strong: mental refreshment, a different approach to problem solving through the importation of fresh experience, new opportunities. Of these the most immediate is the tremendous stimulus of having to learn another new subject.

I joined the Ministry of Transport on 1 April 1968, swapping my town office with its view down Whitehall, and my country office overlooking the parkland at Broadoaks, for a smaller cheaply-furnished pad with a window opening onto an unattractive back street. Only the pictures that had come with me from Whitehall provided any lift for the spirit. The district was equally drab, apart from a few reminders of better days: Southwark Cathedral, a pub where Shakespeare had performed, and the little house on the riverside where Catherine of Aragon had spent her first night in London, and where Christopher Wren had lodged while St Paul's was being built. The district was overshadowed by railway embankments and the Bankside power station, which was still thirty years away from becoming the New Tate Gallery. A whiff of carbolic came from a small soap factory just behind St Christopher House. Southwark had sunk socially over the past few centuries; physically too – in places the sea wall now had to be more than six feet high.

The environment apart, I enormously enjoyed my first few months. It was the first time that I had been concerned with the populace at large, atomic energy and defence having been almost wholly disconnected from the civil side of government. Possible damage in wartime had, of course, been assessed in studies like JIGSAW and at Byfleet; but, so long as defence policy succeeded in avoiding 'hot' war, one could make plans and advance hypotheses with the civilian population entering only as potential 'collateral' casualty statistics. In this new world real people travelled to real jobs, caught real trains, had real accidents. It was more important and more stimulating than the Ministry's lowly position in the government hierarchy at the time might suggest. I felt a new sense of direct responsibility.

The spring and summer of 1968 were months of intense education. I learned about urban and intercity traffic, railways, the dramatic impact on the port industry of containerisation, emerging transport technologies, and how these things interacted with land-use planning. I went for a ride on the footplate of a tube train and participated in an international transport conference that, fortuitously, took place during my first few weeks. At a gala performance for the delegates at the Coliseum, Orpheus descended to the underworld in a Victoria Line train – its automated control system being flavour of the month. All necessary doors were opened by generous colleagues. But I was also under observation; the structure of the research side of the Department was the subject of much discussion.

Our biggest research resource was the Transport and Road Research Laboratory at Crowthorne, under its energetic director Joe Lyons. I was nominally senior to him – a fact reflected in true Civil Service style by a £25 salary differential – but he had the troops and a degree of guaranteed autonomy which made this irrelevant. Relations with TRRL could only proceed on a basis of cooperation. It was a difficult relationship which needed careful handling, but we managed to avoid serious quarrels.

My predecessor, Eric Williams – it was the second time I had followed him into a post – had done his best to smooth my path by securing approval for two senior assistants. I immediately drew these vacancies to the attention of a few past colleagues in defence and atomic energy whose work I admired. Before long I was joined by Alan Goode from Byfleet and Leslie Mullett from Harwell. He had also left me two further legacies. One was an unknown enemy – within weeks of my arrival I received, for no stated reason, an anonymous death threat addressed to 'The Chief Scientific Adviser'. More helpfully, he had worked hard to set up a new interdepartmental Joint Transport Research Committee, through which it was hoped the technical expertise of the Ministry of Technology could be placed at the service of the Transport Ministry. The committee also had the support of a small team of scientists, jointly contributed by the two ministries. This was the Transport Research Assessment Group (TRAG), which was located at TRRL under a former atomic energy colleague, Tony Hitchcock.

What I had not foreseen was the division of headquarters work between the scientists and the economists working under Christopher Foster, who was Director-General of Economic Planning. He was a clever man who had been brought in during Barbara Castle's régime a couple of years earlier. He had built up a highly competent team of mathematicians and economists, who were doing for transport what the Byfleet team had done for Defence. They were, for instance, working on the implied value of a traveller's time, the cost of congestion, and other building blocks that would help to guide new transport investment. While I could only applaud what they were doing – and doing well – it was disappointing that such studies would not be in my bailiwick. In our meetings we remained correct but somewhat distant, while managing to be in each other's hair – a physiological conjuring-trick with which everyone in Whitehall is familiar.

253

The Permanent Secretary, Sir Tom Padmore, was aware that, before long, something would have to be done about the Department's research structure. He was an able and civilised man, who took a noticeably more relaxed approach to his duties than some other departmental heads. He believed that his principal concern should be to appoint the best available people to his staff and, having done so, delegate downwards any decision for which his 'chop' was not essential. He preferred mature consideration to hasty action and knew perfectly well that this had caused him to be dubbed 'the high priest of reaction' during Barbara Castle's early days. I was, however, glad to serve under him, since his style of management added greatly to work interest at the Under-Secretary level – always the engine-room of any government department.

Immediately below Padmore came Jim Jones, a Deputy Secretary universally known as JD. He acted as my guide and sounding-board. He was easy to talk to and helpful, a man whose feet were very much on the ground. Of his Under-Secretaries, I had, at the outset, most to do with Peter Lazarus, who was responsible within the Department for railways. All my administrative colleagues were refreshingly approachable. There were no 'prima donnas' and few vested interests. It was a welcome change from Defence.

It was an interesting time to take up the reins. Across the transport field new technology was becoming available and there were hopes that it might assist in dealing with a whole range of otherwise insoluble transport problems: helping railways to meet the growing competition from the motor-car and, on longer journeys, the aeroplane; congestion in cities; making towns more pedestrian-friendly; reducing noise and pollution; helping the third of the population that was too old, too young, or too disabled to use public transport.

The most evident impact of new transport technology so far had been on the shipping industry, which affected the Department through its responsibility for ports. Freight had traditionally reached this island in ships of around 10,000 tons. Unloading was slow, and ships were sometimes detained for as long as three weeks. In no more than a decade containerisation and full mechanisation had arrived, meaning that ships now needed to stay in port only 48 hours, if that. The ships themselves were also growing in size, being commonly of 30,000 tons or more; they have since grown even larger. Putting these facts together, the number of berths needed was about to fall by a huge factor – at least thirty, and on some counts nearer one hundred. The dockers, a traditional bastion of union power, were putting up a strong fight, but the facts were against them. Nothing could halt the onrush of mechanisation.

Larger ships were also more expensive and more tightly scheduled. Foreign shipowners were no longer ready to accept having their ships held up because of internal British trade union disputes. Militant Bristol dockers once held hostage a New Zealand fruit ship locked in at Avonmouth; the New Zealand authorities immediately embargoed the use of that port. For the same reason ports like Felixstowe, where the berths are in a tidal river and need no locking in, rapidly gained favour over their competitors. Furthermore, since many of the huge new container ships would be visiting European as well as British ports, geography had new implications. The Port of London was too far up-river, Avonmouth too far off the main European shipping route through the English Channel.

I saw some effects of these irreversible trends during an educative visit to Tilbury. There was great activity at the bulk transfer berth, where the 'portainer' crane was feeding a vast queue of lorries. Elsewhere there was equally striking indolence. Was this really the country's export lifeline? I discussed the social consequences with Susan Fogarty, the Assistant Secretary with responsibility for ports policy, during our return through the unmitigated drabness of east London, with its miles of idle wharves. She knew both the problems and the trade union bosses, who, for the most part, formed no part of the solution. She was utterly level-headed in her dealings – a valuable quality given the years of continuing turmoil that the ports industry was evidently facing. She died far too young.

With such enormous forces in play there was little that the Research Committee of the National Ports Council could usefully do. As CSA I was automatically a member, but do not recall making any worthwhile contribution.

Railways were another obvious target for modern technology, and I had not been long in the Department before I was drawn into discussions about what might be possible. As part of my education I was sent to Vienna for a conference on high-speed railways. I naturally felt obliged to travel by rail, but found the thousand-mile journey at normal speeds frankly a bore, the beauties of the Rhine Gorge notwithstanding. The conference did, however, provide an opportunity for a quick trip to Prague to stay with the Michells, who were friends from my own village of Jordans. Denis, as Head of Chancery at our Embassy, had an office near the castle in which Mozart had reputedly worked while composing *Don Giovanni*. It was the time of the 1968 Prague Spring and people were out on the streets celebrating their new sense of freedom. A few weeks later the Russian tanks rolled in.

Our own railways had been pruned by Beeching to make them more economic but, taken as a whole, they were still unprofitable. They had around 10,000 miles of track, but were challenged by 100,000 miles of roads and a rapidly increasing car population. Their traditional freight markets were at risk from several directions; relocation of factories away from rail-connected sidings, loss of train-loads through competition between nuclear power and coal; and, not least, road-hauled containers. Commuter services, particularly into London, seemed irretrievably uneconomic, the trains being virtually unoccupied for half the working day. Yet the major cities needed to function, and there was no alternative in sight.

What did seem possible was to speed up inter-city passenger services to a point where motorists might be persuaded to leave their cars at home rather than continuing to clog the motorways. To this end the British Rail Research Department at Derby was actively studying ways of breaking the technical constraints that so far had limited train speeds to around 100 m.p.h. It was led by the Railway Board's Member for Research, Dr Sydney Jones, who had resolved to bring modern technology to bear on the whole railway operation – vehicles, track and signalling.

It was not before time. The design of railway wagons was so primitive that some became unstable at 20 m.p.h. and were in danger of leaving the rails at only 40 m.p.h. The only means of damping oscillations was the rust in their metal springs. Sometimes corrosion caused them to seize, leaving one wheel flange permanently free of rail contact and ready to derail at the next sharp bend or set of points. The obvious solution – adopting hydraulic dampers such as we take for granted on our cars – was deemed too 'high-tech' for the railways. No-one was prepared to guarantee that they would be regularly replenished with oil – and an unreplenished damper could also lead to derailment. Railway freight was commercially unimpressive, except for train-loads of bulk materials. Railway wagons frequently got lost in transit; even the Research Department lost one of its specially instrumented vans in the Willesden marshalling yards for several days. The rails themselves were unstable and, in hot weather, could buckle suddenly without warning. One train was derailed at Thirsk when this happened and it was only by a miracle that another coming in the opposite direction was stopped in time.

As for passenger trains, their ride was rough and tiring. The traditional British Rail approach had been to design new 'bogie' wheel assemblies for the carriages and hope that they would solve the problem. It was an unjustified hope. In a complete vehicle there are nearly twenty different modes of oscillation, induced by factors such as track roughnesses and wheel imperfections, all needing to be damped down simultaneously. Choosing a new bogie is almost beside the point when what is needed is an integrated mathematical analysis of the design of the vehicle as a whole, and how it would function in a real operating environment. In previous years that had been an insolubly complex problem, but by the late 1960s the necessary computer tools were becoming available.

257

At Sydney Jones's invitation I made an early visit to Derby. Peter Lazarus came with me. It was one of the most exhilarating days of my life. If there was a single centrepiece it was the rolling rig, where, to investigate these instabilities, wagons and coaches could be tested at simulated speeds of up to 100 m.p.h. Having seen a conventionally designed 20 ton wagon oscillating wildly on the rig at only 70 m.p.h., I needed no further convincing of the need for a more sophisticated approach.

That was being provided by Alan Wickens, a mathematical engineer brought in with other colleagues from the aerospace industry. He had successfully removed the instabilities that had initially plagued Blue Steel, one of the early airborne missiles. Now he had shown how to deal with the multiple coupled oscillations found in a conventional two-bogie passenger coach, and the simpler problem of how to make four-wheel trucks run stably at speeds up to 100 m.p.h.

Jones's ambitions did not stop there. He was out to push high-speed technology as far as it could go, and a design for an Advanced Passenger Train was taking shape. The aim was to squeeze as much performance as possible out of the existing rail infrastructure. He argued that by concentrating on well-designed new vehicles the need for expensive new track could be avoided. Jones assured me that the track could safely accommodate speeds 50% greater than were currently in use. The only problem for passengers was that going round curves would be uncomfortable, since the curves could not be banked sufficiently without causing unacceptable discomfort should a train have to halt for any reason on those parts of the line. The solution was to make the train tilt, using rams controlled by sensors. They were an everyday feature of aeronautical engineering and presented no design difficulty. Tilting the carriages would infringe the small British loading-gauge unless the carriages had a considerable degree of what sailors call 'tumble-home'. They would, therefore, be narrower at the top than normal coaches, but still adequate for the task.

The pounding of the track, a growing problem as speeds rise, would be reduced by using lighter coaches made out of aluminium. The maximum safe speed would then be fixed partly by aerodynamic considerations. Unlike aircraft, trains do not always head directly into wind, and side winds create an overturning force that must be kept within limits. Perhaps more important in practice was assured braking, so new ways of dumping the train's kinetic energy were being considered. With everything taken into account an Advanced Passenger Train (APT) running at 155 m.p.h. on the existing rail network seemed entirely within reach. In fact, one APT reached 162 m.p.h. in 1979.

Peter Lazarus – not himself a technical man – could see that I was convinced this dream could be brought to fruition, given a good engineering team and funding that, in comparison with nuclear power or aircraft development, would be almost absurdly modest. But there was a problem. The cash-strapped board of British Rail, unwilling to back such a radical departure from existing practice, was prepared to offer only a trickle of research funds, insufficient for a prototype. Lazarus, with Padmore's strong support, used his Whitehall contacts to see whether the Transport Department might help. Eventually, after some ritual protests, the Treasury – which did not like giving additional subsidies to an already subsidy-dependent industry – agreed to provide several million pounds. With prices at 1968 levels that was enough to make a start – but British Rail was not amused. The Board seemed to regard our initiative as interference and took three months to decide whether to accept the grant, a delay which did not endear us to our Treasury benefactors. Moreover, BR decided that the Advanced Passenger Train should not go ahead on its own, but only in company with a 'belt-and-braces' rival project, which became the Inter-City 125.

Syd Jones and I paid a flying visit to New York, where we set out our hopes for better and faster trains at a meeting of the National Industrial Conference Board – an interesting American institution that ensures that US industry is kept well informed. We also did press and radio interviews. The *Boston Globe*'s enthusiastic reaction was typical; they took everything we said at face value. The British trade mission in New York was delighted.

Unfortunately, events proved our message to be wildly over-optimistic. We had failed to understand the depth of feeling between the old and new railway engineers. The Derby research team was, in effect, saying that much of what had been taken as gospel for decades was simply incorrect. The old-style engineers were on the defensive and, since they were operationally in charge, this inevitably had the effect of according the APT second priority. But, eventually, a prototype was built and trials were begun on a disused, sharply curved stretch of railway line near Melton Mowbray. There was one straight section where 155 m.p.h. could be attained. I attended a demonstration and found that the performance and ride were all that had been hoped for. Unfortunately, the essential next step – careful, systematic and prolonged testing and validation – was skimped. Plans were finally laid for an experimental APT inter-city service, starting in December 1981, long after I had left the Ministry. I was delighted to read that the London to Glasgow run had been completed on schedule in 4 hours 15 minutes. But only days later the papers carried news of a public relations disaster: the tilting mechanism in one coach had failed and the passengers had had to experience the discomfort of travelling for a considerable distance, permanently tilted, round adverse curves. It was a fault that could easily have been rectified, but the will to force the project to succeed seemed to be evaporating. Some work continued and, by 1983, the trains were accumulating mileage satisfactorily, and could have formed the basis for further development. But, despite the fact that the earlier reliability problems had been dealt with, the project was abandoned and much of the excellent technology and experience thrown away.

Eventually, in September 1996, reports began to appear in the British Press that tilting trains were to make a comeback. By then they were in use in Finland, Germany, Italy and Sweden. Whatever design was to be chosen for our own railways, it was most unlikely to be British. The whole sad story of the APT was a national humiliation, when it could so easily have been a triumph.

The outcome for freight traffic was more encouraging. In the summer of 1968 British Rail was still ordering wagons that became unstable at 60 m.p.h. Inevitably, there was a dispute over design between the research team and the traditional railway engineers. To resolve the issue two trains were prepared, one to conventional designs, the other following new Derby practice, and given lengthy tests under actual operational conditions. The new design of wagon emerged as the clear winner, both in technical terms and total cost of ownership. But it was rejected on the grounds that its initial cost was considered too high!

The decline of the railways was only one of the side-effects of the motor-car. At the time – 1968–70 – there were already two cars for every three households (the car population has since doubled). This rising tide was outstripping our ability to provide adequate road space. It was damaging public transport by adding to the congestion with which buses had to contend, as well as draining away their passengers. And the noise, smell and clutter of urban traffic were affecting us all. The Transport and Road Research Laboratory argued strongly that electronic road pricing could offer an acceptable solution. The politicians were not persuaded, nor would they be for the rest of the century.

The car was having another equally important, though more gradual, effect in reshaping our urban communities. By releasing a majority of wage-earners from their previous dependence on public transport for home-to-work journeys – by providing them with a new kind of lateral mobility – it was dispersing cities and breaking down the tight population groupings and established travel habits that, in the past, had made it possible to organise a public transport system. It was already far harder for a public transport authority to deal with suburbs than with a city centre, at least if the services had to pay their way, and the process of dispersal was still continuing.

For a time, the rise of the car was taken to imply a need for ever more multi-lane expressways. But these could cut through established populations and the resulting lines of demarcation could then all too easily become centres of unrest. The 1965 Watts riots in Los Angeles were arguably exacerbated by the sacrifice of previously viable and coherent districts to the requirements of the motorcar.

Against this background I saw the main function of the Joint Transport Research Committee as the exploration of possible new transport solutions. If a wider range of alternatives could be on offer then planners, urban planners in particular, might be more frequently successful when deciding on solutions to their local transport difficulties. In this I was less effective than I had hoped, partly because I allowed the Ministry of Technology to direct the committee's attention unduly towards one overambitious scheme – Cabtrack. This was a project aimed at providing a network of tracked taxi-sized vehicles within our cities. The hope was that such a service would dissuade people from using their own cars, so easing traffic congestion. Because there was no possibility of providing sufficient crews to ensure 24-hour operation they would need to be driverless, automatic and self-routing. However, the proponents made exaggerated claims regarding feasibility and reliability, at a time when the only hardware was a tiny demonstration of a method of routing that did not require actively switched points. It was aimed at allowing cabs to overtake others that had been called in to lay-bys to pick up or set down passengers. Long before we reached a full-scale demonstration the project sank under a growing burden of scepticism within the Ministry.

Another piece of hardware that might have potential for altering town layouts is the moving pavement. Its use in airport terminals is familiar, but there the distances are short and speeds do not need to be high. In practice they barely exceed 1.5 m.p.h. If this could be safely increased to around 8 m.p.h. it could transform the way people move around towns. If such fast walkways could be created they would be a possible substitute for underground railways – slower, it is true, but obviating the need to descend to underground platforms and wait for the next train. The point-to-point block speed might well be much the same. Moreover, these walkways might persuade motorists to park their cars on the edges of shopping centres, before proceeding to swing along three times as fast as they could normally walk to reach their destination.

A slower version had been demonstrated more than half a century earlier at the great Paris exhibition of 1900. There even ladies in long skirts had managed to transfer from a rotating roundabout to a walkway moving at nearly 5 m.p.h. – three times today's speed – and get off again without accident. They entered the roundabout near its axis via a stairway and then walked outwards towards the periphery, accelerating automatically as they did so, thus making it possible to step onto the main belt without difficulty. Dismounting used the same system in reverse. But if the belt is speeded up further the getting-off problem becomes much more intractable. It requires only one infirm person to fall while dismounting for a major accident to occur, as tens or hundreds of fellow-travellers are swept along by the walkway. Attention was therefore concentrated on devices for doing, in a more sophisticated way, what the simple roundabout had achieved for the somewhat slower belts in the Paris exhibition.

The best work was taking place in Switzerland, at the Geneva Battelle Institute, where speeds of over 8 m.p.h. had been achieved. But, even there, during a demonstration I saw Gaby Bouladon, the project engineer, become disoriented while starting to dismount. We shouted, and he reacted just in time to avoid being swept into a barrier.

The mounting schemes that seemed most promising involved a secondary belt that accelerated the passenger to the speed of the main belt in some way. But the faster the main belt was travelling, the larger would be the 'mounting stations'. At Jim Jones' suggestion we decided to see how these structures, and also the stations needed for Cabtrack, might be incorporated into a typical street of a major town. This led to one of those hilarious encounters that help to make life enjoyable.

The work was entrusted to a leading architectural partnership,

Robert Matthew, Johnson-Marshall and Partners – known affectionately as Rum-Jum. Sir Stirrat Johnson-Marshall had done distinguished work for the Department of Education's Development Group soon after World War II, evolving ways of cutting building costs for schools and so making capital investment go further. The partner responsible for our transport study was Andrew Derbyshire, who had started life as a physicist at the Cavendish Laboratory in Cambridge. He had an inventive and practical mind, and it was no surprise when he too was later knighted for his services to architecture.

By way of returning the compliment they invited me to visit York University, which had been their creation. The buildings are laid out round a lake. Towards the end of the visit we were looking out from the music department over the water to the chemical engineering laboratory. I was invited to admire its functional qualities.

'You can infer from the outside what are the structure and the functions which go on inside.'

There was a pause. Clearly I was expected to say something. In desperation I blurted out the first words that came into my mind.

'What is it that you as architects have added, which a civil engineer could not have done himself? Where are the twiddles?'

There was an uneasy silence, and I feared that my remark had caused offence. We then went to lunch in the York Club.

In the panelled dining-room only two tables were occupied. At one of them Lord James, Vice-Chancellor of the university, was waiting for us. A conversation developed about cost and effectiveness in university building programmes – it was the time of the great Robbins expansion. James spoke in a deep booming voice that emerged from the depths of his huge frame.

'These architects have done a magnificent job. They have built to cost, and on time. If the University Grants Committee were to give us no more money for the next twenty-five years, we could still function.' He paused, then raised his voice. 'Not like the University of...' (and he named another of the new

264

universities). 'They let their architect get out of control, knowing that the University Grants Committee would have to bail them out. Dishonest, I call it.'

That was the end of that part of the conversation, and we fell to discussing other matters. But before the meal ended a man rose from the only other table that was occupied and, as he passed us, James called out: 'Next time you come to York come and see a *real* university.'

I asked who he might be.

'That,' said James, in the tone of someone who had just meted out due and very public punishment, 'is the Vice-Chancellor of the University I was talking about.'

There was a small and unexpected post-script to the visit. Weeks later a letter arrived from the partnership. 'We have been thinking about your remark concerning the chemical engineering building,' it said. 'You were right. We have decided that we must change our architectural philosophy.' I could not have been more surprised if I had thrown a treble-twenty blindfold at darts.

Our architects did a thorough job of investigating the impact of new technology on a capital city. Cabtrack was 'installed' – notionally – in the square mile north of Piccadilly Circus, and the problems of insertion into a real urban environment were studied in detail. The results were published in the *Architects' Journal* in May 1971, amid editorial claims of a 'breakthrough as significant as any in technology' – the journal was rejoicing that, at last, architects had actually been consulted. Nothing came of these studies, though perhaps one day growing desperation over the problem of movement in cities will cause the report to be revisited.

The perennial objection to such revolutionary schemes is finance. Yet this should not be an overriding problem, as I realised on the day I took an American visitor up to the tenth floor of St Christopher House to show him the view across the Thames to the City of London.

'Nineteen years ago everything in the City had been knocked flat by Hitler. Now look at it. I conclude that on a twenty- or

thirty-year timescale we can do virtually anything that is needed.'
But I was forgetting the other vital component: political will.

Not long after my arrival at St Christopher House I was
visited by Ken Orski, an American working at the Organisation
for Economic Co-operation and Development (OECD) in Paris.
He invited me to become the UK representative on a new
Consultative Group on Transport Research. It promised to be a
useful forum, with representatives drawn from all over Europe,
as well as America, Canada and Japan. It would meet twice a
year. I accepted with pleasure; it was good to have any excuse
to be back in France. After the first meeting I was elected
chairman, and remained so for the time I was with the Ministry
and for a few months thereafter.

Apart from committee business, which ranged widely over
the whole field of transport, Orski and I cajoled the Group into
organising discussions that led to the publication of a series of
substantial books – of 200 pages or more – each giving an
overview of some part of the transportation scene: traffic noise,
the urban movement of goods, the rôle of buses, how to move
people around 'major activity centres' (which are not necessarily
confined to towns and cities), city-centre airports for vertical
take-off aircraft, rapid transit, etc. Once we went to Washington
DC to study tunnelling – an essential component of many urban
transport schemes. Rapid publication is a useful way of exploiting
the drawing power of an organisation like OECD, which brings
together experts from all over the world. It also avoids the need
for a large in-house research team. I used it again ten years
later when running the Uranium Institute, whose conferences
similarly brought together the world's nuclear power industries.

One significant difference between the British government's
attitude to industry and that of other countries became clear
during these Paris meetings. In some ways ours was the best
transport ministry in Europe, if not in the world, when it came
to ideas and theoretical analysis. Between them the Road Research
Laboratory and Foster's economists and mathematicians had
created a superb understanding of what should rationally be

done. Our views were well received by the OECD group. But our own Civil Service seemed to regard it as improper to invite industrialists to take part, lest one firm might win an 'unfair' advantage over a competitor. We can hardly blame British private industry for failing to lead when for so long it was our own government's normal style to regard its members as second-class citizens. The Americans had no such inhibitions and regularly brought people from their leading firms.

Furthermore, the UK was without a tradition of the long-term planning that is essential if any major transport problem is to be dealt with. We seemed to be content to leave the future to the interplay of market and political forces, while the more *dirigiste* countries of Europe got on with the job of planning and implementation. More than once I returned to London to argue with colleagues who viewed some development as impracticable, telling them that it was actually in hand on the continent.

The Group met in an elegant salon in the old Château de la Muette, where on one occasion we discussed airport access. It was an appropriate venue. On the lawn outside the windows the Montgolfier Brothers had arranged the first successful manned free flight in 1783 – though with understandable prudence they had allowed Pilâtre de Rozier and the Marquis d'Arlandes to be the passengers. I had been lunching with Alex King, OECD's Director-General for Scientific Affairs; he pressed me to take more claret. I pleaded that I had to chair the meeting. 'If you're in the chair you won't go to sleep,' he said; and so it proved.

On another occasion an American economist performed a lengthy mathematical analysis which sought to answer the question: if I use a motorway that does not run straight to my destination – so that I have to leave it at some point – and if the shortest journey time is the criterion, what is the optimal point at which to quit the motorway? After twenty turgid minutes he produced a result that was unexpectedly familiar. He had unknowingly rediscovered Snell's Law of 1621, which governs the behaviour of light at an optical interface: light automatically uses a route that minimises its journey time. It was a perfect example of C.P. Snow's 'two cultures'.

Muette also remains in the memory for its duty-free basement supermarket for employees and delegates. With care I could return home with no fewer than ten bottles of château-bottled premiers crus, at prices that even a British civil servant could regard as most reasonable. We timed parties for friends with these hauls of booty in mind. They had a gratifying effect, in particular on Pat Rance, who later achieved fame as gastronome, maître-fromager and author of two magisterial books on British and French cheeses.

In April 1970 the Group travelled to Orléans to inspect the Aerotrain which was the brain-child of a French engineer, Bertin. This tracked hovercraft was running on a ten-mile test track mounted on pillars about twenty feet high, an arrangement that both minimised land use and protected the vehicles against vandalism. Speeds of 180 m.p.h. were possible in great comfort, and we overtook cars on the nearby main road as though they were standing still. But, like a competing British project, the scheme had virtually no chance of displacing conventional steel-wheel-on-steel-rail technology because of the high cost of new infrastructure. There was also unavoidable anxiety about the design. The vehicle was supported on a concrete girder which, in motion, appeared to pass through the car at very high speed with minimal clearances. It required little imagination to know what would occur if, for any reason, the girder developed even a minor defect.

As time went by I became a well-established feature of the Ministry's scenery, and invitations to lecture and make foreign visits flooded in. I visited Pittsburgh to speak at an international conference on urban transportation, flying at the organisers' expense in great style via Zurich. This had the curious result that, after an early start, by lunchtime I was back 30,000 feet above my starting point, Heathrow, eating lobster in the company of the owner of the 300-strong Wienerwald chain of restaurants. He had three private aircraft: a helicopter, a small Cessna and a Mystère jet. 'That is probably enough,' he told me.

Insofar as urban transport needs infrastructure it cannot rationally be studied except in relation to land-use planning and urban renewal. Pittsburgh, which I was visiting for the first time, proved to be a striking example of urban renewal. In place of the dingy steel town that had existed only 30 years earlier, I saw a shining new city that had grown up on the Golden Triangle, the tongue of land that separates the mellifluously named Monongahela and Allegheny rivers.

The conference organisers had asked for an enormous number of slides. The reason for this became clear at the rehearsal. On each side of the stage were two screens – four in all – and onto these were projected, as I spoke to a script, all manner of photographs relating to the subject of the moment. The effect was almost like being accompanied by a cine-film, though of course it was much easier and cheaper to produce. I marched on to a fine show of tourist shots of London and the sound of a military band playing *The British Grenadiers*. Thanking my audience for these lavish military honours, I reminded them that they too could still be enjoying the aesthetic benefits of the Guards' bands had the inhabitants of Boston been blessed with different tea-drinking habits. They liked that. We met for supper in the house of the impressive and civilised Dean Stone who, immediately following World War II, had been the Administrator of the Marshall Plan – an assignment that would make any man feel proud.

In February 1970 I took a small delegation to Russia under an Anglo-Russian trade agreement. The purpose was ill-defined, except that we should be talking about transport projects. I decided to secure a tactical advantage by taking our own interpreter – an able Russian speaker from Salford University, Richard Pollock. He was so good that after the first day the Russians no longer bothered to bring their own man. With his help we could listen to their informal discussions before they made their next contributions. It was an arrangement that would have been even more valuable in a defence or disarmament context.

Our mission achieved little in the way of tangible trade. But we did attend two ballets, and visited the observation platform at the top of the newly-completed Ostankino Tower (cameras had to be deposited at the entrance!). There followed night train journeys to and from Leningrad. As we were getting into the sleeper on the outward journey, with our people and their Russian colleagues pairing off to go to their bunks, two per compartment, it looked for a moment as though I might have to share with the lady Russian commissar, who appeared to be the political boss. I hissed to Pollock, 'England expects...' But the commissar found a lady to travel with, and Pollock came with me after all.

This was particularly fortunate. We had just put out the light when the door flew open and the burly Chief Engineer of the Moscow Underground burst in, carrying a bottle of champagne in each hand. 'Before you go to sleep you have some work to do,' he announced, brandishing the bottles. He spoke Russian, but with Pollock's help conversation was as easy as though he were speaking English. 'I want to tell you how Russia came to produce champagne. Two hundred years ago a young nobleman from Georgia went to Paris to study French. He developed a taste for champagne and, when he returned home, he realised that the climate was not very different from that of France – perhaps Russia could have its own champagne. So he set to work, married a rich lady, and tried hard for twenty years, only to fail. His wife's fortune was exhausted. But he was a determined man. He divorced that lady and married a rich widow and, after another ten years,' (his voice rose) 'Russia had champagne!' He smiled as he saw our delighted faces and added, regretfully, 'We're not allowed to put up statues to princes any more.'

On our return to Moscow I made an unfortunate gaffe at the final meeting. I told my hosts that I had been particularly pleased to be in Russia in February 'because I wanted to see for myself the General Winter who had defeated Napoleon'.

Our host made a slight grimace. 'We had something to do with it too,' he said.

Seeing my confusion everyone roared with laughter and we parted friends.

Individually, our hosts were charming; but the feeling of Big Brother – and, in our case, Big Sister – was inescapable. On the return flight the moment when tension noticeably relaxed was as we left Russian airspace at Riga and headed out over the Baltic.

At Durham in the autumn of 1970 I gave the British Association a *tour d'horizon* of the transport scene, using the Pittsburgh multi-slide technique. It again worked well and the publicity in the broadsheets the following day was gratifying. Significantly, the comments concentrated on two aspects of transport policy that had occupied much of the time of our Joint Research Committee: high-speed trains and alternatives to the urban use of cars. The Times even produced a leader headed 'The train of the future'. The writer seemed satisfied that we had been justified in seeking special help from the Treasury over the APT. It was too early to know that, in the event, performance would fall short of entirely reasonable expectation.

While there was much in the job that was wholly enjoyable, dark clouds were gathering. During our 1968 summer holiday in Cornwall Jeanie had broken a big toe. We did not think much of it at the time – perhaps she had been careless. In fact, it was a classic medical sign of worse to come. By the end of the year she had no feeling in her legs, and was beginning to worry. Investigations commenced and continued at a steadily increasing pace. On Guy Fawkes' Day 1969 we were at a party organised by Alan Goode who, on safety grounds, had forbidden fireworks and substituted sausages. 'I hope they're not bangers,' Jeanie remarked. But it was not an evening for much light humour. Before she went to bed I had to tell her that the long and short of all the investigations was that she had multiple sclerosis.

It would have been a devastating blow for anyone, but particularly so for her because, over the previous seven years, she had become a skilled studio potter. She was naturally gifted with the attributes for success: manual dexterity, steady hands, a fine eye, a well-formed colour sense, a talent for decoration, and huge determination. Now the underpinning of muscular

271

control was being withdrawn. She wept at the prospect. But before long her character asserted itself and she began to pooh-pooh those who assured her that the illness would be accompanied by a kind of euphoria that would help to make it tolerable. 'Pernicious rubbish. The fact is that if you don't take a positive attitude to life, you're finished!' Her friends looked on admiringly. 'Sheer guts,' said our solicitor from Wallingford, Jack Hedges.

During the months that it took for this terrible news to be confirmed, my position in the Department was eroded as a result of events completely beyond my control. What I had been expecting – what Padmore had led me to believe shortly after my arrival – was that a new Research Council would be set up and that I would, in all probability, run it. 'That should give you the position you want,' said Bill Harris, the Deputy Secretary in charge of road construction. Richard Marsh, who had succeeded Barbara Castle as Minister, was equally encouraging. The uncertainties began when Padmore called me into his office and told me that he had decided to leave the Civil Service early and that Sir David Serpell from the Treasury would be taking over.

The day was memorable for a quite different reason. As we were both going to Whitehall for lunch Padmore offered me a lift. On the way we discussed an interesting conclusion that the Permanent Secretaries – known irreverently as the grey-beards – had just reached. They had been discussing the long-standing issue of whether decimalisation of the currency should be based on the pound or the ten-shilling note. Decimalisation had been successful in Australia and South Africa using ten shillings as the base, without creating any significant inflation. However, the Bank of England and the Treasury both favoured the pound as the basic unit, because of sterling's role as a reserve currency. The National Economic Development Office had warned that the Treasury line would risk creating significant inflation. Each new penny would be worth 2.4 of its predecessors, which would be an open invitation to round prices up. 'There were these conflicting considerations,' said Padmore, 'and we thought about it for a long time. Eventually, one over-riding argument emerged:

272

that the national annual accounts should be comparable year-on-year.' And so the assembled intellectual might of Whitehall decided to recommend to Ministers decimalisation based on the pound, for fear of having to multiply by two! Inflation followed, as NEDO had correctly predicted. It was all of a piece with another Whitehall contribution to inflation, in which a drafting fault in the regulations for inter-bank certificates of deposit led to an explosion in the money supply. So slow was the Conservative government of the day to make a correction that a hard-back text-book discussing the error was already on the bookshelves before any action was taken. Seen from the perspective of ordinary members of the public such avoidable administrative errors provide the strongest reason against automatic inflation-proofed pensions for civil servants – or at least for those working in the Treasury!

Serpell's arrival heralded a sharp change in working practices within the Department. He did not delegate easily. It was as though he wished to examine every corner of what he seemed to fear might be an Augean stable. Suddenly, instead of working one level up from normal, the Under-Secretary layer found itself pushed the other way. In my case there were further worries. Serpell questioned the terms of reference of the Joint Transport Research Committee, my principal power-base. They had been carefully negotiated by my predecessor, with Padmore's blessing, so that both Transport and the Ministry of Technology could feel they shared responsibility for a successful outcome. Serpell disliked divided responsibility for financial matters, even those relating to research and development, small as they were.

Serpell could also hardly fail to notice the competition between some of the economists and my own people, to say nothing of possible clashes with the Road Research Laboratory. He quickly set in train a reorganisation commission under Harry Pitchforth, who had recently left the Treasury to become Controller of HM Stationery Office. Another member of the commission was my Irish friend, Fergus Allen, who was making a name for himself in the Cabinet Office. He later became First Civil Service

Commissioner, in which capacity he survived a mercifully botched IRA letter-bomb attack.

Indications that all would not be plain sailing came quickly. When I met the Commission, Pitchforth asked whether there should be a 'Great Panjandrum', in charge of all the professionals.

'Where would you find such a paragon?' asked HP.

'How does a Permanent Secretary cope?' I countered.

'The job would be more difficult,' said HP.

I refrained from remarking that in that case the post should command Permanent Secretary rates, or higher.

Serpell too had doubts whether one professional could grasp all that would come his way.

'He would be the conductor of an orchestra,' I told him.

'I see,' said Serpell. 'He need not play the oboe himself.'

And with that exchange I unwittingly gave him the green light to place a non-professional generalist, an administrator, in charge of the Department's research.

After a couple of months the Commission decided, not surprisingly, that all the scientists and economists should be brigaded under one Director-General. Foster and I eyed each other warily; it was quite clear that competition for the job would be intense. Although I did not relish the thought, I realised that in such circumstances it would be difficult for any of the existing incumbents to be given preferment. Nevertheless, I lived in hope.

I was not, however, prepared for the news that Serpell gave me on my return from summer leave in Connemara in 1969. He told me that, although I had 'remained in contention until a very late stage', the appointment had gone to John Jukes. His previous appointment was at an end, owing to the imminent abolition of the Department of Economic Affairs, and he now needed redeployment. When I heard the news I was unable to stop myself blurting out, 'Oh God!' Serpell was surprised and asked for an explanation. I told him how ten years earlier I had crossed swords with the Atomic Energy economists over a projected nuclear merchant ship. I had criticised the unreal economic assumptions that lay behind the Atomic Energy

274

Authority's enthusiasm for such a project. Furthermore, a few years later I had rescued John Wright and taken him into the Ministry of Defence when he had found working in Jukes's team difficult. I was now to discover for myself why Wright had so insistently asked for a transfer.

Jukes was clearly delighted with his new job: 'I just happened to fit.' Guidance he gave none. He was likeable enough socially, but committed the unpardonable error of withholding information from his underlings. Within eighteen months of his arrival Transport had lost both Foster and myself.

On the positive side I was to be allowed to keep the title Chief Scientific Adviser, which so far as the outside world was concerned still counted for something. Foster's Mathematical Advisory Unit, one of his major creations, was also to be transferred to me. This softened the blow, but I felt I no longer had a mission – merely a job. A colleague advised me to 'learn how to shrug'. Without much enthusiasm I set about surviving while I identified some other opening. I began to think about leaving the public service on my fiftieth birthday, which would mean tolerating the new regime for sixteen months. It was the earliest date at which I could 'cold-store' my pension.

The prospect facing me was two children who would both need financing at university and a wife who would need an unknown amount of care and money if she were to be properly supported. I spoke again to Monty Finniston, who stressed that there was a worthwhile life to be had outside the Civil Service. That decided me and I followed his suggestion of contacting Peter Matthews, who had recently moved from the Steel Corporation to be Chief Executive of the ailing Vickers Corporation, whose decline the big investment institutions were hoping to halt. Matthews responded favourably and, in the early autumn of 1970, at a meeting with the Chairman of Vickers, I was offered a job as Director of Development and Planning. I noted in my diary: 'I walked to the lift wanting to shout for joy. It had been like a sauna after the claustrophobic atmosphere of St Christopher House.'

To a civil servant the prospects seemed mouthwatering: a chauffered car, a considerably higher salary, and an office at the top of the Millbank Tower looking down on Whitehall and my former colleagues. I pondered a little about working for the first time under a younger man, but the die was cast. On 29 September 1970 I resigned, my departure to take effect three months later on the day after my fiftieth birthday. When I saw Serpell to hand him my resignation letter he seemed genuinely upset, but in a few sentences showed how well he knew human nature. 'You were abstracted at lunch-time.' He took more than a day to respond – he had been checking that there was no alternative. 'Purely selfish,' he explained when I thanked him, adding, 'I should not like you to think that there was not the greatest understanding of the position in which you find yourself.' In this, and in later encounters, he offered me a generous farewell.

In the three months left while I worked out my period of notice I took the only possible course and did whatever I could to ensure that further impending organisational changes would be as successful as possible. Transport was to be merged with Housing, to form the long-foreshadowed Department of the Environment. For two months I was its first CSA. Jim Jones had served in both constituent ministries and was now to be given greatly expanded responsibilities.

'How am I to get ideas?' he asked.

I replied, 'By putting human beings in situations where they will be excited.'

It was encouraging that he not only saw the point, but also had the drive to do something about it.

My last major meeting in the Department was a presentation of their corporate plan by the British Rail Board to John Peyton, the Minister for Transport Industries. One senior colleague thought it improper that I should attend because I was leaving for private industry and might, theoretically, gain some competitive advantage. Certain that there would be not even a scintilla of conflict of interest I insisted on being part of the ministerial retinue.

A principal issue was signalling for the Southern Region. The BR spokesman explained that it was their policy to run trains from as many suburban stations as possible to both east and west London termini. This involved complicated interconnecting train movements, which depended on having a reliable and efficient signalling system. The existing system was wearing out. BR was therefore holding out its hand, hoping the Minister would provide the necessary £300 million.

Having worked in Southwark for the past three years I was aware that the railway embankment between London Bridge and Waterloo had the effect of sterilising development along the hinterland of the South Bank. If it could be removed, the way would be open for major improvements throughout the area. I also remembered Ralph Bennett's comment about operating the London Underground, made while he was Chairman of the London Transport Board. 'There is no problem at all,' he told me, 'about most of the lines: the trains simply run up and down... It is when there are conflicting movements that difficulties arise – as where the Circle has to share lines with the District railway in Kensington, or at Earl's Court. Then, if there is any disturbance, it tends to grow until it can get out of hand ... if you want a railway that will run day in, day out, keep it simple.'

With this in mind I questioned the speaker about the underlying policy of serving both east and west London termini. I suggested that there may be an attractive alternative: to offer services to only one terminal, and put in a new east-west underground link? It need be no longer than about four miles, and could be paid for by property deals made possible by the removal of the embankment. My words were met with stony silence. Afterwards, over drinks, I spoke again to David McKenna of the BR Board. He was a great lover of the arts, was on the board of Sadlers Wells Opera, and always wore a flower in his buttonhole. He hoped I would not persist with the proposal '...because it is only the complexities of our operations that keep us railwaymen on our toes'. More than thirty years later the embankment still disfigures London south of the Thames, and noisy trains still clatter across Hungerford Bridge.

I celebrated my departure with a short skiing holiday in Villars with Jacques and Annie Haas. Jacques, who was then a Colonel in the French Air Force – he later became a General – had been a close friend since my early days in Defence. Moreover, his wife was an excellent pianist, with whom I enjoyed playing duets. I returned to Whitehall in robust good health for the final farewells.

I called on Zuckerman. He said: 'No-one is glad at your going.' He then told me he was going too. 'I've had enough. One thing has killed me: Fulton. Without that I could have succeeded. The Civil Service Department does it all, and so badly.' Clearly he thought that the administrators had 'fixed' the Fulton report on Civil Service reorganisation so that they themselves would not be disadvantaged and that the more level playing-field for scientists that he had hoped and worked for would remain an unfulfilled dream. For me the irony was that it was the Fulton review that he had deployed as an argument when persuading me to take the Transport job rather than go to British Steel.

I entered the doors of my old Department only once more, for a farewell drinks party. I found it a tense occasion, despite Serpell's kind words. Johnny Moore, the Establishments Officer, advised me not to look back with regret: 'The ranks will close...' He had been one of those urging me to remember I would be unlikely ever to have such an interesting job again. He had not intended to wound, but I was already finding that the contrast between Vickers and the Ministry of Transport administrators was unnerving. The womb I was about to leave had been so very cosy – before the reorganisation. My own staff were staying on and we wished each other luck. Eric Williams, my predecessor, also came. After the others left he produced a bottle of whisky, and together we mulled over the results of several years of our joint efforts – some useful, some frankly disappointing. Before we said goodbye, around midnight, the bottle was almost empty.

Twenty years later, I had one more professional contact with transport problems. I was invited to make a survey of the transport scene for the Major Projects Association, which gave me every assistance, including a strong working group of experts. The review led to an inescapable sense of *déja-vu*. Almost every point had already been examined in my days at the MOT. Unlike aviation, surface transport is not a subject where things change quickly, political difficulties never being very far away. As Bacon had observed three centuries earlier in his essay, 'Of Innovations':

Whatsoever is new is unlooked for; he that is holpen takes it for a fortune and thanks the time; and he that is hurt, for a wrong, and imputeth it to the author... it is good also not to try experiments, except the necessity be urgent, or the utility evident.

If I and my fellow bureaucrats in Transport in the 1960s were seriously wrong it was in ignoring Bacon's advice and in believing that changes in transport technology could proceed faster than was technically and politically realistic. It was not until 2004 that the first fast walkway was installed, after months of trials, at the Montparnasse underground station in Paris. Even though its speed was less than 6 m.p.h., of the first 50,000 passengers no less than 40 were seen to fall when dismounting. Nor have driverless transport systems swept the board: our 1990 survey identified only 27 systems worldwide. Practical difficulties have held them back – not least how to deal with the inevitable breakdowns in the absence of any responsible official on the spot. The car has remained dominant.

However, in the spring of 2003 the Mayor of London, Ken Livingstone, took advantage of the ever-increasing power of computers to introduce a radically new toll system in central London. It relied on the automatic reading of vehicle number plates, backed up by swingeing penalties for failure to observe the rules. There was an immediate and striking decrease, by about 30%, in the delays caused by traffic congestion. There was none of the forecast public outcry against this slight constraint on personal freedom. The public knew that the time had come to seek the aid of market forces; and for the first time information technology was sufficiently robust and versatile to provide the means.

Chapter 16

Private Industry

I joined Vickers on 19 January 1971, taking the usual train and travelling as before with my former Whitehall colleagues. A chauffeur-driven car was waiting for me at Marylebone. I climbed into it with slight embarrassment and entered a different world. My large office was on the 29th floor of the Millbank Tower, which Vickers then owned. It was sumptuously provided with a suite of Napoleon III Empire furniture that had once belonged to Sir Basil Zaharoff, the great armourer on whom Shaw modelled Andrew Undershaft in his play, *Major Barbara*. Its windows were on a level with the dial of Big Ben and looked up Whitehall almost to Trafalgar Square. There could have been no greater contrast to the architectural and decorative mediocrity I had left behind in St Christopher House.

By a happy chance I had already worked in the Ministry of Defence with Richard Gibbons, who was to be my closest colleague. He now led a small market research team that answered to me. He was also my mentor, and it was as well that a friend was taking this role, for it was only after my arrival that I began to realise just how little I knew about the ways of industry. For a quarter of a century I had been rubbing shoulders with great engineering firms involved with nuclear or defence equipment. It was only now that I had to concern myself for the first time with how manufacturers managed to stay solvent and invest for the future.

The firm I had just joined was an engineering conglomerate with an extraordinarily wide range of products: nuclear submarines, gliders, printing machines, printing plates, huge cranes for handling containers at ports, office copiers, medical equipment, microscopes, cement-making plant, postal sorting equipment, automatic warehousing, main battle tanks and, in time, cars. But for all Vickers' undoubted metal-forming skills profitability was modest. Far too much activity came from subcontracting to other people's designs, or building under licence with prices driven down by the licensor to an absolute minimum. The lack of internal synergy meant that Group headquarters presided only with difficulty over the disparate operating companies.

The markets on which Vickers had built its reputation were changing faster than the company could react. As shipbuilders the firm had enjoyed a worldwide reputation. But the market for merchant ships was in decline, and the day of the large passenger liner was almost done as long-range aircraft began to take over. There were still cruise ships to be built, but foreign competition was crippling. The Barrow shipyard, with its tradition of naval construction, fortunately had a ready-made cushion in the new generation of nuclear submarines. For this reason Leonard Redshaw, who ran it outstandingly well, knew that his was one of the few parts of the company that could look forward to an assured future, albeit one on a more modest scale than in the past. But another of the Group's operating companies, Roneo, whose name was almost a household word, was being rapidly sidelined by a new generation of copiers based on xerography and electronics. The aircraft division that had developed the successful Viscount and VC10 airliners, and that had once provided a nursery for technologists capable of modernising the rest of the product range, had been lost to the company a decade earlier when it had become part of the newly-created British Aircraft Corporation. At Newcastle a whole community had depended on Vickers, whose Riverside Shops stretched along the north bank of the Tyne for almost a mile. Two decades of something approximating to world-wide peace had savagely

282

reduced the market for heavy armaments. Moreover, there was not only strong foreign competition, but also further domestic competition from the government's own Royal Ordnance Factories, which occupied pole position in any scramble for British orders. As the shops at Elswick and Scotswood became emptier, Newcastle was faced with the social consequences of large-scale unemployment.

The general political and economic background was also unpropitious. I had arrived at a time of extraordinary difficulty for manufacturing industry. The unions were flexing their muscles, with the postal workers asking for a wage increase of 20%. Within a year, at the beginnning of 1972, the miners went on strike. The following month there were electricity blackouts, leading, in February 1972, to the proclamation of a state of emergency and the institution of a three-day working week. Northern Ireland was in turmoil following thirteen deaths on Bloody Sunday. A freeze on wages, prices, dividends and rents was instituted in November 1972. The following year saw a continuation of these industrial troubles. Towards the end of that year a further emergency was proclaimed as power workers struck, adding to the problems manufacturing industry was already experiencing as a result of the Yom Kippur Arab-Israeli war. Oil supplies were affected; prices rose; serious inflation was in prospect. The Heath government brought in measures to control inflation, including a legal limitation on wage increases. This cut short negotiations by the mineworkers. The result was that by November there was a union ban on overtime working in the pits. On the first day of 1974 Heath imposed a three-day working week to save fuel. The situation deteriorated still further and, within a few weeks, the government called a General Election to settle who ruled the country – and lost. Labour was returned to office and bought off the miners with a 35% wage increase.

Against this disheartening background all that industry could do for more than two long years was to batten down the hatches, live frugally and hope for better days. I could hardly have chosen a more difficult time to apprentice myself to long-term industrial planning; short-term survival was all that counted.

Personnel policy was an early casualty. The Vickers apprentice-ship scheme, which had produced generations of British engineers of the highest quality, was axed on the comforting but specious excuse that, with the expansion of the universities following the Robbins Report, government could now be trusted to do an equivalent job. The Barrow shipyard which, like the lost aircraft division, also dealt in high technology and which could therefore have seeded the rest of the company with highly competent engineers and technicians, was effectively sealed off by its management's refusal to allow vacancy notices from other Vickers companies to appear on its notice-boards.

Low profitability meant that funds for research and development were limited and thinly spread. There was a small central research establishment (VRE) under a first-class scientist, Bareford, who had been considerably senior to me at Admiralty Signal Establishment during the war. When he retired I was given headquarters responsibility for VRE, without being able to contribute much to its success. Its links with the operating companies were not as close as they should have been, through no fault of the research establishment. For their part the operating companies must have wondered how our modest central unit could possibly make a significant contribution to their own extraordinarily diverse activities.

In the circumstances it was acquisitions, not research, that held the attention of the company. However, there was no accepted routine for weighing the options that were continually presenting themselves, nor for balancing the costs of acquisition against the kind of internal 'incremental' development that was serving Japan so well. This situation left little scope for constructive headquarters activity, except on the part of the Chief Executive. The heads of the operating groups saw how the land lay and dealt only with him. All in all, Vickers exhibited much of what was wrong at the time with British industry generally: the company was over-extended, insufficiently analytical and insufficiently focused.

Vickers had not yet been dropped from the Stock Exchange indices, but the City institutions – the big investment houses – had made it clear that they wanted a new management to protect their assets. That was why Peter Matthews – 'PAM' – had been brought in from the steel industry. I was one of several recent recruits to headquarters. What I did not know, and was not told for almost two years, was that my arrival had not been welcomed by Len Redshaw. He knew that his profits were a mainspring of the whole Group and wanted no headquarters Director of Planning and Development telling him how to run his affairs. I doubt whether any animus was directed against me personally and he was always polite when we met, but he did once indicate, when another civil servant was proposed as a recruit, that he would be coming 'from the wrong stable'.

His opposition might well have been the reason why I was not offered a seat on the main board. That had not been one of my worries before joining because, in the Civil Service, I had been used to influence being devolved at least three layers down from the top. I soon discovered that in Vickers power was confined to the very top layer, of which I was not a part.

Although not on the main board I was at least on the Managing Director's Committee. It was wholly advisory, and PAM accepted or rejected our proposals as he thought fit. I did not always understand how he reached his conclusions; the habit of logical argument that had made life in the Higher Civil Service so intellectually satisfying was often missing. It was his overriding ambition to buy the Rolls-Royce motor company, for reasons that seemed to have less to do with finance than with prestige and image. Eventually he succeeded.

The corporation's essentially feudal culture had one consequence that verged on the ridiculous. At the South Marston works in Swindon there were several levels of canteen, each hierarchically differentiated from the others. If a move was planned for a worker or manager, before he would agree he would wish to know where he would be eating. Such a culture could not have been more different from what existed in progressive, high-

285

growth companies like the Texas Corporation in America, where every worker had the right to communicate with the Chief Executive Officer. I knew that Vickers was shooting itself in the foot by not dispensing with these outmoded practices, but did not see how to bring about change. Despite all the pampering that went with the job – higher salary, subsidised car, chauffeur at the station in the morning, cordon bleu cooking at lunchtime, a company aircraft to ease travelling to the north of England – it did not take me many months to decide that working for Vickers added up to a less than wholly satisfying existence.

Nevertheless, there was much of interest and much to learn. In one respect Vickers under Matthews strikingly outshone Whitehall: decision-making was braver and quicker than in the Civil Service. If past mistakes needed correction there was no wringing of hands over loss of face or money. The necessary steps were taken and no time was wasted over regrets. But I could not help reflecting that some of the company's problems at the time might have arisen from its past approach to the handling of information – something that the Whitehall machine did incomparably better.

I discussed my doubts and anxieties with the man in charge of the Group's public relations, Sir Harold Evans. We had quickly become friends. He was most congenial and shared some of my Whitehall background, having been Harold Macmillan's press officer at Number 10. Not long after my arrival he told me that he too had come with high hopes, but had found mediocrity in what had once been a great company. I could not help contrasting what I was discovering with earlier impressions of a direct competitor from Germany, the Kraus-Maffei company, which I had visited while at the Ministry of Defence. Like Vickers it dealt in armaments, including main battle tanks. Its directors were not only superb engineers, but also had an intellectual cutting-edge that would have graced a university chair.

Although I feared I had made an error in leaving government service for Vickers, there was no way back. But at least I had a three-year rolling 'evergreen' contract, which meant that there were no immediate financial worries. None, indeed, to hold me back any longer from achieving a life-long ambition to learn to fly. I had done a couple of hours in Tiger Moths in the University Air Squadron and a good deal of light aircraft travel during the war as a naval scientist. That was all thirty years earlier, however, but at least I knew what was involved.

On presenting myself at the Wycombe Air Centre I was introduced to the man who would be my instructor. We greeted each other as old friends. It was 'Mac' – Ian Macdonald – who had been my pilot on many wartime visits to naval air stations. Learning with him was the happiest of master-pupil relationships. Before long I went solo on a beautiful, calm evening in May 1972, during a lull after a black-clouded, stormy day. I came home to a surprised and relieved Jeanie who – not having personally experienced the constant emphasis on safety that underlies every aspect of pilot training – had convinced herself that she was already a widow. Six months later I received my private pilot's licence. Soon afterwards, while holidaying in Cyprus, we hired a small Cessna and explored the island from the air. It is not every day that one can look down and see Othello's tower in the Turkish quarter of Famagusta for the first time. A governor of the city, Christoforo Moro, is thought to have been the model for Shakespeare's hero.

The job had other compensations, the most significant being Peter Matthews' willingness to let me spread my wings in the wider world outside the company, provided that in doing so I promoted the name of Vickers. He agreed, for instance, to allow me to act as chairman of a course on administrative aspects of science in government at the Civil Service College in May 1972. I was interested to find that although there were two French government officials amongst the students, there were no British industrialists. The schism between the British public and private sectors that had troubled me in the Ministry of Transport was evidently alive and well.

I also gave Zuckerman some help in arranging a symposium

on the political consequences of the motor car. I put together a suggested programme while staying at an alpine hotel in Davos, where there was not an internal combustion engine to be heard. Zuckerman accepted the proposals and the symposium was held at the University of East Anglia. A book followed – *Social and Political Consequences of the Motor Car*. It provided what is still a valid conspectus of the huge social changes created by the arrival of cheap motoring.

I was in Davos to attend the second of the annual economic conferences that have since become an established feature of business life. It was the only time I ever went to work on skis. There were the usual 'motherhood' speeches from statesmen and leading industrialists, but what struck me most was the way the EEC's spokesmen were already assuming that a common European currency was just around the corner. They spoke optimistically of completion in 1980, but gave no acknowledgement of what this would entail for the financial machinery of national governments, or for their national sovereignty. This convenient myopia was what first alerted me to the duplicity that lies so often at the heart of the Brussels machine.

The Top Salaries Review Board, which was studying the differences between Whitehall and private industry, invited me to give evidence. In comparing the role of Managing Director with that of Permanent Secretary I said that the MD had a higher level of personal responsibility, a smaller spread of interest, much higher career risks, less able subordinates in general, somewhat greater freedom, fewer holidays, and some 'perks' – though not as many as popularly supposed. The MD was very much exposed to the jobs market; the Permanent Secretary was not – at least not in the same way. Because of these differences it would be misleading for the Civil Service to argue strongly for financial comparability with private industry.

I also did some writing for the *Financial Times*. With astonishing temerity I contributed a piece on Management Science after only nine months in the job. More sensibly, there was another piece on medical engineering, which for a time seemed a possible growth point for Vickers, until financial pressures forced its abandonment.

The most substantial of these extra-mural forays was a series of four broadcasts on the BBC Third Programme in the summer of 1972. They drew on what I was learning about the industrial scene. Living daily with the problems of manufacturing industry, I had begun to make contact with people who were similarly concerned. One was Theo Williamson, whom I met in the autumn of 1971 at a Fabian Society meeting on Science Policy. He was a brilliant electrical engineer, who had the unusual distinction of holding an honorary doctorate of science from Edinburgh, plus a Fellowship of the Royal Society, while being minus a first degree – as an undergraduate he had failed a mandatory paper. He and the National Economic Development Office had recently published a seminal booklet, entitled *Trade Balance in the 1970s – the role of Mechanical Engineering*, in which he documented how British manufacturing exports were falling, while imports were rising. He predicted that these trends, if continued, would mean that the balance of payments in engineering, instead of being comfortably in surplus and contributing one-third of our national net exports, would, by the early 1980s, become negative. I knew from other contacts that his conclusions were being rubbished by at least one Deputy Secretary in the Department of Trade and Industry. 'Williamson is wrong.' Unfortunately for the country, he was precisely right. I resolved to do what I could to help him.

I had already been thinking on similar lines. Soon after arriving in Millbank I had been struck by the difference in attitudes between the public and the private sectors. In Whitehall things could be very 'broad-brush'. In industry details mattered much more. Whitehall could impose a new tax of a few per cent almost as a matter of routine; but those few per cent could take away the whole of an industry's profit margin. The government was toying with the introduction of a new Value-Added Tax, a most cumbersome affair that, apart from the Inland Revenue, would benefit only accountants. I wrote a long piece for Peter

Matthews to use in his contacts with government entitled 'Government action to stimulate the economy', arguing strongly against the introduction of VAT. But even though Vickers was still a major economic player I do not recall the courtesy of any response from the Civil Service.

I decided to use an invitation from the BBC as an opportunity for constructive argument. The invitation was for me to take part in the *Personal View* series of talks. It had fortuitously arisen from my earlier participation in an experimental crisis management programme organised for the BBC about a year earlier by Ian Smart, an old friend from Defence days. It was never broadcast, its scenario having by sheer bad luck been deemed by the BBC management to be too close for comfort to an unforeseen real-life Middle East crisis that blew up immediately afterwards, before the programme could be transmitted. The producer, Roland Challis, was also responsible for other current affairs programmes, including *Personal View* – a fortnightly series of twenty-minute talks during the intervals of Promenade concerts. His brief to me stressed the importance of topicality and, above all, argument. As these were inevitably serious programmes the opening sentences were all-important if listeners were not to switch off. The actual speaking time was eighteen minutes. I was astonished to discover how hard it can be to launch and sustain an interesting argument for that length of time. Compared with television, radio is a very concentrated medium. Topicality was ensured by broadcasting 'live', with a final revision two hours before transmission to work in any last-minute snippets of news that might seem relevant. At the beginning of one broadcast, while the red light was flashing its warning, I heard with special interest the final moments of a concert conducted by Stephen Wilkinson, who had been organ scholar in my first year at Queens'.

The first *Personal View* set out the problem of falling exports that Theo had identified, against the political background of a trades union movement that was out of control and a government that was facing the permanently intractable problems of funding defence, education, transport, health, and law and order. Part of the diagnosis was that the country had provided all manner of comfortable jobs for our best minds, particularly in the new universities, while industry was being starved of talent. The result was a national product range that the foreigner was no longer rushing to buy. We needed more of the country's intellectual cream in places like Vickers. As a nation we had spent too much energy arguing with the unions how the national cake should be divided, too little on how it should be baked.

Immediately after the broadcast Theo telephoned me with obvious enthusiasm. But when I next lunched with Jim Hendin, who ran Vickers Engineering Division, he remarked a trifle testily that I did not seem to think that our colleagues were good enough. I had not meant my words to be taken either personally or in that sense; I was describing a systemic trend that was affecting our national economic performance. My hope was that, in future, people like Hendin might have a wider choice when recruiting their staff. However, my subsequent problems probably began with that broadcast.

Through Theo I met others similarly imbued with a missionary spirit, including John Safford, who soon afterwards invited me to chair a Sector Working Party for the National Economic Development Office.

Listening again to the tapes I realise that the first broadcast was more than a little stilted – I was still at heart a civil servant, reluctant to argue strongly in public. But as the series progressed I began to feel emancipated, as was already evident in the second broadcast. I used as a peg a report on science policy just published by Lord Rothschild, who ran the Central Policy Review Staff in the Cabinet Office. There was an immediate response from His Lordship, who asked if I could be more specific about a 'philosophical' point. I had said I was unhappy about a situation in which we appeared to be content, at the national level, to operate an enormous applied research programme without a specifically stated set of objectives. I told him that on going from Defence to Transport I had been struck by how cheap surface transport development was compared with aviation, but that Transport was one of the 'have nots', and we had never succeeded in getting our hands on the necessary money, partly because Concorde was gobbling up so many resources. Its total operational fleet of only sixteen aircraft underlined the point. I reminded him how the Official Committee on Science and Technology had tried to make a case for a radical realignment of R&D expenditure, and how all their efforts had been discarded when the Conservatives came to power with their doctrine of disengagement. Rothschild invited me to his sumptuous flat in St James's Place, facing Green Park, and we discussed these matters over an evening drink.

Of all these extra-mural activities the one that, in retrospect, gives me the greatest satisfaction was a short talk I gave at the British Association's meeting at Swansea in 1971. It was a contribution to a discussion on Conflicts of Loyalty in Science. I struggled for three weeks to produce a text, but whatever I wrote seemed boring and turgid. Three days before the meeting I was beginning to panic but, while I was taking a shower, a completely new draft suddenly and spontaneously flashed into my mind. It neatly encapsulated everything I wished to say. Shouting 'Eureka!' I sat down at my desk and, a couple of hours later, the job was done. It was a striking example of how the unconscious mind is always there, cleaning up the memory files and working quite independently of any consciously expressed thoughts. *Nature* kindly published the text.

One of my points was that I personally had not experienced intellectual conflict of the kind that other speakers claimed to have known. What I had found was that at the highest levels of political decision-making it was the problems themselves that were intrinsically difficult – if they were not they should have been settled lower down. By way of example I went on to observe that the more I had become familiar with disarmament issues, the less I had felt able to share the certainty of the Aldermaston marchers, admirable people as they doubtless were. Yet they were not wholly without influence; it might have been partly due to their conviction that something should be done that it had been possible to have a serious and, on the whole, reasonably convincing discussion within Whitehall.

I should have known that the Press would seize upon such a passage. *The Guardian*, under a headline, 'Scientists complain of being muzzled', attributed to me a statement to the effect that the Aldermaston marches had led to a reappraisal of nuclear policy in Whitehall. *The Times* took much the same line: 'Aldermaston marches swayed high Whitehall scientific opinion on nuclear policies'. That went beyond what I was implying. The lesson must be to avoid wherever possible any over-subtle nuances when speaking in public.

In the spring of 1972 it became clear that the Vickers subsidiary making printing machinery was in considerable technical and financial trouble. As a result the Chairman, Lord Robens, and I carried out an enquiry, which led directly to the departure of one senior member of the old Group Board. Robens had joined the company shortly after I arrived, another of the appointments made at the behest of the City institutions. For one with such a national reputation he proved surprisingly approachable. This for him was a point of principle. If anyone went to see him in his office, he would move from behind his desk and sit so that there was no obstruction between him and his visitor.

In January 1973 Matthews went away for a five-week round-the-world trip. The effect of his absence was immediately noticeable. Activity at headquarters, never at a very high level, fell almost to zero. I personally found myself with so little to do that I started to think about leaving and even went as far as collecting the names of suitable head-hunters. Then, by chance, Lord Robens saw me in connection with a meeting I had had at his suggestion with Dick Taverne, who had been a junior Labour minister. Robens wanted me to flesh out some of the things I had said in my recent broadcasts. Having heard how the meeting had gone, Robens then asked how Vickers' printing machinery division was faring. I replied that the new management was doing quite well, but went on to mention some recent difficulties.

This was the first the Chairman had heard of them. He suggested that while Peter Matthews was away it would be useful for the headquarters directors to set out their collective views.

When I followed Robens' advice and sounded out my senior colleagues there was general agreement about what was wrong, rather less about what should be done. The upshot was that I drafted a document that was perhaps more abrasive than was expedient. It was intended for Head Office eyes only but, in the event, it was leaked to the operating units. The result was that the apparently constructive atmosphere of our meetings suddenly broke down. One of my colleagues – who had himself contributed to the discussions – developed strong personal doubts and said he must telephone Matthews, his 'best friend.' I, with others, tried to persuade him not to do so; if our discussions were to get anywhere they needed to be conducted coolly. I went off on a visit to Europe for a few days, not without first offering Robens my resignation if the situation warranted it. He refused, saying it was right to set down one's views and have them discussed. If an incompatibility developed that would be a different situation, but first one had to say what one thought – and so it was left.

I returned from Europe on 21 February; Matthews came back the following day. He was apprised of the situation by his friend and met all the headquarters directors a day later to consider my paper. He asked whether I was speaking for the whole headquarters, or merely putting forward a personal view. I could see anxious faces round the table. I suddenly had a strong aversion to working any longer with this team, so I burned my boats and replied that I was speaking for myself. The colleague who had alerted him leant forward and said that it seemed to be an interesting paper and that he would like to peruse it – he who had contributed to its drafting and who had already had it in his possession for several days! Nevertheless, when the meeting broke up most of us thought that a good start had been made. Matthews had conceded that there were points needing consideration and had suggested that we start with personnel policy. The temperature had been kept low and he appeared to respect the reasons for preparing the paper. For a few days nothing happened. Then it became obvious that something had gone completely wrong. Matthews had discussed personnel policy with someone who was not a headquarters director and who thought, wrongly, that he was being criticised. From that moment everything slid out of control. I parted company with Vickers on 23 March 1973.

I sought out my predecessor, Ivor Coates, whom I had not previously met. Over lunch we compared notes. His diagnosis had been closely similar to my own. With some irony he commented that the main difference between us was that he had been shown the door at one hour's notice. I ran into another ex-Vickers man many years later whose experience had also paralleled my own. Such encounters helped a little to repair the self-esteem which had been badly dented.

At Peter Matthews' suggestion the terms of the financial settlement were placed in the hands of third parties. I chose Richard Harvey of Slaughter and May ('...couldn't do better,' said Matthews) and was so pleased with his unruffleable competence that I used him as corporate legal adviser in my next job. My contract brought in a useful sum – sufficient to live on for a couple of years. But what thereafter? It was months before the unfamiliar task of job-hunting came to an end. But all was not loss – in the process I found new friends, and my enforced and unsought leisure gave me, for the first time, a chance to explore the world of political activism.

Chapter 17

Job Hunting

'To make an end is to make a beginning.' So I found. The year following my departure from Vickers was like no other, before or since. I could no longer count on a monthly salary; a solution had to be found before my capital ran out. Nor was there any automatic flow of tasks and problems to provide intellectual stimulus. For the first time in my life everything, without exception, depended on my own unaided efforts. The truth of the ancient Greek dictum – 'work is the way man articulates with society' – was daily borne in on me. When the British Chancellor, Norman Lamont, made his fatuous remark after the 1993 exchange rate fiasco – 'unemployment is a price well worth paying' – I prayed that he too would one day have the spiritual benefit of experiencing it at first hand, as I had done twenty years earlier.

Finding a slot that I would fit would inevitably take time. My career profile was too unusual and I was too senior for any run-of-the-mill job. In any case the economy was in deep depression, with inflation rampant – it reached 25% in 1974. Industry was scraping to save every penny and few companies regarded research or long-term planning as priority items. I explored dozens of possibilities, but had only a handful of tentative offers. They included one to develop and promote a new brain-scanner but, although technically challenging and medically significant, it was too narrowly focused to be exciting. In any case, my days as a technician were almost done; physics was passing on and leaving me behind.

The only viable way of keeping afloat until a worthwhile job turned up was to grasp every opportunity that friends, former colleagues, professional contacts and events might offer. It was essential to circulate. Consequently, whatever else might be said about this period of redeployment, life certainly did not lack variety.

The first to launch a lifeboat was Roger Eddison, whom I knew through my interest in operational research. He was an impressive and very gentle man, similar in build and voice to his distinguished actor brother, Robert. With his partner, Henri Novy, he ran a small business consultancy, with offices only a few miles from my own home. Henri was Belgian by birth and during World War II had been a courier for the Belgian resistance. He possibly held the record for the shortest time between taking his final university paper and receiving his degree: forty-five minutes. The Germans were at the door so, after bowing to the Vice-Chancellor, his next duty was to escape to safer ground. Now settled in England, he had built up a wide circle of business contacts, which he placed at my disposal. But the partnership was too small to attract consultancy offers without a deal of 'prospection' and selling. This I disliked, not least for the expenditure of time. In the end, all the consultancy tasks that kept the wolf from the door came about quite naturally from my own personal contacts. Nevertheless, it was comforting to have Roger's and Henri's experience to lean on, and to have the use of their offices.

Operational research contacts quickly brought in a job to appraise the prospects of a small merchant bank specialising in hire-purchase. It was a business where high rates of interest could be charged, allowing the bank to borrow at somewhat lower, but still relatively high, rates on the overnight and short-term markets and yet make a profit. However, given the economic downturn there was no guarantee that such an uncertain source of funding would continue to be available on the scale needed for even one year ahead, whereas hire-purchase loans might be for as long as three years. Borrowing short and lending long contravenes all normally accepted rules of banking prudence and the directors were understandably uneasy. I had no magic solution to offer, but played the classic role of the management consultant – to set down, from the standpoint of someone with no personal axe to grind, the salient facts which many in the company already knew but had failed to address. Whether what I had to say about strategy was useful I shall never know. But at least the bank did not go under; indeed, its name still survived a quarter of a century later.

For me the most vivid memory of that assignment is of an evening when I had been working late. I left about 8.00p.m., intending to drive away in my small car parked outside (in the early seventies one could still park in the street all day without charge in the quieter parts of the City). Mine was the only car visible. The street had been cordoned off by the police. I asked why.

'That DAF has a bomb in it.'

'How do you know?'

'Because there's a brief-case.'

Absurd! To the fascination of a small knot of onlookers I ducked under the tape, opened the car and drove off.

A consultancy more in line with my experience was a study in 1974 for the National Economic Development Office. It was to be a quick appraisal of the likely effects on the British aviation industry of the huge increase in the cost of petroleum that was taking place following the Yom Kippur war, which had begun a few months earlier on the 6 October 1973. At the time of the study the (duty-free) cost of aviation fuel was expected to treble in little more than eighteen months. Even a doubling of fuel costs would increase passenger fares by 15%. Over and above this direct effect there would be the longer-term consequences of the worldwide inflation that the fuel price increase was already inducing.

The effects on the economics of the fuel-thirsty Concorde

project would be even greater. The aircraft had already flown in the spring of 1969, but it was still two years short of showing its commercial paces. Meanwhile, almost ten thousand people were employed on its development – nearer twenty thousand if all subcontractors were counted. A cancellation with consequences on that scale, at a time of massive recession, was politically almost impossible to contemplate. In any case, high commercial hopes were pinned on the great dart-shaped bird. The sale of as many as four hundred had been projected before the oil price rise. So Concorde continued, to become a technical triumph but a commercial failure – only sixteen were ever operated.

One of the minor delights of holding senior office had been a steady flow of invitations to lecture, and write articles – pontificating to a receptive audience is one of the basic urges of the self-respecting male. That stimulus was now cut off, unless through my own personal efforts I could restore it. This proved not too difficult and, throughout the long months of relocation, this activity did much to maintain my morale. The *Financial Times* published a piece on planning. For British Petroleum I gave a series of lectures at Cambridge dealing with energy and the economic outlook. The venue was close to Oakington, an RAF airfield I had last visited thirty years earlier as an undergraduate member of the University Air Squadron. In February 1974 I seized the chance of doing the journey by air, using my beloved Jodel aircraft G-ATJN – Juliet November.

I had bought the little French-built two-seater in the spring of 1973, shortly before life had been turned on its head. Structurally JN was simplicity itself. There was not even a self-starter; one swung the propeller by hand. There was little to go wrong and JN was almost always serviceable. There was no better therapy, after the sour taste of Vickers, than to take off from Wycombe and fly to the Cotswolds or the coast. All potential adversaries appeared insignificant when viewed from one thousand feet. Moreover, the attention to detail needed for safe piloting meant that little of the brain was left free to worry about where the next pennies might come from.

So I used JN whenever possible, even though that was more expensive and often slower as regards overall journey time than the car. Jeanie came with me to Lands End to join our daughter, Nicky, for a few days' break; and to Edinburgh, where Jeremy was an undergraduate. With my diplomat friend, Peter Smart, I 'went foreign' to Le Touquet and Berck – where my query about overnight hangarage fees was met charmingly with 'rien qu'un sourire, monsieur'. And early one spring morning I took Juliet November to Shoreham, on my way to lecture at Sussex University. The valleys were still covered in mist as the sun rose. Over Farnborough I heard the radio call of another aircraft – Romeo November – coming in the opposite direction, possibly on a collision course. I could not see it because of poor visibility. Shakespeare provided the perfect radio response.

Lecturing and chairing sessions at the Ashridge management college gave other opportunities to rub shoulders with a wide range of mature students. Furthermore, Roland Challis, who had been my producer for the 1972 BBC *Personal View* talks, invited me to be a presenter for the World Service scientific series, *Your World*. The programmes were far-sighted, one even going as far as dealing with genetic engineering years before the subject became a matter of general concern.

In the interests of being seen around I went to hear other lecturers whenever possible – notably Herman Kahn, the American futurologist, in the US Embassy. His message was that Japan, through commendable attention to long-term planning and carefully chosen technological initiatives, seemed likely to become an economic super-power within ten years. To most of his audience the message was so new and unexpected as to be almost incredible. After he had finished there was a torrent of questions. His replies were always thoughtful, but sometimes he broke off as though some new idea had suddenly seized him. One exasperated questioner asked, rather brusquely, 'Why do you never finish a sentence?' Kahn looked at him long and witheringly before replying, 'You don't really need to do so when you're speaking to a sufficiently intelligent...'

300

Zuckerman offered a helping hand. His many activities included a survey of research proposals for the Wolfson Foundation, with a sensible emphasis on useful results in the fairly short term. He invited me to join his panel. He also reminded Wayland Kennet, my old sailing partner, that I was available to serve on the Europe Plus Thirty team. This was an internationally staffed attempt to look into a range of possible futures, describing how the world in general, and Europe in particular, might be shaping around the end of the 20th century. Wayland, who somewhat improbably was both a hereditary member of the House of Lords and a Labour Party member, was convener. Our first meeting was in the French Jura, at Les Salines de Chaux. This was an old royal salt factory, built in 1776 with extraordinary attention to detail and aesthetics by the architect, Ledoux, who had the active support of Madame Du Barry, Louis XV's favourite. This social experiment – the creation of an ideal township – had fallen into decay, but it had been rescued and restored a few years earlier by André Malraux, who was Minister of Culture. Over dinner I found myself opposite Bertrand de Jouvenel, France's answer to Kahn's futurology. He gave me his card and when I saw that his telephone number was Crécy 1 I asked how long his family had lived in that famous village.

'For hundreds of years,' came the reply.

'And what happened after the battle in 1346?'

'My ancestor was wise enough to change sides.'

Two meetings in Italy stay in the memory. At Milan we were in an old convent, just down the road from the monastery of Santa Maria delle Grazie, where Leonardo's *Last Supper* was still flaking away on a crumbling wall. Over the centuries the vast picture had been much restored, and whether anything was left that could be unambiguously attributed to Leonardo was a matter of conjecture. Nevertheless, the grand design was his and to be in the presence of that great manifestation of the high renaissance was a moment to be savoured. The Milan visit was also memorable on a more mundane level. My fee was paid in cash by the EEC, in Italian notes of a designation – 100,000 lire – that had just been withdrawn by the Italian government as a move against criminals smuggling 'hot' money. When I came to present them in London for changing into sterling they were confiscated – no-one was inclined to believe my story that the EEC was itself dealing in this illegal currency. It took over a year before I could convince the authorities that I had come by them honestly. By then the lira had lost a third of its value.

Almost the last meeting of Europe Plus Thirty was at Venice. Jeanie came with me and, although she was by then handicapped by multiple sclerosis, she spent her time gathering treasured memories. Heading the list was the great church of Santa Maria Gloriosa Dei Frari, which rejoices in having Titian's *Assumption* above the main altar. Before the altar is Monteverdi's tomb; a few flowers were scattered over it. Just round the corner was the Scuolo San Rocco with its huge Tintorettos. The artist's attention to everyday detail in his *Crucifixion* brings vivid life to a painting of death. Jeanie marvelled at the glorious palaces of the Grand Canal; negotiated the uneven paving of San Marco; took the vaporetto to San Giorgio Maggiore, where our meeting was held; paid due attention to the church of Santa Maria Della Pietà, where for forty years the choir was under the direction of Vivaldi himself; and rendered homage to the Bellini altar-piece in the water-threatened church of San Zaccaria.

These various self-imposed tasks were, in a sense, a continuation of normal professional activities. A radically new departure came with my first active participation in national politics, albeit initially in a minor role and on an insignificant scale. The trigger was the contact with Dick Taverne that Lord Robens had suggested while I was at Vickers. Taverne had become disillusioned with main-stream Labour politics and was toying with the possibility of putting up a number of like-minded candidates at the next General Election. On 22 October 1973 I lunched with him at the London offices of IBM. There was one other person present whose views seemed to chime strongly with my own. John Hoskyns had been a professional soldier – a Captain in the Rifle Brigade – before joining IBM and later setting up his own highly successful software company. Politically he seemed to incline to the left, but was clearly aware of the damage being done to the country by unbridled trade unions and doctrinaire nationalisation. He had the Wykehamist's willingness to re-examine generally accepted doctrine. I greatly enjoyed our meeting.

Somewhat against Hoskyns' inclinations Taverne pursued the idea of a left-wing mini-party – Democratic Labour – and at the 'Who rules Britain?' general election on 28 February 1974 he fielded six candidates. I was assigned to help John Martin, who was contesting Tottenham. This meant that I had to spend several evenings distributing leaflets, three thousand of them in Greek. In the process I came to sympathise with the humble post-man, who has to run the daily gauntlet of letter-boxes having a remarkably diverse collection of cutting edges in the most inconvenient places.

Martin's fight was hopeless. Tottenham was one of the safest Labour seats and he was pitted against the treasurer of the Labour Party, Norman Atkinson. We polled only a few hundred votes. Taverne kept his seat at Lincoln. Harold Wilson failed to secure an overall majority but, after Edward Heath rejected any thought of a Conservative-Liberal coalition, became Prime Minister. A second election was called seven months later, when Wilson succeeded in winning an overall majority – but a wafer-thin one of only three seats. It was clear that the country was in for an extended period of political turmoil.

When next I saw Hoskyns we agreed that whatever else we might do in politics, helping a splinter group with scant resources to oppose a major party would not form any part of it. Better by far to clarify one's own views and try to sell them to an established party in need of intellectual renewal. Neither of the two main parties seemed yet to comprehend what was happening to the socio-economic structure of the country. They were too blinded by their own dogmas.

During the Tottenham by-election, after long hours spent thinking about the processes that were continuing to drag the country down, I tried to summarise my thoughts in the form of

303

a 'map' of interconnected causal chains (see Appendix). For instance, poor industrial relations and open class warfare were shifting the attitudes of educationalists and students, who were increasingly opting for the 'soft' social sciences and turning their backs on technology and production engineering. Industry was finding itself with an inadequate flow of the people it needed to compete on world markets. Its export record was poor and this was contributing to a falling value for sterling. That in turn created inflation just as surely as careless handling of the money supply was also doing.

To the query understandably posed by those seeing this maze for the first time – 'Where do we begin?' – the answer is: 'Anywhere.' Almost everything is connected, so the starting point does not matter. What is important is to accept that no solution directed at part only of the map can have any hope of success; the time involved for the effects to flow down some of the chains and influence other factors beneficially is simply too long. That is particularly true of the most intractable element, education, where the times involved are counted in decades. It is a measure of Mrs Thatcher's stature that by the end of her reign substantial parts of this map had become outdated.

I took the map with me on my first visit to John's elegant town house on the west side of Clapham Common. When he saw it he gave an enormous chuckle, went to his desk, and came back flourishing his own version. The boxes differed in detail, and his had more chains of causation, but essentially we were thinking on the same lines. It was the beginning of a remarkable friendship that had far-reaching consequences.

As I was getting to know John another figure with political connections entered my life. He was Lord (Wilfred) Brown, who had been Minister of State in the Board of Trade under Harold Wilson from 1965 until Edward Heath took over after the 1970 general election. I met him through Maurice Goldsmith, the founder and inspirer of the Science Policy Foundation. Just what that body did, other than offer Maurice intellectual nourishment, was never wholly clear. But it was held in high regard in places as far away as India and Canada, and at its gatherings one could count on meeting people who were serious, interesting, scientifically literate, and open-minded. Maurice had a wide circle of political friends, most of them, like Wilfred, on the left.

From the moment I met him it was clear that Wilfred Brown was no ordinary, run-of-the-mill politician. He had been an industrialist, and a successful one. Under his enlightened management Glacier Metals, a company making machine bearings, had run smoothly and efficiently for twenty-five years – which included the long period of economically destructive trade unionism. This near-miracle sprang from his insight that trade unions are – or were then – quasi-sovereign bodies, in the sense that no management was in a position to force them to behave as it might wish against their will; they wielded the heavier stick. Wilfred's solution was to carry the analogy further, and introduce – just as in international negotiation – the concept of unanimity (including the union voice) when taking strategic decisions affecting the future of the company or its pay structure. In his fascinating book on organisation he underlines that, at the outset, major difficulties are only to be expected. But once the main players realise that nothing useful will happen unless all can first agree, attitudes change wonderfully. He had run Glacier on these lines for more than twenty-five years with such success that there was no reason to doubt the validity of his analogy, nor the effectiveness of his solution.

Now retired from business, he was applying his managerial talents to the political task of assisting the economy. His main vehicle was the 1972 Industry Group which, as chairman, he urged me to join. This, however, was a Labour Party affiliate. As I could never agree with the notorious Clause IV of the Labour Party's constitution, calling for 'the common ownership of the means of production' – in effect, compulsory nationalisation – I at first refused his invitation. He then explained that the Group also included associate members, who did not at that time need to be members of the Labour Party, providing they were able and willing to help in the task of educating politicians

305

regarding the economy. I was ready to join any group that had such an open mind.

The 1972 Industry Group consisted of around one hundred members, some of them career politicians with an interest in industry, but mostly industrialists and other businessmen. Common sense was much in evidence at their meetings, and it was clear that their easy access to the highest levels of Harold Wilson's Labour government could only be a good thing for the country. Wilfred soon set me the task of collaborating with him in writing a booklet on innovation in manufacturing industry. He believed that a chief executive should avoid spending much time on conventional administration. His main and essential task should be to ensure that his company's products were of the highest standard. That done, much else that was beneficial would follow automatically. We were, of course, simply codifying the precepts that had been developed and honed while he was at Glacier.

I much enjoyed working with him, but still hankered after closer personal contact with parliamentary politics. Being profoundly anti-Wilson I made an attempt to get my name on the Conservative Party's list of candidates. I felt I had quite a lot to offer: wide knowledge of science, Whitehall experience, confidence as a public speaker. But I fell at the first fence. 'Aren't you a little old?' asked the party's Vice-Chairman (I was fifty-three). That was the end of any attempt to enter Parliament, but not the end of wanting to influence what it did.

In the summer of 1974 I received an intriguing telephone call from David Sheppard, an ex-Navy head-hunter whom I had contacted on the advice of Michael Shanks, the economic journalist. 'I've got an odd one here which might interest you.' It was for a Secretary-General – an absurdly over-inflated title – whose first task would be to set up a new London-based international industrial organisation, to be called The Uranium Institute. Sheppard had been engaged by Rio Tinto Zinc, the world's leading mining company. RTZ was heading an association of sixteen mining companies that had decided they needed a collective forum. I knew something of industrial associations

306

from my time at Vickers; anything involving uranium was bound to bring in nuclear energy. It seemed a good fit, but as a precaution I sought the advice of Hermann Bondi, who at the time was Chief Scientific Adviser at the Ministry of Defence – Zuckerman's old job (he was later Master of Churchill College, Cambridge). 'I know nothing of a Uranium Institute. I do know of a uranium club... My advice is that anything to do with RTZ cannot be bad.' I let my name go forward, without understanding the overtones of his reference to a club. They would continue to resonate for almost a decade.

Rumour soon told me that my main competitor was a former Under-Secretary whom I had known well before he retired from the Civil Service. I had the advantage of knowing the technology at first hand; he had great experience in international nuclear negotiations. We were very different, but evenly matched. In due course I presented myself before a selection board, which included an Englishman, a South African and a Frenchman, none of whom I knew. It was not long before this last asked whether I was 'Mike Price's brother'. The initial tension seemed to evaporate. Michel Houdaille had been Michael's assistant at the Winfrith nuclear research station, a member of the international team that was building the Dragon high-temperature reactor; Michael had been responsible for the reactor's fuel. Before long I received a provisional offer of employment, though confirmation was dependent on visiting France and Canada to allow the intending members in those countries to decide whether they would have me ('members' in this context meant corporations rather than individuals).

The meeting in Paris with officials from the Commissariat à l'Énergie Atomique (CEA) seemed to go well. Amongst them was Bertrand Goldschmidt, a nuclear chemist of considerable distinction whom I already knew and admired from our meetings at the time of the 1954 Lancaster House disarmament talks. Canada was an unknown quantity. The people I was to meet were senior mining engineers who were leading some of the most prestigious mining organisations in North America. They were able, tough and hard. The hardness, as I learned later, came from working in an unforgiving environment and from having to direct workforces that would make a Commando unit look like a Sunday school. The principal inquisitor was John Kostuik, a first-generation immigrant to Canada from Poland. He was President of Denison Mines, then one of the world's most significant uranium producers, and chairman-designate of the new Institute. He was tall, white-haired, with intense blue eyes and an engaging smile – which I later found could change in an instant to a fierce scowl. He asked me, in language laced with fascinating malapropisms, to list my strengths and weaknesses. It was the first time I had been subjected to this test, which I did not enjoy. Nor did I warm to him when he struck out of my previously agreed draft contract a clause that would have allowed me to take Jeanie with me on one foreign trip a year – it being understood that the job would entail frequent travel. I needed the job and was in no position to argue. Mixed though my impressions of the Canadian meeting were, I was profoundly relieved when, soon after my return to England, the appointment was confirmed.

Throughout this long period of uncertainty Jeanie's support had been unfaltering and total. To celebrate we flew together to Tel Aviv, to spend a few days with her sister, Wendy, who was married to Sydney Giffard, then the number two at the Tel Aviv embassy. Wendy showed us many of the monuments of the Holy Land: Nabatean caves, the harbour at Caesarea Maritima where the breakwater was formed of columns salvaged from Greek temples, the monastery of Mar-Shabba in the desert east of Bethlehem where no woman – indeed, no female animal of any kind – is allowed through the gates. Jeanie climbed the hill at Herodion, supported on Wendy's arm, to see Herod's palace where Salome danced. We went briefly to Quran, recently made famous by the discovery of previously unknown scrolls. At the rock fortress of Massada Jeanie was daunted to find that above the top station of the téléférique there was still a staircase of some fifty feet to climb. I judged it to be beyond her capabilities, advised her to accept defeat, and promised to film extensively so that she would at least have impressions at second hand of this place where the Zealots had made their last stand against the Romans in AD 73. Half an hour later, as I was filming, I saw through the viewfinder a figure that could only be my wife, hobbling bravely with the aid of a stick, taking in the view of the huge ramp that the Romans had built to bring their siege engines within range. I had forgotten her indomitable spirit.

As we were about to return home relations between Jews and Arabs deteriorated once again. Some kind of terrorist activity was involved. It was a weekend. I treasure the memory of Jeanie's brother-in-law, our Head of Chancery, listening intently to a small transistor radio tuned to the BBC World Service, in an attempt to discover what was happening a few miles up the road. We returned home, and I reported for duty to Rio Tinto's offices in St James's Square on 15 November 1974.

Chapter 18

The Uranium Institute and the 'Club'

I joined the Institute with high hopes of creating an interesting and possibly important new vehicle for exchanging nuclear information worldwide. Only seven weeks later I began to wonder whether it had ever been intended as more than a fig-leaf providing cover for a producers' marketing agreement, known as the 'Club'. It must have been the same Uranium Club that Hermann Bondi had mentioned in passing, without explanation, when I sought his advice about applying for the job. In the early months I wavered between being in denial and reluctantly accepting what others outside the mining industry were asserting – all the while trying to avoid learning too much about the 'Club', and endeavouring to shape events so that the Institute could, in time, look the world in the eyes. It was nearly two years before the full extent of the Club's operations became clear; by a splendid irony, I discovered at much the same time that the reason for its formation was to defend the embryonic nuclear industry against the deliberate exploitation of massive purchasing power by a monopsonistic uranium customer. Once the whole picture was revealed, the Club appeared to be one of the world's more forgivable cartels. This, however, was no protection against years of bad publicity and litigation, into which I found myself unwillingly pitchforked. Also in play were economic forces no one could control: the consequences of war in the Middle East, wild oscillations in the oil market, worldwide inflation, and burgeoning – though only partly justified – ambitions for nuclear power generation. Despite everything – despite the Three Mile Island accident, the Chernobyl disaster, the wave of anti-nuclear sentiment – there was a happy ending. The Institute evolved into a bona fide international non-governmental organisation, which in the year of the millennium was able to celebrate its twenty-fifth anniversary in style. This is the story of how that transformation came about.

The Institute was to be a coalition of sixteen of the world's leading uranium producers. Companies, not individuals, were to be its members. Apart from Rio Tinto Zinc (RTZ) there were Australian, Canadian, French and South African mining companies. I spent the first few days arranging a mid-December preparatory meeting of our governing body, the Council. It was concerned mainly with dry-as-dust constitutional matters: Articles of Association, membership, subscriptions. I was instructed to find suitable offices, preferably in the St James's area of London, and to arrange for the Institute to be incorporated as a British limited company. A further meeting was scheduled for March 1975, to be held in Sydney, Australia. What hardly surfaced as a subject for discussion was the future work programme, though there was some discussion of what we should *not* be doing. In particular we should not 'limit production, fix prices, or interfere with commercial transactions, suppress competition or in any other manner restrain trade'. To my untutored ear it seemed a curiously overemphasised point, but the question of whether the Institute and its members had faithfully observed this provision was to dominate my life for the next few years.

John Kostuik, who had interviewed me in Canada, was elected as the Institute's chairman. Leading for Rio Tinto Zinc was Roy Wright, who, with Sir Val Duncan, had built RTZ into the world's greatest mining house. Amongst the score of people round the table were a Canadian government official, representatives from South Africa and Australia and several Frenchmen from the Commissariat à l'Energie Atomique, including the inappropriately named, immensely tall André Petit. One of his

311

fellow-countrymen, Jean-Paul Silve, from the leading French mining house, Péchiney, seemed to be the most approachable of our visitors; but in trying to elicit his advice on what we should first aim for I had an odd impression that he was being less than wholly forthcoming. Petit, too, hinted that there were things afoot to which I was not, and should not be, privy. I was told that he was secretary of the Club, but there was no word of what the Club did. What was not in doubt was the wealth of the member organisations. We met, and over the coming months and years continued to meet, at only the best hotels and restaurants.

Our French colleagues unwittingly played a part in our choice of offices. While conducting the search I had many meetings with young men waiting on doorsteps in their ultra-long black overcoats – the easily recognised protective winter uniform for estate agents. At one point an office suite just across the road from my own club seemed to offer the best value; it was also conveniently close to Rio Tinto which, as the only London-based member company, would act as my prop and adviser in the early months. However, its address – Trafalgar House, Waterloo Place – put it firmly out of court. The search continued, and by early 1975 we were comfortably settled in the politically neutral ambience of the tenth floor of New Zealand House – three minutes from Trafalgar Square, and a stone's throw from the Athenaeum, where the light-luncheon room conveniently served as my canteen. I was back in the Whitehall village that I knew so well.

The choice of offices also owed something to another Council instruction, which was to draw on the experience of my opposite number at the International Primary Aluminium Institute, on which the Uranium Institute's draft constitution had apparently been modelled. The IPAI, which had been formed three years previously, was already installed in New Zealand House. I admired their offices, and it was hardly a coincidence that we finished up as next door neighbours.

In asking how they served the aluminium industry I was alerted for the first time to the all-pervading importance of US anti-trust law, as it was then operated. Its power stemmed from the fact that few major companies worldwide do not own at least some assets in the USA. If they were to engage in price-fixing or other collusive practices those assets would be liable to forfeiture. Simply writing 'self-serving' words into our constitution prohibiting such practices – as the Council had just done – would not of itself suffice. Independent proof was needed, and there would be no presumption of innocence. A whole regiment of the US legal profession existed to monitor this section of US law and, as became clear from what IPAI told me, the living they made from it was very good indeed. A recent case had established that responsibility for observing these US laws lay not with line managers, but with those at the top of every company. Furthermore, President Ford had recently announced that the drive against illegal practices would be stepped up even further. My IPAI informant left me in no doubt that the Uranium Institute was about to enter a legal minefield.

Apart from providing a meeting-place the main service IPAI offered its members lay in collecting statistics of world production. Aluminium being a well established metal, with millions of users and therefore a stable market, this presented no great problems. Even so, US law made it prudent to have the process and all relevant meetings monitored by independent US counsel. There were several firms of US lawyers operating in London and this was a significant part of their work.

The legal problem only needed to be stated for its ramifications in the case of uranium to be self-evident. There was no established and stable market for uranium for civil nuclear power purposes. Instead, the power industry was in a state of helter-skelter development, as electrical utilities reacted to the oil price rise that had taken place following the Yom Kippur war of October 1973. Before that conflict oil had been a fuel of choice for electricity production. Suddenly oil and, as a result of sympathetic market movements, fossil fuels generally appeared significantly less attractive. As civil nuclear power seemed technically and economically ready to fulfil its long-promised rôle, a massive

313

reactor-building programme was in progress worldwide. A variety of problems, for which I later had a ring-side seat, soon dampened the ardour of the power companies, and the boom was short-lived. Only in France was the original momentum maintained. The result was that in no more than a dozen years, between 1973 and 1985, nuclear power's contribution to French electricity production jumped from 8% to no less than 61% – in splendid conformity with the country's long-term economic plan. This was a rate of expansion that, in my opening weeks at the Institute, had seemed about to take place worldwide. This outlook had immediate consequences for the mining industry, since the uranium fuel for any new reactor needs to be delivered eighteen months ahead of reactor completion, so that the sophisticated fuel assemblies can be manufactured in good time.

With such a volatile market it was clear that providing reliable and legally acceptable uranium production statistics would be not only a considerable undertaking, but also one for which the methodology was far from obvious. What every uranium producer would have liked to know were the expansion plans of his rivals. However, not only was such information commercially sensitive, but its dissemination seemed almost impossible to square with US law. Moreover, anything that looked like setting targets and monitoring progress was forbidden. Unless we could find a way round these problems they threatened to undermine the whole announced purpose of the Institute – which was basically to help the industry to understand the market.

There was also European law to consider. It was on the whole less stringent, and contained a provision allowing the European Commission to bless the work of an organisation such as the UI if it judged that such a blessing, on balance, would be in the public interest, even if there were evidence of producer cooperation. But that would flash red lights in Washington, US law having no comparable halfway house. It was, therefore, not an escape route that the UI could use.

My meeting with the Primary Aluminium Institute was on 13 December 1974. I was still considering the implications of what

I had been told when, on 9 January 1975, I was telephoned from New York by Sam Harris, an American lawyer of immense distinction – he had been a prosecutor at the Nuremberg trials – and a member of the board of Rio Tinto. He told me that the economic journal, *Forbes Magazine*, was about to publish an article headed 'It worked for the Arabs', outlining how a uranium cartel had been operating. This could only be the Club, which up to that point I had not associated with cartel-like activities. In this I was undoubtedly naïve. I should have been alerted by the surrounding aura of secrecy, which made it radically different from any other industrial association that had come my way. Sam Harris's message was not explicit, other than being a clear warning about the extreme urgency of acquiring legal protection for the Institute. He repeated this warning when in London a few days later.

It did not take much imagination to realise that I was being taken for a ride. Although the Institute was itself acting within the law, I was in effect being used to provide cover for what were clearly illegal Club activities. This impression was strengthened when I lunched with John Waddams on 16 January. He worked for the national electricity producer, CEGB. We were old friends from Harwell days and spoke freely. He asserted that the uranium producers were engaging in price-fixing. I was annoyed, not knowing at that time the reasons for the formation of the Club.

I was in no position to entertain the luxury of resignation. The only option lay in playing along, while aiming either to find another job or to transform the Institute into an organisation that the whole of the worldwide nuclear industry, not only the uranium miners, could regard as useful. We faced considerable competition, notably from the Atomic Industrial Forum, a US organisation based in Washington. They purported to be an international body like our own, but made the mistake of selecting their officers exclusively from citizens of the USA. We could only co-exist with them and survive if we aimed to be better, or at least more international. In the end that aim was achieved,

315

but only after some years of worry. Tragically, not long after giving me his immensely valuable advice Sam Harris fell to his death from a high window in New York.

The *Forbes* article led to the cancellation of the second preparatory Council meeting planned for Sydney in March 1975 – the Press had got hold of the news, and there was no point in walking into a hornets' nest needlessly. Instead, the meeting was quietly moved to London. I was able to announce that incorporation formalities were proceeding smoothly, but in other directions there were problems. Five leading US mining companies had told Kostuik that they could not join the Institute in the present circumstances. Perhaps prompted by this refusal the meeting agreed to take on Wilmer, Cutler and Pickering as our US counsel. Theirs was a prestigious Washington firm – Lloyd Cutler later became Presidential Counsel in the White House during the Carter administration. Their London representative was Sam Stern, whom I found most congenial.

From the outset our US counsel's aim was to seek a Business Review Letter from the US Department of Justice, saying in effect that the Department knew of the Institute's existence and operations and that it did not at the time of writing have any plans for proceeding against us. The Justice Department would never go further than this, but to receive such a letter would be tantamount to a Seal of Good Housekeeping. Unfortunately, so much mud had been stirred up by the *Forbes* article, and what had happened subsequently, that it would need a major constitutional change in the Institute and several years of waiting before this ambition could be realised.

During the London meeting I was also given encouragement to engage our first professional staff member, Frank Ticehurst. He knew a great deal about uranium, having been purchasing officer for the British government. He was depressingly sceptical about the Institute, which he noted had virtually the same membership as the Club.

It was September 1976 before I became aware of the true scale of the Club's operations, and then only through a curious concatenation of circumstances. In the intervening months rumours had steadily strengthened and the Club's members had become targets for those opposed to nuclear energy. Eventually, an environmental group stole a large number of documents from the Mary Kathleen mine in Australia; these included the operating procedures of the Club. To give a semblance of normal market operation, bids for uranium contracts would be made by several mining companies at prearranged prices, with a leader and runner-up. The identity of the lead bidder would vary from contract to contract. This I learned during a train journey home from Marylebone Station one evening, when I ran into the Science Editor of the *Financial Times*, David Fishlock, who lived in my village. He handed me a thick bunch of papers – at least one hundred pages – with a comment that I might find them interesting. Indeed I did. They had come from Mary Kathleen via the office of the Attorney-General of California, who had published them to the world's Press. Here were not only the Club's operating procedures, but also a draft constitution for the Uranium Institute.

In the spring of 1975 I did not yet have this additional knowledge. What was clear, however, was that some senior members were already having doubts about the ability of the embryonic Institute to attract additional members in the face of adverse publicity. They concluded that they should bring in a 'strong' Chief Executive, a nominee of Rio Tinto, to run the Institute over my head. They were mistaken. The obstacle to additional recruitment was the legal uncertainty that had been created by our members' own actions as members of the Club. No other company, neither a US uranium producer nor an electrical utility that was a user of uranium, would be willing to make any move in the Institute's direction until the situation was clarified.

Preparations for floating the Institute nevertheless continued. I arranged for it to be registered as a British company limited by guarantee, to provide a legal safeguard in the event of financial difficulty. However, I did not wish to have to append the word 'limited' to our title – it somehow seemed out of keeping with the idea of an Institute. I found it could be dropped, provided words were included in the Memorandum of Association to indicate a 'doing-good' intention.

Formalities were complete by the summer of 1975 and, on 12 June, we met the Press. To one barbed question about a cartel Roy Wright of Rio Tinto responded with a flat denial. Most of the reporters were kind in their comments, but the *Washington Post* ran a story about market rigging. It was probably no coincidence that, within a few days, the US Justice Department and the US Federal Trade Commission started enquiries into restrictive practices amongst the world's uranium producers. This was somewhat ironic, the US having for years, under pressure from its own mining industry, insulated itself from foreign market manipulation by closing its frontiers to foreign uranium.

The enquiry had the effect of making the companies forming the Institute distinctly nervous. Under pressure from the Canadian government the Club was wound up, without publicity, in October 1975. Petit commented that the Institute had now lost its utility. In fact, the Club was hardly missed by the uranium producers, since its main function of putting a floor under the uranium price had by then been overtaken by a rapid shift of the market in their favour. Just why this occurred, and indeed why the Club had been formed in the first place, is one of the most curious stories ever to come out of a commodity market. It also formed a chain of events that had a profound effect on my own life for the remainder of the 1970s.

The Yom Kippur war of 1973 provides a convenient starting point. It took place at a time when nuclear electricity was beginning to seem worth using on a significant scale. One hundred nuclear power-plants had already been ordered in the USA alone, and forward orders for the uranium fuel needed to power them amounted to the astonishing figure of four times the world's annual production. But production levels had fallen in the previous few years by almost 50%, following a reduction in military orders as the nuclear weapons market reached saturation. Several mines had closed.

As with the mining of any other metal, this fall in the price for a time had a direct economic effect on what it was feasible to mine. Metal ores have no value until they are brought to the surface. The cost of doing so varies with the concentration of the ore – dilute ores cost more to mine per pound of the finished metal. So a fall in the price is automatically reflected in a corresponding fall in the economically mineable reserves. That, in turn, for a nuclear industry that had no other choice of fuel, could raise questions about the reliability of future supplies – there being in effect a symbiotic relationship between the nuclear and the uranium mining industries.

The 1973 war triggered an oil price rise, which quickly led to a general inflation of commodity prices. The spot price of uranium oxide leapt from $6 per pound in January 1973 to $40 by April 1976. Zinc, tin and gold all had comparable price rises; in the case of uranium, however, special nuclear factors were at work. One was the uncritical optimism of the industrial countries of OECD that the time had come to switch generally and rapidly from oil fuel to nuclear power. Another was a significant change in the US terms for 'enriching' uranium in the useful fissile isotope, U-235 (the USA had a near-monopoly for this essential step in the manufacture of nuclear fuel). A third factor, one that before long was to impinge on me directly, was the almost simultaneous market reaction to the discovery that the contracts entered into by the Westinghouse company to supply uranium to electrical utilities had not been covered by orders on the mines.

Westinghouse was then the leading manufacturer of nuclear reactors. To increase its market power it had entered into contracts to supply 33,000 tons of uranium in the form of nuclear fuel, but only 6,000 tons had been covered by procurement orders on the mines. 'Going short' on such a heroic scale would play havoc with any commodity market, and uranium was no exception. For a time the result had been most satisfactory for Westinghouse – the price of uranium, already hit by military cancellations, had continued to fall.

319

Eventually, in answer to Westinghouse's exploitation of its quasi-monopsonistic purchasing power, the Club was formed as a defensive producers' association. It had the blessing of the Australian, Canadian, French and South African governments. Its purpose was to share out the available contracts, keep a floor under the price of uranium, and thus maintain the viability of the mining industry, on which the world would shortly be dependent for its civil uranium supplies. Whatever else may be said about the Club it was certainly not a cartel operating from strength. France, which in 1972 had acted as convener, provided a secretariat run by Petit.

The unforeseen uranium price rise following the Yom Kippur war was a potential disaster for Westinghouse. In common with many others who have attempted to play commodity markets the company found itself on the verge of bankruptcy. This became public knowledge in the summer of 1975, soon after the formation of the Institute, when seventeen electrical utilities that were worried about the security of their uranium supplies began proceedings intended to force Westinghouse to honour its contracts. Westinghouse began its defence unconvincingly by pleading 'commercial impracticability', based on an obscure provision in the US Uniform Commercial Code – which, it is said, was identified by a law student on a temporary summer assignment. The cases were still dragging on a year later when the Club documents were stolen from the Mary Kathleen mine and openly published. Westinghouse seized the opportunity of instituting suits of its own in the US courts against Club members. They were for 'criminal conspiracy', which in US law carried a penalty of treble damages. The sums involved totalled $6 billion (in 1976). Unsurprisingly, life in the industry became difficult, and remained so until the lawsuits were finally settled years later.

Despite the complications that the Westinghouse affair brought to my life, the attendant litigation ironically served to show the Club-cartel in a new and more sympathetic light. What became abundantly clear, and a source of great irritation to the uranium miners who were under attack, was that the formation of the Club had been predominantly due to Westinghouse's own actions.

While these storm clouds were gathering one of my jobs was to provide Institute members with a forecast of the likely demand for uranium. Even with Frank Ticehurst's knowledge of the market it was impossible to produce demand forecasts in the detail needed if they were to be commercially useful. We did not have access to the necessary sources of information. We sought the help of our members through the formation of a Supply and Demand working party, but were immediately faced not only with problems of US anti-trust law, but also with other constraints such as commercial secrecy and restrictions imposed by the governments of mining nations. It took two more attempts, and the arrival of new members from the uranium-consuming side of the nuclear industry, before a satisfactory modus operandi and working party structure could be evolved.

One recurring problem was legal costs. US counsel needed to be present at our discussions because of anti-trust law but, before long, lawyers' fees were taking one-third of our subscription income, far more than had been foreseen. The result was that on one never-to-be-forgotten occasion there were insufficient funds in the bank to pay my salary. For a former civil servant this was a wholly novel and unnerving experience. Small wonder that for a time Frank and I assessed the Institute's chances of survival as less than one in three.

Meanwhile, there was one published source of aggregated worldwide uranium demand estimates and, at first sight, its authors' credentials seemed impeccable. It was based on a forecast of nuclear reactor use by the Nuclear Energy Agency of OECD. It predicted a huge expansion of nuclear electricity. However, having examined the figures, Frank and I simply refused to believe them. Our reasoning was so simple as to be almost laughable. Nuclear electricity at that time could be economic only if used for 'base-load' generation; in other words, provided it was switched on for virtually the whole of the twenty-four hours. OECD's basic assumption was that electricity demand would be growing sharply, as it had done in the recent past; we knew with fair certainty that the reverse was likely to be the case. Electricity consumption marches in step with economic activity, and that was suffering from the general worldwide inflation caused by the Yom Kippur war. It followed that the nuclear power stations OECD foresaw could never operate on base-load – the demand would be lacking – so it was an error to assume that they would be ordered. In December 1975, guided by Russell Ackoff's immortal advice – 'forecast the inevitable; you are more likely to be right' – we wrote a short paper disagreeing with OECD and sharply cutting their estimates of demand. John Kostuik, the Institute's chairman, was unwilling to believe us. 'How can you, with your small resources, criticise the considered views of so many governments?' I told him that the people who had contributed to the Nuclear Energy Agency's report would have been, in the main, nuclear energy specialists – enthusiasts who were most unlikely to have taken into account the unwelcome consequences of an imminent world economic downturn. There had clearly been a mutual reinforcement of expectations. While Kostuik insisted that it was 'no part of our job to spread alarm and despondency', we stuck by our lower figures. In the event they themselves proved too optimistic, but they were vastly nearer the truth than those of OECD. The actual figure for worldwide nuclear capacity in 1997 (348 gigawatts) was considerably less than half OECD's forecast for 1990. Since few were ready to believe us, the result was serious misjudgement throughout the industry – which included the miners – until realism supervened a decade later.

The Institute was getting nowhere. The obvious way out of our difficulties was to open full membership to the major electrical utilities. They had shown no interest in becoming Associate Members, as was grudgingly permitted by the original constitution, having no wish to be second-class citizens. If they could come in as full members and then be persuaded to speak frankly, the miners would for the first time have a reliable basis for production planning. Having consumers on board would also help to shake off the cartel image. My proposal received a cold reception. 'How can we,' asked Kostuik, 'sit down with people against whom we negotiate across the table?' There was, however, no alternative. By late October 1975, only four months after the launch date, Kostuik had resigned himself to this outcome and issued a telegram recommending that electrical utilities should be encouraged to join as full members. The lawyers went to work on a revised constitution, with weighted voting to give Consumers (i.e. the electrical utilities) the same total voting power, irrespective of the actual number of such members, as Producers (i.e. uranium miners). This constitution had a difficult birth and the first draft was severely criticised, particularly by one South African. Kostuik, however, now seemed to be on my side. 'Don't worry,' he said adding, in one of his more memorable malapropisms, 'he's a bull in a manger.' The revised constitution was adopted in January 1976 and, almost immediately, the leading German electrical utility, RWE, took up membership.

This crucial development was no coincidence, but the result of sound advice from Bill Cavendish-Bentinck, who had been asked a little earlier by Rio Tinto Zinc to provide the Institute with what help he could. He had been a career diplomat of distinction, having served as chairman of the Joint Intelligence Committee virtually throughout World War II. He also knew the nuclear industry intimately, through being the current chairman of the British Nuclear Forum. He was familiar with Europe generally, and German industry in particular, having been Chairman of British Industrial Interests in post-war Germany. His advice regarding consumer members was engagingly elitist and to the point: 'You should first persuade the nuclear Duke. Then the nuclear Marquesses, Earls, Viscounts, Barons and lesser fry will follow his lead.'

I asked who the Duke might be.

'Heinrich Mandel, of RWE, head of the German nuclear forum.'

So, a month before the change of the constitution, Bill and I travelled to Düsseldorf and succeeded in persuading Mandel that the Institute was about to be remodelled into a body that he would probably find useful. Events followed exactly as Bill had predicted and, within a couple of years, the Institute numbered amongst its membership no fewer than ten electrical utilities from eight countries. Later, Bill himself became the ninth and last Duke of Portland.

The result was a cultural change in the way the Council did its work. The utilities were close to government – in some cases part of it – and their representatives instinctively thought along the public-sector lines I was familiar with. Before long their presence made my job noticeably easier. But for a few months longer I was plagued by the desire of a majority of the producers, led by RTZ, to bring in a placeman over my head in the shape of a completely unnecessary Chief Executive. Luckily for me their choice was not acceptable to the Australian producers, as became clear one afternoon in March 1976. The motion to appoint a Chief Executive was on the point of being railroaded through the Council when Douglas Stewart said that he could not agree without consulting his colleagues back in Australia. This was a crumb of comfort at the end of a difficult day but, despite his intervention, the meeting went on to approve the proposal. It was clear that my insistence on keeping the Institute well away from legal trouble had undermined my position in the eyes of some of the leading miners. I went home uncertain whether my job was about to collapse. The following day I drove with Jeanie to stay with friends in the Lake District. I was to give a public-affairs lecture at Sellafield on nuclear power and was hoping to put the Institute and its worries out of my mind for at least a few days.

On our arrival our host and hostess suggested we go with them the following night to Red How, a splendid house where some Scottish friends, the Dickinsons, were giving a ceilidh. Who should be there but Douglas Stewart, whom I had last seen a couple of days before at the Council meeting. By an extraordinary chance he was father-in-law to the Dickinsons' daughter. He assured me that the Australian miners were certainly not willing to go along with the idea of a Chief Executive being brought in on secondment from a rival mining group. In opposing the proposal they also knew they had the support of their government. A load was lifted from my mind. With confidence brimming over I addressed, for the first and only time, the difficult task of dancing a Scottish jig. Never have I enjoyed a party or a holiday more.

In dismissing the proposal for a Chief Executive so confidently Douglas was in fact ahead of events. It continued to surface at intervals over the coming months, though with decreasing force. Meanwhile, I was occupied with the task of staging a one-day symposium, which was intended to provide, for the first time, a public platform for the Institute before an international audience. I was given exactly three months to make the arrangements, and succeeded only because chance put me in touch with the elegant and omnicompetent Anthea Fortescue. The symposium's modest success owed a great deal to her skill as a conference organiser. The contributed papers were of reasonable standard, though in no way exceptional. But outside the conference hall Anthea provided an ambience that the delegates did not easily forget. The Institution of Electrical Engineers lent us their splendidly appropriate lecture theatre; the nearby Savoy Hotel served a memorable lunch; and, to finish things off, we held a reception and dinner in the Banqueting House in Whitehall, with its throne and splendid ceiling by Rubens. Four herald trumpeters introduced the toastmaster's announcements. 'Complete waste of money,' growled Kostuik. But they added style, and set us apart from the drab uniformity of most business dinners. It was the trumpeters that delegates from America, France and Iran told me they would remember and that, in part, were the cause of their return for the following year's meeting.

Chatting to Kostuik afterwards I pointed to the hall and asked whether, like me, he found it magnificent. 'I don't know. It's rather bare.' So much for the classicism of Inigo Jones that the Japanese delegates found so breathtaking. He then told me that a Chief Executive would, after all, be appointed in the near

325

future. 'Your peers require it.' I broke off to consult Jean-Paul Silve about what should be done. The following day he finessed the proposal by suggesting that instead of a Chief Executive there should be a Vice-Chairman. Voting on the proposal was tied and the matter left for future decision. The balance of power in the governing Council had begun to shift. The combined votes of the Australian miners and two new electrical utility members – RWE and Electricité de France – had saved the day.

That by itself would, in all probability, have ended this trivial and disagreeable domestic squabble, and finally killed off the idea of bringing in a producer-friendly place-man over my head. However, the death of the proposal soon became inevitable for a quite different reason, as threats of litigation arose from the direction of the United States.

The summer of 1976 was marked by steadily increasing pressure from the US Justice Department on our uranium mining members. In early July Kostuik was subpoenaed – due, he said angrily but unconvincingly, to his connection with the Institute. When I received a copy of the document I was astonished by its detail. In August one of the Department's lawyers, Joel Davidow, wrote asking to meet me. For obvious reasons of jurisdiction I refused to do so in the USA and, at the end of September, he came to London. As well as Reuben Clark, who had recently succeeded Sam Stern as our London counsel, I had in support Bob Hammond, who had once been Davidow's boss in Washington. We let Davidow loose on the Institute's files, confident that there was nothing incriminating in them. At one stage I commented that his actions had been widely seen as needlessly stirring up personal animosities. He looked worried – officials in the Justice Department are supposed to remain objective. There was no great difficulty in dealing with his questions. Following the *Forbes* article I had been warned in time by Sam Harris, and had been careful to ensure that the Institute as a corporate body had done nothing wrong. I did, however, mention the generally adverse reaction within the industry to his enquiry which, although undertaken in the name of free trade, was from a country that had sealed its borders to uranium imports. Davidow seemed surprised and a little shaken. Since it was clear that the Press would get hold of the news of his visit, it seemed best to face the possibility head-on. On the Sunday morning of his visit I presented him with a draft Press release. Our openness somewhat surprised him, but he agreed it was 'factually correct'. This defused the situation.

Any feeling of relief was short-lived. On Trafalgar Day, 21 October 1976, Westinghouse named the Institute as a 'co-conspirator' in its Complaint against the uranium producers. The company was fighting for its life and objective justice was not the first consideration. A couple of weeks later I received a similar Complaint and opened discussions with government officials regarding the apparent intrusion by US courts into British jurisdiction. On 2 November I was served with a Letter Rogatory by an official of the British High Court. This was a procedure that was new to me. It is used by the High Court of one country to request the assistance of another by forcing a witness to give evidence; the letter concluded with a promise to offer reciprocal facilities should the occasion arise.

Several board members and executives of RTZ received similar summonses. These included Roy Wright, the driving force behind the Chief Executive proposal – which he was still pushing – and Lord Shackleton, son of the famous Antarctic explorer. Rio Tinto, using its 'deep purse', immediately launched an appeal against any such compulsion. The impoverished Institute was in no position to take similar action, but somehow it was agreed that we should be treated on the same footing as Rio Tinto. The case was heard at the Law Courts in January 1977 before Master Jacob, who let it be known that he was 'inclined to honour the comity of nations'. His judgment, delivered four weeks later, was implacably against RTZ. The case went higher, but although the Court of Appeal made some welcome modifications to the charges against RTZ the outcome was that the company could not avoid responding to the summons. That meant that, as the Institute's embodiment, I too would have to do so. In

327

case things went wrong and I needed an escape route, I called on my old master Solly Zuckerman to tell him what was happening. He had nothing immediate to suggest except, 'Go on fighting. If you break your leg come to me and I'll bandage it up.'

The summons did not worry me unduly because I had a good story to tell. However, RTZ seemed unhappy about my appearing as a witness. I was later told they were afraid that I might seek revenge for the way I had been treated over the Chief Executive proposal. They need not have worried. I knew I would have to give evidence in such a way that I did not appear either a fool or a knave; I also hoped to do no harm either to the Institute or to its corporate members. RTZ did not have the luxury of being so open. The company had large resources in the USA, which might be threatened by admissions of antitrust behaviour. There was one way out – to use the US constitutional provision that enables witnesses to avoid self-incrimination. The hearing, held in London in June 1977, consequently witnessed the bizarre spectacle of a British Knight of the Garter, Lord Shackleton, sheltering behind the US Fifth Amendment.

The proceedings took place in the US Embassy in Grosvenor Square before Judge Merhige, who had gained a considerable reputation for his handling of difficult civil rights cases. That morning I woke early, refreshed my memory by reading my notes in the train and was early enough in London to walk the mile and a half to the Embassy. I took it as a good omen that on the way I chanced to meet Reuben Clark, my own US counsel. Over coffee we ran once again over the position. The Institute was in good shape, with membership more than doubled since its formation. The adherence of no fewer than eleven consumer companies to an organisation which only two years previously had been the object of a great deal of adverse comment was self-evidently a strong defensive point. We also knew we had scrupulously observed every detail of US, British and European company law. The Institute had changed out of all recognition from its original concept and was fast becoming useful to the whole industry, not only to the miners. There seemed little to fear.

At the outset of the hearing there was an argument over the status of the Court – whether it was an English court assisting the US judiciary and subject to British procedures, or the District Court of Richmond, Virginia, meeting on US territory in London. Judge Merhige was quite clear: 'I sit here as a United States judge by virtue of the courtesy and permission of the British courts.' And so matters proceeded under US court rules.

My English counsel, Anthony Hallgarten, began by underlining for the court that I was not present as an adversary witness but as someone who, despite Westinghouse's allegations, was cooperating in the administration of justice. He objected in principle to the breadth with which parts of the Complaint had been drafted and dissociated the Institute from the Mary Kathleen documents that had been stolen in Australia.

My examination began quietly, so quietly that the judge showed signs of impatience. As Westinghouse's counsel proceeded it became clear that the link between Club and Institute was central. I was pressed as to whether I had enquired into the Institute's origins. I replied that the Mary Kathleen documents I had been given in the train were the first detailed documentation ... having read them there did not seem much point in enquiring... by then the Institute was developing along very different lines.

Counsel for Westinghouse went on: 'Regarding the ninth Operating Committee of the Club in Las Palmas, does this paper refresh your recollection, whether the Policy Committee had set up a special subcommittee to form the Institute?'

'I have no recollection to refresh.'

I continued to be pressed.

'You consciously avoided following up these leads concerning the activities of the Club?'

'You can put it like that... I do not wish to pretend to the court that after reading the trade press we were not aware of what was being said in the world at large.'

329

'Did you discuss with any of the Institute members ...the bidding procedures employed by the Club?'

'No. Put yourself in my position. My function was to create an Institute which was as useful as possible.'

'You felt this was a sensitive subject you did not want to explore in great depth?'

'You put it admirably.'

The questioning, which was slower and duller than these extracts might suggest, went on to my seminal meeting with Sam Harris. Did he deny what was said in the *Forbes* article?

'I do not recall any denial.'

'If a denial were warranted you would have received it?'

I threw myself on the mercy of the court. 'May I leave my answer as neutral as I left it then? There are some circumstances where men do not explore all the possible frontiers of knowledge.'

At this the judge commented: 'This may be one of them, be there evidence to the contrary notwithstanding.'

The court laughed. The tension was broken.

Someone said, 'He's as clean as a hound's tooth.'

I asked Reuben Clark later to explain this in plain English.

'It's what Eisenhower said in 1952 about Nixon, who was the Vice-Presidential candidate.'

I did not find the explanation wholly reassuring.

By then Westinghouse's attorney knew he was dealing with someone who genuinely had not taken part in the cartel, and seemed to lose heart. He took refuge in innuendo by asking about a phrase in a document.

'The Institute would seek a location as close to SW1 as possible. How far is that from Rio Tinto?'

'It is in the same general area, but nearer to my own club.'

Counsel looked displeased – witnesses were not supposed to take his questions so lightly. He continued in a desultory vein for a while until the court became restive. A few further questions from my own side enabled me to confirm that, far from freezing out Westinghouse, one of their representatives had attended our first symposium in 1976.

330

So the ordeal ended. I use the word 'ordeal' advisedly because, no matter how well prepared or innocent one might be, responding to questioning from a hostile counsel is never something to be taken lightly. I rushed home to let Jeanie know how well things had gone. That evening the Athenaeum was for the first time holding a joint party with the Reform Club. We sat on the wide staircase with John and Thérèse Wright, rejoicing in what could only be regarded as a great escape.

A few days later the Institute held its second conference. It was already known as the 'Annual Symposium', which coming from such a young organisation may have seemed pretentious. To us the title was indicative of a challenge successfully accepted. In the year 2000 the Institute held its twenty-fifth symposium.

I summed up the proceedings myself. Mandel, who following the earlier constitutional revision had succeeded Kostuik as Chairman, was flattering. I felt a warm glow. That evening we again dined in the Banqueting House, Whitehall. The mood – friendly and promising – could hardly have been more different from that of the previous year.

Chapter 19

Politics and the Economy

The Institute's disappointingly slow start had one positive aspect. Without neglecting my duties I had time to pursue what had become an absorbing personal interest: why was the British economy failing? I had grown up with high technology, and considered it obvious that this should be one of our prime markets. But other countries were proving dangerous competitors.

The problem lay in both our management style and our political institutions. The trade unions were ruthlessly exploiting their negotiating muscle, and Labour's hirelings in Parliament did little to stop them. The checks and balances promised by Mr Asquith when the Trade Disputes Bill was debated in 1906 were long forgotten. Industrial management was too often a reflection of outmoded quasi-feudal traditions. There were too few technically qualified company directors – technologists were on tap rather than on top, as they often were in Germany, Japan and the USA.

Too great a proportion of national resources was still devoted to indulging Ministers' vanity, so that they could 'punch above their weight'. The essentials of Britishness – the grit and toughness that had seen us through two world wars – were being eroded by pussy-footing idealism and the ceding of power to Brussels. Parliament, which should have been the powerhouse of the nation, was caught in the crossfire between factions reflecting the opposing sides of industry. Both political parties had contributed to the destruction of industry's investment resources by creating inflation – Labour and the unions by their negotiating muscle, the Conservatives through poor management of the economy. The Civil Service was content to be doctrinally subservient to Ministers' wishes. The Cabinet Secretary himself had spoken of the 'orderly management of decline'.

This was how things appeared in 1974. My views had been hammered out in frequent discussions with John Hoskyns and Theo Williamson. They were more than friends; we had a basis of common understanding that made every meeting an exhilarating exploration. We hoped to find a way of doing something about the situation before national failure developed into calamity. We had no locus and were rowing against the political mainstream. Our only advantage was that we were wholly independent. With persistence and a little good luck we succeeded in giving a small shove in the right direction. Much remained unchanged, not least Parliament itself, but the unions were brought to heel. In the process John Hoskyns became head of Mrs Thatcher's Policy Unit in Number 10. This is the story of my part in the events of seven exciting years, from 1975 to 1982.

In early 1975 the Labour government seemed incapable of effective action. As F.M. Cornford noted in 1908 in his amusingly cynical essay, *Microcosmographia Academica*: 'Nothing is ever done until everyone is convinced that it ought to be done.' The country was not yet at that point. Meanwhile social, educational, technological and political factors were inextricably entangled, all contributing to a spiral of decline, as the causal-chain 'maps' that had brought me together with Hoskyns attempted to illustrate.

In the spring of 1975 I published an article in *Futures* discussing these issues, including my own version of the 'map'. This led to an invitation to speak at the August 1975 meeting of the British Association for the Advancement of Science. My talk, 'Operating a Technological Economy', drew on my contrasting experiences in the Civil Service and the private sector:

I saw at first hand the extraordinary difference between helping to govern and being governed. I had spent half a lifetime dealing

333

with big science for government, but it was the switch to private industry that opened my eyes to the problems of planning when the umpire keeps changing the rules... I saw the denuded state of British industry, compared with the prodigious intellectual wealth I had left behind in the Civil Service. I began to question the uses we were making of our technical resources.

Western industrial nations like Britain were experiencing a permanent change of economic climate. Developing nations were learning our tricks. I listed the way in which we were governed as one of the factors needing to be changed. The Civil Service was, I said:

> ...graced by its brilliance, but cut off by it. The absence of practical experience of the operational levels of the economy in the great economic departments of state has been one of the hidden factors in our decline. Our factories are the teeth arms of the economy, and the generals ought to know something about them.
>
> We have not been sufficiently innovative, and it shows in our market performance. We have not been short of technologists. Our research effort was running at twice that of Japan during her economic breakout in the sixties; but no less than 50% of our industrial research and development effort was associated with only 5% of industrial turnover... The opportunity cost of Concorde must have been a decline in the medium-technology mechanical engineering industry which [at the time was] our single most important export industry. Moreover, if we insist on organising much of our research [in government laboratories] that are divorced from production, we must not be surprised if too few attend to the ticklish problems of getting the goods out of the factories at reasonable cost.

I was echoing what a handful of others, notably Theo Williamson and Sir Ieuan Maddock, Chief Scientist at the Department of Trade and Industry, had been stressing for the past four years. But the country was showing no interest in their message.

Other countries had been more successful. Economic planning

needed continuity of policy, which was what France had enjoyed for the past thirty years. Our own auction of votes at each general election made such an approach all but impossible. As the left-wing politician, Richard Crossman, caustically observed, 'The real tragedy of British politics is not promises that are broken but promises that are kept.' The country needed to protect itself by some kind of administrative invention – I called it a 'flywheel' – a set of procedures and conventions that would keep the wheels of the economy turning smoothly irrespective of which party happened to be in power. The French planning system involved thousands of people in a task that in Britain would be regarded as the prerogative of a few in central government. They had applied it continuously since 1946. Our own National Economic Development Office (NEDO) was by comparison still an infant. I was particularly hard on the advice given by economists:

> The frequent inability of economics to prescribe courses and policies, unless hedged about with language worthy of Old Moore's Almanac, cannot have helped its voice to be heard. If the subject could be made more prescriptive it would command greater attention. (I remember hearing the same point made to an economist by – of all people – a meteorologist!)

The talk had a good press. The crack about Old Moore appeared in the *Observer*'s 'Sayings of the Week'. Anthony Harris of the *Financial Times* was particularly kind, in an article entitled 'No Experience Required'. He began by recalling a meeting at which a very senior Treasury economist explained why Government investment had to be planned five years ahead – the diseconomies of chopping and changing were too great. And why, asked a business economist, was it assumed that private industry could be forced by alterations in taxation to chop and change without incurring similar costs? Harris went on:

> What brought this encounter to mind was a very provocative address to the British Association... Terence Price's observations

may not individually seem very new; taken together they are far more suggestive. Price believes that one cause of our decline is the lack of practical operational experience among those who run the great economic departments. He accuses the public sector of draining the private sector of intellectual talent. In technology we have misdirected our effort. Government policy is both opaque and capricious. What is unusual about this familiar catalogue of complaints is Price's insistence that they all connect up ... through a great matrix of cause and effect; but his remarks also suggest a rather different approach – an attempt at self-knowledge ...

There followed a coruscating critique of British economic management, wholly consistent with what I had been saying, and concluding:

... the luminous intelligence of our senior civil servants combined with their profound silliness in practical affairs reflected the qualities of donnishness ... Like dons, they are impatient of outside views, because they are cleverer than those with whom they deal ... Above all Price wants patience and persistence, less faith and more hopeful hard work, a process of learning to make our administrative methods effective. This is perhaps the hardest suggestion to put into practice: dons did their learning years ago; they now research and teach.

Wilfred Brown was delighted with the reception I had been accorded and asked me to repeat my talk for the 1972 Industry Group. Early in 1976 Wilfred and Arnold Gregory, Secretary of the Group, suggested I should bring together a drafting team with the intention of producing a 'policy-action' piece that might be smuggled into Number 10. It was too good an offer to refuse. Theo Willamson and John Hoskyns came as two whom I could trust implicitly (though I omitted John's name from the list of authors, to avoid spoiling his relations with the Conservatives). Nigel Beard, then directing the Docklands Project, had been one of my bright stars at Byfleet; he later became a Member of Parliament. Eric Duckworth from the Fulmer Research Institute and Gordon Fryers from Reckitt and Colman represented manufacturing technology. Arnold Gregory himself brought enthusiasm and political flair to our work. Alas, he died suddenly while our report was still taking shape.

After several changes of title we settled on *Rebuilding British Industry*, with *A Coherent Socio-Economic Approach* as sub-title. The paper pulled no punches. It emphasised that although the Government's stated policy was to ensure a massive shift of resources to industry, the country did not yet have a feeling that everything hung together. Conflicting economic advice showed that the problems were imperfectly understood. The pound was sinking because this was the only circumstance in which price competition could be used to substitute for what was lacking in design, marketing, delivery, servicing and other aspects of competition. This was especially true of engineering products, which at that time played a determining role in setting the value of sterling. If we had spent more time in asking ourselves what makes an economy effective at the operating level, instead of concentrating on macro-economic policies, we could have avoided crisis as surely as West Germany had done.

The paper went on to list many of the factors that needed to be recognised as relevant: the arbitrary chopping-and-changing policies of the Treasury, the need to use the Government's own massive purchasing power to encourage specifications with export potential, the importance of middle-range technology, the inappropriate distribution of professional manpower, the remoteness of the Civil Service and universities, the inadequate margins for industrial investment, the importance of encouraging professional mobility as a factor contributing to innovation, the significance of pensions policy, the role of education... Everywhere changes were needed. The one constraint that there seemed to be no way of avoiding was the Socialist doctrine that lay behind the work of the National Economic Development Office. It gave spurious emphasis to the role of the trade unions as partners in policy-making. Three years later the arrival of Margaret Thatcher provided the signal for a wholesale clearing of the decks, but in

1976 the real world was one in which this doctrine could not be easily abandoned.

By the time the report was ready for distribution a major change had taken place in the political scene. Harold Wilson had resigned unexpectedly and, in April 1976, James Callaghan had moved from the Foreign Office to Number 10. Before he was taken ill Arnold Gregory had arranged that our paper would be given to the new Prime Minister, provided it arrived before the summer recess. With a great effort on the part of Marcelle Bradshaw, my secretary, I got it to Number 10 on 4 August and heard, a couple of days later, that it was on Callaghan's desk.

The Prime Minister was anxious to do whatever might be possible to stem the economic decline and welcomed this contribution from outside the normal bureaucracy, particularly as it came so early in his tenure of office and from a Labour-friendly source. Five weeks later we received his congratulations. Zuckerman, although he read our piece 'with admiration', was less convinced that our proposals were politically realistic. 'Where's the leadership coming from?' Nevertheless, he asked for an extra copy to be sent to the Palace and, in due course, allowed me sight of some shrewdly realistic comments from 'a certain source' – by which I assumed he meant the Duke of Edinburgh.

Callaghan was on weak ground, in charge of a party that was in thrall to the unions, but he did his best to educate his supporters in a speech to the autumn Party Conference that directly reflected our paper. On 14 October 1976 he minuted the Chancellor of the Duchy of Lancaster, Harold Lever, saying that our report's value lay in the way it brought together a wide range of suggestions into a coherent programme:

> If we can reach favourable decisions on many of these suggestions and announce them in a single document, that could prove much more effective than the series of announcements which is otherwise likely... I should be grateful if you could find time to chair a Group of Ministers whose task would be to add a political

dimension to the ideas ... while at the same time bringing in Departmental assessments... The exercise should be a quick one. The group might make it their first task to see if any points should be picked out for inclusion in a national recovery programme.

In the weeks that followed I was not privy to what was being said, but in May 1977 a friend who worked in Number 10 told me that 'few documents have had such a far-reaching effect'. In June I heard from another direction that the Lever Committee 'had reported very favourably on our paper'.

This was gratifying, but by then Hoskyns and I had become convinced that the Labour Party was too cluttered with baggage from the past to be able to lead the country to economic salvation. On the day before Callaghan gave a brave speech to the party conference Denis Healey, the Chancellor, had been forced by an economic crisis to return from Heathrow while on his way to a Commonwealth Finance Ministers' meeting. The pound fell sharply and, a few days later, the bank rate jumped by two per cent. Labour's economic policy was in ruins. If the future lay anywhere it could only be with the Conservatives. We had already made contact with them several months earlier, before the 1972 Industry Group had unexpectedly provided us with an opportunity for influencing the Labour government. Hoskyns decided that any further time spent in helping Labour would be time wasted. Though politically neutral I was more personally committed through my friendship with Wilfred Brown, but my links with Hoskyns were closer still. In time I managed to loosen my contacts and drift away without causing too much hurt to Wilfred.

Chance had played a part in our switch from Labour to Conservative. In the summer of 1975 I had been taken as a guest to a lunch-time current-affairs discussion of the Romney Street Group, which was then meeting weekly in the Reform Club. The Group had been founded towards the end of World War I by Tom Jones, deputy secretary of Lloyd George's cabinet, with the *pro bono publico* rôle of thinking about the post-war future. It had continued to meet ever since – in private, and without political commitment, since this is the most efficient way of discussing difficult issues. I was intrigued, and became a member. There I met Alfred Sherman, who told me he was helping Sir Keith Joseph, the recently-appointed policy guru of the Conservative Party, to set up a new Centre for Policy Studies (CPS). Its Chairman was Margaret Thatcher, who had succeeded Edward Heath as Conservative leader a few months earlier. While the new body would be centre-right in its views, it would not be bound by any pre-existing Tory dogma – its task was to bring in new thinking. I expressed my interest and, shortly afterwards, met Sherman again at the Centre's house in Wilfred Street, not far from Victoria Station.

It did not take long to discover that the new CPS was regarded as an undesirable upstart by some at the Conservative Central Office. Alan Howarth took the view that Wilfred Street was redundant, since Central Office already had eighty (sic) working parties. The CPS was also 'too much imbued by the spirit of the Holy Grail. It had been set up before the change of leader as a protest. It was no longer needed'. A similar feeling of scepticism emerged at a meeting with Christopher Patten of the Conservative Research Department. Patten characterised Sherman as a 'theologian'. He said there were no grounds for thinking that the Conservative Party would pull itself together in time for the next election, even though that was still three years away. Thatcher was no radical and it was unlikely that she would ever seek to reform Parliament. Hoskyns and I walked back feeling depressed, but in no way deflected from our intention of working with Sherman in the hope of inducing some shift in political thinking.

It was my good fortune that I was given the chance to work with the CPS at a time when my views were formed and embodied in my British Association speech. Sherman was delighted to see that they chimed with his own thoughts on monetarism. He was particularly intrigued by the 'map'. He seemed to be just what we needed. His verbal dexterity and journalistic and political contacts were guarantees that our ideas would have some chance of bearing fruit. It was not many days before I introduced Hoskyns to Sherman and, for the next few years, the three of us formed a closely knit team.

To listen to Sherman for the first time was to draw a great breath of political fresh air. For anyone so closely connected with the Tory leadership he came from the most unlikely background. Born into a Jewish family from the East End of London, and in his early years a Communist by conviction, he had at the age of eighteen become a machine gunner in the International Brigade on the Republican side in the Spanish Civil War. In the 1950s he had been on the economic staff of the Israeli government and a leader writer for the *Jewish Chronicle*. More recently he had been filling a similar role for the *Daily Telegraph*. He was now in his mid-fifties, heavy of build and with measured speech, but his mind was quicksilver.

When speaking of himself he was utterly realistic. 'I'm a purveyor of second-hand ideas,' he would say. 'Like second-hand houses and second-hand cars they help make the market for first-hand ideas.' Regarding nationalised industries he was scathing: 'British Shipbuilders provide work simulation stations: we subsidise ships for Poland so that the Poles can build the Russian Navy!' He hated statistics and statisticians: 'The average person in this country has one breast.' Economists too were his target: 'People confuse economists and witch doctors; witch doctors have a higher success rate... Friedman [the monetarist] is a friend of mine, but truth is a greater friend... The UK is a mediocracy.' His conversation was larded with quirky proverbs: 'Obstinacy is the opposite of courage... A clever man can escape from a predicament that a wise man might not have created... Tell a fool to pray and he bangs his head... We need more law, but not more laws... If justice cannot be done it is all the more important that it should be seen not to be done.' Words for him were a passion, but he was alert to the way they can deceive when used thoughtlessly. He was scathing about the Liberals, dubbing them 'a party of protest'. And he was ever-

341

conscious of his origins: 'Like a Jewish buffet supper, there's enough to go round provided you get there early.'

The months that followed were among the most exciting of my life. My frequent meetings with Sherman were the more remarkable and agreeable because they coincided with the darkest days of the Uranium Institute, when the uranium producers were still striving to use it as a front for their cartel, and when their threat to appoint a nominee as Chief Executive still hung over me.

Through Sherman's good offices John Hoskyns and I soon met Sir Keith Joseph, the co-founder of the CPS. Sherman explained with an impish smile, 'When we started he did not know where we were going. If he had known he wouldn't have wanted to go there.' Joseph was the most cerebral member of Margaret Thatcher's shadow cabinet, with a publicly announced special responsibility for 'policy'. What exactly that implied was unclear, but it provided the opening we were looking for. He had read a paper that Hoskyns had prepared for the meeting, and his attitude was warmly welcoming. He took our notes 'as read'. The conversation focused on how to convert our diagrammatic representation into political reality.

'Has anyone done this before?'

We thought not.

'How *strong* are you? We must confront you with an *advocatus diaboli* – Rothschild perhaps. Not Zuckerman – he's one of those responsible.'

That remark surprised me: I did not see how Solly, despite his enormous influence, could possibly be held responsible for the state of the country. Hoskyns underlined that it was the act of comprehending the import of our 'map' that could be the biggest single step forward. I suggested that stability should be an important target.

'Most exciting,' said Keith, and went off to make a speech.

When he had gone Alfred made mouth-watering suggestions about political careers for the two of us. But we were unconvinced that our future would lie in the Palace of Westminster. For myself, although I had been trying for some months to escape from the seemingly discredited Uranium Institute, I thought it safer to regard his suggestions as no more than friendly commendation.

Partly to test our strength, partly to introduce ourselves to the Conservative Party, we met a month later – 11 November 1975 – with Keith Joseph and several of the brightest young Tories. The group included Christopher Tugenhadt, David Howell and Leon Brittan, all of whom later had distinguished careers. John led off and I followed. We found it difficult to judge how deep an impression we had made, though another meeting was helpfully suggested. Our own impression was of politicians caught in a House of Commons trap where truth could hardly prevail. Indeed, in a subsequent meeting we reached the sad conclusion that even the purest truth would be pilloried if uttered there by a politician. 'Impossible' figured too largely for my liking in Keith Joseph's comments. Clearly we were not about to take the Tory citadel by storm – though someone did express the encouraging thought that the best contribution, for the moment at least, might come from 'technicians' from outside normal politics.

A fortnight later we met the same group again. The atmosphere was warmer. By then Hoskyns, Sherman and I had been joined by Norman Strauss, one of Sherman's important discoveries. For someone interested in wielding political influence Strauss had a most unusual background. He was an advertising specialist, a rôle that bored him to distraction. Nevertheless, he had launched a new soap so successfully that in three months it had jumped from being an untested brand-new product to becoming market leader. His skill lay in talking up to the public. His aim was always to present them with 'new data', incisively worded. This approach was to have more than a little to do with Thatcher's eventual success at the polls.

Our meeting suffered from lack of an agenda. When I tried to deal with the politicians' obvious bewilderment over the relevance of a 'systems' approach I was slightly upset to hear Strauss whisper 'too early'. He was probably right; it *was* still very early days. As the meeting broke up I was given a thinly disguised offer to work as special adviser to the Select Committee on Expenditure – impossible to accept, but an encouraging straw in the wind.

When we met Keith Joseph again just before Christmas 1975 we made a somewhat confused, but bold, bid to put these preliminaries behind us and get right into the middle of Tory thinking. Keith was enthusiastic and talked grandly of a Commando Unit, or more grandly still of a Central Synoptic Unit. The details did not matter – things were beginning to go our way.

As 1976 arrived and the months rolled by I became worried lest the policy thinking that my friends and I were still doing under the aegis of the 1972 Industry Group should be regarded by our new Tory associates as treasonable infidelity. Shortly after delivering *Rebuilding British Industry* to Number 10 in August 1976 I went to see Keith Joseph at his house, to explain. After his initial surprise he took what I had to say calmly.

'Are you a member of the Labour Party?'

'No.'

'Is your piece political or analytical?'

'Analytical.'

'Then it might well be helpful. If it improves Callaghan's thinking it might make it unnecessary for us to contradict him.'

It was a warmer, more generous and more sophisticated response than I had expected. He drove me to Marylebone station. I felt I had spent the evening with a gentleman and a patriot.

I found his civilised pragmatism attractive. He did not bridle at criticism: 'I have no toes.' But he was depressed by his inability to put across the message that the Unions were creating unemployment by pricing their members out of jobs. 'What must I do? Must I make a speech saying that I don't eat babies for breakfast? Well, not before breakfast.'

At the same time there were difficulties in communicating. His background and experience were so very different from my own. I relied on ideas and facts, insofar as I could be sure of them. He was more interested in communication as an art form in its own right. 'Are you a wordsmith?' he once asked. Even more strangely: 'Are you a polymath?' He had accepted monetarist views on economic policy, I thought, too unquestioningly. Other countries did not necessarily lie back and rely on the workings of Adam Smith's 'invisible hand'. They, including the United States, were not averse to government subsidy and intervention. More than once Keith chided me for what he saw as my wish to intervene. It was an odd view coming from a politician whose job could be viewed as doing precisely that.

John Hoskyns and I were reasonably certain that we were thinking on the right lines; we nevertheless took whatever opportunities we could for cross-checking with others. Not all union leaders were unthinking ultra-leftists. John Lyons, of the Electrical Power Engineers Association, spoke and wrote soberly on politico-economic subjects without ducking difficult issues. He had read economics and was chairman of a working party at the National Economic Development Office. Later he became a member of the TUC General Council. From the autumn of 1975 we saw a good deal of him, and were delighted to make common cause with someone from the other side of the political spectrum. He did, however, remind us that in public he might have to watch his words, to avoid creating trouble with his Trotskyite members.

Sir Geoffrey Vickers was another special person. In World War I he had won the Victoria Cross. In World War II he had been Head of Economic Intelligence at the Ministry of Economic Warfare, and a member of the Joint Intelligence Committee. He had then joined the National Coal Board as their legal adviser, and was later in charge of manpower policy. This wealth of experience had led him in retirement to write extensively – and most elegantly – on the socio-economic predicament in which modern society found itself. I had especially enjoyed his analysis of changing values in an unstable society, *Freedom in a Rocking Boat*, and had told him so when we first met. He smiled: 'Cream to a cat.' He was now eighty-one and, although still vigorous, was unable to drive at night. In February 1976, by dint of a logistics effort of Herculean proportions, Geoffrey and the two Johns met at my house in Jordans for a memorable discussion, made all the more enjoyable by a gastronomic tour de force on the part of Jeanie. It provided the perfect antidote to a sour meeting earlier in the day, when I had encountered fierce opposition from an influential member of the Uranium Institute to my accepting an invitation to chair a Sector Working Party at the National Economic Development Office. I had made clear that I would, nevertheless, accept.

Throughout the summer of 1976 I was doing my best to keep the Institute afloat, while assuaging the US Justice Department's suspicions regarding its mining members. I was willing to pursue my political interests by working well into the night, but could not continue to match the contribution that John Hoskyns – whose time was his own after the sale of his successful software company – and Norman Strauss were able to make. A change in the division of our work came naturally when they had their first meeting with Margaret Thatcher in August. It went well and led on to other meetings. From then on I worked through Hoskyns whenever I had anything useful to say.

It was mid-term in a Parliament in which Labour had won a wafer-thin majority: Labour 319, Conservatives 276, Liberals 13, others 27. Labour were able to stay in power only through the pact they had made with the Liberals. They were running the country so badly that I wondered whether Mrs Thatcher might just possibly be able to spring a surprise, if she made a speech aimed at detaching at least some of the Liberals from their otherwise automatic support of the government.

Shortly afterwards, in March 1977, she put down a vote of censure which she failed to win, even though the government majority had fallen through by-election losses to just one, excluding the Speaker and his deputies.

Later in the year *The Economist* preached the need for Parliamentary revival. But it is a matter of record, and of regret, that in the quarter of a century since then the standing of the House has not improved. The Executive governs, untrammelled by effective scrutiny. More and more laws are passed after less and less deliberation. The lack of parliamentary consideration of the torrent of European legislation has become farcical. In the summer of 2002 the Father of the House, Tam Dalyell, bitterly and publicly criticised his Prime Minister, Tony Blair, even though they were from the same party, for his contemptuous attitude towards the legislature.

As 1977 began, the recently appointed chairmen of the National Economic Development Office's working parties were invited to Number 11 Downing Street, to meet the Chancellor. Denis Healey, who had been my Minister in Defence, greeted me cordially with the words, 'Glad to see you're getting your hands dirty.' He was right; trying to find ways of simultaneously satisfying the aspirations of both management and unions was proving an educative experience.

The underlying thought of the paper that had gone to Callaghan was that the country was failing to nurture its potentially innovative industries in the way that Japan and France were doing so effectively. An opportunity came in March 1977 to spread the message in a lecture to the Confederation of British Industries. The following day the *Financial Times* quoted me with relish: 'I am not, of course, speaking about the public sector, where survival after death is a well-documented phenomenon.'

It was becoming all too easy to be emotional about the state of British politics. So it was perhaps timely to be reminded that we were no more culpable or inefficient than other countries and institutions. By chance, I ran into an Italian who worked at the European Commission and whom I knew and liked through his interest in science. He too was depressed: 'There's a huge volume of "bumph". We collect opinions like butterflies. It's the philatelic approach to policy-making.'

In July 1977 Callaghan gave a reception at Lancaster House for those involved with the National Economic Development Office. He spoke well and to the point. All the main issues we had examined in the '72 Group paper were covered in the discussion. Even the trade unionists were on their best behaviour,

347

one notable Left-winger, Hugh Scanlon, making the unexpected admission that the unions, by their actions, had fuelled inflation in 1974. The one group that did not seem to agree on the need for change in their own stance was the Civil Service. Sir Eric Roll believed we had gone too far in our paper for Callaghan, when giving our prescription for a Service that would be more aware of the effect of its actions on those who had to make the economy succeed. Another Treasury luminary felt it would be a 'calumny' to suggest that the country's inflation record might well have been different had not the Civil Service been protected by inflation-proof pensions. Fortunately, we had the Government behind us. Before the year ended I had an opportunity, along with other members of the '72 Industry Group, of discussing with the Minister responsible the practical possibilities of importing outsiders from business into the Service.

I listened to Callaghan once more, at the end of 1977. I had the impression of a fundamentally honest man who wanted to do his best in his last job, particularly in stopping key unions from holding the country to ransom. He, of course, had opposed Barbara Castle's attempt to bring the unions under the rule of law in 1969, with her White Paper, 'In place of Strife'. Now the country was paying the price, and he had belatedly become a reformist. 'I don't know if the country wants it. But that's what it's going to get. It needs only one vote of censure and I'll go.'

Meanwhile, starting in August 1977, Hoskyns and Strauss had been working on a new strategic approach to future Tory policy. They called it 'Stepping Stones', a title suggested by Keith Joseph. Its purpose was to clarify Tory thinking and to induce a public perception that something quite new was stirring on the Right of British politics. I took no direct part in this work but, during our frequent meetings, I fed to Hoskyns whatever thoughts seemed likely to be relevant.

Some words of my US lawyer, Reuben Clark, still ring in my ear: 'Nothing will come right in your country until the unions are brought under the rule of law. We did it in America. You can do it here.' At a CPS meeting I repeated his words, only to see some of the mainstream Tories shaking their heads. Fortunately, Hoskyns and Strauss were made of sterner stuff. Early in the evolution of 'Stepping Stones' they had come to the conclusion that controlling the unions was an essential step towards re-energising the country. By the end of November 1977 they had secured Thatcher's support – though Jim Prior, the shadow minister dealing with employment, and Lord Thorneycroft, the party chairman, remained sceptical and apparently in fear of what the unions might do. At one point Thorneycroft unsuccessfully called for all copies of the 'Stepping Stones' papers to be called in and burned. More than once during the summer of 1978 Hoskyns told me he was thinking of throwing in the sponge, so tired was he of the 'highly articulate crap' he was forced to listen to from the politicians.

How 'Stepping Stones' finally succeeded in weathering the doubts and uncertainties of the Shadow Cabinet is the subject of one of the most arresting chapters in Hoskyns' fascinating account of the Thatcher revolution, *Just in Time*. It also speaks of his tenacity and clarity of vision. Despite the poor economic performance of Labour the Tories were not obviously sweeping ahead in the opinion polls. It would have been only too easy to be discouraged. Hoskyns was, nevertheless, convinced that they would succeed at the next general election. They should, therefore, make clear to the unions that they would be disciplined by law – and should do so early, so that the unions would understand there was no point in attempting to bully an incoming Tory government, and might even make moves towards reconciliation before the election.

In the summer of 1978 I was preoccupied with producing two major papers, one on the management of national scientific resources for the British Association meeting at Bath, the other for a Salzburg Seminar on the control of nuclear proliferation. Driving home from Bath I heard Callaghan addressing a restive Trades Union Congress that was angrily opposed to any pay limits (15% had been proposed). Although busy, I managed to

349

keep a toe-hold in the Centre for Policy Studies, helping Keith Joseph and David Wolfson (Chief of Staff of Mrs Thatcher's political office) and, of course, John Hoskyns. They were thinking about how to make the best use of the Civil Service once the election had been won. Wolfson asked whether it would be feasible for new Ministers to enter Whitehall with a set of self-consistent dossiers already prepared, or whether the better course would be to wait and ask the Civil Service to do the job. If the former (which I favoured) what scale of effort would be needed? I gave him my estimate: three two-hour working party meetings for perhaps fifteen policy areas, plus drafting time. If the party were seriously interested in governing in the near future, that should be well within reach. He seemed convinced. The following day – it was towards the end of October 1978 – I lunched with John Hoskyns, who was in low spirits. Without rancour he said that he had written hundreds of pages contributing to Tory thinking, every one of which had more content than they seemed able or willing to contribute. The time had come to hold up a mirror. So we wrote down a stream-of-consciousness list of topics that would need to form part of any coherent approach. There was no difficulty in doing so; it just needed a little determination to allocate the necessary time. For David Howell I listed a number of questions, the answers to which – assuming the Tories could produce them – would go a long way towards settling future policy. He was warmly appreciative.

I also wrote to the *Times* on wages policy. It was a long letter and was published in full. It suggested that the crude, self-destructive bludgeoning the country was receiving from the unions could have been avoided. But coolly academic counsels stood little chance of being heard through the wage-dispute turmoil that was gripping the country as 1979 dawned. There were rail strikes. Mobile pickets were blocking the ports. Water workers were on strike in the North. So were a million and a half public service workers. Some hospitals were being picketed and ambulances refused entry. Some dead were left unburied. And the Civil Service, which was supposed to be helping

Ministers to administer their anti-inflation policy, was making a wage claim of between 26 and 48 per cent. In Number 10 there was sad resignation and acquiescence in inevitable defeat.

Towards the end of January a judge gave the country a small element of relief, by granting an injunction against the leader of a secondary picket. 'There must be some limitation,' he said, 'otherwise there will be anarchy. Parliament would not have legislated to bring about its own destruction.'

In the midst of this mayhem Callaghan had to leave for a summit in Guadeloupe. In the tube going home I saw a slightly tipsy man waving his arms about.

'All this crisis and they're in Gawdaloop. They're on 'oliday... It's yer veg yer wants to worry abaht... This 'ere.' (He patted his stomach.) '*Turnips*. Turnips at 18p. Brussels 40p. And frawsted. The country's bent, and we're all in enough agro.'

The doors opened. He swayed unsteadily on to the platform knowing, as the country knew, that the government was on its last legs.

The Tories had an open goal. Their new strategy of attacking the privileged position of the unions was beginning to pay off. On 9 January 1979 the *Financial Times* published a favourable first leader. But Alan Howarth – who had once told me that Central Office had eighty working parties, and that the Centre for Policy Studies was not needed – now had a worrying message. In Conservative Party headquarters in Smith Square all was chaos. Mrs Thatcher had little organising power and the hierarchy was riven with jealousy. Nevertheless, policy integration was essential. Our '72 Industry Group paper had shown what could be done with relatively little effort, and, as Thorneycroft's assistant, Howarth had seen how the 'Stepping Stones' project had been the result of a limited but concentrated effort on the part of a few determined clear-thinkers. Someone senior needed to take a grip.

I drafted a letter to Sir Keith Joseph and took it to the House of Commons. David Howell had agreed to pass it on. John Hoskyns was elated: 'How to build Rome in a day!' But when I received a summons from Keith Joseph our meeting was

351

disappointing. 'I am still not at one with you. You are too interventionist.' He asked why I thought the Tories were not organised. 'We are,' he insisted. 'Hoskyns wouldn't know.' Clearly he underestimated the power of the grapevine. Afterwards, I rang Zuckerman and told him I had run into the sand.

'Yes, it does sound like the sand,' was all he could say.

A timely dinner at Oxford provided a little light relief, for there I heard a story of a vastly less frenetic approach to an election. Roosevelt was due to give a final speech on the radio. He had only ten minutes, but the Republicans had booked the whole of the next hour. FDR was unflustered. 'The enemy have delivered themselves into our hands.' He spoke for seven minutes; there was a one-minute prayer and two minutes of organ music. Roosevelt won.

The enemy were delivered into Margaret Thatcher's hands on 28 March 1979, when Labour lost a motion of no confidence. An election was called for 3 May. It was time to consider how far changes in the Whitehall machinery might be needed. Hoskyns and Strauss were uncertain about the best way to use the Central Policy Review Staff (CPRS). I persuaded them that the Staff constituted a resource that was ready and waiting. There would be no problem about making a case for new staff and, if properly used, the CPRS might prove invaluable.

Hoskyns began to wonder whether I could be drafted into the CPRS. Would I be prepared to report to him?

'Yes, personally,' I told him.

But I was worried that the Civil Service might see difficulties. The CPRS was a component of the Cabinet Office; John would be in Number 10. The two were closely linked, but organisationally separate; it would be a new arrangement. I advised him to discuss the possibilities with John Hunt, the Cabinet Secretary, naming no names so that the conversation would be more clinical.

In a discussion a fortnight before the election I told Hoskyns that there was too much exposure of the 'leader' and that she was harping too much on 'freedom'. I remembered how Churchill had lost the 1945 election after his unconvincing warnings about a Labour 'Gestapo'. Her words about 'wreckers' needed softening, to take account of the many who felt forced to join the far left out of fear for their jobs. Her broadcast four days before the election was a disappointment – to me, at least.

On election day itself I was in Germany for a Uranium Institute meeting. It was at Assmannshausen, in a riverside hotel situated exactly where the Rhine begins its descent through the Rhine gorge. By midnight seventeen results had been declared, too few to be a guide to the future. Throughout the following morning calls to London made it increasingly clear that the Tories would soon be home and dry, and with a comfortable working majority. Before our meeting broke up Margaret Thatcher had been called to the Palace. The work of Hoskyns and Strauss on Stepping Stones had not been in vain. Nor had it been unappreciated. On 5 May the Prime Minister found time to write to John:

Over the past two years your experience has brought a new dimension to the way the Party thinks and operates... It has been invaluable, and I greatly appreciate what you have done with the help and loyal support of Norman Strauss and Terry Price.

On 7 May John Hoskyns rang to say that he had had an hour with the Prime Minister, who appeared not to know whether or not she wanted him to join her staff in Number 10. But before long he became Head of her Policy Unit. The Prime Minister had also discussed the Central Policy Review Staff. Hoskyns told her that he wanted me to run it. That was exciting news. Shortly afterwards there was a meeting between Hoskyns, myself, and Sir Kenneth Berrill, the existing head of the Staff. It got off to a questionable start, involving turgid details about terms of employment. Then we got to the meat. I fired questions at him, gradually getting him to admit how little it had been possible for the CPRS to do for Labour.

'We were in the same bed, but our dreams were different.' We talked about the need for a political vision. Could CPRS help to create it? Berrill thought that it could. Feeling that he and I were thinking on similar lines I withdrew, leaving the rest to Hoskyns. They talked about Berrill's successor. He thought it should be someone from outside the Civil Service and preferably a scientist. Hoskyns went back and wrote to the Prime Minister. I heard later that Berrill had spoken favourably about me to a colleague.

However, as the days went by it became steadily clearer that my future did not lie with the CPRS. Hoskyns, in *Just in Time*, does not attempt to conceal his annoyance:

> I was successful with Norman, but not with Terry, I think because Keith and Margaret thought that with his Civil Service background he would be too interventionist [as the new head of the CPRS]. We thus wasted someone who had been involved in all the 'Stepping Stones' thinking, had himself run a Ministry of Defence think tank, was highly intelligent, numerate and had the advantages of a scientifically trained mind – all too rare in Whitehall. Although Terry did not return to Whitehall, I consulted him on many questions throughout my time at Number 10.

A month after the election I took Hoskyns to the London Zoo for lunch with Zuckerman. He did well, and Zuckerman warmed to him. The conversation rambled – flew rather – over personalities and industrial and economic issues, before alighting on what was still Zuckerman's main concern, controversial defence issues: SALT, Polaris, cruise missiles, defence expenditure, the immobility of the Scientific Civil Service. He still feared that the world might blow itself up. I envied John for the huge canvas that was now his.

At the beginning of 1980 I picked up a suggestion of Keith Joseph's and set up, within the Centre for Policy Studies, a study group to consider the forces that had been preventing the country from exploiting its undoubted innovative skills. Alfred Sherman provided me with a ready-made team – the Enterprise Culture Group (ECG) – that rapidly became, in Alan Howarth's words 'the best dining club in London'. We usually met for a buffet dinner and talked non-stop from beginning to end, the conversation stimulated by a rioja of Alfred's choosing – a throwback to his time as a machine-gunner during the Spanish Civil War.

The ground the ECG was to cover was familiar. Five years of passionate conversations with Theo Williamson and John Hoskyns had taught me how varied were the causes of our economic decline and how deeply they were embedded in the structure of British society. My NEDO sector working party was also throwing up examples of industry's creaking joints – in particular, poor product quality and indifferent marketing. Drawing on such experiences I set out the chapter headings of a possible book.

The Group met for the first time on 28 January 1980. The meeting went well. Drafting tasks were handed out and I had a hope that a small book could be finished by the autumn. I said as much in a presentation by the various CPS chairmen to the Prime Minister a few days later. Organisationally that occasion was unique – thirteen speechlets in the space of fifty minutes. I pruned my remarks down to 350 words and managed to raise a couple of laughs. The Prime Minister was more impressive than I had expected, somehow radiating morality and common sense. I was introduced to her and thanked her for her 5 May letter.

'John is marvellous,' she said, several times. 'Stepping Stones got us where we are today. Of course it was Jim Prior who was the trouble even then.'

A few more friendly words and she was off. Even though I had been a contributor to 'Stepping Stones' – as an off-stage member of the family – I could not help wondering whether she was in the habit of criticising one of her own Cabinet to someone whom she was meeting for the first time. I said as much to Hoskyns as we walked over to Downing Street. He had just come from talking to a BBC man, who had said, 'Of course you should be clobbering the unions. But you won't. And in 1983 they'll tear you to pieces.'

He underestimated the Thatcher team, which was just beginning to comprehend what might be done now that they had their hands on the levers of power. Privatisation seemed an attractive option that offered a real chance to reduce the Public Sector Borrowing Requirement. But for the moment the economy was in a mess. Inflation was running at over 20%. A steel strike was in progress. Unemployment was already two million – and on course for three million. The Treasury's remedies fell short of what was needed.

On St Valentine's Day 1980 I sent a short paper to Hoskyns. It was called 'Economic Policy: is it carrying us in the wrong direction?' The covering letter said: 'I hope I'm not misleading you. I can't think I am, even though this is way off my own field. One develops a nose for when something is not properly understood, and here is such a case if I ever saw one.' My paper described another kind of 'map': a vicious circle involving a monetary squeeze, with inflation still rising; high interest rates leading to a high pound on the exchanges; more imports – therefore more unemployment – leading to higher public spending on social security; reduction, therefore, in tax revenues and so further upward pressure on interest rates; which completed the circle by keeping the pound too high. I queried whether £M3 was the correct monetary measure by which to steer the economy. It included interest-bearing deposits, and so could grow on account of the very measures – high interest rates – that were intended to squeeze the economy and so make the money-supply shrink. I added that there were some people in Switzerland who might have alternative advice to offer. Hoskyns kindly describes this letter as 'extraordinarily prescient'. It seems to have had some beneficial effect on the thinking that preceded the 1981 budget.

A fortnight later, on Leap Year Day, I went to Number 10 soon after lunch, and left after a four-hour discussion with John Hoskyns, his assistant, Andrew Duguid, and three economists. Amongst them was Christopher Foster, whom I had not seen since my Transport days. Looking two years ahead, the possibilities seemed encouraging, with a huge decrease in the PSBR possible. But there was an immediate problem in the level of the sterling exchange rate, which was crippling British business. Ideas emerged as they could never have done in a normal Whitehall meeting, where so much is 'given' in advance. I walked happily down Number 10's Queen Anne stairs, looked up at the balconies to fix them in my memory and went out past the watchman's chair into Downing Street.

I was soon back again in Number 10 for a discussion with Hoskyns and Douglas Hague, who had been acting as Margaret Thatcher's economic adviser. The subject was the stabilisation of the economy. As accountants and economists did not seem able to create the stability that was needed, I wondered whether it might be time to call in the control engineering profession. Control engineers had wide experience, in many different fields, of damping out unwanted oscillations. I do not know whether the suggestion was taken up, but clearly the complexities of 'squeezing out inflation' were not understood by the Chancellor – nor, presumably, by the Treasury either. The new government had failed to grasp the public expenditure nettle when it first took office and now, a year later, the consequences were evident all around.

In mid-June Hoskyns and I again had dinner together. He had been trying to get the Prime Minister to think in terms of economic stabilisation. She did not take kindly to the idea.

'I don't like the word, "stabilisation". It sounds like "stagnation".'

'Funny,' he replied, 'it sounds like "stabilisation" to me.'

Something was certainly needed. The decline in our engineering products that was such a concern of Theo Williamson was continuing. Foreign car imports were showing a year-on-year increase of 31%. Hoskyns was working hard preparing a list of 'accelerators' for discussion in a Cabinet Office economic committee. The country somehow had to avoid repeating the symptoms of the Dutch disease: a nexus of problems, including the exchange rate, North Sea oil (which had just started to flow), imports, industrial regeneration... It was largely the same list we had presented to

357

Callaghan. The government had changed but the battle was still the same, except that Thatcher had greater freedom to deal with one very central problem – the trade unions.

I passed on John Hoskyns' *cri de coeur* to Alfred Sherman, who was soon to have a meeting with the Prime Minister and, the following day, sent him an aide-memoire on what might be done. Within a few days this had been expanded to over ten thousand words – perhaps inappropriately long, but a measure of how much required improvement. The drafting problem was to explain to her why change was needed without making her 'switch off'. I tried introducing some oblique flattery; but Jeanie, who was checking my drafts, wrote 'flannel' in the margin.

The piece for the Prime Minister was finished at last and I walked it over to Number 10. On the way I met Sherman and congratulated him on that day's *Telegraph* leader.

'How did you know I wrote it?'

'Your style is unmistakeable.'

He beamed. Hoskyns was pleased with my draft. 'So many points, and how true.'

But when I spoke a couple of days later to Norman Strauss he was discouraging. 'It's all over. Until she realises that she can't do it all herself there's little hope.'

Hoskyns pressed for an opportunity to speak informally and without pressure of time to the leading members of the Cabinet at Chequers, and in mid-January 1981 he was given the chance. There was one small snag. He wanted to use a flip-chart, but rang to tell me that the whole resources of the Civil Service were incapable of providing him with flip-chart paper. Could the Uranium Institute assist? Not for the first time Marcelle took a taxi to Number 10 and did her patriotic duty.

Pessimism was easier to find than optimism. Strauss was particularly depressed. He was due to leave Downing Street within a few months, and would have preferred to leave on a 'high'.

'We're watching authority drain,' he said despondently.

Theo Williamson was equally down. 'High technology is now

only ten per cent of the British economy. Japanese workers don't fear for their jobs, and so work without restrictive practices. This means *growth*. A man who leaves for more pay simply finds himself blocked later on.'

I told John Hoskyns my political morale was low. He invited me to a meeting on 4 March 1981 to discuss how the PM could be persuaded to face up to the need for a more rational approach to running the country. More cohesion and coordination were needed – but she was resolutely setting her face against anything approaching reorganisation. It was perhaps the most extraordinary policy meeting I ever attended. Her six closest non-parliamentary advisers were wringing their hands, desperately searching for ways of saving her from herself. The general conclusion was that she would probably not change. I felt quite sick. So did Alfred Sherman – and he had helped to make her.

Meanwhile, the Enterprise Culture Group was continuing with its work. At its third meeting I thought it might be useful for them to hear something of industry's problems, so I brought along a professor of engineering, Alec Chisholm, who had kindly produced a paper for discussion. To my surprise it was not well received. I felt that the non-technologists round the table showed no understanding of what was involved in conceiving and successfully producing a modern industrial product, nor the extent to which market constraints play their part in engineering. Alec was surprised and upset; I felt I owed him an apology. Afterwards Sherman said how much he regretted that I was not with the Central Policy Review Staff, and could I help with strategy for the next election? The suggestion was meant kindly but was premature; anyway, the government would be judged on its deeds, not its words.

The Enterprise Culture Group included Tony Flew, who was Professor of Philosophy at Reading. He was the son-in-law of Vernon Donnison, who had played such a large part in my life while I was at Harwell. I had been at Tony's wedding. In those days he had been a centre-leftist of the Crosland variety. Now he was politically on the far right and anxious that we should attack Labour party philosophy, and do so without mincing words. He produced a stream of elegantly drafted polemics which, to my surprise, Alfred Sherman seemed somewhat unwilling to support. Flew had the better of the argument and I encouraged him to continue.

It was at the Centre for Policy Studies (CPS) that I encountered Denis Thatcher for the first time. I thought him shrewd and honest. He was unwilling to speak about the Prime Minister, except for one direct quotation: 'We may not win next time; but by God we'll make it impossible for them to reverse most of what we've done.'

The CPS brotherhood also included Christopher Bailey, a ship repairer. He gave dinner on board his 160 foot motor yacht, *Welsh Falcon*, for the Minister of Transport, Norman Fowler. We were moored alongside HMS *Belfast*, and the view was all that one might wish for, with the Tower and Tower Bridge both illuminated. Christopher, a larger than life personality, had once stood against Jim Callaghan, whom he knew personally. During the campaign he had gone into a pub where the Red Flag was being sung. When it was ended he picked out the largest man and said, 'Put that table there.' He did so. 'Now put that chair on it.' Again he did as instructed. Christopher mounted the chair. 'I've heard you sing. Now you're going to sing my song.' And he launched into 'Lloyd George knew my father, my father knew Lloyd George'. They all joined in. The country needs more candidates like that.

One bright light amidst the gloom came from a meeting with Keith Joseph, who was now Secretary of State for Industry. The subject to be discussed was telecommunications, and a few of us from the CPS hoped to use our privileged positions as political insiders to plead on behalf of manufacturers for the Post Office to specify more internationally marketable equipment. Representations to the Post Office over the years had achieved little; now we were to speak directly and in confidence to the Minister concerned. With no civil servants present the discussion flowed easily. It proved to be the first move towards a sea-change in our national approach to telecommunications and digital equipment.

The mood of pessimism was spreading to my own Enterprise Culture Group. In mid-April only four attended. We spoke about what purpose, if any, could still justify our book project. We concluded it might be something to do with the 'vision' that the government had so far failed to project. But I had personally begun to doubt the value of continuing. To do so would tie me to the Tories, whom I was beginning to doubt were any longer worthy of support.

The rot continued. In May the 'First Eleven' – Sherman's hand-picked team of CPS leaders – showed signs of disintegration. The PM was not interested in their forward thinking, in which case they had no purpose. For me the meeting was saved by the presence of R.V. Jones. 'R.V.' had worked directly to Churchill as a young scientist during World War II, and now poured out a constant flow of fascinating Churchillian aphorisms: 'Honour a poor man's medals: they are his escutcheon.' In approaching his war-time duties Churchill liked 'diagnosis'. He had despaired of the Civil Service – 'the hierarchical attenuation of experience'.

Rather to my surprise, Wayland Kennet rang in July 1981 to ask whether I could assist with the conversion of the 1972 Industry Group into one that supported the newly-formed Social Democratic Party. Wayland had been one of the inaugural Committee of One Hundred that had engineered the SDP's breakaway from the Labour party. I doubted whether I could help him, but he held out the prospect of dinner with Shirley Williams. Four days later she spoke to the 1972 Group, giving a dazzling performance and putting not a foot wrong. The following day Zuckerman lunched me at Brook's Club, and the conversation was entirely about the new Social Democratic Party. That in itself was significant, as he did not waste his time on trivia. Roy Jenkins, the leader of the SDP, was staying with him; Zuckerman would mention my interest.

My political life seemed to be taking a new turn. I confessed to John Hoskyns, who was sympathetic. He saw little point in staying with the Centre for Policy Studies. If the Prime Minister went he would go too – the Whitehall culture was wrong. Like me he was aware of the predictions that because of the economic turmoil under Thatcher the Social Democrats might well win next time by a landslide.

In September 1981 I took Alfred Sherman to Beoty's restaurant in St Martin's Lane for a dinner marking the sixth and final anniversary of my connection with the Centre for Policy Studies. I told him I was at the end of the road and wished to shed the Enterprise Culture Group. We agreed on a possible follow-up chairman. He compared Thatcher to a good platoon commander, who was failing at the Field Marshal's job. She was insufficiently analytical. '*Omnibus dubitandem*' should be, but was not, her motto. But he did not share my interest in the Social Democrats.

As 1981 drew to a close John Hoskyns was wrestling with the decision to resign. He felt he had done, to the limit of his abilities, everything possible to help launch the Prime Minister successfully. She was later to show her warm appreciation by honouring him with a knighthood. But, like Alfred Sherman, he had never reconciled himself to her inability to think analytically. In all-important matters of state he felt very keenly the need for quiet, rational argument. Before long, the next general election would begin to cast its shadow; he did not relish the thought of taking part in the trimming that could hardly be avoided. He decided to quit. The Prime Minister invited John and his wife, Miranda, to Chequers and spent a long evening trying to persuade him to change his mind, but to no avail.

In the event the future in general, and politics in particular, proved as unpredictable as ever. A year after their formation the Social Democrats reached 50% in the national opinion polls and, on 25 March 1982, Roy Jenkins won a by-election at Glasgow Hillhead. But only a week later, on 2 April, the Argentinians invaded the Falklands. In doing so they transformed Margaret Thatcher's reputation and prospects. The country responded warmly to her courage and sheer guts, and by forgetting about the Social Democrats destroyed them politically. Just as

362

surely the invasion led swiftly to the overthrow of the Argentinian dictatorship and the restoration of democracy in that sorely tried country.

On 29 April 1982 John's friends assembled in the Pillared Room of Number 10 to wish him and Miranda goodbye. Despite her Falklands preoccupations the Prime Minister was there to do them honour, as were several Cabinet colleagues. I found it an emotionally charged occasion. So much had been attempted and successfully carried off; so much had failed. But life can only be lived in the real world; regrets were pointless. John was right to set a time of his own choosing for his departure.

As I walked out into Downing Street I found myself in the company of a fellow guest whom I had not previously met. We walked up Whitehall together chatting, and I discovered that he too had been at Vickers, where his treatment had exactly mirrored my own. By the time we arrived at Trafalgar Square tube station I felt so encouraged by our evident similarity of views that I quite forgot to ask his name.

Chapter 20

The Institute Matures

Politics had been enormously exciting, but my livelihood depended on the more prosaic task of keeping the Institute afloat. Moreover, Jean's health was continuing to deteriorate, and no-one could say what the future might involve. In any case there was a strong element of personal pride in what had so far been created and a determination to ensure that the Institute did not fail. Given our successful rebuttal of Westinghouse's attack at the US Embassy hearing, and the election a few days later of Heinrich Mandel as the first chairman to come from an electrical utility – someone, that is, who shared my own background and to whom I could speak easily and freely – there seemed to be a real chance of making a fresh start. Kostuik added to this impression by withdrawing his proposal to bring in someone over my head. He used the face-saving formula, 'in view of progress now being made', but in fact he had no other option. To have persisted with the proposal would have meant losing the consumer side of our membership – as Mandel made quite clear to me.

The Institute was not alone in seeking to create a worldwide nuclear association; to succeed it would first need to outpace the opposition. This became clear in the early days of Mandel's chairmanship, during a World Energy Conference at Istanbul. In the course of a magnificent evening reception in a park overlooking the Bosphorus I was approached by a representative of the

Atomic Industrial Forum. He said that the Institute, with its controversial record, could never hope to succeed. It would be more sensible to merge with his own organisation. It was already successful; its membership was larger and its subscription smaller; and its base was in the US, the main centre for the nuclear industry. It was now seeking to develop as an international body. However, since all its officers were US nationals, to merge as suggested would have compromised the Institute's multi-national character. I dismissed his offer, while inwardly wondering whether my confident words would be justified by events.

Before flying back to London I joined a short cruise along the Bosphorus as far as the Black Sea. Along much of its length beautiful houses were built only a few feet above the water level, a kind of linear Venice. As the ship headed out into the Black Sea for a few minutes before returning, it struck me as quite extraordinary that, in the middle of the nineteenth century, the British had allowed themselves to be drawn into the Crimean war, which involved ferrying men and equipment three hundred miles further still into the Eurasian land-mass.

I settled down to working with Mandel to make the Institute more generally useful. The original unannounced purpose of providing cover for a uranium producers' marketing agreement had failed. What remained possible would be to develop an educational rôle, aimed at improving the general understanding within the nuclear industry of how the uranium market worked. That implied collecting statistics in a way that was consistent with US and European law. The essentials for self-protection would be open publication of whatever was put together and legal monitoring of the process of collection and analysis. Initially, the miners were uneasy – running the Institute cost money and to offer such information openly seemed irrational. They were somewhat mollified when assured that there would be no objection to selling the information at a reasonable price; first, however, it had to be collected.

That meant a small research staff. We already had a young geologist and an economist, but needed a couple more people

365

with broader experience. We were lucky. In answer to an advertisement the formidably able and articulate Jan Murray arrived in my office. She was from Australia and a graduate of INSEAD, Fontainebleau. During lunch on the *Old Caledonia*, the last remaining paddle-steamer on the Thames, she subjected me to a searching interview, before agreeing to join us. In the fullness of time she followed me as Secretary-General.

Because the industry was affected on a day-to-day basis by government reactions to issues such as nuclear proliferation we also needed someone who knew the international scene. Jim Bedore, an American, was fortuitously finishing an assignment at the Royal Institute of International Affairs. He stayed with us for five all-important years, during which the Institute established itself as an international clearing house for ideas on nuclear policy.

Any research team needs an information base. The suggestion that we should build up a specialised library had earlier met with opposition from Kostuik: 'Every member already has one.' However, we persisted. Only a few years later people came from as far away as Sweden to consult our collection. So, incidentally, did a Russian intelligence officer who nominally ranked as a diplomat. The library undoubtedly became a major contributor to the Institute's success.

Before the US Embassy hearing in June 1977 a half-hearted attempt had been made to assess the future balance between uranium supply and demand. It had failed, partly through weak chairmanship, partly because our lawyers had ruled out any discussion of production capabilities and, not least, because there was almost universally muddled thinking about how nuclear electricity would develop. Mandel's arrival as the Institute's chairman provided an opportunity to recast this side of our work. The important decisions were taken in South Africa during the first of the Institute's annual foreign meetings in November 1977.

Ironically Mandel was not present, for reasons that were never entirely clear. The general assumption was that, as a prominent member of the German scientific community, he had been told by his government not to go, relations between Germany and South Africa being distinctly cool at the time. Or it may have been his position as, reputedly, the second most important target for terrorist attacks after Chancellor Schmidt. His life must have been almost intolerably difficult. For security reasons his car's number-plates were changed weekly, and his children went to school under armed guard. In South Africa Kostuik deputised for him, and Jean Féron, of Electricité de France, spoke for the electrical utilities.

The meeting was a considerable success, administratively as well as socially. An equitable and easily workable system was instituted to guarantee an orderly alternation of officerships between the mining and the nuclear electricity members, and a new committee system was agreed.

In technical visits we were shown how uranium is extracted. In South Africa it is a by-product of deep gold-mining, which is the economic underpinning of the Rand area around Johannesburg. We were taken down to a depth of 9,000 feet, where geothermal heating is a major problem. The mine cannot be cooled by air because of the phenomenon of adiabatic compression, with which every cyclist is familiar. In being taken down to that level, where the atmospheric pressure is much greater than at the surface, the air becomes too hot to be useful. Iced water is used instead, both as a coolant and as a lubricant for rock-cutting tools. At the working face everything was clean and quiet. White engineers and black labourers worked together in a spirit of mutual trust. When a small rock-fall occurred as a rock-face exploded under the huge overlying pressure, team-work quickly restored safe working conditions.

Back at the surface we watched the chemical extraction process leading to the production of 'yellow cake' (ammonium or sodium diuranate, the form in which uranium is marketed). We also watched the pouring of gold ingots under tight physical security and visited a mining camp, where miners from other African countries lived away from their families for months at a time.

There was a lavish social programme, including visits to a winery at Stellenbosch and to the Kruger National Park. By making membership enjoyable as well as useful the South African visit helped enormously to strengthen the organisation. It set a standard which, to our members' considerable delight, other host countries sought to emulate in their turn.

On the last evening I was taken to the airport by Stuart Young, who had been a colleague at Harwell twenty years previously. The darkness of the sky was punctuated by frequent explosions. 'Guy Fawkes,' he explained. I had forgotten it was November the Fifth. I was watching a cultural leftover from the days of Empire.

Following the Johannesburg meeting the Institute's Supply and Demand Committee (SD) was radically overhauled. Féron's appointment as its strong and effective chairman – he was Director of Production at Electricité de France – effectively answered all charges of cartelism. In February 1979 the Committee published a sixty-page report reviewing supply needs for the following decade. Its ten-year estimates, giving upper and lower bounds for uranium consumption, satisfactorily straddled the actual out-turn.

The committee's firm view was that although many aspects of nuclear power were open to opposition (reactor siting, operation, reprocessing, waste disposal, recycling, etc), the broad case for proceeding was very strong. Part of the Institute's expanding role would be to assist in making that case. With membership already embracing a substantial part of the worldwide nuclear industry – by 1980 there were forty-eight member organisations from twelve countries – it could do so with authority. Two more committees were established to deal with non-market aspects of nuclear policy.

One major issue was widespread public fear that power reactors might be used as covert sources of nuclear proliferation. A Committee on International Trade in Uranium (ITU) was set up to record what was already being done to police the proliferation danger. It was an issue with which the industry was already familiar, since most of the nations supplying uranium imposed contractual obligations, and in some cases physical inspections, directed precisely towards that end. The committee's first report, 'Government influence on international trade in uranium', was followed by a steady stream of more detailed documents. Always in the background was the question of how day-to-day commercial transactions could be kept in line with the obligations of the Nuclear Non-Proliferation Treaty (NPT) of 1968. The Committee played an important role in rehabilitating the Institute in the eyes of the International Atomic Energy Agency (IAEA) in Vienna and its participating nations.

The committee's field of work was given renewed urgency by the passing of the US Nuclear Non-Proliferation Act of 1978, which sought to put the USA in the rôle of world policeman. The USA possessed the necessary leverage through being a main supplier internationally of nuclear materials and services. However, the Act took no account of other countries' laws or operational needs. Sweden had a Stipulation Act (1977) that required agreement about what should be done with the waste from a reactor before authorisation for start-up could be given. German law required reactor operators to define their proposals for spent-fuel management six years ahead of fuel discharge, whereas under US legislation this would be the subject of a case-by-case decision at some time in the future by persons yet to be appointed. The ITU Committee's numerous reports approached such problems from the viewpoint of industrialists who were charged with delivering electrical power reliably from nuclear stations on a day-to-day basis. They added a practical perspective to the often theoretical and political views of governments.

The US 1978 Act created a furore. In an attempt to calm international opinion President Carter instituted an International Nuclear Fuel Cycle Evaluation, based on the International Atomic Energy Agency in Vienna. To the ITU Committee's credit two of its papers were regarded as sufficiently authoritative to be accepted as INFCE documents. A few years later equally close cooperation between the Institute and governments occurred

369

during the run-up to the Third Review Conference on the Treaty on the Non-Proliferation of Nuclear Weapons (NPT). The Institute issued a special commentary that was thought so helpful that several thousand copies were requested by the IAEA. In the event, the hurdles of the Third Revision were successfully negotiated.

A third Institute committee, on Nuclear Energy and Public Acceptance (NEPA), dealt with other issues affecting public attitudes. The public was having understandable difficulty in judging how to react to an industry that depended so greatly on obscure scientific detail. Thus NEPA became even more necessary from the moment in March 1979 when the Three Mile Island (TMI) reactor accident spread alarm amongst the US public, even though there was no loss of life and a negligible escape of radiation.

In this process of establishing the Institute as a respectable body I was given invaluable help by our US lawyers – Wilmer, Cutler and Pickering. Cutler, the senior partner, was one of the most distinguished and versatile members of the US bar – indeed of US society generally. As well as being a member of the executive board of the Metropolitan Opera he was close to the US political scene (at one time he was spoken of as a potential Secretary of State) and was clearly fascinated by the impact of the nuclear industry on world politics.

As chairman of the Salzburg Seminar in American Studies he invited me to speak there in September 1978 and to direct my remarks towards the need to ensure that trade in nuclear fuel did not contribute to nuclear weapons proliferation. The Seminar was housed in the magnificent Schloss Leopoldskron. The students were mature professionals from many different countries. One of the brightest, Pierre Lelouche, later became a Gaullist member of the French Parliament. The faculty members included Bertrand Goldschmidt, whom I had known since my Harwell days, and David Fischer, who at the time was Assistant Director-General for International Relations at the International Atomic Energy Agency. In the informal atmosphere of the Seminar I was able

370

to ask him whether he thought the US government would ever agree to lifting its reserve on the inclusion of the Uranium Institute as a non-governmental participant in the Agency's work. He must have used his good offices for, a couple of years later, I was able to represent the Institute at the IAEA's annual meeting. Having helped, while still a civil servant, with some of the planning prior to the Agency's creation, it was a matter of personal satisfaction that the Institute could at last come in out of the cold.

Shortly before Salzburg Cutler arranged for Joseph Nye to take part in a discussion on nuclear weapons proliferation at our third international conference. Nye was then a senior official in the US State Department and his text had been cleared in advance with the White House. It was subsequently read into the Congressional Record and was also quoted by the Japanese Prime Minister during a speech in Iran. Nye followed the current US policy – that all reasonable steps should be taken to avoid the use of plutonium recycling because of feared proliferation dangers. In taking this line he was not asking the US to give up any technical advantage, but the positions of the UK and France were more closely affected. Both countries had devoted great efforts to mastering nuclear fuel recycling; this was of course the purpose of the Sellafield project. So there were marked differences of view between Nye and Walter Marshall, deputy chairman of the UK Atomic Energy Authority, over what technical developments could be regarded as necessary, desirable, or safe. In his own speech to the conference Marshall made his position clear: 'Much of the general concern about plutonium is emotional and non-factual ... proliferation arguments are ... amenable to analysis.' Marshall had the wider experience of nuclear matters and was a powerful speaker. Most of those present felt he had won the argument.

For many months the Institute's lawyers negotiated with the US Department of Justice over the issue of a Business Review Letter. In terms of anti-trust law this would be the equivalent of a certificate of approval. They made their first approach early in

371

1977. It was premature, but after the London Embassy hearings relations with the Department became warmer. When I went to Washington in the winter of 1978 we were more optimistic, not least because the Florida Power and Light Company had decided to join the Institute. The meeting with the Department went well. I left by a side door, crossed the road, turned and looked back. Next to the Justice Department's offices a small shop was displaying a slogan in large letters over its window: PRICE IS RIGHT. I took it as a good omen. The sought-after Letter was issued in January 1979.

The Institute was becoming better known. Nevertheless, I was surprised to receive a letter addressed to the 'Geranium Institute' asking whether the writer could register a new flower that he had successfully cultivated! In May of the following year, just before the dramatic rescue by the SAS of Iranian diplomats held captive by terrorists in their London embassy, something far less innocent occurred. A message was left on our answer-phone by someone whose voice resembled that of the terrorist I heard speaking later during a television report – possibly Salim, the only English speaker amongst them. The voice threatened us all with death. It would have been ridiculous to lose one's life because of a spelling mistake so, for several days, until the situation was resolved, an armed guard protected us.

Much of the credit for the enormous step forward in the Institute's reputation was Mandel's. But he did not have long to live. He was taken ill just before my visit to the Justice Department; two months later was dead. I went to his funeral, where his friends played a string quartet. He had been a good violinist and I had been looking forward to playing Mozart or Brahms with him – but it was not to be.

By the time of his death there were already well over 100 gigawatts of nuclear-electrical capacity working around the world. This was an economically significant figure – roughly double the total electrical capacity of the UK. The outlook appeared rosy. But on 28 March 1979 there was a serious accident at the Three Mile Island reactor at Harrisburg, Pennsylvania. An error during maintenance of some non-nuclear equipment had affected two main feed-water pumps. The reactor had then been shut down correctly, and the operators had believed it to be safe. However, they had failed to notice that a drain valve had been left open, allowing nearly a million gallons of cooling water to escape. The nuclear fuel elements were left without the coolant that is always needed, even in a shut-down reactor, because of the residual heating that arises from the intense level of radioactivity. The fuel melted and half the reactor core was destroyed. Despite this, only a negligible amount of radioactivity escaped from the large containment pressure vessel surrounding the reactor, which was there to provide the final line of defence. There were no casualties and no adverse health effects of any consequence.

Although the safety design of the reactor had done its work, that did not protect the US nuclear industry, the largest in the world, from having to live with the consequences: reappraisal of safety requirements, delays in licensing until higher safety standards were met and, inevitably, a great strengthening of the anti-nuclear campaign. In the lawyer-dominated system of separated powers by which the USA is administered, those who were opposed to nuclear energy were able to mount a degree of opposition which greatly hampered further expansion. However, it is worth remembering that the significant improvements in reactor design and operator training that have underpinned reactor safety in later years had their origins in the many months of industry self-appraisal that followed this accident.

For me personally the accident could hardly have occurred at a more embarrassing time. I was in Australia for the first Institute meeting in that country. While there I was due to launch a new series of public lectures at Geelong University and, a few days later, to give a Guest of Honour broadcast on nuclear power on the national radio network. By the time I came to deliver the Geelong lecture on 30 March too few details of the accident had emerged to make it worthwhile to change what I had prepared. The broadcast a week and a half later was a different

373

matter. By then TMI had become a matter of worldwide concern and could not be avoided.

In preparing for the broadcast I was fortunate in being able to draw on the advice of Erik Svenke, a distinguished Swede who knew a great deal about the political ramifications of nuclear power. We were visiting the Jabiluka uranium ore-site on the East Alligator River in the Northern Territory. Jabiluka is one of the better-known of the world's wildernesses, having been the location for the film, *Crocodile Dundee*. One hot, still afternoon we took a canoe, paddled through closely packed water-lilies into the middle of the wide river, and spent an hour discussing what I could usefully say in the broadcast. The only viable line of argument seemed to be that while nuclear power is admittedly a difficult technology, it is necessary to persist and master it, because oil supplies are finite, world energy demand and world population are both rising steeply and global warming is becoming a threat, one to which nuclear power does not contribute. We paddled back reasonably satisfied with the discussion. It was only then that I remembered the wildlife in the river. The worry was not alligators – the river's name is taken from the Royal Navy ship that made the first marine survey – but from the many salt-water crocodiles that can grow up to thirty feet in length. Fortunately, as we learned later, they sleep in the afternoons. But before dawn the following morning our lawyer Reuben Clark went out in a motor launch and saw several pairs of eyes shining in the light of his torch.

Harold Macmillan, when Prime Minister, once remarked that what he found most difficult were 'events'. So it was with our relationship with our lawyers. Professionally, they could not be faulted – though some of our members begrudged the expenditure on fees for legal advice, particularly after the free-wheeling days of the old Club. But such worries were as nothing compared with what was about to happen on the litigation front. Following the 1977 hearings in the US London Embassy Westinghouse still retained unjustified suspicions that the Institute was holding back documents that might incriminate our mining members.

They delivered a bombshell when, in December 1979, they subpoenaed Institute documents held in the Washington offices of Wilmer and Pickering, our lawyers.

By then Cutler was no longer the senior partner, having been appointed as Presidential Counsel in the White House. There he had the unique experience of sitting with President Carter on the last night of his presidency, while the Iranians dragged out the final stages of the release of the US hostages. He told me with a smile, 'At least I've slept in the Oval Office.'

The American court order enforcing the subpoena was issued in the face of the normal convention of client confidentiality. Our lawyers smarted from the thinly disguised, and wholly undeserved, implication that they had facilitated cartel operations. Moreover, the subpoena involved them in a huge amount of paperwork which, of course, cost money. The issue of who should pay came at an awkward time. Only one of our member companies was American. To the remainder the US court order came from a foreign jurisdiction. I also knew from my contacts with the British Government that it was displeased by what it saw as an attempt by a US court to exercise extra-territorial powers.

I did my best to maintain good relations with our lawyers, who had given us such excellent guidance and support; but, by early 1980, rupture of the client-lawyer relationship and withdrawal of our only American member were both inevitable. I feared the incident would lose me the friendship of Reuben and Mary Ellen Clark, which I greatly valued. But that did not happen and, a quarter of a century later, they both crossed the Atlantic to join us at our Golden Wedding.

As the Institute developed I received a stream of invitations to take part in energy conferences. One, as unexpected as it was intriguing, came from the Middle East, inviting me to an Arab Energy Conference in Amman. It took place in April 1981. The oil sheiks had doubtless noticed that, as a reaction to the oil market instabilities created by the Yom-Kippur War, nuclear power had begun to displace oil in commercially significant quantities for central electricity production. The invitation must have been sent in the spirit of getting to know their commercial enemy.

There was clearly an enemy of another kind, as the conference door was guarded by machine-gunners. The talk posed no difficulties – I simply described the current state of the nuclear power industry. My Arab hosts were charming and, as a matter of courtesy, used English for their discussions whenever possible. One subject that came up constantly was Israel. The name, however, was never mentioned – the reference was always to 'the enemy'.

The numbers attending the Institute's Annual Conference were growing, making it no longer possible to hold the farewell ceremony in the Banqueting House in Whitehall. But for a time it was still large enough to host the welcome reception. In 1979 we were all relaxed and enjoying ourselves when, halfway through the evening, the music was interrupted by a stranger, who seized the microphone and started haranguing the assembly about the dangers of nuclear power. We were caught off guard but, after perhaps twenty seconds, I ran with a few others to throw him out. He eluded us, ran down the stairs, jumped on his bicycle and pedalled off up Whitehall. We were settling down again when a whiff of rotten eggs grew steadily into the stench of hydrogen sulphide. It took some minutes to clear. In searching for the cause – several small chemical flasks – we found a note from the intruder, who claimed to represent The League of Invisible Radiators.

Two days later the conference farewell banquet was held in the Middle Temple Hall, one of the greatest rooms that London has to offer. A hatch-cover from Drake's *Golden Hind* is built into the wooden screen. One of the tables was given by Queen Elizabeth herself. As we left the hall we were assailed by a demonstration whose theme was 'yellow cake' – the form of uranium we had witnessed being produced in South Africa. The demonstrators were holding small cakes, each with a candle. They were goodnatured and disciplined, but the Benchers of the

Middle Temple took serious offence. When, a few months later, I tried to book the hall for the following year I was reminded that the demonstration had taken place on private property, that we were a controversial organisation, and that we were no longer welcome.

I was in a quandary. Because the Institute did not yet have a great deal commercially or technically to offer its members I was using such historic surroundings whenever possible as an additional inducement. To have nothing suitable yet arranged so close to the deadline for issuing the next conference prospectus was disquieting. While there are other historic halls in London, few match the Middle Temple Hall in size or ambience. The one alternative which clearly outranks it is the Guildhall, but this seemed so far out of reach as to be hardly worth considering. However, by a happy chance the Lord Mayor of London for that year was chairman of a mining company. I wrote to him and, to my delighted surprise, received a favourable response. There was only one stipulation – should the Queen need the Guildhall she would take precedence over us, however short the notice. Our informant added helpfully that the Royal Family always took their holidays at Balmoral in Scotland during the first week of September. We settled the date of the 1980 Annual Conference accordingly, booked the Guildhall, and were able to offer members and guests a setting which could hardly be bettered anywhere in the world. Moreover, the move from July to early September had a further advantage: coming immediately after the holiday period in the Northern Hemisphere, our conference became the accepted rendezvous for the world-wide nuclear fuel industry at the beginning of the autumn working season. When, just before retiring, I attended my last Banquet as Secretary-General, I made a point of thanking the demonstrators whose appearance had first prompted me to apply for the Guildhall.

In 1980 the Japanese occupied a particularly important position in the Institute, with no fewer than twelve member companies – one quarter of our total membership. So the time was long overdue for one of their countrymen to speak during the annual conference. Many of the younger Japanese had worked in England or America and would have had no difficulty with English, the working language of the meeting. But in Japan seniority is all-important, and few of their elders could match them. The most senior Japanese representative, Ichiro Hori of Tokyo Electric, spoke English only haltingly, but if anyone were to speak it would be he. I offered to help and, on that basis, he agreed. But when I received his script, only a few days before the conference, my heart sank – it was sadly in need of recasting. That done, I recorded a tape and sent it back via a Japanese courier, just in time to catch Hori before he left for London. He practised in the plane and when he came to speak he was fully understandable. Having attempted the near-impossible, he was delighted to have succeeded. In a gesture of gratitude he wrote an account of his adventure for the Japanese electrical newspaper, which is a substantial daily with a circulation of over one hundred thousand. His engaging title was 'The friendship of a cassette tape'.

The rhythm of Institute life now comprised the Annual Conference in London in September, the ongoing work of the three committees and a Spring meeting in some other member country. In 1982 our hosts were the Canadian miners, led by John Kostuik. The visit coincided with the Argentine attack on the Falklands, a couple of days after the sinking of the *Sheffield*. I was distressed by the thought that during my three years at Byfleet I never once remembered having studied the potential lethality of surface-skimming missiles. There were one or two possible 'fixes' that might improve the situation; so I spent half an hour on the phone talking to Tom Kerr who, since we had been close colleagues, had become head of the Farnborough aircraft research establishment.

It had become customary for members' wives to accompany them to Institute meetings. This created an emotional difficulty for John Kostuik, since a visit to the No. 2 shaft of the Denison Mine at Elliot Lake, Ontario, was scheduled as part of the technical programme. 'Goddamit, Terry,' he exploded, 'I have been a miner for forty years, and no woman has ever been down any of my mines. Not even my wife. It's bad luck I tell you. And now the Uranium Institute comes along...' His voice tailed off. He was deeply distressed. Nevertheless, he allowed his duties as host to take precedence and gave a gracious welcome to the few hardy wives who chose to make the descent.

Denison was a traditional deep mine, where the ore was embedded in hard rock, which had to be crushed before the uranium could be extracted. However, the search elsewhere for military uranium had identified ore-bodies of an entirely different kind – at or close to the surface, of much higher uranium content, and far more easily worked. Production costs were correspondingly lower and there was also less of a threat to the workforce from radon inhalation. A huge ore-body of this kind was in process of being opened up at Key Lake, in Northern Saskatchewan. It was about to become the largest uranium mine in the world. Since it was owned by a public corporation that was an Institute member, the new mine was naturally included in our technical visits. Relations between Kostuik and this publicly owned company were noticeably cool. One reason was the natural reaction of all private industry to public funding, which can so easily become public subvention. There was also the matter of professional pride. I once heard Kostuik comment that a mining engineer who took part in surface or near-surface mineral extraction was 'demeaning himself'. But there was no denying that mines such as Key Lake held the economic trump cards, and that technically more difficult mines like Elliot Lake could only hold their own so long as the uranium market remained buoyant. By the time I returned to Key Lake in the summer of 1984 production had begun.

June 1982 found me in Lausanne for a European nuclear energy conference. Bill Cavendish-Bentinck ('C-B'), who by then had become Duke of Portland, was also there. He remarked that it was his first visit to the town for sixty years. 'I was here in Curzon's delegation for the Treaty of Lausanne – the settlement with Turkey after World War I. France was represented by

379

Poincaré, Italy by Mussolini. Curzon and Poincaré arrived at Lausanne station as arranged, but Mussolini was not there.' Mussolini was playing a political game. He had just come to power, following his March on Rome three weeks earlier, and wished to impress Italian public opinion by making the other statesmen dance to his tune. 'Word came that he could meet them at Territet, a few miles further on, just beyond Montreux. The moment they arrived the cameras clicked, and Mussolini strutted before the press. That done, he was content to complete his journey to Lausanne.'

Bill Portland went on to give us his own highly personal account of how World War II had come about. At the time of the 1922 meeting in Lausanne the French were proposing to occupy the Ruhr as a form of war reparations. The British regarded such a move as political dynamite; so, during the Christmas recess, Curzon was asked to call at the Quai d'Orsay on his way back from Lausanne and counsel caution. 'He put up at the Ritz – whose walls, as you will know, are far from soundproof. The next room was occupied by a Romanian couple, who spent most of the night doing what comes naturally. Curzon got not a wink of sleep. Next morning our dead-tired statesman called on the French; his sixteen-inch gun failed to go off; the French occupied the Ruhr; the Weimar republic followed; then Horst Wessel and the rest; and inevitably Hitler. All because of the thin walls of the Ritz and a certain Romanian couple.'

C-B was a frequent and welcome visitor to our London offices. He usually came just after lunch (or, as he always preferred to call it, 'luncheon'). After he had succeeded to the dukedom in 1979 the end of our meetings would be signalled by his edging towards the door as three o'clock approached. Asked where he was going he would reply, with a mischievous smile, 'To legislate.'

It was at Bill Portland's suggestion that I found myself, just before retiring, giving evidence to a House of Lords committee which was studying nuclear energy policy. Another friend on the other side of the table was Solly Zuckerman. Portland had enlisted the help of some European members of the Uranium Institute who, like Jan Murray and myself, were able to provide a worldwide perspective for their Lordships' discussion. He was hoping to offset British nuclear pessimism with the more 'can-do' attitudes from across the Channel.

After the Committee I had a chat with Zuckerman, who was in good spirits, having almost finished his autobiography. He seemed nostalgic about the past. 'I think you won't mind what I wrote about you.' He reflected on '...the awful agony of the last two Wilson years'. A propos of nothing in particular he remarked, 'I'm not ambitious. I've never had time to be ambitious. I've always been too successful.'

I responded: 'I'll use that in my book.'

SZ came back at once. 'Come to think of it, it's not bad. I'll use it too.'

Shortly before Bill Portland's death at the age of ninety-three I was his guest for luncheon. Over coffee we were discussing nuclear policy. Bill was leaning back in his chair when a thought struck him. He pulled himself upright and began, as he often did when passing on advice, 'Now look here...' He paused. I waited. He slowly relaxed and his eyelids closed. As seconds turned to minutes I signalled my plight to the waitress. She knew exactly what to do. Standing close to his chair she said in a loud voice, 'Is there anything else, your Grace?' He woke. That was the last time I saw my much-loved friend.

Our legal troubles seemed to be at an end, but I had forgotten the extraordinary ramifications of the US legal system. Just before Christmas 1982 a dossier arrived accusing me of deliberately misleading the US Department of Justice. It originated from lawyers representing the Tennessee Valley Authority (TVA), a large electrical power producer. A few days later we became aware of a fresh attempt to subpoena our documents. Then on 21 January 1983 an American lawyer, Neil Peck, rang from Denver, asking if I could give evidence in the case of TVA versus Gulf Oil, for whom he was acting in the litigation. I told him I knew nothing of either party.

'Nevertheless, you are right in the middle of this case.'

I asked why.

'It is alleged that you are organising a world-wide uranium cartel.'

I pointed out the fatuity of the charge. Jean Féron, who was now the Inspecteur-Général of Electricité de France, had succeeded Reg Worroll (a miner) as the Institute's chairman, and was hardly likely to organise a cartel operating against his own interests. I invited Peck to come and see for himself. We met for a memorable meal ten days later at the Connaught Hotel. It was the beginning of a warm friendship that has continued ever since.

There were tactics to be settled. I already knew that the British Government would not take kindly to yet another attempted exercise of extra-territorial jurisdiction by an American court. We could, of course, have refused to cooperate, but my freedom to travel to the US might then have been impaired. If we decided that I could give evidence, with the purpose of demonstrating publicly that the Institute was whiter than white, our own government was likely to disapprove and, moreover, to be unable to offer protection. I had several meetings with the Board of Trade without reaching a firm decision. Finally, I flew to Paris to see Féron and, after a lengthy argument over lunch, he agreed that it would be best for the Institute if I were to give evidence.

I caught my plane back with seven minutes to spare, and spent a most enjoyable evening at the Inner Temple as guest of my friend, John Burrell. It was a very different kind of encounter with the legal profession. Like his father before him John was now a Bencher, albeit the most junior. It was an extraordinary evening of silver and ceremony. At one point the Master Treasurer rose and said: 'Master Burrell: the Queen.' Pointedly John did not reply. Later John rose and said: 'Master Treasurer, have twenty minutes elapsed?'

'Yes, Master Burrell.'

I asked John what this was all about. 'We can now smoke.'

I thought of what my own lawyer, Jack Hedges, had once told me: 'Every profession is entitled to its own mystery.'

It did not take Peck long to conclude that the Institute had nothing to hide, whatever some of its members may have done individually in the past. But he suggested that we should do more than simply establish a negative. We should also aim to underline the positive side of our work. This fitted well with the mood of our Executive Committee, which was thoroughly irritated by TVA's charges and by the way their lawyers were seemingly able to drag out discovery processes long after they had ceased to be even remotely plausible. In the hope of putting an end to this nonsense once and for all it was decided to give Gulf Oil any documents they needed. The list ran to well over one hundred items. To avoid any appearance of taking sides in a dispute that had nothing to do with us, Jean Féron ruled that if TVA requested any documents the same facilities should be given to them. The Executive also agreed that I could give evidence in London, in the form of a videotaped deposition.

At the end of May 1983 the contending parties met in London, and for several days I was deposed by Peck. It was an immensely boring process. The titles of book after book, document after document, were read into the record, while I confirmed that we had transferred them to Gulf and that they were authentic Uranium Institute documents. Only lunch at Sweetings, the idiosyncratic fast-service fish restaurant in the City, provided light relief. After several days of this farce Van Beek, TVA's attorney, accused us of colluding with Gulf. I blessed Féron for his foresight.

'The Chairman of the Institute decided that if TVA asked for our documents you were to be treated on an equal footing with Gulf. The fact is that you didn't come through our front door.'

Peck said that when this passage was replayed to Gulf's other lawyers back in the USA they judged that if it were ever heard in court its effect on TVA's case would be devastating. In the event the dispute was settled out of court.

As the days wore on I felt increasingly confident; indeed, rather sorry for TVA's attorney. I said as much to my own lawyer. I had expected to receive his congratulations. Instead he made a grimace, as a teacher might when scolding an inept pupil: 'You *educated* him.'

With the legal tussles behind us the way was open for the Institute to develop as a normal international association – insofar as any organisation dealing with nuclear power could be regarded as entirely normal. Few other industries operate under such powerful constraints, nor do so with a greater sense of public responsibility. If expansion was to be our target it was not for the sake of revenue alone. We had views on nuclear policy to offer to the politicians and knew that we should be listened to with greater attention the larger our membership.

Jean Féron, who had given me the greatest support, was now at the end of his chairmanship. To mark the occasion Electricité de France organised a formidable display of history and technology. We assembled in Paris and dined in the Conciergerie, where Marie Antoinette had been held captive before her execution. Although it was a gala occasion I found it hard to forget the hundreds of deaths for which this building had been a staging-post. The museum upstairs confirmed that the reality was as terrible as I had imagined.

The following morning saw us at the Gare de Lyon, where the departure board listed the '8.18 Train Spécial: Institut d'Uranium'. We had a TGV to ourselves! From the driver's cab we were able to experience the sensation of travelling at over 150 m.p.h., and observe how the controllers communicated their instructions electronically to the driver.

A stop was made at Chalon-sur-Saône for a visit to the Framatome factory, where nuclear reactor pressure vessels were fabricated. One was being annealed, rotating slowly while gas jets kept it just below red heat. It was a carefully managed operation, but I saw nothing in it to support British doubts about setting up our own production line. That lack of confidence had helped to keep us away from the pressurised water type of reactor that the rest of the world had adopted.

The main difference between French and British nuclear policies lay in France's willingness to trust her technologists

384

and to make long-term plans stretching over a decade or more. We had scoffingly dismissed this as 'dirigisme', but it worked. France, with few energy resources of her own, had been shocked by the 1973 oil crisis into adopting a crash programme of conversion to nuclear electricity, initially using US pressurised water technology. Britain, being more blessed with energy resources, had felt under less compulsion, despite the high cost of coal. We were also seduced by the overstated benefits of competition into ordering no fewer than three competing versions of the Advanced Gas-Cooled Reactor, thereby significantly increasing programme costs. In contrast, France settled on one standardised design and ordered large numbers. Three-quarters of French electricity was now nuclear. The Framatome visit was a sobering experience.

Lunch was at the nearby royal glass-works of Marie-Antoinette, where one of the two huge kilns had been converted by a former owner into a small theatre. Then on to Avignon where, on the following morning, our Council met, appropriately, in the Council Chamber of the Palais des Papes. The ambience was memorable, the acoustics verging on the impossible.

The following morning there was an early start for the Lodève uranium mine, northwest of Montpellier. On the way we passed the village of Cartels where, in view of the early history of the Institute, I could not resist the temptation to stop the bus while a photograph was taken of the Secretary-General – me – leaning on the village name-board. Before leaving the mine and dispersing I told our French hosts that they had trumped all our aces.

At a farewell dinner in the Dongeon of the ruined Chateuneuf-du-Pape we listened to an initiation ceremony in medieval French, while two of our senior members were admitted to an impressive-sounding gastronomic fraternity. I whispered appreciatively to my French neighbour how remarkable it was that these traditions had been kept alive through the centuries. 'That's kind,' he replied, 'but actually we invented this ceremony fifteen years ago with the help of the local university, as a tourist attraction!' The main course began strikingly, as a whole pig, roasting in a red-hot brazier, was carried round the dining-room. The local vignerons served half a dozen different vintages of the famous wine, illustrating in the most practical way how the maturing process develops its flavour and quality. As I climbed into the bus the clock told me it was 1.23a.m.

According to the Institute's rules Féron, as someone from an electrical utility, would be followed as chairman by a miner. The choice fell on Anthony Grey, a Canadian mining entrepreneur who had settled in Sydney. His company hoped in time to exploit the Jabiluka uranium deposit on the East Alligator river, where Erik Svenke and I had canoed amongst water-lilies, and possibly crocodiles.

Grey was married to a lady of striking beauty from Hong-Kong, so it was convenient for all concerned for our regular administrative meetings to take place at that half-way point. I had not been there since 1946, nearly forty years earlier. In that time the population had increased ten-fold, and both the island and the New Territories had new towns consisting almost entirely of high-rise apartments. David Akers-Jones, brother-in-law of Sebastian Pease, my musician friend of long standing, was the home affairs minister in the colonial administration. He showed me round Shatin town with evident pride, drawing my attention particularly to specially built high-rise workshops suitable for light industry. He and his wife Jane lived at Island House. It was connected by a small causeway to the mainland, and faced a glorious bay. They had a tame macaw, a bird with cardinal-red plumage, which would fly down when called and perch on Jane's shoulder.

At the end of Grey's two-year chairmanship the Australians did their best to outdo even the French as hosts for the Institute's spring meeting. After dealing with the usual formal business in Sydney we made our way to Adelaide and from there to Olympic Dam – a classical deep gold and uranium mine. Two aircraft took us on to Ayer's Rock – 'Uluru' to the Aborigines – where we arrived in time for champagne sundowners in the bush. The full moon was rising behind the huge red outcrop and a lunar eclipse was beginning as we turned in. Come morning, those of us who were fit enough climbed the 1,100-foot high rock before breakfast.

Two hours' drive east of Darwin, in the Northern Territory, lay the Ranger surface uranium mine. It had its own airstrip, where we landed. At a nearby hotel, over a dinner which included my favourite fish, barramundi, I learned that a helicopter would be flying the following morning to a potential mine-site about forty miles away. I was successful in hitching a ride. The take-off from the road-side was memorable. Instead of climbing away normally the pilot, for sheer impish fun, drove his machine along the main east-west road, a couple of feet off the ground, underneath a long archway of huge trees for perhaps a quarter of a mile. The road was empty, but I wondered what would happen if a large Australian road train appeared round a not-so-distant bend. Luck was on our side and, after rounding up some water buffalo as a demonstration of how this could be done, we dropped off the others at the ore-body. The pilot then took me to a road junction in wooded country, close to some Aborigine cave paintings, which the rest of the party would be visiting. The descent had to be absolutely vertical, the road junction itself being the only place where there was room for the helicopter blades. I said farewell and started to walk towards Nourlangie Rock. Five minutes later the rest of the party arrived by bus, cheering as they saw my ridiculously inappropriate brief-case. It was as well I had arrived before them – it would have been a day's march back to the hotel. At the Rock we duly admired the paintings, reputedly thousands of years old. 'But,' said an Aborigine guide, 'the paints are water-soluble, so we have to touch them up every twenty years or so.'

To round off the visit the party took a motor-launch along Yellow Waters to view the crocodiles. Jan, my Australian-born deputy, had invited a friend from Darwin. When we were introduced this lady said, 'Your address is . . .' and repeated it correctly.

I asked how she could possibly know that.

'I was addressing an envelope only last night.'

This seemed absurd; we had only just met, and time's arrow appeared to be pointing the wrong way.

'I was at medical school with your daughter.'

That evening there was a farewell open-air dinner at which some of the old uranium hands expressed delighted astonishment at the progress of the Institute, particularly, as they emphasised, given the tensions that had existed at the outset. I reminded them that it was undoubtedly the Australian members who had saved us from foundering, following the ill-conceived attempt to impose a redundant 'Chief Executive' from the mining side of the industry.

These frequent overseas visits were a sign of the Institute's international orientation, but as a result my contacts with the British establishment were in need of refurbishment. Discreet enquiries and a little arm-twisting led to the Institute becoming a corporate member of the Parliamentary and Scientific Committee. This is a typically British device for keeping some kind of liaison going between parliamentarians from both Houses and the engineering and scientific community. It meets in the Grand Committee Room, just off Westminster Hall, the historic centre of British parliamentary life. I was occasionally able to justify our membership by making comments supporting nuclear power.

The Royal Society – the oldest scientific society in the world – provided another regular point of contact through its discussions on important scientific issues that were open to non-members like myself. More special was a dinner at which I was invited to speak about nuclear fuel and fast reactors to a dozen Fellows. They included my musical friend, Sebastian Pease, who had received a Fellowship for his work on nuclear fusion. Peter Medawar was also there; no scientist should fail to read his small book, *The Limits of Science*. Being somewhat disabled he, perforce, remained seated for the Loyal Toast, excusing himself with the words, 'At least I tried to *look* loyal.'

I was sitting next to Viscount Hailsham, the Lord Chancellor, who towered over me. Having never met him previously, I wondered whether we would manage to find common conversational ground. I made the opening move.

'What interests you most?'

It was an inspired choice. 'Being a judge. I'm the top boy, you know.'

For twenty minutes I was regaled with all manner of fascinating legal and parliamentary anecdotes.

The Institute was running smoothly and I felt somewhat underemployed. Meeting Sir Keith Joseph at an annual meeting of the Centre for Policy Studies I said as much. Soon afterwards the Ministry of Education wrote asking if I would be willing, as a part-time task, to undertake an appraisal of the Council for Educational Technology. The name sounded interesting, so I agreed. In clearing the proposal with the Institute's governing body I was pleasantly surprised to have the support of one member with whom I had frequently crossed swords: 'Just the kind of *pro bono* thing our Secretary-General should be doing.' Here was evidence indeed that the culture of the Institute had radically altered since its claustrophobic early days.

The CET had been set up seventeen years previously as a national focus for the rapidly developing uses of information technology in education. It did not take long to identify the main problem. The Centre was attempting, with a small staff, to stay in the forefront of a revolution that was being driven worldwide by huge armies of bright-minded enthusiasts. The task was beyond its resources and, unless it altered its approach, it could only flounder.

The analogies with the Uranium Institute were self-evident. We too were a small group trying to keep abreast of a fast-developing industry. But because our staff was proportionately even smaller we had been driven to adopt the only viable course – exploiting our privileged position within the industry to provide a forum where, in committees and conferences, the main players could keep themselves up to date. I concluded that the CET should move in a similar direction, using its position close to government to ensure that action followed its recommendations.

I submitted my report to Sir Keith in February 1985. It was the subject of an arranged question in the Commons – and was

389

duly lodged with the Library. It was inevitably unpopular with the CET staff. I was asking them to act as a conduit and to forgo some of their ambitions as individual researchers. I did not attempt to monitor the effects of the report. It had taken up a good deal of spare time and, meanwhile, Jeanie's mobility problems were becoming more severe. Finding ways of mitigating her difficulties was now the main challenge out of office hours. I sought no more *pro bono* investigations.

Growing confidence in the reputation and future of the Institute led to a suggestion that a medal should be struck and used to honour individuals who had made significant personal contributions to nuclear energy. Responsibility for its production of course fell to me. It was yet another of the many interesting, unexpected and non-delegatable tasks that brighten the lives of people who run small organisations. A word with the Royal Mint led me to Christopher Ironside, who had been responsible for the Britannia design on the English seven-sided 50p coin. A few days later, as we met for the first time, I realised that creating a medal was unlike anything I had yet encountered. His question, 'What do you want me to depict?', while obvious, was one that I had not foreseen in sufficient detail. I told him about uranium mining and nuclear reactors, and sent him a packet of photographs of mine-workings, nuclear stations, fuel element transport flasks – indeed, anything that came readily to hand. We soon had a plaster prototype the size of a plate, with suitably symbolic references to the various sides of the industry. Any thoughts that the medal could be of 22-carat gold were abandoned once the cost was calculated. Eventually, four 9-carat medals were struck, each two and a half inches in diameter. The first was presented to Erik Svenke, in recognition of his leadership of the Swedish nuclear waste fuel storage programme, which was easily the most advanced in Europe.

At the last spring members' meeting before I retired our generous hosts were the Italian members. Their lavish programme included a reception at the Castel Sant'Angelo. Its construction was begun by the Emperor Hadrian in AD 130, and it was there that he was buried. During the Pillage of Rome in the sixteenth century Pope Clement VII escaped through the passageway connecting it to the Vatican. In Puccini's opera Tosca falls to her death from the highest terrace – where we were served cocktails by magnificently attired Swiss Guards. I could not help being distracted from the usual small-talk by the breathtaking view of the city, the Vatican and the Tiber. Some of us went on to visit a reactor under construction at Montalto di Castro, about eighty miles northwest of Rome. At the time it was the Italian flagship project; before long, however, national politics and a further jolt to public confidence in nuclear power caused it to be cancelled, even though three-quarters of the cost had already been incurred.

The publication of a vacancy notice in the *Economist* was a reminder that my retirement was less than a year away. It attracted an astonishing number of applicants – further proof that the Institute now occupied a respected place within the nuclear industry. Having short-listed them as best I could, I decided to spend one week meeting candidates who lived on the European mainland. On four successive days I left home at the usual time and returned at the usual time, but lunched with applicants in Paris, Pisa, Rome and Munich. None, however, struck me as likely to combine the ambassadorial functions of the job (the easy part) with acceptance of the inescapable year-in-year-out slog to which any successor would have commit himself – or herself (the candidates included my hard-working deputy, Jan Murray). I was not personally involved in the final decision, but was well pleased when the Executive Committee offered her the succession. Bill Portland wrote to say that he looked forward to attending the funeral service of the Australian who had said that Jan would be appointed 'over his dead body'.

Between the *Economist* announcement and her appointment an event occurred that added a new word to the language, and stopped nuclear development dead in its tracks: Chernobyl. On 28 April 1986 I had been due to visit the Swedish waste facility serving the nuclear reactor at Forsmark, sixty miles north of Stockholm on the

391

Baltic coast. At the airport I received a message saying that the reactor was shut down and the visit cancelled. I went instead to Stockholm where, as the afternoon progressed, first rumour and then hard news began to clarify what had happened.

The reactor had been shut down because monitors had detected abnormal levels of radiation. At first the operators assumed that their reactor had failed in some way, though no fault was obvious. Then they realised that the radiation levels inside the reactor building were lower than in the air outside – the cause lay elsewhere. From analysis of the radioactive contamination the Swedes were soon able to estimate roughly when the accident – for accident it must have been – had occurred. The evidence pointed to a major disaster in the Soviet Union. The truth could not be suppressed for long. Moscow eventually confessed that an explosion had occurred at Chernobyl, in Belorussiya, at 1.23a.m. on 26 April. That was two days before my visit to Sweden, and during the whole of that time Moscow had remained silent.

Chernobyl had major repercussions in the West, but its consequences within the USSR were far more radical. It destroyed the myth of Communist Party omnicompetence even more surely than the recurring food crises. It induced a new mood of humility and self-examination that was the one encouraging feature of the meeting of experts arranged at Vienna by the International Atomic Energy Agency in August 1986, which I attended. Valerii Legasov's presentation was a model of clarity, even through the distortions of simultaneous interpretation. He made no attempt to gloss over the gross violations of operating procedures, nor the fundamental instability of the Russian reactor design. He seemed, however, astonished when an Italian delegate informed him that in some Western countries such flagrant disregard of safety requirements would be a criminal offence. Sadly, on the day after the second anniversary of the accident Legasov committed suicide in a state of depression, but not before writing a personal memoir that flayed the Soviet establishment for its complacency and sins of omission. Across the world the need for peer-group review of reactor design and operation was seen as self-evident.

Symbolically, it was in Moscow that a new World Association of Nuclear Operators was inaugurated in May 1989.

A month after this Chernobyl meeting the Institute held its eleventh annual conference, starting with a presentation on the causes of the disaster. A booklet, *Understanding Chernobyl*, followed. The conference proceedings closed with another Guildhall banquet, my last as Secretary-General, at which I made a short speech thanking those who had helped to make the Institute such a success – not forgetting the protesters who had made me *persona non grata* with the Middle Temple. A fireworks display in the Guildhall courtyard rounded off the evening. One journalist told me: 'You went out with a bang!'

In the four months remaining before retirement forward planning was no longer my business. Jan Murray was now almost in the saddle; for me there was a crowded period of tidying up and nostalgic farewells. The Institute's constituency being world-wide, it was with gratitude that I received the Executive' Committee's blessing to make one last round-the-world goodwill trip. It began memorably, as I was driven to Heathrow by a driver who announced proudly that he was the UK's champion 'banger' racer. Alarmed, but still alive, I boarded the plane and slept all the way to Toronto where, at the Yacht Club, fourteen friends and colleagues were awaiting me.

A couple of days later Mary Ellen Clark, Reuben's wife, met me in Washington and drove me to her wine-producing farm at Charlottesville. It lay in a small valley. Everything within sight, up to the skyline, was hers. Reuben greeted me warmly, and we relived the struggles of the early days, when we were trying to save the Institute from internal mistakes and external attacks. He took me to see Jefferson's stylishly beautiful Rotunda at the University of Virginia, the lawn surrounded by cloisters, and the ingenious garden walls that rely on corrugations for their strength while being only one brick thick.

The timing of the trip had been arranged so that I could fly the Institute's flag at an Atomic Industrial Forum meeting in Washington. As I was not speaking I had few cares. The worldwide nuclear circle of colleagues and friends whom I had known for a quarter of a century or more was gathered there. The outlook for nuclear power was not as promising as we had once hoped, but great things had already been achieved and we were certain that the world would yet come to rely more fully on nuclear power. That evening I played for one last time the Brahms F minor sonata with my splendid clarinettist friend, Max Isenburgh – 'Moose' – in his glorious music-room on Massachusetts Avenue.

There followed three crowded days in Japan. It was eleven years since I had first been there, and in that time I had gained many Japanese friends. One of them, Naomi Ohno, was showing me round the Ginza restaurant district when we stopped in front of a toyshop. In the window, astonishingly, was a large model of a British railway steam locomotive, six or eight feet long, and carrying the name of the distinguished railway engineer, Sir Nigel Gresley. Ohno gazed at it appreciatively murmuring, 'A4 class Pacific 4–6–2.' I was amazed by his unexpected erudition. He explained, without a hint of bombast: 'My father was our ambassador in London. We used to take the *Railway Magazine*.'

A young pianist, Yumiko Ohta, took me to lunch with her family. I had known her for about ten years. Her uncle, while attending an early UI conference, had given me a tape recording and had asked for my comments. She had a magnificent technique, but showed scant understanding of European music. She needed a Western teacher. The British Council put her in touch with a professor who regularly visited Tokyo. In due course she gave a recital in London's Purcell Room.

After lunch Yumiko took me to a Tokyo district rarely visited by tourists. It was a warren of narrow alleys, with microscopic two-roomed houses – one up, one down – and paper-thin walls. In one of them was living for the time being my niece, Teresa, the daughter of Jean's sister, Wendy. We walked round the quarter, absorbing the atmosphere. She introduced me in fluent Japanese to her friends, the shopkeepers. One eighty-two-year-old lady treated me with almost embarrassing deference.

Teresa is no ordinary woman. From an early age she had been fascinated by the circus, and had worked as a clown. Moreover, she is probably the only British clown to have worked in a Japanese circus – and to have done so from the residence of the British Ambassador. She joined me at my hotel for supper. We were in a lift when it stopped at the fourth floor and an English colleague from the nuclear industry entered. In England we lived only a quarter of an hour's drive from each other. We exchanged greetings in matter-of-fact tones, as though such accidental encounters 7,000 miles from home were an everyday occurrence. I introduced Teresa.

'Brian, this is my niece.'

He looked at me enquiringly.

'Brian, this is the British Ambassador's daughter.'

His gaze relaxed.

My duties during the visit involved commuting up and down the Shin-Kansen high-speed railway, visiting the offices of our Japanese members and doing my best to recruit one more electrical utility. These meetings were easy, with friends everywhere. It was all so different from my first visit to Japan, when I was trying to recruit members against the discouraging background of the Club. Then I had, of course, been received courteously, as is the Japanese way, but it had been clear that the electrical utilities were weighing the benefits of easy access to the nuclear fuel industry against possible future legal embarrassments.

Australia was next on the visiting list. Tony Grey took me for a meal at the Royal Sydney Yacht Club and we reflected nostalgically on the work we had both put in to bring the Institute to its present stature. At Melbourne Hugh and Liz Morgan were my hosts. Professionally, Hugh was Executive Director at Western Mining; politically, he was a leader of the New Australian Right and, as such, had recently joined the select band whose pictures appear on the front cover of *Time* magazine. Their country house was filled with a glorious collection of abstract paintings by recently graduated arts students. I envied their sureness of touch as collectors and had no compunction in breaking the tenth commandment.

In the morning Hugh took me to the ABC studios in Melbourne where, before flying on to Hong Kong, I was to make a recording on the prospects for nuclear power. On the way we drove through a burnt-out patch of countryside where, only recently, people had died when fire had travelled an almost unbelievable thirty-five kilometres in twenty minutes. My journey onward was in an Australian aircraft, whose captain periodically gave out the latest test-match scores to a cabin full of cricket enthusiasts.

At Hong Kong I changed to a China Airlines plane. Its public address system, improbably, was playing 'Greensleeves' as we flew in over mountains and vast river beds to Taipeh. Smiling faces that I had seen only a few weeks before in London's Guildhall were waiting for me. I was to be the guest at lunch of David Chu, the amiable guiding spirit behind Taiwan's active nuclear reactor programme. The meal was a gargantuan feast in the former Prime Minister's house. David presented me with a gold watch of quite extraordinary accuracy, which remains amongst my treasured possessions.

I remembered how, three years earlier, I had visited mainland China, which was showing an interest in the world uranium market. I had been given every courtesy, including the tourist round of the Great Wall, the Ming Tombs and the Forbidden City. I had also visited their national geological centre, where I learned to my surprise that no fewer than fifty thousand geologists were looking for uranium. Our discussion of the possibility of Chinese membership of the UI had run into the difficulty that the Taiwan Power Company was already a member. Taiwan's claim to be known as the The Republic of China was deeply resented by the mainland government. I sought the Foreign Office's advice, but learned that this was an apparently insoluble problem that troubled many other international organisations. We never did manage to hit on a mutually acceptable nomenclature.

I was to return through Hong Kong. It being almost certain that I should never go there again it was one last opportunity for exploration. In glorious weather I took a hovercraft to the still unspoilt north end of Lantau Island and spent the day walking. The ferry took me back to Hong Kong Central, where I looked for memories of 1946. The Hong Kong and Shanghai Bank building, that had once seemed so daringly high, was dwarfed by huge new skyscrapers. Only the Cathedral was unchanged. Inside an organ was playing. Opening the only unlocked door I found myself immediately behind the organ console. A young Chinese woman was practising. I asked if I might stay, adding that I had once played there long ago. She replied welcoming any help I could give her; she was worried about having to play for the Governor's funeral. With growing confidence she worked through two Chorale Preludes by Bach.

Home again in London all that remained was to finish off my handover to Jan and plan my farewell party. I made a point of inviting my friend, Brian, and of briefing sister-in-law Wendy to comment when they met that she had heard he had been associating with her daughter in Japanese lifts. During the party the anxiety I felt about the unknown condition called 'Retirement' was slightly eased by an invitation to act as an expert witness in a pending arbitration dispute. A Syrian acquaintance also unexpectedly invited me to make the keynote address at a forthcoming energy conference in Aleppo. Such small gestures were some kind of reassurance that professional life would not entirely come to an end on the day I left office.

My twelve years at the Institute had not been the easiest. But they had given me a worldwide perspective matching anything that the Civil Service or industry could have offered. With the help of many friends from across the world, and in the face of all the difficulties, we had succeeded in creating an institution robust enough to survive in a difficult world. In the year 2000 the Uranium Institute held its twenty-fifth and final annual conference. In the following year, recognising that its purview had become far wider than the original title seemed to imply, it appeared in new guise as The World Nuclear Association, with Hans Blix as its President.

Chapter 21

Poco Rallentando al Fine

On the morning of my retirement party I felt an acute sense of loss. Life had been so exciting, so full of action and so often unexpected. Henceforth, it seemed likely to be stale, flat and, in all probability, unprofitable. A few days earlier a tactless woman friend had made things worse by reminding me that I 'no longer mattered any more'. Suddenly, I understood the sour reply a former Permanent Secretary had given when I asked why he was looking so unhappy as he walked along Pall Mall: 'Life's terrible. I have no IN tray.'

I was somewhat luckier. The two leads that the retirement party had produced both seemed worth following up. Even so, I was a long way from matching the standard advice to the recently retired: always have too much to do. However, that other feature of retirement – the loss of a secretary and her precious filing system – was already making its own special contribution to filling my days.

There was one other piece of advice that I had carried with me for four years, since an evening in Delhi when I had unexpectedly been invited to an Indian coming-of-age party. The father, Abdul Rahman, was widely respected not only for his contributions to science but also as a philosopher. He told me his two guiding principles: to live life as though every day might be his last – unless he had some great project on hand, when he tried to act as though he were immortal. The first proposition posed a difficulty that fifteen years later was still imperfectly resolved: how to winnow my papers so as to present only a moderate burden to my executors. The second was easier to handle: in time I wrote a couple of books that each took charge of my life for four years, exactly as *Radiation Shielding* had done in the Harwell days.

I took the question of being an expert witness to my recently acquired Hungarian lawyer friend, Laszlo Gombos. He had appeared one day asking for help with an international conference on energy law in Australia. I put him in touch with one of the Uranium Institute's leading figures, who did what was needed. Laszlo was some years my senior and our new friendship did not have long to flourish, but while he was still alive it was never for a moment dull. When he died in 1992 Lord Weidenfeld paid him as fine a tribute as I have ever heard:

Whenever I think of him I see before me that man we all knew: impeccably dressed, chivalrous in his comportment, hectoring yet lovingly loyal, the unforgettable friend, the stubborn perfectionist.

Laszlo was indeed a striking figure. He was a lawyer who had left Hungary before World War II. Being well-connected, he had, before long, become involved in an attempt on the part of the British establishment to find cause for preventing a divorce for Mrs Wallace Simpson, in the hope of blocking a marriage with the Prince of Wales. He left that story tantalisingly unelaborated.

He was more willing to speak about two wartime incidents. He had worked for the BBC, monitoring enemy radio transmissions. Following the exploits of the German commerce raider *Graf Spee* in the South Atlantic there was particular interest in the movements of the supply ship *Altmark*, which was known to be carrying men from the ships that had been sunk. A report from Bergen alerted him to the movements of a mysterious vessel that somehow seemed not to fit into the normal pattern of coastal traffic. He concluded this must be the *Altmark*, even though photo-reconnaissance showed a vessel with the wrong number of funnels. He spoke directly to Churchill, then First Lord of the Admiralty, stressing that, while reasonably confident, he could not be absolutely certain. Churchill reflected for a moment, then said, 'My boy, I'm going into action.' On 16 February 1940 the destroyer *Cossack* attacked. Laszlo had been right – it was the *Altmark*. Many seamen were freed as a direct result of his tenacity.

He had a second, less happy, encounter with Churchill later in the war. By then he had been given reponsibility for broadcasting a special coded message to the resistance movements on the continent, warning them that the Allied invasion was imminent. Some weeks before D-Day it became clear from incoming calls throughout the morning that his secretary must have inadvertently made the coded call-to-arms transmission while doing her daily teleprinter practice, having failed to check that the machine was switched off. Laszlo had no choice but to ring Churchill to confess this grave breach of security. Churchill thought for a while, then said, 'This is unfortunate, but it will provide a test of whether our security has been breached. We will see whether the enemy reacts.' Laszlo recalled that there might have been some reaction, but that the Germans had probably concluded it was part of a disinformation exercise. When the D-Day invasion actually occurred there was nothing to suggest that its surprise had been compromised by his secretary's error.

Now I was seeking his advice over the invitation to be an expert witness in a contractual dispute involving uranium. Laszlo smiled. 'For every expert witness who is prepared to make an assertion, there will be another to assert the opposite,' he said – and so it proved. I did my best, but our opponents were dangerously well-informed. Fortunately, the case was overtaken by a wider settlement.

The second invitation, to be the opening speaker at an international workshop on energy at the University of Aleppo, had a more lasting influence. Aleppo being a city with an intriguing past, I eagerly accepted and threw myself into preparing a review paper on the global energy scene. But I wondered why an Arab conference should be so interested in someone with a background in nuclear energy.

The reason must have had something to do with what happened after the Arab-Israeli Yom Kippur war in October 1973, most strikingly in France. At the time imported oil accounted for 46 per cent of French electricity production, nuclear power for only 8 per cent. The oil price had been 3 dollars a barrel; three months later it had risen to 12 dollars and, following the 1978 Iranian crisis, it reached over 30 dollars. In resolving to free the country from oil price instability the French government authorised the construction of five or six nuclear reactors per year. By 1985, 61 per cent of French electricity was nuclear, exactly as planned. Other countries reacted similarly, though more slowly. Worldwide, nuclear power took several million barrels of oil per day out of the market. The oil price slumped.

The Aleppo workshop was due to take place in October 1987, nine months after my retirement. Drafting the paper took up most of the summer. By the time it was finished it had grown to 20,000 words, and I was far better informed about the world energy scene. I wrote to the organisers and awaited the University's reply. When it came they promised to send me air tickets; none arrived. My diplomat friends advised me on no account to foot the bill myself. A week before the workshop was due to start it became clear that it had been cancelled – or, at least, my own participation in it. This was profoundly irritating. I seemed to have wasted several months' work. However, on reflection I realised that what I had written could easily be adapted to become the opening chapters of a full-length book on nuclear energy.

A fascinating and splendidly complicated story was waiting to be told: the worldwide interplay of technology, economics and politics, and the extraordinary progress that nuclear power was making, despite the set-back of the Three Mile Island accident in 1979. The book would need to appear fair to any reader with an open mind. Problems would not be glossed over, energy alternatives given their proper place. The nuclear

401

proliferation issue – which had occupied so much of my professional life in the fifties and sixties – would be confronted squarely. So would nuclear power's economics. I was fortunate in being able to draw on the resources of the Uranium Institute – not only the library, which had grown into an impressive repository, but also personal contacts with my worldwide friends, who helped to clarify the convoluted and complex political backgrounds to nuclear power in a dozen countries.

The job took until August 1990. The book was published by Oxford University Press and, after the initial print-run was exhausted, the Uranium Institute bought the plates and gave it a fresh lease of life. The book turned out to be what I had hoped for, and I wrote the Preface with some confidence:

> The story that emerges is of a nuclear industry that has rarely been guilty of dereliction of duty, though it was undeniably complacent in not addressing sooner the causes of the public's entirely reasonable anxieties. The anti-nuclear lobby has been skilled in debate, and sometimes extraordinarily percipient; but less than fair in failing to acknowledge the industry's achievements and its willingness to learn from past mistakes. As for the politicians, the book contains many examples that show how the flames of controversy can be deliberately fanned when there are votes to be gained. The story has few heroes, but within the industry fewer villains than the public has been led to believe.

I called the book *Political Electricity*. The reviews, when they came, brought home the difficulty of pursuing rational argument in a field where fear and politics had reigned for so long. The centre-left press simply did not want to listen – nor, very clearly, in some cases even to read what they were purportedly reviewing. But there were sufficient commendations from people whom I valued to leave me with the feeling that the three years following the Aleppo farce had not, after all, been wasted.

Following publication John Maddox offered me a couple of pages in *Nature* in which to encapsulate the pros and cons of the nuclear argument. It was an interesting exercise in précis-writing which, because of its compression, brought out the inconsistencies in national nuclear policies even more clearly than in the book. Writing in 1991 I pointed out that nuclear power was already making about 17 per cent of the world's electricity – about as much as had come from all sources in 1957. French nuclear exports were keeping the Italian grid in balance. Fiercely anti-nuclear Austria was drawing on Czech nuclear stations, just as environmentalist Denmark was using Swedish electricity, which was 50 per cent nuclear. Clearly the disparity between perception and reality would have to be dealt with before nuclear power could make its proper contribution. But the need for energy is far from static, and the world's population is growing rapidly. Even allowing for conservation and efficiency, 50% more energy will be needed by 2025. It cannot come on that scale from the renewables. Only coal, gas, hydro and nuclear power can produce really big packets of energy. There is scope for at least a doubling of nuclear electricity over the first half of the twenty-first century. I concluded that, despite post-Chernobyl worries, the ever-growing pressure for more energy would lead to a new wave of nuclear orders soon after the second millennium.

Rather to my surprise I was finding little difficulty in 'always having too much to do'. A chance meeting put me in touch with the Major Projects Association – a group of industrialists interested in large engineering projects. I was asked to chair a review of surface transport, with a view to predicting what might be expected to happen over the next twenty years. An expert group of engineers and other professionals would be helping me. A year later, by Christmas 1990, the job was done.

Twenty years earlier I had been chairman of the OECD Transport Research Committee, so the field was already familiar. Even so, I was surprised by how little that was really new emerged from our discussions. Clearly transport is not a field that changes quickly, except where progress can be accommodated without much social upheaval – as with containerisation in the 1960s, and the more recent development of high speed trains. If

403

there was a systemic bias in earlier predictions it lay in believing that innovation would proceed more quickly than was, in fact, politically possible.

The problem is that transport touches so closely on the social and economic fabric of the community. I have long felt a need for a new 'Chatham House' for transport – having the same constructive relationship to the transport and environmental departments as the Royal Institute of International Affairs does to the Foreign and Commonwealth Office, and the International Institute for Strategic Studies does to the Ministry of Defence. Our report attempted to give a shove in that direction. But policy has remained confused and the country's transport system is still irritatingly mediocre. It is not British engineering that is to blame – we are perfectly capable of creating first-class transport infrastructure overseas. The problem lies in British politics, and the absence of long-term investment plans. Every new Parliament feels it has to demonstrate its political purity by tinkering with its predecessors' plans.

As long as Zuckerman was alive my hands were never idle. He was always bubbling with ideas for improving the world. In 1989 he suggested that I should try my hand at advising how the Loss Prevention Council should aim to develop. I had never heard of that body; when he told me that it was the forward-looking research arm of the British insurance industry, on which the economy depended for much of its investment, the potential interest was immediately clear.

The industry was facing a future that no longer seemed to be a simple extrapolation of the past. It was not simply a matter of soaring crime rates. Insurers had also been shaken by heavy losses involving other kinds of risk that had not been given proper weighting. Some had been created by new technologies that were imperfectly understood. There were also clear cases where business – of a kind – had been generated by low premiums set on a basis of virtual ignorance.

In addition, there were some previously unconsidered risks that were now seen to be significant, even though they had very long times of expression. The climate was beginning to change.

There were more claims for flooding. The water table in London was rising, threatening even the British Library. There was a new problem of 'sick' buildings, where innovative techniques were proving vulnerable to medium-term effects of decay, corrosion and even, in a few extreme cases, collapse. There were outbreaks of Legionnaires' disease traced to ageing air conditioning systems.

Insurance law was changing. There was a new legislative trend towards greater corporate liability which, in effect, placed the insurers at the mercy of the operators. Professional liability was an area of huge uncertainty. Personal liability had become comparable to fire risk. There was even legislation allowing employees to resuscitate wound-up companies for the purpose of making claims. In conventional insurance fields there were problems of setting standards, even of deciding whose responsibility that should be. And there was the further complication of new European regulations.

Feedback from operating experience was deficient. Little first-hand fire investigation was carried out centrally by the insurance industry. So there were no good data demonstrating how much it was worth spending on fire protection, at a time when fire losses in the UK were running at half a billion pounds a year. Eighteen months after one huge fire in which the sprinkler system had been overwhelmed no proper analysis had been carried out – so no lessons had been learned.

It did not take long to appreciate that, in its existing form, the Loss Prevention Council had little of the organisational clout that the situation demanded. Its staff was small and excessively preoccupied with servicing too many committees. It was a familiar situation and it was not difficult to suggest a better way. The principal obstacle was the Byzantine complexity of the relationships that had grown up between the insurers, the industry that manufactured protective equipment, and the regulatory and legislative aspects of Government. Eventually, I produced a report I hoped would have some chance of assisting the insurers. A meeting was arranged, and not for the first time I found

405

myself working in Zuckerman's Kensington home late into the night. He quickly concluded that one essential key to a more effective future would be to enlist the services of a senior scientist with sufficient personal authority to make a difference. The name of Dr Harry Atkinson came up. He too had worked with Zuckerman in Whitehall. He became involved, and when I last spoke to him was enjoying the experience.

Zuckerman was not the only friend to make an interesting suggestion. Laszlo Gombos wrote wondering whether I could help with some courses on Energy Law being run by the University of Dundee. I already knew this was his special interest, but the Dundee connection was new to me. It turned out that a decade earlier he had been behind the creation of the now pre-eminent Centre for Petroleum and Mineral Law Studies. My job would be to give the students some feeling for the international rules regulating trade in uranium, intended as a discouragement to nuclear proliferation. I accepted, and from 1988 to 1993 spent occasional days reliving my atomic energy past. The students were well-informed and intelligent, the assignment a delight.

Thanks to these projects retirement was proving personally enjoyable and professionally rewarding. But even Zuckerman was mortal – in April 1993 his life came to an end, a month short of his 90th birthday. His shrewd and sympathetic biographer, John Peyton, recalls that on the previous day he questioned his doctor's readings of his blood pressure, telling him that he should take them again, because if correct he was already dead. 'It showed a side of him,' says Peyton, 'questioning, quizzical, and never far from laughter, both at life and himself.' His memorial service was held at the Liberal Synagogue in St John's Wood. The congregation was a roll-call of the country's Great and Good. Roy Jenkins delivered the eulogy. The organist played a fanfare by William Walton, another of his friends; it was dedicated to 'Solly – lion of lions'.

While writing *Political Electricity* and doing these assorted studies some juggling was needed to avoid crowding out my primary duty of safeguarding Jeanie. There was an ongoing game between us of seeing how many normal activities she could still enjoy. Transport for her wheelchairs was the key. Back in 1981, when walking had first become difficult and then all but impossible, I had concluded that it would be sensible to buy a one-ton delivery van. When Jean saw its strikingly aggressive green colour she announced that its name would be 'Sprout'. Adapting Sprout to her needs – fitting a ramp, a kitchen, a bookcase and other necessities – was a labour of love.

No sooner was all ready than I bore her off on a tour of Northern Italy. The trip gave her a treasure-chest of memories that have remained undimmed ever since. They included such gems as driving her outdoor wheelchair around the great basilica at Assisi; dismantling the bathroom door in a Pisa hotel so that her smaller wheelchair could enter; and pulling her in that chair manually up a straight outside flight of stairs – fifty-three treads – at the Bargello museum in Florence. Jeanie, whose resilience and courage were never in question, had wanted to see Verrochio's 'David' on the second floor. Taking her all the way up proved almost beyond my strength, but a German student came to our rescue just in time. Going down was even more daunting, particularly when the rubber hand-grips began to work loose.

With Sprout's assistance we were able every summer to visit somewhere exciting and new. In 1985 we were invited by two friends from Jordans, Peter and Joan Smart, to stay with them in Prague. Peter was Head of Chancery in our embassy, a posting he had specially asked for. Prague's place in musical culture had led him to forgo a more senior position. Sprout bore us across Europe, but we arrived thirty minutes late. Peter was waiting impatiently in the road. 'Hurry! The Menuhins are coming in a few minutes. Then there's a London Philharmonic concert. The Prague Festival Ballet will be in for drinks afterwards.' That was the pace at which we lived for the next week.

It was the second time I had been in his house. Another Jordans friend, Denis Michell, had held the same post twenty years earlier, and I had stayed with him in 1968, following a

High Speed Train conference in Vienna. It was Denis who had told Peter about the city's cultural delights.

Peter had been in Prague long enough to know personally most of its leading musicians, whether they played classical music or jazz. On one memorable occasion he had two special guests for lunch: Petr Eben, a leading composer and virtuoso organist, and Jiří Stivín, a jazz flautist. Both enjoyed improvising in their very different musical idioms. They had never before met, but Peter persuaded them to improvise as a duo. The result was a total success. He also asked Eben to show off his improvising skills at the keyboard. 'What theme shall I improvise on?' As we were in Prague the obvious choice was 'Good King Wenceslas'. For the next twenty minutes the good King appeared and reappeared in the style of Bach, Beethoven, Scarlatti, Schumann, Chopin, Debussy. Eben's only failure was a bashful refusal to improvise in his own musical idiom. Later he published some organ variations on the same theme, dedicating them to Peter, who heard them played in a London church a few weeks before his death in 2002. Stivín told me he was shortly coming to England for a jazz festival at Bath. I invited him to dinner. As we left the club he paused on the steps, took several deep breaths, and said, 'Freedom. You can smell it!' The Velvet Revolution in Czechoslovakia was still four years away.

Just before we left Prague Peter took us to St Agnes's fountain, where we filled Sprout's water containers. At Glyndebourne a few days later we were able to offer our supper guests a choice: Perrier or St Agnes? Crossing the Czechoslovak frontier proved frustrating. We were held for more than two hours before the guards were satisfied. The moment we reached German soil we too smelt freedom.

The Smarts were such perfect hosts that I needed no prompting when they invited me to the Seychelles in 1988. I was nearing the end of *Political Electricity* and spent many hours in their garden in the cool shade of a giant banyan tree, wrestling with a difficult chapter. Overhead, fruit-bats winged their leisurely way to and from their roosts.

Peter was now the British High Commissioner and, through his good offices, I was able to spend two happy afternoons flying a small Seychelles Air Force monoplane, learning how to perform stall turns with an English instructor, Roy Marsh. We lunched on Frégate, an island with a minimal and badly obstructed runway, where it is advisable to check for giant tortoises before committing oneself to landing. Marsh told me how he was once piloting Ernest Hemingway on a tourist visit to the Victoria Falls. The two agreed that it would be amusing to dive into the canyon below the falls. However, they failed to notice a wire stretched between the canyon walls. The plane's windscreen was broken, and Marsh feared the worst, but it stayed airborne and they managed to make a precautionary landing at a nearby grass strip. A couple of hours later a twin-engined Rapide came to see why they were overdue and, having spotted them, landed to take them back to their base. 'However,' said Marsh, 'half-way down the runway it became quite clear that the overloaded plane was not going to leave the ground.' It was a write-off. One of its engines, still rusting in the grass at the turn of the century, was featured in a BBC documentary about the author. Hemingway never flew again in small planes.

From the Seychelles Peter went to Fiji, as British Ambassador. His invitation in 1990 was irresistible, the experience unforgettable. The British Crown is held in the highest esteem in the islands, as became evident on 11 November, when we watched a Remembrance Day parade. The ceremony was conducted with the pride and dignity of a Guards battalion. When it ended we visited the Suva war graves cemetery. Every headstone had its poppy.

Fijian politics at the time reflected the racial tensions between the Polynesian and Melanesian indigenous people and the Indians. The latter were descendants of the labourers whom the British had brought in to work on the sugar plantations after the islanders had sought attachment to the British Crown in 1874. By the time of my visit the Indian population had increased to a point at which it slightly exceeded that of the Fijians. A general election in 1987 had brought in a coalition government with an Indian Prime Minister. One month and two days later, on 14 May, a thirty-eight-year-old army officer, Lieutenant-Colonel Sitiveni Rabuka, staged a surprise bloodless coup and took over the government for a period of seven turbulent months, before relinquishing power to a reshaped civilian government – though remaining in charge of the islands' security forces. During my stay he was one of Peter's lunch-time guests. It was a memorable encounter, during which he was heard to regret the feudal nature of Fijian society. He had not been born into the hereditary élite – the Ratus. I drew his attention to the modern British system of life peerages and suggested the idea might have value for Fiji. Rabuka was clearly interested. His personal charm and savoir-faire ensured that he remained a potent force in Fijian political life throughout the next decade.

Holidays apart, life at home had acquired a new focus through the purchase of a two-manual electronic organ, with built-in reverberation, that allowed me to produce a passable imitation of a classical church organ in my own sitting room. For the first time I could practise seriously without fearing I might be interrupting other peoples' prayers. Quite soon, in the summer of 1995, I felt able to accept an invitation to give a lunch-time Bach and Hindemith recital at St Mary de Crypt in Gloucester. It was my home town, and the church hall had been the original location of my grammar school when it was founded in the mid-sixteenth century. Bob Feilden, one of Whittle's original team of jet engineers, kindly came along in support with his wife Diana. To my delight she arranged for me to have a couple of hours on the Gloucester cathedral organ. What I found striking was the enormous range in the building's acoustics, between the organ loft – where, being close to the pipes all the voices are clearly differentiated – and the nave, where the cathedral's six-second echo masks the intricacies of contrapuntal writing. The organist and the congregation have two quite different musical experiences.

With Sprout's aid I was able to take Jean to the theatre in London and to the opera at Glyndebourne. There was an annual

410

pilgrimage to Cornwall's superb West Penwith. Her outdoor wheelchair seemed undeterred by any kind of terrain. It was her delight to drive to the very edge of the cliffs and look down on Nanjizel, or Treen, or Cape Cornwall; or, nearer home, to watch from Hock Cliff the gathering of the Severn tide into its mighty Bore. In Scotland her buggy took her without difficulty, amongst hundreds of sea birds, to the far end of the magical shingle bank that is exposed in Loch Fyne at low tide.

By the autumn of 1994, fourteen years after she had taken to a wheelchair, Jeanie was still triumphantly facing down whatever multiple sclerosis threw at her. It was time for a celebration, and her seventieth birthday provided the occasion. Sixty of our friends gathered for a concert given by the Nossek Quartet, a young group with a growing national reputation. They played Shostakovitch and Beethoven. It was a memorably happy evening.

In retrospect, it marked a watershed in our lives. Some months later, at midnight on 22 May 1995, her condition dramatically worsened. She had just gone to a 'hotel' run by the Multiple Sclerosis Society so that I could take a short holiday. The following morning I was rung very early. She had collapsed and was in hospital. I went immediately. She was unconscious, and remained so for three days. Our doctor daughter, Nickie, warned me that she would be lucky to survive. I sat long hours at her bedside, feeling useless, but speaking quietly, remembering stories of cases where patients who were in a coma nevertheless sometimes seemed to react to familiar voices. On the fourth day she was sitting up in bed, seemingly alert and little changed. But when we spoke it was obvious she had suffered a grievous blow. Her memory was almost destroyed and she no longer knew she had multiple sclerosis. Worse, she was totally paralysed from the neck down. For reasons that were unclear the sodium content of her blood serum had fallen below the level needed to maintain normal functions and her central nervous system had been damaged. It seemed an appalling prospect.

But she convalesced and in three weeks was back home, her memory partially restored. I took stock and found, to my surprise,

411

that in nursing terms less had altered than I had feared. By the high summer of 1997 we were sufficiently on top of managing her condition to feel able to celebrate our Golden Wedding. Once again the Nossek Quartet was summoned to provide a pre-supper concert. It was a great gathering. Reuben and Mary Ellen Clark came from Virginia, our splendid first *au pair* – Inge – from Germany. We reminisced with John and Miranda Hoskyns about my brief political interlude; with Bas Pease about Harwell; with Pat Rance on gastronomy; and with several others about the Sabrina choir that in the 1950s had so unexpectedly helped to shape my career. It was, and was intended to be, a 'this-is-your-life' experience.

As multiple sclerosis took its inevitable toll, caring for Jean involved more time. We thought about nursing homes, only to dismiss the very idea. There was no way in which a nursing-home bedroom could take the place of her own study, with its shelves displaying her studio pottery, its hundreds of carefully chosen and much-loved books, and a new page-turning machine – an electro-mechanical miracle made by Harold Wroe, a retired Harwell engineer – that allowed her to pursue her passion for reading. In this, at least, she could still be autonomous and in control.

By the summer of 2000 Jean was experiencing problems which clearly needed surgery, but the advice available locally was that any operation would be difficult and probably dangerous. However, Nickie remembered that a friend from medical school was now a leading specialist. He assured her that in the right hands Jean's condition could almost certainly be dealt with. He also reminded her that the relevant teaching hospital was only twenty miles away at Harrow. The surgeon, Robin Phillips, Dean of the hospital, warned us that because of problems over anaesthesia (connected with her MS) he might not be able to complete the operation – but he was willing to try. We liked his spirit and, having nothing to lose, told him to go ahead. The following morning I was greeted by a smiling surgical team.

So, in the spring of 2001, looking after Jean at home again

became a possibility. But it would be time-consuming, and would mean that after fifty years my part in the world of action and my links with London's chattering classes would have to be accepted as things of the past. There would be no more fascinating periods of concentrated familiarisation with new subjects: electronics, atomic energy, defence, disarmament, transport, aviation, mechanical engineering, mining, education, insurance. It was time to bow out.

I have no regrets for having chosen a life in and close to science. It has not been an avenue to wealth, but I have been privileged to experience, year after year, the stimulation of working with colleagues who were almost always objective, sometimes brilliant, and, in a few cases, possessed of extraordinary intellectual courage. I have also seen at first hand how truly Zuckerman spoke when he characterised science as the greatest force for change the world has known.

I can still surprise myself by reflecting that my own life-span, which is in no way unusual, stretches more than half-way back to the earliest days of the railways – to before Brunel completed his line from London to Bristol. I have lived in a period of astonishing and marvellous invention. When I first went to school cars were a rarity, trains still steam driven, air travel hardly begun. The silver screen was silent, home entertainment in its infancy. Then, in quick succession, came radar, the turmoil of war, nuclear fission and the atomic bomb, civil nuclear power, rocketry and space engineering, the green revolution, computers, the communications revolution and the world-wide web, decreased infant mortality, an extraordinary extension of the human life span in advanced countries, the 'pill' and all that has stemmed from it, and now the beginning of an understanding of the basis of life itself. Max Planck, the father of quantum physics, once remarked that science advances 'funeral by funeral'. Its astonishing speed of development is because there are more technologists alive today than have ever lived in the whole of the world's previous history. The dynamic of change they have created extends far beyond the merely technical – there are also the

413

most far-reaching social and political consequences. Zuckerman's aphorism simply encapsulates the incontrovertible evidence we see all around.

Where has this brought us? To a world that emphatically bears out the truth of Bacon's observation in his essay, *Of Innovation*: 'Things that have long gone together are, as it were, confederate within themselves; new things piece not so well.' Every day the earth is being made to carry a fifth of a million more people. The world's population has grown three-fold since I first went to school, from 2 billions to 6.5 billions, with every prospect of three more billions before a halt can be called. And this despite a near-halving in female fertility in some countries. Better medicine and proper attention to safe water supplies have so far proved a stronger influence.

It is a world where demands for a higher standard of living imply the consumption of ever more energy, the production of ever more carbon dioxide, the growing probability of a degree of climate change that could prove counterproductive for many species, our own not excluded. By our own choices we in the developed world may be generating the conditions for forced migration on a scale unknown in world history.

Even the most apparently desirable new creations have their downside. The motorcar has destroyed the compact geographical relationships that once supported daily and community life; made it easier for criminals to raid places where they are unknown by sight; destroyed the safety of the streets that my parents took for granted. Computers, by easing the handling of paper, have greased the slide towards bureaucracy and Soviet-style centralisation of government. The internet, that astonishing offshoot of the exchange of scientific research, spreads terrorism and pornography as well as knowledge. Television has fatally weakened the diverse institutions that, before World War II, provided this country with its entertainment, local debate and leisure-time education. For a time the BBC maintained high standards, which I saw at first hand. But growing demand has led to a saddening deterioration. In a manner reminiscent of

Gresham's Law in economics, bad practice is driving out the good. England is busily throwing away its great traditions of literature, art, music and intellectual debate, exchanging them for the banalities of televisual football, quiz games, soaps, violence and sound-bite pap. That is not how young minds are developed, imaginations set on fire, a nation encouraged to thrive.

One can forgive the young for living for the day. Science has called into question the validity of previously accepted religious teaching. Nuclear weapons and instantaneous annihilation lurk only just off stage. The strict controls that kept world peace during the Cold War crumbled when it ended. Terrorists wait for the chance to replace democratic freedom with their own brand of theistic bigotry. It is difficult not to feel deeply pessimistic – until one lifts one's eyes from immediate preoccupations, and thinks of the longer-term. The human race became dominant in the world through its capacity to survive in the face of even the greatest disasters: the super-volcano eruption in Sumatra 70,000 years ago; the Santorini explosion in Minoan times; ice ages, drought, pestilence, the invention of gun-powder. We know that life on earth hangs by a thread; that one day there will be an asteroid collision that may bring all to ruin; that in a time very short on the geological scale the Yellowstone Park super-volcano could lead to another extinction. But, short of total disaster, our descendants may well prove as competent as our ancestors. That at least must be our hope.

In the certainty that nothing I now do will have the slightest effect on the outcome, for good or ill, I shall therefore follow Candide's excellent example: *cultiver mon jardin*. I shall play out my time in the pursuit of the many happinesses that are still here to be enjoyed.

I shall practise the organ seriously, until I can once again deal adequately with Bach's G major Prelude and Fugue ('The Great'), which has been an all-purpose accompaniment to important ceremonies in my life: my daughter's wedding; my great friend Vernon Donnison's funeral. I shall seize any chance of taking

415

part in chamber music: accompanying the Brahms F minor clarinet sonata that sealed my friendship with 'Moose' Isenbergh those many years ago in Washington; or the César Franck violin sonata, that happy wedding present to South African friends which I learned during World War II, my Blüthner piano in a Surrey garage, flying bombs droning overhead. I shall work at Italian and Spanish; feast my eyes once more on the view over the Vallée Blanche; renew my acquaintance with the Cotswolds and the Severn bore; and perhaps occasionally fly again. I shall cherish my friends and do my best to preserve dear, courageous Jeanie.

As for personal conduct, Voltaire will remain my guide. I shall oppose those who peddle political correctness and staunchly support every man's right to speak as he finds – even when I disapprove of what he says. I shall remember that the best is the enemy of the good, and that the superfluous is often necessary. If exhorted to renounce the Devil and all his works I shall adopt Voltaire's defence that this is no time to make fresh enemies. And I shall try to remember that the most certain way for an author to bore his readers is to go on too long.

Appendix: The Causal Chain 'Map'

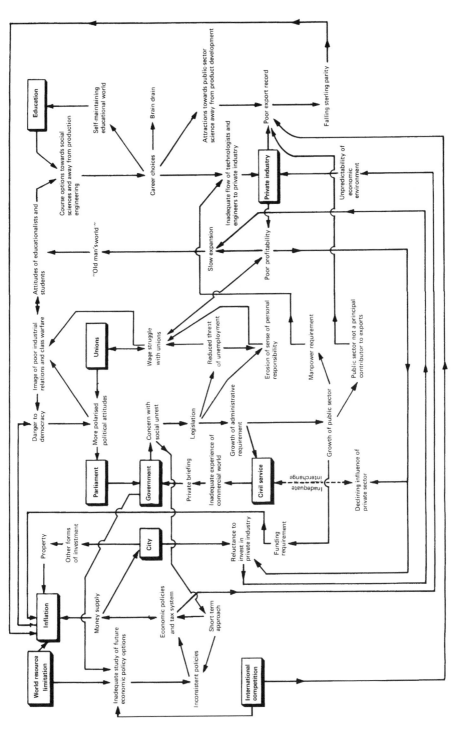

Socio-political factors affecting Britain's economic performance in 1974 (see Chapter 17).

Index

Names in the main text are those used at the time of the events described. Where titles are known to have been subsequently conferred, they are included in this index.

419

420